Fictions, Philosophies,
and the Problems
of Poetics

Fictions, Philosophies, and the Problems of Poetics

PETER J. McCORMICK

Cornell University Press

Ithaca and London

PN
3326
.M39
1988 / 62,823

First published 1988 by Cornell University Press.

International Standard Book Number (cloth) 0–8014–2204–3
International Standard Book Number (paper) 0–8014–9519–9
Library of Congress Catalog Number 88–47783

Printed in the United States of America

Librarians: Library of Congress cataloging information
appears on the last page of the book.

The paper in this book is acid-free and meets the guidelines for
permanence and durability of the Committee on Production Guidelines
for Book Longevity of the Council on Library Resources.

to Moïra
and for Laure, Anne, and Hélène

μόνος δ᾽ ἔτι μῦθος ὁδοῖο
λείπεται ὡς ἔστιν· ταύτῃ δ᾽ ἔπι σήματ᾽ ἔασι
πολλὰ
—*Parmenides*

Ἔσπερε πάντα φέρων ὅσα φαίνολις ἐσκέδασ᾽ αὔως,
φέρεις ὄιν, φέρεις αἶγα, φέρεις ἄπυ μάτερι παῖδα.
—*Sappho*

Contents

Preface

This book inquires into the natures, kinds, and roles of several cardinal fictions in the light of contemporary literary theory and philosophical reflection. It investigates some of the central conceptual interactions between literature and philosophy on a series of shared themes in recent Anglo-American and continental philosophy. The goal is to point up the ineluctable place of the arts in critical philosophical work as well as the necessity of philosophical thinking for understanding and appreciation of the arts. Although my focus is clearly on the give and take between literary presentation and philosophical representation, with necessary qualification the "argument" of this extended essay is, I believe, generalizable to most if not all of the other arts as well.

The Introduction sets out seven working hypotheses with the help of an extended analysis of an unfamiliar twentieth-century Korean poem. Chapters 1 to 7 investigate each hypothesis. The first four concern distinctions between fictional and nonfictional discourse, putative truths derived from fiction, questions about fictions and belief, and the effects of some fictions on feeling. With these particular considerations as background, a second group of three chapters focuses more sharply on the larger themes of the role of fictions in action, fictions and selves, and fictional worlds, with the help of case studies on poetic presentations of these themes in the lyric poetry of T. S. Eliot, Rainer Maria Rilke, and Wallace Stevens. Finally, in the Conclusion, the cumulative results of the preceding investigations are drawn together in a different order to generalize the argument, with the help once again as in the Introduction of other unfamiliar twentieth-century poetry, this time Japanese, to a consideration of fictions, relativisms, and rationality. Each of the seven chapters includes detailed appendixes to focus attention on technicalities without interrupting the movement of the essay as a whole.

This book attempts to identify in twentieth-century modernist literature and especially poetry, both in the European and the Oriental traditions, several presentations of central philosophical issues. These fictions are then used as benchmarks for taking the critical measure of recent philosophical work on important themes in both analytic and continental reflection. In each case I suggest that taking such fictional representations seriously involves a willingness to think twice about the satisfactoriness of our usual philosophical idioms. Thus, the larger concerns of this book center not just on the details of our various philosophical accounts of language, truth, knowledge, emotion, action, the self, and the world but on the rich and perhaps inexhaustible solicitations to revise some of our as yet insufficiently critical philosophical idioms in the light of poetic fictions and their challenges to those particular eighteenth-century interpretations of rationality which make up the stamp of modernity, still the contour and shape of our minds today.

Some of the ideas for this work first took shape during my two-year tenure of a senior fellowship of the Alexander von Humboldt Foundation in the Philosophy Department at the University of Konstanz. I thank the foundation for its support and my colleagues—Friedrich Kambartal, Jürgen Mittelstrass, Gottfried Gabriel, Wolfgang Iser, and Hans-Robert Jauss—for their hospitality. A major step in the realization of the work was taken thanks to the support of a joint program between the Social Science and Humanities Research Council of Canada and the Centre Nationale de Recherche Scientifique of France and the kindness of my hosts in philosophy at the Université de Provence in Aix-en-Provence, Gilles Granger and Louis Guillermit. The final elements have come into view thanks to the Taniguchi Foundation of Japan, which has allowed me to test these ideas with Japanese colleagues and friends in Kyoto and Tokyo each fall over the last seven years—with Tomonobu Imamichi especially and with Koichi Tsujimura, Shinro Kato, Megumi Sakabe, Ken-ichi Sasaki, and Ryosuke Inagake. I owe much as well to the criticisms of colleagues in the United States and Canada, to Joseph Margolis, Nicholas Wolterstorff, John Fisher, Ted Cohen, Calvin Seerfeld, Francis Sparshott, and to my year as visiting professor in the Graduate Program of Comparative Literature of the University of Toronto at the invitation of Peter Nesselroth and Mario Valdez. The editorial assistance of Edward Tingley has proved invaluable, and the patience of colleagues and students at the University of Ottawa in both the English and Philosophy departments has helped me greatly. My largest debts are to my teachers William Hill, William Richardson, Hans-Georg Gadamer, Gilles Granger, and, especially, Paul

Ricoeur—each of whom I thank sincerely for his encouragement over many years.

I have also benefited greatly from comments, criticisms, and conversations with many other friends and colleagues in various universities both here and abroad whom I do not have the space to mention here. I hope they will forgive me these constraints and find in this work some small reflection of all the many kindnesses they have extended me.

PETER MCCORMICK

Acknowledgments

Excerpts from "Burnt Norton," "The Dry Salvages," "East Coker," and "Little Gidding" in *Four Quartets*, copyright © 1943 by T. S. Eliot; renewed 1971 by Esme Valerie Eliot. Reprinted by permission of Harcourt Brace Jovanovich, Inc., and Faber and Faber Ltd.

Excerpts from *Murder in the Cathedral* by T. S. Eliot, copyright © 1935 by Harcourt Brace Jovanovich, Inc.; renewed 1963 by T. S. Eliot. Reprinted by permission of the publisher and Faber and Faber Ltd.

Excerpts from "Ash Wednesday" and "Choruses from 'The Rock' " in *Collected Poems, 1909–1962* by T. S. Eliot, copyright © 1936 by Harcourt Brace Jovanovich, Inc.; copyright © 1963, 1964 by T. S. Eliot. Reprinted by permission of the publisher and Faber and Faber Ltd.

Excerpts from *The Palm at the End of the Mind: Selected Poems and a Play* by Wallace Stevens, copyright © 1971 by Holly Stevens. Reprinted by permission of Random House, Inc., and by Faber and Faber Ltd.

Excerpts from *The Selected Poetry of Rainer Maria Rilke*, translated by Stephen Mitchell, copyright © 1982 by Stephen Mitchell. Reprinted by permission of Random House, Inc.

The poem "Still Life" by Yoshioka Minoru and an excerpt from the poem "First Love" by Shinazaki Toson, in *Modern Japanese Poetry*, translated by James Kirkup, edited and introduced by A. R. Davis, published by the University of Queensland Press, 1978, reprinted with permission of the publisher.

The poem "The Man with the Green Face" by Tamura Ryuichi is reprinted by permission of Howard Hibbett.

The poem "Still Life" by Yoshioka Minoru is reprinted by permission of the translator, Sato Hiroaki.

The poem "Face at the Bottom of the World" by Hagiwara Sakutaro, from *Face at the Bottom of the World and Other Poems* (Tokyo: Charles E. Tuttle Co., Inc., 1969), is reprinted by permission of the publisher.

Excerpts from the poems "First Love" by Shinazaki Toson and "Remaining Fruit" by Miyoshi Tatsuji, in *Dawn of the West* by D. Keene (New York: Henry Holt and Co., 1984), reprinted by permission of the publisher.

The poem "Sickly Face at the Bottom of the Ground" by Hagiwara Sakutaro reprinted by permission of the University of Tokyo Press and the translator, Sato Hiroaki.

The poem "Mountain Hut" by Han Yong-un appeared in *A Handbook of Korea*, 5th ed. (Seoul: Ministry of Culture and Information, 1983).

For permission to use articles of mine that have been revised for this work, I acknowledge the following journals and publishers: *The Journal of Aesthetics and Art Criticism* (Temple University, Philadelphia), for "Real Fictions" (46:1988), "Feelings and Fictions" (43:1985), and "Moral Knowledge and Fiction" (41:1983); *Literature and the Question of Philosophy* (Baltimore: Johns Hopkins University Press, 1987), for "Philosophical Discourses and Fictional Texts"; *Journal of the Faculty of Letters* (University of Tokyo), for "Literary Truths and Metaphysical Qualities" (8:1983); *Revue Internationale de Philosophie* (Tokyo), for "Future Selves, Virtual Persons" (4:1986) and "Moral Justifications, Self-Identity" (2:1984).

Sections of my paper "Interpreting Intentional Actions" are reprinted with revisions from Evan Simpson, ed., *Anti-Foundationalism and Practical Reasoning* (Edmonton, Alberta: Academic Printing and Publishing, 1987), by permission of the publisher.

Grateful acknowledgment is made to Sven Linnér and Gilles Granger for permission to quote from their personal communications to me.

P. McC.

Introduction

Here is an unfamiliar poetic text, a meditative twentieth-century Korean lyric.

Mountain Hut

Forsake this dusty world, they said,
And I would achieve oblivion.
So I hewed the crags to build a hut,
And delved the rocks to dig a well.

The clouds are entertained as guests,
Who freely come and freely go
And the moon, although no sentinel,
Keeps watch all night above the gate.

The song of birds my music is,
And the world among the pines my lyre—
As they were wont from ancient times.

None but my pillow knows
My rue for love of thee which stays
And haunts me through the sleepless nights.

O solitude of the vacant heights!
Whence do you bring this silent grief?

Rather give me that tranquil grief
Without the song of nightingales!
O solitude of the vacant hills![1]

[1]Han Yong-un 1926.

When we read this poem, translated here poorly into English, we may notice in a subjective way a series of particular features. Intuitively, we may say that the situation the speaker describes involves many elements. Unnamed persons have counseled the speaker to try to realize an ideal, presumably a spiritual ideal, by seeking solitude. The speaker has followed this advice by building a hut in the mountains and digging a well. And as a result of this activity he, or she, has apparently recovered a freer relation with the world of nature—the pine trees, the nightingales, the clouds, the moon. But this relation is not the realization of his spiritual ideal (perhaps the speaker is in fact a man) because he remains troubled— he goes sleepless and grieves silently for someone he loves. In distress, he addresses the "solitude of the vacant heights" to ask the source of the wordless grief that solitude has brought. And finally, the speaker prays that he be granted neither the freedom to participate in the primal world of nature nor freedom from his own grief but a "tranquil grief," a grief no longer unsettling.

This paraphrase brings out what seems to be a central suggestion in this poem—that some genuinely spiritual ideals may well be incompatible with human love. Suppose, when the specialists had each finished his or her critical reading of the poem (and especially the correction of its curious translation), a consensus crystallized among them that this suggestion, or one very much like it, was entirely plausible. At that point some other readers might well question whether such an intuitive and subjective reading of the poem is adequate. Before such readers would be ready to reflect further on the poem and its "suggestions" they would require, if not an objective rereading, at least one more anchored in the text than this one.

This brief unfamiliar poem is just an infinitesimal element in twentieth-century Korean literature. Still, "Mountain Hut" is significant in the sense that Korean literary scholars have selected this poem and very few others to represent Korean literature in the most authoritative source available outside Korea today.[2] Accordingly, I focus my reflections with the help of this work whose very unfamiliarity may incite us to articulate our reflections more carefully.

Many things about this poem could be of interest—perhaps the lan-

---

[2]See "Literature," in *A Handbook of Korea*, 5th ed. (Seoul: Ministry of Culture and Information, 1983), 282–92, with bibliographies on 812–13. I have restricted myself here to "modern literature" because, unlike earlier Korean literature, which developed under the influence of Chinese literature, many modern works have evolved in close proximity to currents in Western literature. For background, besides the Chung Han-mo and Chang Duk-soon contributions to *A Handbook of Korea*, see Lee 1965. More generally, see the appropriate articles and especially the updated bibliographies in the *Encyclopaedia Britannica* and the *Encyclopedia Universalis*. My reading here of "Mountain Hut" has gained much from extensive discussions with Jung Myong-Hwan, Paik Ki-soo, Jung Jaeg-won, Hwang Jae-Woo, and Kim So-wol.

guage, the translation, the disposition of the text on the page. Traditionally, scholars have distinguished various aspects of such texts (linguistic, psychological, historical, sociological), their disparate contexts, their many themes, their unusual effects, and so on. Each individual reader or audience selects different sets of features as a function of certain interests. Thus, the literary historian may choose to explore certain lyric affinities between this poem and other related texts, whereas the literary critic may choose to center attention on each text in isolation.

My interests here are mainly philosophical. I am less interested in the genesis of such a text, its constituents, its contexts and affinities than I am in how understanding such a poetic text and indeed any work of art in a particular time like our own would seem to depend on thinking twice about basic issues concerning language, knowledge, emotion, action, the self, and the way the world is. More specifically, unlike the interest of the historian of art or the sociologist, psychologist, or linguist, my concern lies in exploring the possibility that understanding some artworks involves scrutinizing the revisionary effects such a process would seem to work on our antecedent convictions about how certain basic issues in philosophy are to be articulated.

This concern arises from a general hypothesis that informs this book and that I spell out in greater detail in Part III. Some students of contemporary history, economics, and politics agree that many societies are now undergoing radical and widespread social changes.[3] Indeed, some critical observers have persuasively argued that societies in Europe, North America, and Japan are undergoing fundamental transformations. When such basic changes—as in the Renaissance sequel to the medieval religious synthesis or as in the seventeenth-century scientific sequel to Renaissance humanism—involve the replacement of one fundamental comprehensive pattern for integrating the quasi-totality of facts, events, relations, and institutions with another equally fundamental and comprehensive pattern, we may speak of a cultural revolution. Thus, a cultural revolution transforms a culture by gradually substituting a new paradigm of rationality for an older one. Such a revolution leaves virtually nothing unchanged.

If such observers are largely correct, then philosophy is also caught up in this process of radical cultural transformation. But what sense does such a general way of talking about philosophy make? Can part of the fundamental changes transforming societies today, and with them the practices of philosophy, be understood more concretely in the shapes that some philosophical problems assume? More specifically, if the practices of philosophy are undergoing radical change,

[3]See Neville 1971.

then are at least some such things as philosophical problems themselves being transformed?

The present moment, then, is, as one philosopher has recently put
the matter, "a very curious moment in intellectual history. On the
one hand, we are witnessing, in all explanatory disciplines, a profound retreat from the principal sources of conceptual assurance and
stability regarding the fixed canons of science; and, on the other, we
are witnessing an equally profound disbelief in the capacity of theoretical and metaphysical anarchy to account for the palpable successes
of orderly inquiry. . . . In short, methodological speculation has produced a vacuum, and efforts to fill it have conceived a chaos."[4] My
working hypothesis is that our ongoing reflection today on the various intersections between philosophy, literary theory, and the arts is
indeed taking place in a particular time, a time of radical cultural revolution. One consequence is that what is to count as a philosophical
or theoretical version of certain central matters is fairly controversial.
Another is that thinking fruitfully about such matters today may well
require a new openness on the part of philosophical and theoretical
reflection to the various ways in which works of art suggest thoroughgoing revisions in their still uncritical formulations.

My aim, then, is this: to exhibit a series of different yet related questions
about one kind of art only, the verbal art of lyric poetry, questions that
arise from reflection on the interaction, at least in contemporary philosophical reflection on the arts, between two contrasting philosophical
approaches: those of analytic philosophy and those of hermeneutic phi-
losopy. And my plan is to investigate this contrast in a preliminary and
introductory way with the help of the distinguished and yet largely unfamiliar text I have begun with here while restricting for the moment my
concerns with both analytic and hermeneutic approaches to the work of
Nelson Goodman and Paul Ricoeur.

I turn, then, to a summary formulation of the seven topics in this book—
art and language, truth, knowledge, emotion, action, the self, and the
world. In each I first describe a stage in an elementary linguistic description of our text, then show how this analysis raises a problem about our
understanding of the text, and finally suggest how such a problem invites
a thoughtful reformulation in terms of at least some current exchanges
between analytic philosophy and hermeneutics. My purpose in this introduction is to provide an overview of many but not of all the results I
try to work out in the following chapters, and to use an unfamiliar poetic
fiction as a means for focusing on widespread, largely uncritical, and
philosophically provocative aspects of our intuitive thinking about verbal
works of art.

[4]Margolis 1986:187.

ON ART, LANGUAGE, AND DISCOURSE

In his meditative poem "Mountain Hut," the poet Han Yong-un (1897–
1944) represents for us a fictional character who speaks about a fictional
situation. Instead of describing this situation in more detail or calling
attention in an impressionistic way to several of its interesting features,
I wish to proceed more systematically, to sketch the lineaments of a varied
and broad approach to literary works which has become increasingly
important for providing a space where different philosophical reflections
on the arts might interact. I shall simplify here and for convenience call
these various currents "the linguistic approach."

Trying to understand a text like "Mountain Hut" involves working out
answers to several questions. One question that arises here concerns the
kind of context in which the text is situated. What exactly is the context
here? Our initial response, on the linguistic approach, is that the most
fundamental context is the communication process itself.[5]

This process is construed as involving several different factors. First,
the process consists of a person intending to communicate a message to
another person. More particularly, the message is understood as encoded
in an organizational sequence of signs. Thus, at the beginning of the
process there is an encoder, and at the end a decoder. Central to the
communication process is the sign sequence encoded in such a way as
to be understandable by both the encoder who sends the message and
the decoder who receives it. These three elements are constitutive of the
communication situation that is the context of the poem. Moreover, the
encoder and decoder are both said to be aware of the communication
relation in which they stand and to be concerned actively with maintaining
this relation. Finally, the message that is encoded in the sign system of
the text is taken to convey information about a variety of matters.

Like texts of all kinds, this text is verbal and includes both an explicit
code and an implicit context. The character of a verbal text, however,
differs depending on whether it is primarily oriented *to* and conveys
information *about* the encoder (the emotive function), the decoder (the
connotative function), the context (the denotative function), the code (the
metalingual function), or is oriented simply to its own composition as a
text (the poetic function). Other functions may be formulated (for example, the so-called "phatic function," which serves at the beginning of
a telephone conversation to establish contact). Often more than one function is present at the same time. Much can be said to fill out the details

---

[5]This first stage in the linguistic description of a poetic text derives mainly from the work
of R. Jakobson, especially Jakobson 1971 and 1976. In general, I have relied heavily for my
description of the linguistic approach and for diagrams on the composite and yet studiously
consistent terminological presentation on Krajka and Zgorzelski 1974, hereafter referred to
as "KZ."

of each of these functions. But the basic claim of the linguistic approach here is threefold: in a text one function is primary; further, in a literary text, the poetic function is primary; finally, the effect of reading a literary text is pleasure in the text for its own sake. When viewed in this linguistic perspective, a literary work may be described, then, as "a text encoded in accordance with certain sign systems, which by virtue of the dominance of the poetic function contains a certain amount of additional information and thus becomes the source of the aesthetic experience of the decoder" (KZ:16).

In terms of this linguistic approach to the verbal text, "Mountain Hut" can clearly be seen as situated in a communication process. The author has encoded a message in the organized signs of the verbal text, and the reader in turn is to decode this message. A problem may seem to arise from the fact that the verbal text here was first presented in the sign system that is the Korean language and hence can be understand preeminently only by a reader who knows Korean. But this problem does not affect the central claim; so long as some decoder can understand the message, even if the receivers require that the original message be further translated into another sign system, that claim holds. Moreover, "Mountain Hut" also illustrates the different functions of the verbal text which depend on the various possible orientations of the text.

The emotive function is evident in the beginning, the middle, and the end of the poem. By contrast, the connotative function seems to be absent—no injunction or appeal seems to be directed to the decoder of the text. The denotative function is hardly present because the text conveys very little objective information about the empirical world. Moreover, since the text does not refer explicitly to the code used in its construction—it does not say, for example, that "solitude" is another word for "oblivion"—the metalingual function also seems to be absent. The poetic function, however, seems predominant. For the text exhibits many parallel constructions, repetitions, and small variations that in the communication of information are largely redundant. Consequently, the text concentrates the reader's attention on its own features, on the peculiarities of its own articulations.

This response to an initial question about the fundamental context of the poem—namely, its situation as a multifunctional sign system in a process of communication—could of course be articulated in much more sophisticated terms and in much greater detail. But whatever its final satisfactoriness inside a particular and more fully developed linguistic framework, the idea here of the verbal text as part of a communication process remains essential to the linguistic approach. And it is this idea that in its own right raises a question of a different order. This new question does not concern the satisfactoriness of a particular linguistic theory, but the understanding of language which that theory would seem to incorporate. For what reasons are there for justifying the interpretation in this account of the language of a poetic work as most fundamentally a matter of communication? Our experience as readers often seems to belie such a conception. Far from being solely a means of communication, the language of a poetic work especially is often not communicative enough—even not communicative at all. The language of many poetic works, even after repeated readings, is often revealed as extraordinarily dense, opaque, even incomprehensible. The larger question here, then, concerns the issue of providing a satisfactory account of one notion of the language of the poetic work, that is, one that will at the very least do more justice to our repeated experiences with the language of poetry as only sometimes a means of communication and at other times something altogether different. Put quite baldly, without any of the required nuances, the linguistic response to our initial question about the poetic work raises a larger question about how we are to characterize the differences between fictional and nonfictional texts.

The standard answer to this question in recent years has been an analysis of these putative differences in terms of speech-act theory. Without repeating the details of that analysis, we may summarize one version of that account as follows. What makes a text fictional is its representation of the performance of illocutionary acts—roughly, utterances that communicate some message and at the same time generate a particular act. In the illocutionary act "thank you" I both say something and do something. Since, however, a fuller account would need to incorporate a sharper articulation of what a text is as well as some indication of whether any internal objective features allow a distinction between a fictional text and a nonfictional text, the standard answer to our question usually includes technical qualifications. Thus, what makes a text fictional is the nature and not just the use of certain markers and conventions of a text type structured in no one way other than to ensure that a community of readers in a culture takes those, among the many cardinal sentences of the text which are speakers' illocutionary performances, in a certain way. These illocutionary acts are taken as putative illocutions, finally incomplete ones, and therefore not authorial but textual representations of illocutions understood inside the continuing history of an interpretive community. Certain linguistic and epistemic marks ensure that competent readers of such a text construe its supposed illocutions as representations and not as performances.

But this response to the more general issue that the linguistic account raises is not without some serious difficulties of its own. For this view relies on an understanding of language which does not allow it to deal perspicuously with the opacities, contradictions, paradoxes, indeterminacies, and silences of such poetic works as "Mountain Hut." One element in this speech act analysis of the nature of fictional discourse which seems to cause such difficulties is the reliance on an overly instrumental understanding of the nature of language.

Why not, then, explore the possibility of articulating a general account of the fictional language of poetic works which complements this instrumental notion of language (as representing or objectifying) with a different view of language (as nonrepresenting and nonobjectifying)? The idea here is to construe the distinctive use of language in poetic works in both those analytic terms proper to a scientific understanding of language and those hermeneutic terms more appropriate for a meditative understanding of language.

This larger, more meditative, view of language is evident—to take one example only—in some of Paul Ricoeur's critical yet sympathetic readings of the work of Nelson Goodman. In *The Rule of Metaphor* and in an article published in French and English before the appearance of his three-volume work *Time and Narrative*, Ricoeur calls attention to the richness of Goodman's reflections on reference. At one point Ricoeur marks his agreement with Goodman in *Languages of Art*: "My own approach," he wrote in 1979, "is in agreement with this book's general thesis that symbolic systems 'make' and 'remake' the world, and that our aesthetical grasping of the world is a militant understanding that organizes the world in terms of works and works in terms of worlds."[6] Ricoeur goes on to make his own suggestions about the reference of language as sometimes productive rather than merely representative, and the uses of language to change, to expand, and even to increase "reality" through processes such as the semantic innovations of metaphor and the transformations and refigurations of "reality" through the workings of narration. This revisionary work of Ricoeur draws inspiration from many sources, most of which are different from the various works (like those of Carnap, Tarski, and Quine) which have nourished Goodman's reflections. The central ones are the meditations on language in the later Heidegger and the development of that work in the hermeneutics of language in Gadamer.

Part of the value, then, of Ricoeur's reading of Goodman, I suggest, is the promise it makes of formulating an account of poetic language in less encumbered terms than those of language as a means of communication only, and yet in sufficiently engaging ways that draw critically on more than one philosophical tradition (as the speech-act theory does not). Such an account, if coherent and persuasive enough, might enable us both to take the critical measure of what seems to be lacking in the standard philosophical account of fictional discourse and to reorient the current linguistic description of the poetic work. Such an account would also enable readers to seize upon such possibilities in their interpretations and appreciations even of such unfamiliar works as "Mountain Hut."

[6]Ricoeur 1979:123, citing Goodman 1978:241.

In the light of these summary remarks, my hypothesis about art, language, and discourse serves as a guideline for further reflection:

> 1. The differences between the fictional discourse of a poetic work and nonfictional discourse are less a matter of observable or implied properties of the representation of illocutionary speech acts as of meditative uses of nondenotative varieties of so-called productive reference, or refigurational readings.

I detail this hypothesis more fully in Chapter 1, where I argue the serious credibility of this suggestion.

Part of what some competent readers respond to in such poetic works as "Mountain Hut" is not so much the communication of certain messages as what one philosopher has cryptically called the speaking of language itself. When we construe language too narrowly as merely a means of communication, whether in the context of a linguistic description of the poetic work or in speech-act analyses of such a work, we cannot respond satisfactorily either to the question these theories are addressed to as putative answers or to some of the central experiences with language which communities of competent readers reliably report.

On Art, Knowledge, and Truth

A second question that arises about "Mountain Hut" and similar texts concerns its peculiar status not just as a literary text but as specifically a poetic text. For if a literary text is to be understood as a multifunctional organized series of signs, and if the poetic function is taken as what predominates in a poetic text, then how exactly does the poetic function work? The answer on the linguistic approach is: by the operations of selection and combination.

On the linguistic view, the encoder must select a series of appropriate signs in the natural language at hand.[7] He or she does this by applying the principle of equivalence according to which the meaning of a sign is either similar to or different from the elements about which the encoder wishes to convey information. The encoder must then combine the selected signs by applying the principle of contiguity according to which signs can be combined only according to the appropriate rules of a grammar.

We can understand the particular kind of organization which determines the poetic function of a text with the help of several examples from

---

[7]This second stage in the linguistic description also derives from Jakobson. See KZ, 16–18.

our poem. Compare "So I hewed the crags to build a hut" with "Although I hews crag for build hut." With respect to selection, both sentences follow the principle of equivalence; both sentences comprise choices of appropriate signs from the entire range of such signs in, say, a dictionary. But with respect to combination, only the first follows the principle of contiguity. The second sentence violates the principle by juxaposing incontiguous elements such as "I hews, hews crag," "for build," and "build hut," with the result that the second sentence is ungrammatical. Now compare "So I hewed the crags to build a hut" and "So I quarried sufficient stone on the mountain in order to construct a small lodging." Here, with respect to combination, both sentences observe the principle of contiguity; both sentences are grammatically correct sentences in English. But with respect to selection, only the first applies the principle of equivalence. For the first sentence superimposes on one of the ordinary ways of organizing and articulating such a sentence an inhabitual kind of order, diction, and rhythm which the sentence exhibits in different ways—for example, in its stress patterns, syllabic lengths, repetition of vowel sounds, brevity, ellipsis ("to" for "in order to"), choice of words ("hewed"), and metonymy ("crags" for "stone"). Consequently, the decoder's attention is drawn away from the informational content of the sentence to certain features of the text itself.

The two operations of selection and combination, together with the two principles of equivalence and contiguity, are central to the ways in which a coded verbal text orients the decoder's attention to the text itself. The poetic function of the text consists in this kind of orientation. Since, however, many functions can be at work simulataneously in the same text, the text itself is properly characterized as not just a literary but indeed a poetic text only if the poetic function dominates whatever other functions are also at work. The poetic function is understood to dominate these other functions the text may have when it subordinates most if not all of those operations to its own by a process that is usually called "superposition."

When we read "Mountain Hut" in this perspective it is evident that the text is the result of both a selective and a combinatory process. Moreover, the two principles of equivalence and of contiguity are applied concurrently. More interesting is when we focus our readings, as we will shortly, on sentences that are strikingly similar—not just lines 3 and 4 or 9 and 10 but especially the text's concluding five lines. Here, this kind of linguistic approach enables us to bring out in great detail similarities and differences by scrutinizing how the principle of equivalence is used in the process of combination. The result of such scrutiny is the recognition that the poetic function of this text subordinates the other functions by superimposing on the usual organization of texts, where the communication of information is paramount, another kind of organization, in which the features of the text itself are paramount.

In particular, we can choose any of the six stanzas of the poem or take the poem in its entirety and we will find that each sentence is grammatical and also somewhat unusual in more than one way. Thus, both the principles of equivalence and contiguity are illustrated. This would undoubtedly remain the case even were the translation carefully reworked by critics whose native language is Korean and again reworked by a prominent Korean poet. But as the poem stands we can already observe, in stanza 3 for example, both principles in operation. Despite the inverted word order in lines 1 and 2, and despite the position and the syntactic role of the additional clause in line 3, the entire complex sentence is grammatically correct English; no incontiguous elements are juxtaposed. Yet the inhabitual word order and the sequence of clauses themselves, together with the use of conventional terms ("lyre"), epithets ("the song of birds"), archaisms ("wont"), and rare passive verbal terms ("were wont"), show that the author has subordinated the usual selection process to a much less familiar one; an inhabitual kind of order is superimposed here on the ordinary uses of language in such a way that the language calls attention to itself.

Thus, to the question of just how the poetic function operates, the linguistic approach proposes an answer in terms of two processes, two principles, and an operation called "superposition."

But this linguistic answer again raises a question in its own right. And again the question concerns not so much the details of the linguistic approach but certain implications that flow from this account. For how can a literary text such as "Mountain Hut," which is construed here to be specifically a poetic text in the sense that it predominately calls attention to its own linguistic peculiarities—instead of conveying information about the empirical world to which language refers—be properly described in cognitive terms as a genuine source of not just insignificant but indeed important knowledge? For it may well appear on the linguistic account that just because a poetic text is defined as one that predominately conveys no important information about anything but itself, a poetic text cannot properly be described as cognitive at all. A text is cognitive, one wants to say, to the degree that it provides its readers with knowledge of truths about the way things are. And such truths are held to be found in the contents of nontautologous propositions whose truth value is subject to various controls.

The standard answer to this question is straightforward: a question about the truth or falsity of a statement or suggestion in a poetic work is simply misplaced because, to recall the Renaissance poet and critic Sir Philip Sidney, poetic statements and even suggestions are neither true nor false. More strictly, we may argue that truth value depends on the propositional contents of sentences. But sentences that are used to represent nonfictional states of affairs are not properly described as having propositional contents in the same sense as those sentences that are used to represent fictional states of affairs. The first set of sentences occurs inside a domain governed by a major speech act called pretending, whereas the second set does not. Consequently, when a fictional state of affairs like the situation the poet represents in "Mountain Hut" includes a statement or gives rise to a particular suggestion, that statement or suggestion is not judged appropriately as either true or false. It lacks truth value because it is not a statement or a suggestion at all—it is the pretense of a statement or a suggestion.

But this standard response is not without some difficulties of its own. For our readings of such poetic works as "Mountain Hut" and sometimes even the role of such texts in our lives suggest that something more is going on than simply the assertions or even pretended assertions of truths. Why not investigate the possibility of disassociating the notion of truth in some cases from the domain of assertions and statements, the domain of truth functions? For at least two claims are central in the linguistic account of the cognitivity of literary works of art: the claim that truth is restricted to the domain of assertions and the claim that apparent assertions in literary works, because they are not genuine assertions, are neither true nor false. But as Nelson Goodman argues in his recent work, when we are dealing with predicates as categories, rational appraisal involves the notion of rightness of categorization. And when we are dealing with an entire system of categories—a categorial system—rational appraisal involves fitness in exemplification, or projectability, or simply considerations of whatever the categorial system can do.[8] Once one notices the curious criteria mentioned here of "rightness" and "fitness," then it seems that even within one of the cardinal works in analytic philosophy some larger sense of truth than the truth of statements is not absent. The value of this suggestion, taken from Ricoeur's critical yet sympathetic reading of Goodman, is that it offers the chance of incorporating into a richer account than the standard one resources from at least two philosophical traditions, the analytic and the hermeneutic.

I take such reflections as opening up a path to the understanding of art, knowledge, and truth, to the notion of putative fictional works as being true to life and not just as being truth-functional. We might formulate a second hypothesis as follows:

> 2. Those peculiar beliefs that some works of fiction seem to generate may be taken as beliefs about what is true to life, which communities of readers come to entertain in their understanding of fictional works.

Part of what some readers come to believe in reading Han Yong-un's poem "Mountain Hut" is that the demands of some personal ideals may well be inconsistent with the demands of human love. And on this account

[8]See Ricoeur 1980:114–15.

a poetic work is cognitive in the sense that it can be the source not so much of truths as such but of truthlike views such as this one. When we construe cognitivity too strongly in terms of knowledge and truth functions we do indeed have great difficulty in accommodating the intuitions of many readers that some literary works do provide knowledge. But we do not always need to construe cognitivity in such strict terms. For as the several recent discussions between analytic philosophy and hermeneutics show, cognitivity in the case of literary works as opposed to scientific ones can be interpreted in legitimate although weaker terms as truth to life rather than truth-functionality. We may understand a literary work such as "Mountain Hut" as a genuine source of beliefs about, let us say, the compatibility of different personal ideals with the exigencies of human love, beliefs whose truth is more a matter of responsiveness to and coherence with a certain experience of life than one of truth-functionality.

ON ART, KNOWLEDGE, AND BELIEF

If a literary text is to be understood as an element in a communicative process, and a poetic text as a literary text in which the poetic function dominates, we need to pursue our questioning further about the nature of this poetic function. How are we to understand the cognitive aspect of this poetic function as a source if not of truths then of beliefs? On the linguistic account, the poetic function not only involves the superposition of the operations of selection and combination, which raises questions about cognitivity and truth; it also raises questions about cognitivity and belief by varying the extensions of different words and phrases through the process of foregrounding and backgrounding.[9]

On the linguistic view, the poetic function needs to be analyzed further with the help of a distinction between the standard uses of language and its poetic uses. As we have seen, only the latter functions in such a way as to call attention preeminently to itself. This implies that poetic uses of language turn on a contrast between the standard uses as a background against which the poetic uses stand out as deliberate and systematic distortions. More specifically, "The function of poetic language consists in the maximum of foregrounding of the utterance" (JM, 19). Unlike the occurrences of foregrounding in nonpoetic uses of language, poetic language never subordinates foregrounding to our objective of communication but always accents the expressive objective. Moreover, the poetic

[9]For this third stage in the linguistic description of a poetic text, I rely on J. Mukařovský's criticism and on developments of Jakobson. See especially Mukařovský, in Garvin 1964:17–30. Hereafter this seminal article is cited as "JM."

function maximizes the foregrounding effect not by multiplying the number of foregrounded elements but through "the consistency and systematic character of the foregrounding" (JM, 20).

The consistent and systematic foregrounding of certain components results in the establishment of one component that dominates all others, that is, the dominant, the "component of the work which sets in motion, and gives direction to, the relationship of all other components" (JM, 20). But with the maximization of foregrounding, the background itself assumes a fuller profile. For it now consists of both the standard uses of language and those extratextual conventions, themes, and traditions that resist the emergence of the dominant. The line between language and subject matter breaks down, this story goes, so that the subject matter stands centrally in a relation to the semantic structure of the work rather than to any extralinguistic reality. The result is that "the question of truthfulness does not apply in regard to the subject matter of poetry, nor does it even make sense" (JM, 22–23). Still, the relationship between the standard and poetic uses of language changes with time, so that "the structure of a work of poetry can change completely from its origin if it is, after a certain time, projected against the background of a norm of the standard which has since changed" (JM, 27). Hence, although "truthfulness" on this account is not a pertinent consideration, nevertheless the changing relations between the dominant of the poetic distortions and the norm of the standard opens the text out onto history, ideology, and belief.

When we return to "Mountain Hut" with this account in mind, we stumble of course on all the difficulties that arise from reading a text in a hesitant translation from an extremely unfamiliar culture. Specifically, the distinctions between standard and poetic uses of language are extremely hard to sustain in a case where the reader has to deal with translation. Nonetheless, certain effects of foregrounding can be seen in the way the inhabitual diction of this poem contrasts with the usual expressions of everyday communicative speech. As we saw earlier, expressions such as "hewed," "delved," "wont," "rue," and perhaps "whence" are striking in the way they stand out against the background of the standard terms most often used in these contexts. Most striking perhaps is the insistence in the final stanzas on the carefully contrasted phrases "silent grief" and "tranquil grief" in the complex context of personification and apostrophe ("solitude"). Here the strong impression is one of a dominant component of the text which links a longed for "oblivion" with the tension between the silence of one kind of grief and the tranquility of another. The main effect is one of complex suggestion about the shifting relations in the text between changing understandings of "oblivion" and "solitude" on the part of the lyrical persona. The foregrounding of the dominant also works an associated effect on the reader's understanding of the same opposition between "oblivion" and "solitude." But what specifically are the devices by which the poetic function succeeds in foregrounding a particular component as the dominant one of the poem? If we were to agree that the dominant in "Mountain Hut" is the dynamic relation between "oblivion" and "solitude," then the foregrounding of this component follows not from any quantity but from both "the consistency and systematic character of the foregrounding" (JM, 20). As to the first, we find in "Mountain Hut" both a careful selection of lexical terms and the establishing of an uncommon semantic relationship between these items in a particular context. And as to the second, the progressive ordering of the textual components in a series of interrelationships results in the constitution of a hierarchy among the components. Thus, the foregrounding in "Mountain Hut" of the opposition between "oblivion" and "solitude" follows from the consistent and systematic regimenting of a hierarchy of importance among the inhabitual semantic tensions set up between particular lexical items. Thus, to the question as to how the poetic function accommodates a cognitive interpretation in terms of belief if not of truth, the linguistic account urges an answer in terms of interconnections between a dominant component foregrounded in the poetic text and antecedent norms of a standard understanding of nonpoetic uses of language which readers bring to the text.

But this account once again raises difficulties in its own right. For the account is continually threatened by a thoroughgoing tension between its formal character and not exclusively formal interests. The problem is, then, to maintain the interpretation of the connections between the textual and the extratextual in "semantic" terms only and yet allow for the centrally important dimensions of social, cultural, and historical change. More particularly, how can the poetic function of language in a poetic text such as "Mountain Hut" be properly described in terms of foregrounding a dominant component without making a central place in the account for more than formal "semantic" concerns only? "Truthfulness" may be construed as an irrelevant consideration, but how, then, are we to accommodate the cognitive interplay of the reader with the text on which this detailed account of poetic function depends?

These reflections suggest the need to scrutinize freshly in a philosophical and not just linguistic vein the talk here of the "semantic" dimension in the poetic function of a text. I propose a third working hypothesis as follows:

> 3. The cognitivity of some works of fiction concerns the question of whether many works can be sources not of knowledge as truths but of knowledge as beliefs of whatever kind about the extratextual world on the part of historical communities of readers.

Part of what readers come to accept in reading Han Yong-un's poem is not any putative truth about this or that but merely the idea that the demands of certain personal ideals may conflict with the demands of human love. A poetic work thus is cognitive in the sense that it can be the source not of truth or even truthlike views but of plausible beliefs only.

ON ART, EMOTION, AND FEELING

If a literary text is to be understood as an element in a communicative process, and a poetic text as a literary text in which the poetic function dominates, and the poetic function as the foregrounding of a dominant component, we need to ask next just how such a text is organized—just what is its structure. On the linguistic account, a poetic text is organized as a hierarchy of formal structures, and the poetic text exhibits a variety of different formal structures, and the initial point to be made about such structures is that their sum does not result in a mere product, some kind of aggregate. Rather, when taken together all of the structural elements constitute a whole unified in such a way as to become more than and different from the sum of its parts. In other words, certain properties may rightly be predicated about the whole which cannot rightly be predicated about the sum of the parts.

The poetic text may then be considered as a set of elements and relations. These elements and relations are equally semantic units in the sense that individually or in various combinations they contribute to the meaning of the text and to the text's various transformations of meaning across different traditions, times, and readerships. Even though these elements and relations are mainly to be understood as structural factors of the poetic work, each factor, even when taken in isolation from its interconnections, has a meaning. "No meaningless element, factor or constituent can appear in a structure, and the traditional dichotomy of 'form' and 'content' turns out to be a misleading concept: each unit within a structure is both 'form' and 'meaning' " (KZ, 19).

Although there do not appear to be any convincing reasons why the number of such elements and relations should be less than infinite, practically speaking any given poetic work contains a limited number of such elements and relations organized in a hierarchical structure. This structure may involve such different types of relations as those between elements, or those between an element and the whole, or between an element and a relation, or between relations, or between a relation and the whole. Moreover, these relations may themselves be of different types, whether directional within the whole, or integrative of the whole, or multilateral. Thus, relations of a directional type might be represented as $A{\rightarrow}B$, or $B{\rightarrow}A$, or $A{\leftarrow}B$, or $B{\leftarrow}A$, and so on. Relations that integrate as a whole might be represented in triangular form

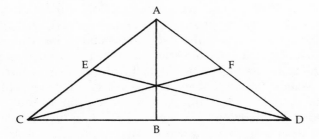

as the relations $A{\leftrightarrow}B$, $A{\leftrightarrow}C$, $B{\leftrightarrow}D$, $C{\leftrightarrow}F$, and $D{\leftrightarrow}E$, and so on. Finally multilateral relations in a simple version might be represented in rectangular form

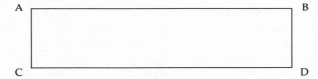

as the relations AB, AC, BD, and so on (KZ, 20ff.).

Besides the notions of a unified whole of formal elements and relations in a hierarchical organization, a final notion needs to be added to this linguistic idea of the structure of a poetic text: the notion of depth. Here again we may borrow another diagram:

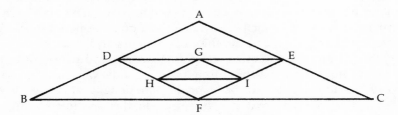

The point of this diagram is to represent each successively inscribed triangle as being "deeper" than its predecessor. Thus, DEF is deeper than ABC, and GHI is deeper than DEF. The notion of "depth" is hence that the number of relations proliferates with every increase in the level of resolution of the poetic analysis.

On the linguistic account, then, we have the notion of a verbal artifact organized as a hierarchical structure of various elements and relations descending deeper with every increase in the level of analysis. "Mountain Hut" is a poetic work organized as a formal hierarchy of the sort just described. The whole of the text is more than the sum of its parts in the sense that we can rightly predicate certain properties and propositions about the poem as a whole that we cannot about the poem as a mere aggregate. Thus we may plausibly claim that the poem as a whole succeeds in communicating, among other things, the idea that some personal ideals such as speaker's "tranquil oblivion" are irreconcilable with the commitments of love, even though this idea is not the sum of the ideas of the poem's parts. Similarly, we recognize that the structure of the poem includes a set of elements (the world, the mountain, clouds, birds, the ocean, the gate, pine trees) and relations (those between the man and the gate, the world and the mountain hut, the nightingales' song and the world and the mountain hut). Some relations in the poem, moreover, are directional (from the world to the mountain, not vice versa), others are multilateral (silence and grief, tranquility and grief), and still others are integrative (solitude and the vacant heights, solitude and the vacant hills). And finally, the number of relations would indeed seem to multiply as we increase the level of resolution in our analysis from, say, an initial inventory of certain relations holding among the various natural phenomena represented in the poem (such as the speaker's relation to the clouds, the birds, and so on) to a deeper consideration of certain abstract relations (between, say, the speaker and his successive frames of mind) to an even deeper attention to relations between general human states (kinds of solitude, kinds of spiritual disorder, and kinds of inner peace). In short, "Mountain Hut" seems to be formally organized in such a way as to accommodate the linguistic account of poetic structure.

But once again this linguistic answer to a question about the nature of poetic structure raises a question in its own right, this time a question of another order. For how can a poetic text such as "Mountain Hut," which is formally structured in such a way as to include an apparently endless series of formal hierarchies consisting of elements and relations in their various kinds and permutations extending deeper and deeper into the poetic text—how can a text structured in such a static way be what many competent readers take it to be, namely, emotionally affecting? For it seems, to the contrary, that just because, on this account so far, the structure is fixed once and for all in strictly formal and static organizational patterns, it could not genuinely move readers. The kinds of formal units and their organization into various hierarchies might indeed arouse the admiration of readers in the way the details of an extended mathematical demonstration might occasion the appreciation of a mathematician. But this reaction would be very different from the emotionally moving experience many competent readers often report.

The usual philosophical response to this kind of difficulty in the linguistic account is as follows. When we say that we are genuinely moved by a literary work of art such as "Mountain Hut" we are responding emotionally to the contents of sincere beliefs in our own minds. These beliefs are based on the representation of certain fictional states of affairs in the poetic work. But the contents of these beliefs, although they arise from meanings in the poetic work (understood as the senses of fictional sentences), are not identical with those meanings. In short, the contents of these beliefs are not fictional because they are not identifiable with the contents of certain sentences occurring in the poetic work. Rather, these contents are nonfictional—they are located in the minds of real readers and not in the features of the poetic work. Thus, just as some things may frighten us even though we sincerely believe that nothing actual corresponds to such things, so too the contents of our beliefs can genuinely move us without there being anything actual corresponding to these contents.

But as before, this standard philosophical response is not unproblematic. For this rather ingenious account skips over a central problem with reference: specifying the interpretation of reference as denotation only. What is said to determine the thought-contents that in turn are said to move us genuinely are the senses of the fictional expressions within a text.[10] And those senses, unlike the senses of nonfictional sentences, are taken to be neither true nor false. We have, then, a parallel between the truth-functional values of assertions and beliefs on the one hand and the lack of such values in the senses of fictional sentences and thought-contents on the other. A fictional work like this poem does not, properly speaking, refer at all because fictional sentences are said to lack reference. The poet not only pretends to describe and to assert; he also pretends to refer, because the nature of fictional sentences is such that he can refer within the fictional state of affairs alone and not outside the poem in the actual world. Yet just as the earlier account of truth depended on an overly narrow construal of truth as truth-functional, so too this description construes external reference much too narrowly on the model of one kind of reference only, reference as denotation.

But why not work toward a fuller and less restrictive notion of reference than the one to which the current view of fictional feeling is committed?[11] For the suggestion in the exchange between analytic[12] and hermeneutic views is that not only denotation but also exemplification and expression involve reference. Ricoeur's notion of productive reference presents a valuable alternative to the more restrictive notion of reference, permitting us to talk of fiction not as representing feelings but as remaking emotions, as rendering a world. A fourth hypothesis comes into view:

[10]Cf. Lamarque 1981:298.
[11]See Evans 1982.
[12]Goodman 1976.

4. Those peculiar feelings some poetic works arouse may be taken
   as both the intensional referents of the various uses of language
   in poetic discourses and as the extensional referents of the contents of readers' emotions.

Part of what moves us in Han Yong-un's "Mountain Hut" is what the
speaker's sufferings refer to. This may well be the real sufferings of the
families and the friends of the readers themselves. My suggestion is that
when we construe the emotive character of a poetic work in terms of
reference as denotation only, then we once again have serious difficulties
in arriving at an account of art and emotion that does justice to our
intuitions. But we need not restrict reference to denotation: we have at
our disposal a series of nondenotational interpretations of reference as
exemplification, expression, and even productive and figurational reference which enables us to account for how poetic texts can move readers
genuinely, sincerely. Thus, we can understand some readings of poetic
texts such as "Mountain Hut" as sincerely moving in the sense that the
organization of elements and relations in formal hierarchies (the key to
the text's structure), far from falsifying the reader's reaction, is essential
in soliciting active supplementations from the reader's own emotional
experience of the emotive aspects of the fictional situation.

On Art, Action, and Praxis

A fifth question arises: if all literary works that are poetic are structured
hierarchically in the sense the linguistic approach details, how is it that
each work of this kind is nonetheless organized in a different way? The
answer from the linguistic approach is that, although the structure of
every poetic work is a unified hierarchy of formal elements and relations,
poetic structure is individuated as a function of its dynamic hierarchy.[13]
   In order to clarify this initial response we need to note that the elements
of meaning are arranged not just in a static hierarchical structure but also
in a dynamic hierarchy of importance. This internal dynamism is the effect
of the opposing forces of two or more semantic tendencies or fields in
the poetic work. And it is this internal dynamism that is taken to be the
most characteristic feature of literary structure. "These tendencies," a
recent account goes, "function in the text as its organizing principle,
because they determine the structural functions of particular elements.
. . . The meaning of a literary work arises from the semantic tensions
between the organizing principles and between each of these principles

[13]KZ:73. "Structure" here is a technical term. For this fourth stage in the linguistic account,
see especially Ingarden 1973a and 1973b. For other key texts of Ingarden and critical discussions, see the Ingarden selections and the bibliography in McCormick 1986a.

and the set of elements subordinated to them. The tensions of the former type are caused by the structural oppositions between the organizing principles, while in the latter the source of dynamism resides in the tension between the deformation of meaningful factors by their organizing principle and their tendency towards semantic 'independence' " (KZ, 21–22). On this view the distinctive structure of a particular poetic work is preeminently a matter of the dynamic structural functions of its meaningful units. But the linguistic notion of what accounts for the distinctive structure of a particular poetic work is technical in comparison with the discussions of context, poetic functions, and formal structure of the poetic work. Moreover, it depends heavily on the consistent use of some theoretical notions that are unfamiliar. We will find it useful therefore to borrow once again a diagram to illustrate the most important feature of poetic structure, its internal dynamism:

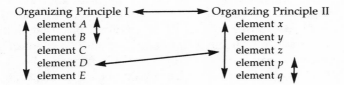

Consider first the left-hand side of the diagram alone. Notice that each element of the poetic work is a meaningful element arranged in a certain hierarchical order. Further, within this hierarchical order several elements coexist in a certain tension with one another. The result is the presence within the organizational hierarchy of at least two forces, one that attributes to each element a determinate place in the hierarchy, and an opposing force between two elements that puts that general determination under pressure of dissolution. Thus, the organizing principle is always in a certain tension with some members of the set of elements it subordinates.

Consider the two sides of the diagram together. Notice that in a poetic work at least one other organizational hierarchy coexists in opposition to the first. Since these two hierarchies consist of elements of meaning, they may be referred to as two opposing semantic tendencies within a single work. The meaning of the literary text is the result not just of the opposition between these several hierarchies, each one of which exists with the independent tension of its own internal elements. Rather, the close juxtaposition of these semantic orders results in an element from one exercising force on an element in the other. Hence the meaning of a poetic work is the resultant of three kinds of tensions: that between elements in the same hierarchy and the hierarchy's organizing principle, that between the organizing principles of each hierarchy, and that between elements in hierarchies organized by different principles. The source of the internal dynamism in the structure of a poetic work, on this linguistic account, is precisely "the tension between the deformations of meaningful factors by their organizing principle and this tendency toward semantic 'independence' " (KZ, 22).

Return now to Han Yong-un's poem "Mountain Hut."

Besides the situation the poet represents for us here—the inability of the speaker to achieve his personal ideal by following, say, the counsel of his chosen guides—the work in its own right exhibits several interesting features. Among the many details that a complete analysis would need to touch upon, consider just four.

First, the text exhibits a series of oppositions. A short list would have to include the plain/the mountain, crowdedness/emptiness, nature as a means/nature as an end, the world of art/the world of nature, the past/the present, and language/silence. Second, the text opposes to this series of divisions a basic dichotomy between the multiplicity of a rich natural world and the simplicity of a spiritual world, with the oneness of its endless and timeless domain ("the vacant heights . . . the vacant hills"). Third, the text juxtaposes two kinds of oblivion, one that the speaker seeks and finds and which leaves him troubled with "a silent grief," and another that the speaker cannot find but which can only be granted to him—this second oblivion alone will bring him peace in a "tranquil grief." And fourth, the text emphasizes, with its striking repetition of an even more striking apostrophe ("O solitude . . . O solitude"), what seems to be an alternative spiritual ideal to the ambiguous oblivion the speaker seeks, the just as ambiguous "solitude." This word "solitude" marks the major turning point of the poem and marks also the poem's conclusion. Moreover, the word occurs each time within almost the same sentence form, in an invocation whose repetition changes one word only, the last. And thus the poem closes on a final opposition between the "solitude of the vacant heights" and the "solitude of the vacant hills."

The point of the linguistic account of the essential structure of the poetic work as an internal dynamism can now be seen more clearly. For each element in each of these various pairs stands not just in a static but in a dynamic relation to its opposite. Moreover, each pair is itself arranged within a certain dynamic hierarchy of importance within the poetic work. And finally, each of these hierarchies stands in a dynamic relation not only to the other hierarchies but especially to its own organizing principle. What is called the structure of the poetic work is not a merely static formal organization of semantic elements and relations, but a very highly articulated series of internal tensions within and among these.

Notice, however, that this linguistic response to the question of how a poetic work can be structured in a unique way gives rise to yet another problem of a philosophical nature. For how exactly can either a direct statement or an indirect suggestion that arises from the internal dynamism and tensions among multiple semantic tendencies within the structure of a poetic work, a work in which the poetic function predominates, be a reasonable ground for human action? It would seem that any statement or suggestion of that kind necessarily lacks the central causal links with the empirical world that would allow one to claim for such utterances the status of being a reasonable basis for action. How can an idea derived from the complex representation of a fictional state of affairs be a reasonable ground for acting in the nonfictional everyday empirical world?

The usual answer to such a question is "it cannot." And the grounds for such an answer are not difficult to find, for we need only insist on one basic fact about a poetic work as I am using the term, precisely its fictional character. As we have seen, this notion of a poetic work does not exclude some correlations holding between elements of the fictional world and those of the nonfictional one—nightingales are to be found in both. But the essential character of the poetic work as fictional is that the states of affairs it represents do not exist in the same way as in a non-fictional work. Now, some would argue on just this basis that whatever the suggestions that might arise from reflection on a nonexisting state of affairs, they are not properly taken as reasonable grounds for action. Rather, grounds for action are reasonable to the extent that they are clearly linked, indeed causally linked, with the way the actual world really is. But whatever links there may be between the fictional world of this poem and the actual world within which its readers must act, these links at best can be extremely tenuous only and certainly not causal ones.

The problem with this standard philosophical reply, however, is that it fails to do justice not so much to the reasonableness of actions but both to the nature of action and to its connections with language.

In general, many philosophers today are sympathetic to a set of views we may summarize as follows. Although actions arise from the intentions of individuals, some necessary conditions for these actions are social aspects or roles. These two elements are intimately connected. Accordingly, explaining actions requires explaining their contexts. Moreover, accounting for actions seems to involve both explanations of causes and interpretations of intentions. Further, actions not only bear a reference to contexts, they occur within contexts. And finally, one needs to distinguish between theories of action which try to account for single actions and those that try to account for interactions, and to distinguish also between explaining actions through causes and understanding actions through reasons.[14]

The connection between explaining and understanding actions and the necessary appeal to contextual elements, whether as parts of complex causal chains or as series of reasons, shows that the usual dismissal of

[14]See Fløistad 1982 and Tuomela 1982.

the suggestion that artworks can constitute reasonable grounds for action
is overly hasty. For part of the context of some real actions is the world
of the fictional works with which the agent is acquainted. Moreover, these
works are verbal artifacts that include ambiguities arising from the open-
ended, historically developing character of the natural language in which
they are formulated.[15] However, these ambiguities cannot be resolved
without an appeal to the larger speech contexts in which they occur, so
that these contexts themselves become part of the contextuality of reasonable actions.

Now, instead of construing reasonable actions as a function of necessary
and sufficient causal warrants, why not work toward a larger understanding of *reasonableness* than the one that holds sway widely today?

In his discussion of Goodman, Ricoeur calls attention to the importance
of understanding correctly what Goodman calls "the making" of a world.
This notion is central for Goodman, because it is carefully linked with
certain theses about perception which arise from his analysis of the perception of motion as an illustration of "how perception makes its facts."[16]
To make a world is no more and no less than to articulate "in words,
numerals, pictures, sounds, or other symbols of any kind" a world-
version.[17] Ricoeur seizes upon this idea of making and underlines the
related fact that for Goodman "the way in which an object or event
functions in certain circumstances as a work of art through certain modes
of reference is a part of the way it contributes 'to a vision of—and to the
making of—a world.' "[18]

In other, more recent works Ricoeur returns to this connection between
works of art and reasonable actions. Basing his preliminary analyses on
historical narrative, then going on to literary narrative, Ricoeur argues
that the reasons for actions must not be found or even reconstructed;
they must finally be placed "within the configurational whole of a narrative." But such a configuration itself already presupposes the prefigur-
ation of an antecedent world and thus contributes to the refiguration of
a subsequent world.[19] Placing an action within a configuration, then, can
be seen in part as redescribing the world with the help of those interconnections that exist between the world of a text and the world of a
reader. Again, the attempt to incorporate into a unified account some of
the individual resources of both an analytic account of action and a hermeneutic one offers a way past a difficulty.

World here becomes the context in which the reasonable grounds for
action are to be identified, for the refigured world is, as Ricoeur writes,

[15]Kambartel and Schneider 1982:161.
[16]Goodman 1978:89.
[17]Ibid., 94.
[18]Ricoeur 1980:112, citing Goodman 1978:70.
[19]See Carr 1984.

"the totality of reference opened up by the different sorts of descriptive poetic texts I have read, interpreted, and loved."[20] Thus, for Ricoeur the goal in the interpretation of a text becomes that of grasping the text's world. "What must be interpreted in the text is a proposed world which I could inhabit and wherein I could project one of my inmost possibilities."[21] Accordingly, we may try the formulation of yet another hypothesis:

> 5. Those peculiar actions that some poetics works present may be taken as reasonable not on empirical or causal grounds but on the pragmatic grounds that such actions would lead to the refiguration, in praxis, of a scenario whose possibility has been glimpsed in imaginative interactions with the configurations of a fictional world.

Thus, I claim that when we construe the reasonableness of actions strongly in terms of their necessary and sufficient causal antecedents, we are not able to account for enough of what our own experience and that of others reliably reports—namely, that some poetic works sometimes serve as reasonable grounds for action. But just as in the case of language, knowledge, truth, and emotion, so too in that of action we need not restrict ourselves to causal explanation. For we also have available, as some of the interaction between analytic philosophy and hermeneutics shows,[22] a strategy for interpreting actions intentionally. When we investigate these possibilities, we find that, far from being unreliable as grounds for human actions, some poetic works present their readers with scenarios for reasonable courses of action which can be interpreted satisfactorily in just these terms.

On Art, the Self, and the Person

If we return once again to our example, keeping in mind the linguistic description of a text in a communication situation in which a poetic function dominates and is structured in both static and dynamic ways so as to call attention largely to its organization as such, a further question arises: in what ways can such a description be elaborated so as to account

[20]Ricoeur 1983–85:1.121.
[21]Ricoeur 1981:142.
[22]See Stoutland 1982:45–72.

for the complex phenomenon in many such works of the author's voice and the speaker's voice? The suggestion on the linguistic account is that the speaker's voice is to be explained mainly in terms of a set of codes which is imposed on the primary set established in the ordinary usages of a natural language.

A literary work uses some signs in such a way that they function simultaneously in more than one system.[23] Such signs are points of intersection between various codes. When the meaning of a sign is determined in one code only, some linguists speak of a system; and where a sign's meaning is determined as a function of the intersection of two codes, then the linguist speaks of a primary and a secondary system. A primary system is designed to avoid ambiguity through the use of signs with univocal meanings, whereas a secondary system is designed to foster the "semantic potential" of each sign through the fashioning of signs with multiple meanings. In a poetic work the secondary system is constructed through the interplay of various codes in such a way that its own code is unique. This means that a secondary system functions in more than one sign system at the same time, thereby establishing a unique semantic code. Often this unique code consists of a "complex network of semantic equivalences" (KZ, 31).

Each sign system orders its semantic information in view of accomplishing a specific task. The task of the primary system is to select and to order from an infinite variety of materials a set of information units in a sign system in such a way that the communication process can proceed without ambiguity. To each and every distinct sign in the system one and only one meaning is to be assigned. Thus we may say that the semantic tendency of a primary system is toward univocity. By contrast the task of the secondary system is to superimpose on the univocal meanings of the signs that are selected and ordered in the primary system a multiplicity of additional meanings. Each sign in the secondary system is, we may say, charged with a semantic potential it did not possess as long as it was confined to the primary system. Thus, the semantic tendency of the secondary system is toward multiplicity.

Equivalences among signs in a primary system depend on the signs sharing a common empirical denotatum, with the result that one sign can be interchanged for another where both are synonymous—they refer to the same object or state of affairs in the empirical world. But in a secondary system equivalences among signs depend on the signs sharing a common intentional designatum, with the result that signs are able to be interchanged not because of synonymity but because they refer to the same designatum in the text even though this designatum lacks a denotatum in the empirical world. What happens is that a particular sign in a primary

[23]For this fifth stage in the linguistic approach, see especially Lotman 1976 and 1977.

system is recoded in a secondary system and subsequently no longer functions the way it did antecedently. Such a recoding involves the substitution of a designatum for a denotatum. In losing its denotatum the recoded sign loses its reference to the empirical realm; it retains, however, a relation to the intentional realm. This phenomenon of recoding a set of elements and relations selected, defined, and revealed as a code in the primary system is taken to be central in the understanding of the speaker's voice in the poetic work. For such understanding involves recognizing how two different systems, each with its own opposed semantic tendency, coexist in the same verbal text. The primary system is the natural language whose semantic register corresponds to the author's and reader's own linguistic competence, whereas the secondary system is poetic discourse whose semantic register results from the superposition of multiple meanings on the semantic register of the primary system. The speaker's voice in the poetic work is the result of the interaction between the preeminently linguistic codes of one primary system and the cultural codes of the secondary system, and the speaker's voice of the poetic work is taken to be that of a fictional self.

When we turn back to "Mountain Hut" we may observe the interactions between the two systems at work in the poem. For on rereading the poem we notice two semantic organizing principles operating in opposition to each other: the description of the mountain hut is a metaphorical embodiment of one interpretation of the personal ideal of solitude, whereas the expression of the poetic self's restlessness, questioning, and prayerful invocation is a metaphorical embodiment of a different interpretation of solitude. The theme of the poem seems to ask the question how the speaker is to achieve a kind of peaceful and personal emptiness, but the word "emptiness" is not in the text. How, then, does the poem communicate the meanings associated with the unspoken theme of personal emptiness? It does so, on the linguistic account, by superimposing on the primary semantic system of the author and reader a secondary semantic system of the poetic self.

We have already noted a striking parallelism in the last two stanzas of this poem—its last five lines—which now requires a closer look. Notice that the first and last lines are almost exactly alike. Both consist of complete sentences, both are exclamations, both exemplify the rhetorical figure of apostrophe. But the last line substitutes the epithet "vacant hills" for the first line's "vacant heights." The effect is one of careful and deliberate contrast (an effect, we have noticed, reinforced by the positions of these lines both in the poem as a whole and in their respective stanzas) together with a distinctiveness in rhetorical character. Hence the major principle at work here, despite the parallelism, is that of semantic differentiation whose main function is to dynamize through repetition a network of disequivalences between the last two stanzas and to multiply the meanings that arise from the combination of the closely similar but not identical elements in the two epithets.

In the primary system the word "vacant" means "empty," in the sense of there being nothing present in a particular place at a particular time. But in these epithets the word cannot mean what it ordinarily means— that is, what it means for the author—because the speaker has already informed us that the mountain is no longer quite "vacant": he has built a hut there and it is now inhabited. With this realization the secondary system comes into play with the suggestion that the word "vacant" is here recoded; it carries a different sense than the one that bears it in the primary system. Here this code links the word "vacant" with the much earlier word "oblivion" in line 2, "rue" in line 13, "without" in line 18, and especially (because the word is repeated) with the two occurrences of "solitude" in lines 15 and 19. The suggestion, then, in the secondary system is that each of these terms has to be understood in a different way than it ordinarily is. And explaining such meanings involves accounting for the speaker's voice and the newly established codes of the poetic self as opposed to the author's voice and the ordinary codes of the author's natural language.

This linguistic description of how a poetic work communicates a peculiar tension between one semantic pattern characterizing the author's voice and a different semantic pattern that is that of the speaker's voice can of course be elaborated much more fully. But even in the summary form in which we have it here, this linguistic response to a question about the poetic work provokes in turn a more general question: how can a poetic work such as "Mountain Hut," which achieves some of its central effects by recoding the primary sign system of the author in terms of a secondary system that largely pertains to the speaker, be instrumental, as many readers reliably report, in the critical articulations of their own identity as persons? On the linguistic account the matter of the speaker's voice arising from a fictional self is to be understood in immanent terms only as the result of the superposition of an aspect of the secondary system on the relevant part of the primary system. Yet the phenomenon of the fictional self whose voice is to be heard in the speaker's voice within the poetic work seems often to be closely related to the nonfictional identities of many readers themselves. In short, the linguistic description raises general questions about the nature and genesis of future selves.

The usual response to this issue is to construe the notion of a fictional self as a way of referring to possible future states of a particular individual's identity as a person. Thus, talk of a fictional self outside the poetic work is on this view a way of accounting for the fact that persons change over time while remaining "the same person." In other words, persons are said to maintain both psychological and physical connectedness and continuity between their past, present, and future states. Brain states as well as memories, intentions, desires, character states, and so on persist. At one time, however, a particular person can imagine different possibilities for himself in the future, including different possible identities as a person. In this context one may talk of any one of these future identities as a fictional self in the future. Similar accounts can be developed for a person's necessarily partial and imperfect reconstructions of his or her identity in the past. Once again, one may speak here of any one of these past identities as a fictional self in the past. The place of the poetic work in all this, for the philosopher, is simply that of a source of inspiration. Reading poetic works, or more often works of narrative fiction, allows some readers the opportunity to explore imaginatively different possible interpretations of their own identities as persons. Some readers then come to entertain different fictional selves as possible scenarios either for the partial reconstruction of their past identities or as indeterminate scenarios for their future identity. In such a philosophical context, then, talk of the voice of the poetic work, the lyrical voice of a fictional or poetic self, suggests no more than a rhetorical figure, metaphor, or metonymy for what is properly an analytic task of providing necessary and sufficient conditions for the identity of a person over time as one and the same person.

But just as in the previous cases this familiar philosophical account of personal identity, and the specific issue of the nature and genesis of future selves in connection with poetic works, is not unproblematic. For our own reading of "Mountain Hut" and similar works suggests that the connection between the fictional selves (whose lyrical voice we ourselves and not only the implied reader hear) and our own identities as persons in the future is much richer, more substantive, and more functional than the standard account is able to acknowledge. Part of the difficulty in the philosophical account seems to arise from making talk of future selves depend much too directly on the kinds of analyses which seem fruitful in accounting for the identity of actual persons in the present.

But why not investigate the possibility here of disassociating much more radically than the current account would seem to permit the notions of self and person from an interpretation of identity in terms of two undifferentiated uses of physical and psychological connectedness and continuity (an interpretation that leaves too little room for indeterminate identities)? For it may well turn out to be the case that accounting for the nature and genesis of future selves is not necessarily the same kind of task as accounting for the identity of actual persons.

A suggestion along these lines can be developed from reflecting again on one of the central interactions between analytic and hermeneutic philosophy. In his most recent work Ricoeur has concerned himself less directly with the work of Goodman than earlier, but in some sense he has made one of Goodman's own working principles explicitly his own.

At one point in his examination of the notion of narrative action and temporality he refers to the title of the first chapter of Goodman's *Languages of Art*, "Reality Remade," as an effective guideline for his own work. He refers also to Goodman's idea that fictional works are to be thought of in terms of worlds and worlds in terms of works.[24]

Ricoeur's comment here is a preliminary indication of a theme that preoccupies him throughout the three volumes of *Time and Narrative*. Perhaps the most relevant part of that extended discussion for our concern with personal identity is the idea that a poetic work (to use our term) involves an element that points beyond its own confines; a poetic work has what Ricoeur calls a *visée*.[25] Later, in a much more central passage, he talks of the work involving a certain "finality" (2.150). The idea is that understanding a work satisfactorily involves grasping a certain intentionality or directedness in the text which is not reducible to the set of intrinsic elements and relations which the text comprises. This directedness is what points beyond the work itself to the domain of its readers. Further, it is this directedness that invites the readers of the work to articulate a fictive experience of certain matters such as time. Finally, Ricoeur makes the major claim (2.151) that some of the variety of such matters as time can only be explored through the construction of such fictive experiences, of what he calls later "virtual ways of inhabiting the world that the literary work projects by its power of self transcendence" (2.233).

Much of this talk needs, to say the least, careful sorting, some of which Ricoeur has himself undertaken in his Gifford lectures in 1986. But even in this initial form such reflections offer a promise once again of elaborating an account of fictional selves and personal identity which draws upon more than one philosophical tradition, spells out more fully the conceptual background of the linguistic descriptions of the poetic work, and may even open up further areas in our understanding of individual poetic works.

Thus, we may formulate another hypothesis as follows:

> 6. Those peculiar entities that some poetic works generate as the subjects of their various speakers' voices may be taken as bases for selfless persons, kinds of indeterminacies which communities of readers come to explore through imaginative variations in articulating their past and future identities as persons.

Part of what some readers of "Mountain Hut" come to understand in understanding this poetic work is certain virtual states of their own identities as persons. When we construe personal identity too strongly in

---

[24]Ricoeur 1983–85:1.122, n. 3.
[25]Ricoeur 1984:2.130. Further references are given in the text, volume before page number.

either reductionist or nonreductionist terms alone, we have serious difficulty in accommodating the experiences many competent readers reliably report of appropriating fictive experiences for their own repeated
attempts at increased self-understanding. But such a choice between reductionist and nonreductionist accounts is not required. For as several
recent discussions in this domain also make clear, personal identity, at
least with regard to the nature of a person's future states and their connection and conformities with his or her identity in the present, can be
interpreted on the less restrictive terms of some future selves, as selfless
persons, as fictions of a peculiar sort. Thus, coming to understand poetic
works such as "Mountain Hut" leads here, as elsewhere, to raising central
questions about the adequacy not just of our current linguistic description
of such texts but of a current philosophical interpretation of at least one
central concept on which these descriptions turn.

On Art and the World

Finally, when we reflect further on a poetic work as a verbal text in a
communication process where the poetic function predominates, a text
structured as a dynamic and unified set of tensions among opposed
groups of semantic tendencies whose signs are articulated in social, cultural, and artistic as well as linguistic codes, and whose unique code
results from the superposition of a secondary system on a primary one,
still another question arises: how are we to explain the fact that a poetic
work characteristically makes use of polysemic signs in such a way as
often to yield the construction of a fictional world and the opening up of
the possibility of enhancing our experience of the real world? On the
linguistic account, we are to explain such matters by understanding the
systems of a poetic work as modeling systems and the constructions of
such works not as copies but as models.

In order to elaborate this special use of the term "model" we need to
return to our discussion of primary and secondary systems (KZ, 42–43).
These systems are more properly understood as primary and secondary
modeling systems. The former is largely used to convey information about
the empirical world through the use of univocal signs, whereas the latter
conveys information about a model of the world through the use of poly-
valent signs. More simply, we may say, as earlier, that a primary system
is a natural language consisting of a very large set of signs, each element
of which communicates some meaning; whereas a secondary system is a
poetic discourse consisting of a much smaller set of signs, each element
of which communicates a much larger quantity of information and whose
meanings are more complex than those of its counterparts (KZ, 52, 59).

For besides interacting in terms of different codes in such a way that a secondary system superimposes a set of inhabitual schematic tendencies on the ordinary ones of the primary system, the intervention itself is said to bring about the formation of a new semantic code that cannot be reduced to either of its separate components. The new code is in fact a specific function of the ordinary and univocal semantic tendencies of the primary system and the unusual and multiple semantic tendencies of the secondary system. This fusion comes about differently in each reading of the text, with the result that for any one reading there is one unique code only, the specific effect of the specific intention of the component semantic tendencies at that time.

The unique code of the poetic work may be understood as a peculiar kind of semantic field in which a new network of equivalencies is generated, within which signs that are similar but not identical are combined. When the signs of the primary system are recoded as a result of the interactions between the two systems, these signs, as we have noted, lose their referential connections with empirical reality, their denotata, and become signs with designata only. The unique set of these designations still stands in relation with empirical reality because the set preserves some genetic connections with the denotative signs of the primary system from which it derives. This relation, however, can no longer be understood in the same way. In whatever way the account of the antecedent relation between denotative signs and empirical reality may have been qualified—as imitation, as representation, as picturing, as configuration—the subsequent relation between designative signs and empirical reality must be redescribed differently. For the two relations are fundamentally distinct.

The linguistic proposal is that this relation be called a modeling relation. The set of designative signs is a construction of empirical reality in the sense that it is a model of that reality. The formulation of this relation differs somewhat according to the specific theory at issue, but the central functions of such formulation are evident in the following summary. "In those created semantic fields the signs of the primary system lose their referential connection with the objects' empirical reality—they become devoid of denotation, and so their set does not pretend to be a copy of the reality; instead it forms a model of a reality in itself. Thus, a literary work does not so much 'reflect' the world, as create it; there is rather poiesis than mimesis . . . a construct, an effect of selection, combination and interpretation—in a word, a model of a world" (KZ, 45; emphasis omitted and translation slightly corrected).

The most important element in this view is the idea that the model is not a copy of the empirical world even though it is articulated with the help of ambiguous signs, some of whose interpretations may include denotata and hence some connections with the empirical world. The accent is on the difference between the model and that world; "the poem brings into existence not only its own communication system but also its own model of reality different from that of the empirical world" (KZ, 64–65). This model of reality is what we mean when we talk about the fictional world of a poetic work. And it is this fictional world that is finally recoded in the superposition of the secondary modeling system on the primary one.

One final point needs to be added to the linguistic account of a world as a fictional world—the idea that it is often against the background of such fictional works that readers of poetic works are enabled to perceive the empirical world in novel ways. This central thesis is muted in the linguistic account but nevertheless can be clearly heard when questions of aesthetic and artistic value arise. On one version, the fictional world is seen as exhibiting a special value that is reducible neither to the properties of the poetic work itself nor to certain kinds of expectations on the part of the reader. Rather, the value of a fictional world consists in the relationship between textual features of the work and textual features of the readers' changing awareness across history. The "value of a literary text is proportionate to the force and dynamism between the literary text and the expectations of the reading public for whom it is intended; between the tendency toward innovation and the system of literary conventions and aesthetic norms operative in that society" (KZ, 170–71). The value here is called aesthetic value because the responses of readers and their communities is essential, unlike the artistic value of a work that depends on the internal dynamic structure of the text itself without any reference to readers' attitudes or responses. A fictional world, then, enhances the possibilities of experience in the empirical world to the degree that it is invested with a kind of value resulting not just from the interaction between its two semantic systems but between its immanent structure and its transcendent readership as well.

Return, then, one last time to "Mountain Hut." Here as elsewhere we would ultimately have to delve much more deeply into the original language of the poem and its distinguished readings over the several generations since its publication to articulate well enough the construct the poem achieves. But once again several elementary observations of what the poem exhibits even in translation, as opposed to what the poet represents, call our attention to a certain power in this work to project a model that may seem to offer some readers the possibility of enriching their own experience. Thus, quite generally, the model here may be construed in part as a fictional world in which unique tensions hold between the realization of certain personal ideals and the fulfillments of a human love. More particularly, some readers may find here a fictional world that opens out onto the possibility that in the nonfictional world some personal ideals that are granted in contrast with those that are too actively sought may be entirely compatible with human love. Consider by way of one example only several details.

Besides the parallelism between "vacant hills" and "vacant heights" which we examined in the previous section, the last two stanzas include another central element, the pair of opposed terms in the epithets "vacant heights . . . vacant hills." The "heights" are opposed to the "hills." Thus, the suggestion arises that the vacancy in the first epithet is not of the same order as the vacancy in the second. Since both epithets occur in the exclamations addressed to "solitude," it follows that the meaning of the "solitude" in the last line is no more to be identified with that in the preceding line than the meaning of "vacant" in the last line is to be identified with that of "vacant" in its predecessor.

Thus, the dynamic tension here between two modeling systems suggests to attentive readers the idea that, whereas the first interpretation of oblivion as a solitude of the vacant and "lofty" heights must fail because it is envisioned as something the speaker sees himself as achieving through unaided personal effort, the second interpretation of oblivion as a solitude of the more prosaic hills may well succeed because it is envisioned as something that can only be granted to the speaker independently of his strivings.

Without losing ourselves in too much speculation, we may pursue this suggestion by looking finally at one of this poem's central terms, "mountain hut." Although the phrase as such is used explicitly in the title only, the word "hut" occurs prominently in the first stanza, is evoked indirectly in the second ("gate"), and is understood throughout the second half of the poem as the place where the speaker passes his "sleepless nights" meditating on love and solitude, on grief and tranquility, on vacancy and emptiness. The poem constructs a model, the linguistic account claims, of the empirical world. This model is a fictional world that, though similar, is centrally different from the empirical world. Further, this fictional world may enhance the possibilities of experience. Here one specific suggestion seems to be that the concrete ideal of a mountain hut as opposed to the mundane hut at the beginning of the poem can be realized only through a transformation in the speaker's understanding of his own personal ideal. And this transformation itself must incorporate a radically new relation between an understanding of solitude as a restless and vacant emptiness and that of solitude as a peaceful and fulfilled nothingness.

But once again, the linguistic answer to the question about how a poetic work constructs a fictional world raises a question. For how exactly can the model of a fictional world, which the harmonious conjunctions of different and dynamically opposed semantic hierarchies in the structure of a literary work construct, connect effectively with the everyday historical and empirical world of its interpreters? How can the fictional world be effectively connected to the nonfictional world? For again it would seem that any such construction at best could be of no further use than as an object of disinterested contemplation, an artifact of the interaction between a writer's articulation of an intentional object and a reader's projection, through that complex state of affairs, of a possible world only.

One standard response to this question, which has become increasingly important in analytic aesthetics, goes like this. The "world" of a literary work is one of a number of possible worlds. Possible worlds, this view goes, are nothing more than sets of ideas. Some of these may well have correlates in the actual space-time world. And when they do such ideas invite an imaginative supplementation and exploration. In more technical terms this view of the literary work as a possible world has been formulated as follows: "the world of a work is a complex state of affairs, or complex proposition—thus a complex Fregean *Gedanke*. It consists of those states of affairs which the inscription of the text was used to propound with one or another illocutionary force, plus whatever is appropriately extrapolated therefrom."[26]

This view of the nature of a fictional world as a possible world is certainly plausible. It relies in fact on a sophisticated understanding of language and logic. Moreover, it allows for the fact that some elements in fictional worlds may have nonfictional counterparts. But this philosophical view has problems of its own. For it leaves the nature of fictional worlds, such as the one the poetic work here presents, open to too large an array of ontological interpretations. Fictional worlds are various. But unlike merely possible worlds, they are both more particular and more closely related to the actual world of their authors than are their counterparts.

Why not then work toward a less general but more adequate understanding of the connections between works of art and the actual world by rethinking the notion of the world of a work not in terms of possible worlds but in those of fictive and fictional worlds? In Ricoeur's discussion of Goodman's ontology we may find still another suggestion, this time as to how we might deal more adequately with fictional worlds.

Ricoeur calls attention to a curious asymmetry in Goodman's expressions "world-versions" and "versions of the world" on the one hand, and "chimera-versions" and "versions of a chimera" on the other. He suspects that Goodman's insistent attempts to do away with *the* world by talking of world-versions is finally no more than an artifice of language. "The irreducible difference," Ricoeur writes, "between world-versions and versions of the world arises from the connection that no version exhausts that which requires to be, literally or metaphorically, described, depicted, exemplified, or expressed. Otherwise why throughout cultural

[26]Wolterstorff 1984:152.

changes would men (and women) have wanted or needed to make new kinds of versions and new versions of the known kinds *again and again*?"[27]

Ricoeur's suggestion here is that we need to pay much closer attention to the repeated attempts of writers of fiction continually to render a world. What stands behind these attempts, he wants to say, is not so much *the* world, which Goodman rejects, nor even the plurality of worlds, which he advocates. Rather, we can entertain the notion of *a* world that, though never reducible to any one world-version or even to classes of such versions, remains nevertheless always and eluctably part of a particular world-version. It is this notion of *a* world which may do better justice to the perceptual inexhaustibility of world, "the interplay between all the perceptual fields, the movement of attention which dilates and contracts alternately and the indefinite flight of the perceptual horizon" (188). And it is also this notion of a world which also addresses the opacity of the world, its unrelenting resistance to our repeated scrutiny. In short, world-versions are versions of a world as a horizon.

With such a notion of world as a horizon we may be better able to deal with the difficulties of making out the distinction I alluded to earlier between fictional worlds and possible worlds on the one hand and fictional worlds and actual ones on the other. I suggest a formulation of a final working hypothesis:

> 7. Those peculiar worlds that poetic works represent may be taken as neither possible nor actual worlds independent of some descriptions, but as virtual worlds that can only exist within world-versions and yet whose horizons always surpass their articulation in particular versions of a world.

Part of what we come to be at home with in the unfamiliar world of Han Yong-un's "Mountain Hut" is nothing more or less than a horizon of our own real world. My claim, then, is that such a model must remain in the domain of contemplation alone only so long as we understand this model in the powerful terms of possible-worlds theory. But as a sample of a discussion between analytical philosophy and hermeneutics shows, other alternatives for understanding these models are available. Thus, interpreting such models not so much as possible worlds but as scenarios—configurations of conceptual alternatives for figuring the everyday world of daily experience—allows us once again to recapture the force of our intuitions. Some poetic works enable their readers to explore imaginative alternatives for the rearticulation of their own worlds. The models that poetic works present us with in presenting their fictional worlds,

---

[27]Ricoeur 1980:117.

even though they have intentional existence only, remain nonetheless intimately connected with the so-called really existing world.

Here, then, are seven suggestions taken from different contexts and perhaps indicative of further resources in contemporary aesthetics for advancing our reflections on problems with literary works of art. We have, thus, a notion of fictional discourse based on reference as productive rather than strictly denotational, a notion of truth as truth-to-life, a notion of cognitivity of literature as more a matter of belief than knowledge, a notion of the feelings that some literary works may arouse as involving both extensional as well as intensional referents, a notion of reasonable grounds for action as intentional connections rather than just causal links, a notion of fictive selves as indeterminate entities of a peculiar sort, and of world as a fictional model, rather than world as merely model whether possible or actual. Each remains to be articulated in the more richly detailed context of specific concerns with literature and philosophy. But it seems already clear by anticipation how each may well present a serious alternative to corresponding notions in the prevalent account of poetic works.

1

Fictional Discourses

> In a word, the task is to consider philosophy also as a particular genre.
> —JACQUES DERRIDA

> In the case of the distinction between fiction and non-fiction, the relation is one of logical dependency. One could not have the concept of fiction without the concept of serious discourse.
> —JOHN SEARLE

> If we could imagine dissonance become man—and what else is man—this dissonance, to be able to live, would need a splendid illusion, that would cover dissonance with a veil of beauty.
> —FRIEDRICH NIETZSCHE

Below are excerpts from two familiar works, one usually taken as fictional and the other as nonfictional. In the interests of comparison it will prove useful to have both texts before us in paragraph form.[1] The first text reads:

> . . . it is only in the midst of this world that a new transfiguring illusion becomes necessary in order to keep the animated world of individuation alive. If we could imagine dissonance become man—and what else is man—this dissonance, to be able to live, would need a splendid illusion that would cover dissonance with a veil of beauty. This is the true artistic aim of Apollo in whose name we comprehend all those countless illusions of the beauty of mere appearance that at every moment make life worth living at all and prompt the desire to live on in order to experience the next moment. On this foundation of all existence—the Dionysian basic ground of the world—not one whit more may enter the consciousness of the human individual than can be overcome again by this Apollinian power of transfiguration.

[1]See Dickie and Sclafani 1977.

And the second goes:

> There are three conditions which look alike yet differ completely, flourish
> in the same hedgerow: attachment to self and to things and to persons,
> detachment from self and from things and from persons; and, growing
> between them, indifference which resembles the others as death resembles
> life, being between two lives—unflowering, between the live and the dead
> nettle. This is the use of memory: for liberation—not less of love but
> expanding of love beyond desire, and so liberation from the future as well
> as the past. Thus, love of a country begins as attachment to our own field
> of action and comes to find that action of little importance though never
> indifferent. History may be servitude, history may be freedom. See, now
> they vanish, the faces and the places, with the self which, as it could,
> loved them, to become renewed, transfigured in another pattern.

These two texts, the first from a work of philosophy (Nietzsche's *Birth
of Tragedy*) and the second from a poem (Eliot's *Four Quartets*), are said
to differ in kind in that the first is an instance of nonfictional discourse
and the second of fictional discourse. It is difficult, however, to say in
just what this difference consists. In what follows I try to articulate the
nature of this distinction, working through successive approximations to
revise our standard account of the distinction between fictional and nonfictional discourse. I test the established account in terms of three putatively nonfictional texts from eighteenth-century philosophical aesthetics,
to reconstruct it accordingly, and finally to highlight some underlying
difficulties the reconstruction indicates in traditional philosophical reflection on fiction.

A Standard View of Fictionality:
Speech-Act Theory

The general question here is just what makes the second of these texts
and not the first an instance of fictional discourse? One recent view, which
we may call hereafter the standard view,[2] is a contemporary variation of
Sidney's defense of poetry against the Puritans. What makes a text fictional is that it "nothing affirms." Or, in modern parlance, Eliot does not
perform illocutionary acts in "Little Gidding"; rather, he represents the
performances of illocutionary acts.

The cardinal notion of an illocutionary act invoked here is relatively
familiar. Some conventions allow speakers to make a single utterance do
double duty. Those familiar with the conventions of, for example, chris-

---

[2]Standard in the sense that, without being the only view available, it remains one of the
few comprehensive and influential accounts on record which continues to solicit sympathetic
critical qualifications.

tening, which is to say with certain specifiable social, psychological, and physical conditions governing a particular utterance and with certain rules for the production of a well-formed utterance, are able both to communicate with other persons and at the same time to confer a name on a newly launched ship. In making an utterance of a certain type, a speaker both performs an act of communication and at the same time conventionally generates an act of christening. With some simplification, the first act is called a locutionary act and the second an illocutionary one. An utterance, moreover, can just as well be an act of writing or of gesturing as one of speaking. Since a locutionary act can generate an illocutionary one only if all the requisite conditions and rules for the generation of that kind of illocution are satisfied, some putative illocutionary acts may be incomplete. And when a locutionary act is performed in such a way as to invite a hearer or reader to recognize the concomitant production of an illocutionary act without satisfying all the conditions and rules required for the generation of such an act, the result is a quasi-illocutionary act, or what the standard account calls a fictive illocutionary act.

In the case of fictive illocutionary acts two elements are crucial. First, the text must include sufficient markers (for example, sentences in the form of assertions) which clearly invite the hearer's or reader's supposition that appropriate conditions and rules might generate an illocutionary act. And second, the text must also include sufficient markers (for example, a subtitle such as "a novel") which clearly indicate that some of the appropriate conditions are lacking and/or that some of the rules are not being followed. The result is a text that includes utterances representing genuine illocutions, while not itself actually presenting genuine illocutions. Such utterances are instances of what the standard account calls fictional discourse, that is, "discourse in which there is a make-believe illocutionary action, but in fact no such action is performed."[3]

We now need to look at several aspects of this initial formulation more closely. Here is a first formulation of the standard view:

> 1. What makes a text fictional is its representation of the performance of illocutionary acts.

This view of fiction focuses on the nature of a particular text and not just on how a reader or a community of readers in a culture takes a text. For even though some community of readers may approach virtually any text within a certain set of common expectations such that the text is taken as fictional, it is another and more difficult matter to say whether virtually any text may appropriately be taken as fictional.[4] Just as not any text can

[3]Beardsley 1978b:170.
[4]Beardsley 1981:292.

properly be described as literary, so too not any text can properly be described as fictional. It is true that the fictional text, like the literary one, is a language game set within a frame.[5] And of course someone somewhere may always choose to set any language game whatsoever within a frame, perhaps by viewing the language game at issue from a particular perspective or with a certain attitude. But on the standard view these facts do not entail that any text whatsoever is fictional: that a text may be considered fictional does not make it fictional; further, that someone may take any text as fictional does not entail that a community of educated readers will follow. Thus, some texts on this view cannot be properly taken as fictional at all.

The standard view incorporates a particular interpretation of what a text is. A text here is construed as an oral or written "syntactically ordered string of words in a language."[6] More precisely, the text is "not an individual inscription or utterance but a text-type, of which inscriptions and utterances are instances" (293). A text is produced in order to perform an illocutionary act, that is, an essentially rule-governed act of a particular act-type such as promising, inviting, regretting, and lying. Fictional texts as opposed to nonfictional ones represent the performance of such illocutionary acts, where the term "represent" is used by analogy with its use in the visual arts. Thus, a fictional text is said to represent those performances in the way that a painting is said to depict a scene: "it is a matter of selective matching—some shapes, colors, line segments, regional qualities, or gestalts are captured and perceived to be those characteristic of the kind of object or event depicted" (295). So the sense of representation which is central in fictional texts is representation not as denotation but as a selective similarity relationship between symbol and referent.

The standard view also tries to address the question of whether any objective features distinguish fictional from nonfictional texts. Most discussion so far has focused on fictional prose narratives. The accent has not fallen on external markers such as the subtitle "a novel" indicated earlier but on internal markers only. And the working assumption continues to be that, although the aesthetic intentions they manifest may suffice to distinguish such texts as literary, they do not suffice to distinguish them further as fictional.

Five such features stand out. One mark of fictionality is said to be the use of indirect discourse about the mental states of characters. Such a practice implies an omniscient narrator or speaker. And no nonfictional speaker can rightly claim omniscience. Thus, the occurrence of an illocutionary speech act in such contexts must be construed not as the per-

---

[5]Fish 1980.
[6]Beardsley 1981:293. Further references are given in the text.

formance of such an act but as its representation. Another mark is the use of narrated monologues that transform performances of illocutionary acts into their representations. For such monologues contract the past and future tenses of verbs into a fictionally present time. Third, some putative descriptions of particular events in fictional texts are not required to satisfy the same epistemic conditions that govern descriptions in non-fictional texts. A further objective mark of fictionality is said to be the presence in fictional texts of nonreferring names or descriptions, that is, sentences containing names or descriptions of what does not exist. The illocutionary acts at issue in such sentences can only be represented and not actually performed. Finally, still another mark of the fictional text is the aspect of address without access. The author of a fictional text, while wishing to communicate by the very fact of writing and publishing such a text, deliberately withdraws from the occasions and circumstances that would allow personal access to an individual reader. "We hear a personal voice," this account goes, "but we know that it cannot be speaking to us, since we have not received the text from the author, but found it in a library or book-store or magazine" (303).

With these observations in hand we may now detail the initial statement of the fictionality theory more fully:

> 2. What makes a text fictional is the presence in the text-type itself of certain external and internal conditions that together insure that a community of readers in a culture (a) takes the relevant sentences as illocutionary performances, (b) recognizes that at least some requisite conditions are not fully satisfied, and (c) goes on to construe these illocutions not as genuine performances but as represented ones in the sense of some relevant features being selectively matched ones only.

If this is a fuller statement of the standard theory, what are the central qualifications? Some fictional texts may be used to perform illocutionary acts—for example, to make a political statement by being read aloud at a political rally. But such a use does not change the nature of the text; it remains a representation of the performance of such acts and not a performance in its own right. More interesting is the case in which the composition of a fictional text is used to perform an illocutionary act. For example, in writing a fictional text the author is understood to be inviting through an act of pretense his or her readers to consider certain fictional entities in a particular set of fictional states of affairs.[7] Here again, however, the composition of such a text, like its performance, can be an illocutionary use of a text that is not itself an illocution.

[7]See Krukowski 1981:328.

Second, we should note that the standard theory does not include the claim that fictions contain only representations of illocutionary acts. For some fictions include both representations of such acts and the acts themselves. But the theory does include the related claim that the speakers in fictional works and not the authors perform the illocutionary acts in question. This, however, remains very general in that no attempt is made to explain just how speakers' statements in fictional texts can be absolved from bearing authors' intentions.[8]

Still, the function of the distinction is clear. For the speakers most often direct their illocutionary acts at characters in a work and hence cannot assume responsibility for the seriousness of such acts. And by merely representing illocutionary acts instead of performing them the author need not assume such responsibilities either. Hence the notion that fictional texts involve the suspension of speakers' and authors' responsibilities.

A third qualification turns on the distinction between a text being fictional and a text becoming fictional. The standard theory attempts to do justice to both kinds of works, the readily recognizable and the puzzlingly experimental. Thus, the basic task is to plot "a comprehensive, yet limited and explicit set of characteristics that both identifies and describes fictional works" (328).

A text is fictional if it exhibits most but not necessarily all of such characteristics. But this set of characteristics is not fixed. And as times change innovatory pieces may provoke the addition of further elements to the original set. A text, then, becomes fictional by exhibiting some traditional characteristics and forcing interpretive communities to consider adding novel elements to the original set of characteristics (324).

A fourth qualification touches on the structure of fictional works. For the standard theory of the fictional to hold not all fictional works need to be structured as first-person narratives. This case of course is the central one in such a theory because first-person narrative illustrates very clearly just how the distinction between fictional speakers' performances and authors' performances arises. But other fictional texts are in fact structured in other ways. It is sufficient for the standard theory that many but not all fictional texts, whatever their basic structure, exhibit the fundamental distinction between those illocutionary acts that fictional speakers are represented as performing and those performances that authors represent.[9]

A fifth qualification is the distinction between what an author may represent about characters in a fictional text and what he or she may represent about him or herself in a fictional text. For "just as we can assert of ourselves what is not true, so too can we fictionalize of ourselves what is not true" (316). This distinction is important, for it addresses the often remarked fact that at least some sentences in any fictional text can be

---

[8]Ibid., 325.
[9]Wolterstorff 1981:322.

parsed satisfactorily only on the hypothesis that they in part reveal something about the teller of the tale and not just about the speaker in the tale. "Literary discourse," this thesis reads, "cannot be viewed solely as telling a story. Discourse has significance beyond story" (318). And part of this significance attaches not just to the figure of the narrator but also to the author specifically in the guise of fictionalizing something about himself or herself in the various stances of pretending.

A final qualification turns on just who or what is doing the representing in the text. For even when we gloss representing as a selective similarity relationship, we need to distinguish between what the author represents and what the text represents. On the standard view, the author initially represents what the text ultimately goes on to represent in a process called "the detachment of reference." The author intentionally devises and uses various modes of referring. However, "once the convention becomes understood and accepted in a community, the focus of reference is shifted from person to the object used to refer and unintentional reference becomes possible" (296). This qualification allows the standard view to accommodate the usual kinds of concerns which arise about so-called intentional fallacies, failures of reference, pretended reference, and so on.

With these qualifications in mind we can now restate the fuller account more carefully as follows:

> 3. What makes a text fictional is the nature and not the use of certain markers and conditions of a text-type structured in no one way other than such as to insure that a community of readers in a culture takes those among the many cardinal sentences of the text which are speakers' illocutionary performances in a certain way. These illocutionary acts are taken as putative illocutions, finally incomplete ones, and therefore not authorial but textual representations of illocutions understood inside the continuing history of an interpretive community.

Thus, what makes Eliot's text fictional is the nature of certain linguistic and epistemic marks that insure that the readers of "Little Gidding" construe the text's supposed illocutions as representations and not as performances.

The View Applied: Three Nonfictional Texts

What we have so far is an account of what makes a text fictional. This account continues to undergo critical testing, but the version elaborated here already incorporates much of the most recent criticism. In short, we have an account that, whatever its weaknesses, can be taken as a serious working view of what currently distinguishes fictional discourse from the nonfictional.

We should now be in a position to scrutinize several philosophical texts from the perspective of what presumably makes these texts *non*fictional. Let us examine three eighteenth-century philosophical texts from a seminal period in the philosophy of art which together trace the important notion of taste across the successive figures of the tasteful critic, the judge of taste, and the connoisseur. Each philosophical text is, we assume, nonfictional, and each is an example of excellent work by the philosopher concerned.[10] I examine these texts in the light of the standard account, the hypothesis to be tested being that they are nonfictional because they do not exhibit those features that on the standard account make up fictional discourse.

The Tasteful Critic

> ... though the principles of taste be universal, and, nearly, if not entirely the same in all men, yet few are qualified to give judgement on any work of art, or establish their own sentiment as the standard of beauty. The organs of internal sensation are seldom so perfect as to allow the general principles their full play, and produce a feeling correspondent to those principles. They either labour under some defect, or are vitiated by some disorder; and by that means, excite a sentiment, which may be pronounced erroneous. When the critic has no delicacy, he judges without any distinction. . . . the finer touches pass unnoticed and are disregarded. Where he is not aided by practice, his verdict is attended with confusion and hesitation. . . . where he lies under the influence of prejudice, all his natural sentiments are perverted. Where good sense is wanting, he is not qualified to discern the beauties of design and reasoning. . . . Under some or other of these imperfections, the generality of men labour; and hence a true judge in the finer arts is observed . . . to be so rare a character: strong sense, united to delicate sentiment, improved by practice, perfected by comparison, and cleared of all prejudice, can alone entitle critics to this valuable character; and the joint verdict of such . . . is the true standard of taste and beauty.[11]

This text from Hume's "Of the Standard of Taste" (1757) is generally understood as part of a nonfictional, indeed a philosophical, work. The philosophical character of the text is said to be evident in the preeminently argumentative style in which the text is elaborated. The speaker begins with a carefully qualified thesis. He proceeds to adduce reasons in support

---

[10]We do well to choose expository prose pieces and to leave aside more ambiguous texts such as Plato's *Dialogues*, Augustine's *Confessions*, Anselm's prayers in the *Proslogion*, Descartes's *Meditations*, the *Dialogues* of Berkeley and Hume, Mill's *Autobiography*.

[11]In Dickie and Sclafani 1977:601–2.

of the thesis. Moreover, these reasons are not merely stated; they are ordered in such a way as to make their point evident. Further qualifications are noted. The central elements are gathered into a summary conclusion and underlined in the reformulation. And further argumentative discussion is motivated.

The text of course is not just argumentative. For readers usually respond as well to several of its striking literary features. For example, the text turns on a well-observed contrast between two characters, the critic and the judge. Both finally give way to a third character, the judicious critic, who unites the key elements of his predecessors. Another literary feature is the rhetorical use of careful parallelism in the construction of the sequence of three relative clauses each beginning with a "where" and all reaching a minor crescendo at the very center of the text.

Even if the text has literary elements, however, it is still, at least on the initial formulation of the standard view of fictionality, to be judged as nonfictional. And the reason quite simply is that Hume's text does not include any representations of illocutionary acts.

On reflection, this verdict seems too simple. For even though we must grant that the text includes no such explicit representations, still the use of identifiable characters even in a third-person narrative might be taken together with other factors as warrant enough for inferring that the text includes implicit representations of illocutionary acts. Such a case of course needs detailed support. But without trying to provide that support just now, we can at least see the possibility of arguing such a case.

But the standard theorist might not require us to go so far, for he has at hand a simpler move. He may allow the possibility of implicit representations of illocutionary acts and yet still claim that the possibility is not actualized in Hume's text because that text does not conform to the second and fuller statement of his theory. Consider this move in more detail in the light of a second putatively nonfictional text, this time on the nature of the judgment of taste.

The Judge of Taste

The delight which we connect with the representation of the real existence of an object is called interest. Such a delight therefore, always invites a reference to the faculty of desire. . . . Now, where the question is whether something is beautiful, we do not want to know, whether we, or anyone else, are, or even could be, concerned in the real existence of the thing, but rather what estimate we form of it on mere contemplation (intuition or reflection). If anyone asks me whether I consider that the palace I see before me is beautiful, I may, perhaps, reply that I do not care for things of that sort that are merely made to be gaped at. . . . All this may be admitted or approved; only it is not the point now at issue. All one wants to know is whether the mere representation of the object is to my liking, no matter how indifferent I may be to the real existence of the object of this representation. It is quite plain that in order to say that the object is beautiful, and to show that I have taste, everything turns on the meaning which I can give to this representation, and not in any factor that makes me dependent on the real existence of the object. Everyone must allow that a judgement on the beautiful which is tinged with the slightest interest is very partial and not a pure judgement of taste. One must not be in the least prepossessed in favour of the real existence of the thing, but must preserve complete indifference in this respect, in order to play the part of the judge in matters of taste.[12]

Kant is at pains here, in his *Critique of Judgement* (1790), to show how the quality of the attention we pay to the object of a judgment of taste (for example, "this picture is beautiful") differs from that which we pay to the object of any other kind of judgment (for example, "this picture is expensive"). As in the Hume text, we can note here as well a number of features that seem to distinguish the text as philosophical and hence presumably nonfictional—a sustained argumentative structure, a fastidiousness about distinctions, the recourse to a technical vocabulary, a high resolution in the level of analysis, and so on. By contrast, literary elements with few exceptions (one example is the use of a brief illustration) are noticeably lacking: where are the characters, where is the plot, where are the rhethorical and persuasive uses of language?

Reading this text, a standard theorist might press his earlier point: even though some implicit representations of illocutionary acts might possibly be teased from such a text, the efforts would be insufficiently justified; consequently, the so-called implicit representations should be judged implausible. For on the second and fuller account of the standard theory this text does not exhibit the marks of those conditions and constitutive rules that invite uptake on the part of cultivated readers. This uptake normally results in the recognition that certain illocutionary actions can be construed "by filling in the gaps of the text in a reasonable way."[13] But here he fails. Consequently, the original verdict that the standard theorist brings down on the Hume text is now extended to the Kant text on the same but more detailed grounds.

But though no longer too simple, the verdict now seems short-sighted. For granted that Kant's text lacks virtually all the literary elements that might have invited Hume's readers to infer the possibility of his text representing illocutionary acts implicitly, still Kant's text turns in part on a remarkably suggestive syntactic feature that the verdict of "nonfictional" has overlooked—the play of personal pronouns.

The text in fact abounds in variations not only in the selection of pro-

---

[12]Ibid., 644.
[13]Beardsley 1981:307.

nouns but in the specification of their referents. Notice first the variety: the movement is from "we" to "anyone" and again to "one." And now notice the various referents of those pronouns. One pronoun ("we") refers to both the speaker and the implied readers of the text; another ("anyone else") refers to everyone who could be in the situation at issue; one pair ("me" and "I") refers to the author; another pronoun ("one") also refers to the author; still another ("I") refers to the speaker; and finally we have a pronoun ("everyone") which refers to all those rational persons who concur with the conclusions of Kant's argument.

This analysis is of course elementary and could be developed in greater detail. But even as it stands, reflection on the play of pronouns raises a serious question about the satisfactoriness of the standard theorist's second try at substantiating his "nonfictional" classification of philosophical texts. For even without examining the consequences of change of person or shifts in quantification or modal variations, this pronominal play is itself suggestive enough to solicit uptake on the part of some community of cultivated readers. Hence some marks, *pace* the standard theorists, do seem present in the text and thus can be construed as allowing the inference that the text implies the representation of illocutionary acts even if it does not explicitly incorporate these representations. Accordingly, the question resurfaces: is such a text as this properly construed as fictional or nonfictional?

The standard theorist, however, may still rejoin that, despite the objections to a verdict of nonfictionality based on the first two formulations of the standard theory, philosophical texts may finally be seen to be proper instances of the nonfictional if we appeal to the third and most detailed formulation. Thus, granted that some philosophical texts include markers that may seem to invite fictional uptake, still the relevant markers for fictional texts are not present in philosophical ones. Consider this final rejoinder in the context of one last philosophical text, this one not on the standards or judgment of taste but on its limits.

The Connoisseur

> ... since the work of art is not ... meant merely in general to arouse feelings (for in that case it would have this aim in common, without any specific difference, with oratory, historical writing, religious edification, etc.), but to do so only in so far as it is beautiful, reflection on the beautiful hit upon the idea of looking for a peculiar feeling of the beautiful, and finding a specific sense of beauty. In this quest it soon appeared that such a sense is no blind instinct, made firmly definite by nature, capable from the start in and by itself of distinguishing beauty. Hence education was demanded for this sense, and the educated sense of beauty was called taste which, although an educated appreciation and discovery of beauty, was supposed to remain still in the guise of immediate feeling. ... Yet the

depths of the thing remained a sealed book to taste, since these depths require not only sensing and abstract reflections, but the entirety of reason and the solidity of the spirit, while taste was directed only to the external surface on which feelings play and where one-sided principles may pass as valid. Consequently, however, so-called "good-taste" takes fright at all the deeper effects of art and is silent when the thing at issue comes in question and externalities and incidentals vanish. For when great passions and the movement of a profound soul are revealed, there is no longer any question of the finer distinctions of taste and its pedantic preoccupation with individual details. It feels genius striding over such ground, and, retreating before its power, finds the place too hot for itself and knows not what to do with itself.

For this reason the study of works of art has given up keeping in view merely the education of taste and proposing only to exhibit taste. The connoisseur has taken the place of the man of taste or the judge of artistic taste.[14]

Like those of Hume and Kant, this text from Hegel's Berlin lectures on art in the 1820s exhibits some of the generally recognizable features of philosophical prose—an argumentative structure, the careful considera- tion of alternative views, the use of historical material for speculative turns, indications of the evolution of an abstract idiolect ("in and by itself," Hegel says, "the concern for validity"), and so on. And once again, like Hume's text but not like Kant's, Hegel's makes some room for such literary elements as the movement of a narrative, the use of rhetorical devices, a sensitivity for the use of historical and period echoes. But, the standard theorist would urge, this text includes no explicit representations of il- locutionary acts. Nor does it include any of those relevant linguistic mark- ers that would authorize proper fictional uptake. The pronouns are not at play here. And even should someone try to make something of the interesting shifts in tense halfway through this text, closer analysis would, the claim is, be able to explain away such shifts in other terms than those of the requisite markers for fiction. So, once again, the original verdict should remain unchanged—philosophical texts are nonfictional. But now it is justified by an appeal to the carefully qualified features of the standard view's third formulation.

The verdict is no longer either simple or shortsighted. But after reflec- tion I still do not think it will do, for the verdict now seems blinkered. Even in such cases as the Hegel text, where either the requisite markers are missing or no discrete markers are present at all, the text can still work, on some community of cultivated readers, such effects that it may properly be taken as fictional in part. Here the signal may be construed in two ways. A reader may attribute to the text nonperceptual properties such as "having been composed by students and not by Hegel himself"

[14]Hegel 1979:34–36.

or "being intended to illustrate Hegel's mature thoughts" and accordingly construes the generalizations in the text as implied representations of illocutionary acts. Or a reader may observe in the text diffused signs rather than discrete markers—recall in the text the juxtaposition of the central generalizations with the evocative personification of genius in the suggested metaphorical guise of the Russian spirit driving Napoleon back from Borodino—such that the generalizations are contextualized in such a way that they can be once again taken as implied representations of illocutionary acts. In either case it remains an open question whether the absence of specific linguistic markers of fictionality is sufficient warrant for construing such a text as nonfictional. For some markers are epistemic, not just linguistic. And epistemic markers may be other than explicit; they may in fact be implicit. Thus, the justice of the repeated verdict of nonfictionality on these representative philosophical texts remains in doubt.

Detailing the Standard View

Objections may be brought to bear on the perspective I have been sketching about what is said to make a text fictional. There is, first, the question of possible omissions (see Appendix 1A, "Genre as a Criterion of Fictionality"). Someone, for example, may wish to insist on the need for a more detailed discussion of the place in this account of so-called markers and their conditions and rules. And still someone else may require a more thorough analysis of the cardinal distinctions in the account between implicit and explicit representations of illocutionary speech acts. Each of these critical concerns is reasonable. Yet each is more a request for detail than a fundamental objection. Thus, in this section I increase the level of conceptual resolution on the speech-act theory already before us. I begin with some general distinctions and recall the main lines of Searle's theory of fictional discourse. I then call attention to some recent criticism of this theory and proceed to provide a larger context in which the theory can be reconstructed. Finally, I offer a partial reconstruction of the speech-act theory.

Before looking at the details of this theory, we need to make several distinctions. Distinguish first between literary works and fictional works.[15] Clearly the first concept is not the second. For some fictional works are not literary in one sense or another, nor are some literary works fictional. Some forms of journalism, for example, are literary but not fictional, and many would argue that comic strips are fictional but not literary. Part of the problem is that the expression "fictional work" is easily mistaken as

---

[15]Searle 1974 mainly, but see also Searle 1975a, 1975b, and 1976. Hereafter references in the text are to Searle 1974.

any work of the genre fiction. But the expression "fictional work" is broader than the expression "work of fiction" where what is meant is a novel and not a lyric, an epic, or a play. Our concern is with the broader concept. We are concerned with fictional works rather than works of fiction, and so include poetic works. Moreover, we need to add that we are concerned with fictional works independent of whether they have more or less of what is called aesthetic value. Finally, we are not centrally concerned with the still broader notion of literary works.

Searle's interests are different. Part of the explanation for this difference derives from his Wittgensteinian views about the impossibility of defining literary works. Searle gives three reasons why such works can't be defined. He argues, first, that it is impossible to find necessary and sufficient conditions for a work being a literary work since such works have no traits in common. Moreover, he holds that the expression "literature" refers not to an internal property of a work but "is the name of a set of attitudes we take toward a stretch of discourse" (320). Finally, he claims that, since there is hardly any demarcation at all between the literary and the nonliterary, "the literary is continuous with the non-literary." But these claims are not uncontroversial. In any case, they cannot be accepted without argument and reconstruction. Consequently, Searle's interests need not be ours.

A second distinction we require is that between fictional discourse and figurative discourse. Both include metaphorical expressions; but only the first need occur in a nonserious context, that is, in a context where the speaker is not committed to the truth of what is being presented in non-literal terms. Moreover, the first kind of discourse is much broader than the second, for the first may include both metaphorical and literal utterances and expressions. Our concern again is with the broader of the two.

A third and related distinction has also been introduced, that between nonserious and serious discourse. As we have noted, only the first does not entail truth commitments on the part of the speaker.

A final distinction can also be mentioned briefly. Thus we need to distinguish between fictional discourse and discourse about fictional works. Only the second is serious discourse.

We have, then, fictional work, fictional discourse, and discourse about fictional work. Our concern is with the kinds of discourse which occur in fictional works and not with those that occur in discourse about fictional works. The latter are not instances of fictional discourse at all because, unlike the former, they can be verified by reference to the fictional works. The literary critic can check the truth of a claim about a fictional work— does the rose garden imagery occur in "Little Gidding"?—by referring to the poem, not the author.

With these distinctions in hand we can now turn to Searle's account of the differences between fictional and nonfictional discourse.

On the basis of sentences occuring in the *New York Times*, Searle isolates one kind of illocutionary act which is called an assertion.[16] He then specifies both the syntactic and the pragmatic rules that govern assertions. "An assertion," he writes, "is a type of illocutionary act that conforms to certain quite *specific semantic* and *pragmatic* rules [my emphasis]. These are (1) the essential rule: the making of an assertion commits himself (the speaker) to the truth of the expressed proposition. (2) The preparatory rule: the speaker must be in a position to provide evidence or reasons for the truth of the expressed proposition. (3) The expressed propositions must not be obviously true to both speaker and the hearer in the context of utterance. (4) The sincerity rule: the speaker commits himself to a belief in the truth of the expressed proposition" (322). For an utterance to count as an assertion in nonliterary discourse, all four rules must be followed. And for the assertion to count as proper, all four rules must be followed completely; otherwise the assertion is defective—either false, or lacking sufficient evidence, or pointless, or a lie.

Searle's second move is to examine the statementlike utterances that occur in a particular section of a fictional work (here, Iris Murdoch's novel *The Red and the Green*) in which all of the utterances are literal and not metaphorical. This restriction guarantees that complicating questions about metaphorical expressions may be kept from confusing the issue. The result is a problem. Here is the careful way Searle formulates the problem. "If, as I have claimed, the meaning of the sentence uttered by Miss Murdoch is *determined by the linguistic rules* that attached to the elements of the sentence, and if those rules determine that the literal utterance of the sentence is an assertion, and if, as I have been insisting, she is making a literal utterance of the sentence, then surely it must be an assertion; but it can't be an assertion since it does not comply with those rules that are specific to and constitutive of assertions" (323; my emphasis). In short, "the linguistic rules" and the "specific semantic and pragmatic rules" are opposed.

Before we note Searle's solution to this problem, we must in all fairness point to the somewhat artificial nature of his problem, at least as Searle states it here. For if there are definite rules for sentences to count as assertions, we should be able to list these rules fairly completely. When we do so, no conflict should arise between this inventory and some other set of considerations. For the considerations are, however interesting in other contexts, simply irrelevant to the determination of the rules for assertions. Had any one of these considerations been relevant, it would have been included in these rules since the rules were cataloged as completely as possible. Perhaps, then, Searle is suggesting that there are two

[16]See Austin 1971 and Searle 1969. But notice the controversial status here of propositions. Cf. Nishiyama 1975.

different kinds of rules, the "linguistic rules" and the "specific semantic and pragmatic rules." But this is speculation. The simple point here is that Searle's problem is poorly stated.[17] We shall see further on that the basic difficulty has to do with the claim that rules for meaning are said to determine the nature of the illocutionary acts in the text.

Regardless of this difficulty, Searle goes on to propose a solution, the key to his account. He first rejects the suggestion that fictional works characteristically exhibit, as in this case, one kind of illocutionary act (telling a story), whereas nonfictional works characteristically exhibit another (making assertions). Such a view, Searle argues, entails that the words occurring in fictional discourse do not have their ordinary meanings. And this conclusion is highly problematic because it implies that an entirely new set of meanings would have to be learned for all the expressions in a fictional work were a reader to be able to understand it. This argument is interesting for at least two reasons: the conclusion itself follows from how we construe the nature of an illocutionary act, and the corollary doesn't seem to follow at all.

Consider the corollary first. Even if it were true that the expressions do not have their ordinary meanings (but if they don't then why has Searle taken pains to point to literal expressions that occur in fictional works?), it still would not necessarily follow that "a new set of meanings for all the words" in the fictional work would have to be learned. For these meanings are almost all already known. We bring to our readings of fictional works an experience of language which is far larger than any overly narrow construal of "ordinary meanings." This comprehensive experience of language enables us to understand from the fictional work itself whatever the novel uses are to which antecedently unfamiliar expressions are put. A fortiori, then, Searle's attempt to develop immediately an *argumentum ad absurdum* does not follow either: "and since any sentences whatever can occur in a work of fiction, a speaker of the language would have to learn the language all over again, since every sentence in the language would have both a fictional and non-fictional meaning" (314). Searle also provides a somewhat different argument against the claims that the difference between fictional and nonfictional discourse is a difference between two distinctive illocutionary acts. I look at this argument below.

But let us return now to the conclusion from which this corollary is supposed to follow. Regardless of the theory of illocutionary acts whence it is supposed to derive, the conclusion as stated is simply wrong in the case before us. For the expressions here do have their ordinary meanings at the outset. In fact, that is exactly the point of Searle's efforts to keep the confusion of metaphorical expressions out of consideration. Searle himself has set up the example in such a way that the expressions in question are to be understood as

<hr/>

[17]Related issues arise in the exchange between Grice and Ziff. See Grice 1957, Ziff 1967, and on Searle's understanding of rules and conventions Loar 1982.

literal expressions. And whatever the nuances we may wish to quibble over, construing literal expressions as having "ordinary meanings" is uncontroversial enough to show that the conclusion Searle's argument arrives at is mistaken. The proposal Searle thinks is to be excluded is thus not defeated by the arguments he turns against it.

But what, then, is Searle's own proposal to get around the problem of explaining the apparent assertions that occur in literary discourse? If the speaker is not asserting in such cases where his utterances include literal statements that have the form of assertions, what is he doing? He is, says Searle, pretending to assert in the precise sense of engaging in a performance "which is as if one were doing or being the thing and is without any intent to deceive" (324). Moreover—and this is how Searle's position differs from the one he rejects—the act at issue here is not "telling a story" but "pretending," and "pretending" is not a distinctive speech act in the sense in which asserting is.

From this account Searle derives four conclusions. I will omit his discussion and gather these conclusions together.

> S1. "The author of a [fictional] work pretends to perform a series of illocutionary acts, namely of the representative type (statements, assertions, descriptions, characterizations, identification, etc.)."[18]
>
> S2. "The identifying criterion for whether or not a text is a [fictional] work must of necessity lie in the illocutionary intention of the author. There is no textual property, syntactical or semantic, that will identify a text as a [fictional] work."
>
> S3. "The pretended illocutions which constitute a [fictional] work are made possible by the existence of a set of conventions which suspend the normal operation of the rules relating illocutionary acts and the world."
>
> S4. "The pretended performance of illocutionary acts which constitute the writing of a [fictional] work consist in performing utterance acts with the intention of involving the horizontal conventions that suspended the normal illocutionary commitments of utterances." (325–27)

I have already pointed out some difficulties with the discussions that lead to these conclusions. But the major difficulty must still be spelled out.[19] This difficulty derives from what has been called Searle's "determination principle," the principle that the kind of illocutionary act a sentence is used to perform is determined by the meaning of that sentence.

---

[18]See Searle's 1975 papers.
[19]Here I follow Currie 1985 closely. Further references to Currie in the text.

"The illocutionary act (or acts) performed in the utterance of a sentence is a function of the meaning of the sentence. We know, for example, that an utterance of the sentence 'John can run the mile' is a performance of one kind of illocutionary act, and that an utterance of the sentence 'Can John run the mile?' is a performance of another kind of illocutionary act, because we know that the indicative sentence form means something different from the interrogative sentence form."[20]

This principle lies behind Searle's reflection on the claim that the difference between fictional and nonfictional discourse is the difference between performing the illocutionary act of, for example, asserting and performing the illocutionary act of telling a story. For since both writers may use the same sentence form—for example, the indicative—the meaning of the sentence would not determine the nature of the illocutionary act it is used to perform. The same sentence meaning in the sense of sentence form would in such a case determine two different illocutionary acts, thus violating the determination principle. This principle, however, can be seen to be false once we advert to the familiar fact that the same sentence form is used to make different speech acts depending on the context. Thus, the sentence "You are going to camp this summer" may be used to state a fact, ask a question, or give an order. Moreover, it has also been shown that Searle's theory controverts his own principle. For Searle, "the same sentence with the same meaning can occur in nonfiction as the result of the illocutionary act of assertion and again in fiction as the result of an act which is not an illocutionary act at all. So sentence meaning (i.e., meaning in the sense of sentence form) does not determine the illocutionary act performed" (386). Finally, modifying the determination principle even in drastic ways does not overcome the arguments against the principle. The result is that Searle's central claim—fictional discourse is the result of pretended but not fully fledged illocutionary speech acts—is left without sufficient support. And since Beardsley's understanding of fictional discourse, which I referred to earlier, relies on an uncritical acceptance of Searle's distinction between asserting and pretending to assert, his version is also left without sufficient support.

On the basis of these criticisms and a basic concern with what conditions must prevail for an act of fictional communication to be successful, Currie has recently proposed a revision of Searle's theory. The basic idea arises out of distinguishing carefully, as neither Searle nor Beardsley do, between the author's performance of a speech act in his own right and the readers of a fictional text performing a speech act. Currie argues that, unlike the reader, the author does not pretend to perform a speech act but actually does perform a speech act, and a distinctive and fully fledged speech act at that. Moreover, in performing such a speech act, the author

---

[20]Searle 1975:64; cited in Currie 1985:385.

intends that the reader adopt a certain attitude with respect to further speech acts he represents in his text, and that the reader recognize that the author intends him to adopt such an attitude. The author's speech act is properly described not as pretending but as "inviting to pretend" or (in Walton's terms) as "making believe." Thus, the author invites the reader to recognize his authorial intention that the reader adopt an attitude of making believe with respect to some if not all of the illocutionary acts the author represents the speaker as performing in the text. The qualification "some if not all" is necessary because the author sometimes intends the reader to believe some of the utterances he represents the speaker as making (for example, "Napoleon was uneasy before the Battle of Borodino") while intending the reader to make believe others.

In order to account for some problem cases Currie elaborates this account further. Thus, to account for possible discrepancies between the prevailing intentions of a community of readers at some time and the author's intention, he distinguishes between fictional discourse in the primary or core sense (that defined by the author's intentions) and in a secondary sense (that defined by a competent community's practice of conferring fictional status on a particular discourse). Moreover, some texts can be fictional works by accident, as when a historical novel turns out by accident to relate some things that are true. To rule out such cases Currie adds a qualification that a work is fictional only if it "is not related by an information-preserving chain to a sequence of actually occurring events" (389). Further, making use of both Grice's work on conversational implication and Lewis's on propositions being true in a fiction, Currie goes on to nuance the kind of stance the reader is to assume with respect to the text. These main qualifications bring him to a fuller articulation of his account. Thus, we may add an additional claim to the previous four from Searle (making it prime):

> S'5. A work is fictional in the core sense if and only if it is not related to a sequence of actually occurring events by an information preserving chain, and is the product of the specific illocutionary intention of the author that the reader
>   a. recognizes that the author is inviting the reader to assume a certain attitude with regard to the represented illocutionary acts of the speakers in the text,
>   b. that this attitude is one of making believe these represented propositions, and
>   c. that adopting this attitude also involves assuming "an obligation (ideally) to make-believe certain things not explicitly stated in (or controversationally implicated by) the text." (391)

Such a theory is seen to be superior to Searle's and Beardsley's in that it does not depend on the seriously flawed determination principle. Moreover, this theory is also more powerful in that it allows one to distinguish the actions an author performs in writing his or her work from those, for example, an actor performs in reciting the text. And finally it accommodates, as Searle's and Beardsley's theories do not, the curious fact that readers of fictional works can transpose utterances represented in the work in one illocutionary key to a different one, one that corresponds to the author's intention. Recognizing that the author's intention is to invite the reader to adopt an attitude of make believe toward some of the utterances represented in the text and then actually consenting to play a kind of internalized game in so adopting such an attitude is what secures "illocutionary uptake" (387).

FURTHER DIFFICULTIES: CONVENTIONS AND LITERARY NORMS

This revised theory is superior to the earlier one, but this is not to say that there are not some difficulties still remaining. I call attention briefly to three such difficulties before looking more closely at a fourth.

Notice first that the revised speech-act theory turns on a number of distinctions. Although Currie spends time not only with Searle's version, in which pretended speech acts are prominent, but also with Beardsley's in which the accent falls on represented speech acts, and although he criticizes Beardsley for not distinguishing between the nature of the author's speech act and that of the reader's, he himself pays far too little attention to the further distinction between the performance of speech acts by authors and readers on the one hand and the representations of such performances by speakers in a fictional work on the other. In the description of his theory I have already included this further distinction, so we need not enlarge on it now. Nonetheless, we need to keep straight in a speech-act theory the differences among those who are said to perform a speech act (authors, readers, communities of readers, speakers in a work) as well as those among different acts themselves, some of which may not be illocutionary speech acts at all (performing an illocutionary speech act, pretending to perform an illocutionary speech act, inviting someone to pretend to perform one, re-presenting the performance of one, and so on).

A more important problem has to do with intentions—their nature, kinds, and recognition. Notice here that, however intentions are finally parsed,[21] the revised account includes more than one kind. Thus, we have authorial intentions and the intentions of interpretive communities which this account mentions explicitly. We would also have to include intentions that the author may represent speakers in his text as having, although these are not mentioned explicitly (388). Further, the revised account

[21]See Searle 1983.

makes room for a further opposition, one "between serious and nonserious intentions to deceive" (389). Again, we may leave aside the question about how to determine the exact nature of these intentions. But we
may not dodge the issue of just how at the very least [the author's]
intentions are to be recognized. For the reader's recognition of authorial
intentions is essential to the revised account.

Currie himself would concur, for he devotes some space to the matter.
"The reader may recognize this intention [the author's] in a number of
ways through his perception in the work of certain familiar elements of
fictional style, or simply by noting that the work is represented and
advertised as fiction. The author may even make an explicit avowal of
his intentions . . . and of course the reader may misperceive the author's
intentions" (387) with the consequence that no illocutionary uptake occurs. But these comments are not satisfactory because they are insufficiently detailed. Further, they contrast starkly with Currie's opening
remark: "while stylistic or generic features may certainly count as evidence
that a work is fiction rather than nonfiction, they cannot be definitive"
(385). In fact, the revised account is close to begging the question it
purports to answer—how to distinguish fiction from nonfiction—because
it does not provide us with a full enough description as to how at least
the central cases of relevant intentions, authorial ones, are to be
recognized.

A third difficulty concerns the unclear notion in this account of "make-
believe." Recall that the expression was introduced in apposition to the
phrase "the author is inviting us to pretend, or rather to make-believe
something" (387). Currie went on to state that in his account "I shall
make relatively uncritical use of the idea." But is this use sufficient? To
make believe something may well be very much like to pretend something. But this is not evident, especially when Currie himself has already
singled out the term "pretend" in his criticism of Searle's use of the
expression "pretended speech acts." Are we to understand that just as
the expression "distinctive, fully-fledged speech act" (385–86) is the opposite of "pretended speech act," so too "distinctive fully fledged" is the
opposite of "pretended" *tout court*? This does not seem right. And yet
without a fuller gloss on exactly what is meant here, we will continue to
have difficulty in making out what is going on when the author of a
fictional work is said to invite the reader to make believe that many
statements in a fictional work are true, true in a fiction. Without pushing
this further now, we should note in passing that reference to Walton's
most recent work and to its critics[22] shows that Walton's own ideas of
make-believe have changed. Just as in the case of how authorial intentions
are to be recognized, so too in the case of what sense we are to make of

[22]See the discussion in McCormick 1986b.

pretending as making believe, the present revised account of speech-act theory needs more work.

The most important issue, however, with the present account is more a matter of its working assumptions than of its acknowledged incompleteness and pragmatic character ("my aim here is to present the outlines of a program," Currie writes on page 388). This assumption has to do with the situation of communication. "In order to understand what distinguishes fiction from other kinds of discourse it may be helpful," Currie writes, "to inquire into the conditions which must prevail in order for a successful act of fictional communication to take place" (385). We need to get a better grasp of what is involved in the background of this assumption.

A useful way of surveying that background is to recall a basic disagreement about how the linguistic rules that govern assertions are to be understood.[23]

In his 1969 inaugural lecture at Oxford, Strawson discusses two different ways of raising questions as general as the following ones: "What is it for anything to have a meaning at all, in the way, or in the sense, in which words or sentences or signals have meaning?" "What is it for a particular phrase, or a particular word, to have the meaning or meaning it does have?"[24]

Strawson arranges a confrontation between those who, like Grice, Austin, and the later Wittgenstein, would explain linguistic meaning with the help of a certain theory of the intention of communication (communication intention), and others who, like Chomsky, Frege, and the early Wittgenstein, would do so with the help of a particular theory of formal semantics. Searle, it is essential for us to note, is a member of the first group. The two groups agree that linguistic meaning is a conventional meaning, that is to say that linguistic meaning is a function of semantic and syntactic rules. They disagree on the question about how these conventions must be explained. The first group insists on the fact that rules must be explained by their necessary reference to the social function of communication. The other group thinks that such rules must be explained by the necessary reference to their truth conditions. The controversial point that separates the two, as Strawson understands it, is "whether the notion of truth conditions can itself be explained or understood without reference to the function of communication" (13). The second group must be able to propose an explanation of these truth conditions without presupposing an essential reference to communicative speech acts. The first group must be able to explain the concept of communication intention without presupposing the existence of structured linguistic rules. Strawson thinks that the second group has not yet accomplished its task be-

---

[23]I rely here in part on a reworking of some material first presented in McCormick 1971.

[24]Strawson 1970:4. Further references are in the text. See also Strawson 1964, Grice 1957, Grice 1968, and Armstrong in Schiffer 1972.

cause no explanation has yet succeeded in separating linguistic meaning from the concept of communication intention (24). The first group, on the other hand, has succeeded. Strawson thinks that conventional meaning can be explained in terms of the utterer's meaning without presupposing the existence of structured linguistic rules. His strategy consists in providing an explanation of preconventional meaning by taking on the question of how "primitive communication intentions and successes give rise to the emergence of a limited conventional meaning system, which makes possible its own enrichment and development which in turn makes possible the enlargement of thought and of communication needs to a point at which there is once more pressure on the existing resources of language which is in turn responsive to such pressure" (9).

For my part, I think that Strawson's arguments against theories of the formal semantic type are clear, forceful, and convincing. His arguments, however, in favor of versions of the group-of-meaning intention do not seem so strong. More exactly, the explanation Strawson proposes of preconventional communication seems both mysterious (as Strawson admits himself) and excessively speculative. And to the degree that Currie's guiding assumption shares Strawson's views, Currie's theory also suffers from a similar problem.

However, Strawson has also defined an utterance as "something produced or executed by an utterer; it need not be vocal; it could be a gesture or a drawing or the moving or disposing of objects in a certain way" (6). If we allow at least provisionally this definition of utterance, and if we draw the conclusion that certain things do not have a meaning just by virtue of saying but by virtue of showing (see Appendix 1B, "Saying, Showing, and Speaking-of"), then it would seem that a way is opened toward a simple and nonmysterious explanation of preconventional communication in terms of language that is at times gesture rather than language that is always sign.

RECONSTRUCTIONS

In the light of these criticisms and contexts, what changes seem called for in Currie's revision of Searle? We may proceed by rewriting Searle's theory.

As regards the first of Searle's theses we need a reconstruction:

> S'6. The author of a fictional work when writing fictional discourse is not pretending but actually performing a series of illocutionary acts.

Searle's second thesis takes up the question of intention. Searle believes that pretending entails intention. "One cannot truly be said to have pretended to do something," he writes, "unless one intended to pretend to do it" (325). But this applies just as well to actual illocutionary action as to pretended ones. So we need have no difficulty in accepting this as long as we agree on a nonpsychologistic interpretation of what intentions are, and as long as we specify the nature of the mental acts involved. A second qualification, however, is in order. Where Searle speaks of intention as "the identifying criterion," we need to speak more cautiously of "an identifying criterion." For the nature of a fictional work must be construed at least partly in terms of its historical and cultural context in the life of a particular human community. Finally, we need to add the notion of genre to the list of those items that are unable to identify a discourse as fictional. With these qualifications we can then say:

> S'7. An identifying criterion for fictional discourse is authorial illo-cutionary intention. These intentions, however, are expressed in discourse about fictional works and not in fictional discourse itself. Neither textual properties nor generic notions can properly identify a discourse as fictional.

Searle's third thesis is more complicated, for it tries to explain how "pretendings" are possible. Searle suggests that in the case of assertions we should imagine the rules for assertions "as vertical rules that establish connections between language and reality" (326). The rules for the pre-tended assertions that occur in fictional discourse may be termed con-ventions. Conventions are not semantic norms that govern the meanings of expressions, but what we might call pragmatic, nonlinguistic strategies. These strategies "enable," as Searle writes, "the speaker to use words with their literal meanings without undertaking the commitments that are normally required by these meanings" (326). These strategies thus may be pictured as horizontal conventions of fictional discourse which cut across the vertical rules of nonfictional discourse. Pretending to per-form an illocutionary act is different from lying because the latter is a violation of one of the so to speak vertical rules for the performance of any speech act (the sincerity rule), whereas the former is an instance of a so to speak horizontal convention. The convention, however, is not evident in the literal utterances of fictional discourse because these are indistinguishable from the same literal utterances in nonfictional dis-course. Rather, the convention is operative at the level of the illocutionary act and not at that of either its mental contents or real counterparts.

We have to avoid a confusion here, however, between "convention" as a norm that governs pretended assertions and "convention" in the sense of, say, either style (the rhyme schemes of sonnet kinds, the diction of ballads) or structure (presenting the main figure of a pastoral poem as a shepherd) or theme (the attitude toward death in the Elizabethan lyric). Convention in this larger sense may be defined as "any characteristic of the matter of technique of a poem [read throughout 'fictional work'] the reason for the presence of which in the poem cannot be inferred from the necessities of the form envisaged but must be thought in the historical circumstances of its composition."[25]

I propose, then, to use the term "literary norm" as our adaptation of what Searle calls "convention." We may say:

> S'8. In the case of fictional discourse a set of literary norms governs in a pragmatic and nonlinguistic way the author's sincere pretended illocutions. The contents of these mental acts as well as their nonmental counterparts in sentences are governed by a set of semantic and syntactic rules which are not suspended but which operate normally.

With similar qualifications we can reformulate Searle's fourth thesis:

> S'9. In the case of fictional discourse, the author's performances of assertions consists in willingly invoking literary norms in addition to the usual linguistic rules when making such illocutionary acts and involves the normal illocutionary commitments of utterances.

Besides this larger context and these particular reformulations, are there further qualifications that should be introduced? For a modified speech-act theory further semantic precisions are indeed in order.

One area in which semantic theories can provide help is supplementing the account of "pretending," where the pretending now at issue is not that of the author but of the reader. We have already noticed an ambiguity in this expression (deceiving versus acting as if). And indeed in Searle's original account no great weight is put on this term alone. Writing of the Murdoch example Searle says: "She is pretending . . . to make an assertion, or acting as if she were making an assertion, or going through the motions of making an assertion, or imitating the making of an assertion. I place no great stress on any one of these verb phrases, but let us go to work on 'pretend,' as it is as good as any" (324). We already have at our disposal, then, a series of parallel expressions. But can we be more precise?

Suppose (modifying the suggestion found in Heidegger [see Appendix 1B again] of a distinction between speaking of and speaking about) we distingish between speaking about and speaking as if. Speaking about we may take as asserting and speaking as if as pretended asserting. And instead of contrasting these expressions in terms of their rules and conventions, as we have done so far, we may extend the contrast to one

[25]Crane 1953:198, n. 62.

between the referents of assertions and the pretended referents of pretended assertions.[26]

Assertions may be classified in part according to the kinds of referring expressions they make use of. Thus, assertions may include only
one or more of at least the following: proper nouns ("Dr. Zhivago"),
singular definite descriptions ("the mistress of Dr. Zhivago"), plural
definite descriptions ("the children of Dr. Zhivago"), singular indexical expressions ("I", "my," "this"), and plural indexical expressions
("we," "ours," "these"). The expressions, moreover, are articulated in
the form of predicate expressions ("Dr. Zhivago has a mistress").
Such expressions are used correctly only when there exist individual
or factual spatio-temporal counterparts for such expressions. Furthermore, when using such expressions the speaker must intend to refer
to such existing individuals or facts. In fictional discourse talk about
fictional states of affairs does not involve a proper use of referring
expressions because each of these two conditions is violated. The
reader, then, in speaking of fictional states of affairs does not involve
a proper use of referring expressions because each of these two conditions is violated. The reader in speaking of fictional states of affairs is
pretending to make an assertion in the sense that he or she is improperly but nondeceptively making use of referring expressions.
Moreover, in pretended assertions whatever predicative expression is
made up by the referring expression is also used improperly but nondeceptively. We may conclude then:

> S'10. In the case of the reader, pretending to perform an act involves
> suspending not only the general linguistic rules that govern the
> use of assertions but also the particular semantic rules that govern
> the use of referring and predicative assertions.

In short, the author of a fictional work in the context of a communicative
situation in writing a work performs a series of sincere illocutionary acts
in inviting readers to make believe that what the fictional discourse of
the work represents as being the case is in fact the case. The reader by
virtue of his or her antecedent knowledge of certain elements in the
communicative situation—namely, pragmatic, nonlinguistic norms for
reading certain kinds of texts—comes to recognize the author's intention
and, when successful, consents to take up the invitation. The reader does
so by performing a series of pretended illocutionary acts, acts of make-
believe, with respect to the states of affairs represented in the fictional
discourse of the text while keeping straight the distinction between the

[26]Gabriel 1975.

speaker's represented performance of illocutionary acts and the author's implied but actual performance of illocutionary speech acts. In the light of these revisions we may say roughly that a work is fictional:

> if it is not related to a series of actually occurring events by an information preserving chain; and

> if it is the product of the sincere and not pretended performance of illocutionary acts of the author to communicate to the reader (through the representation of the performance of illocutionary acts of speakers in a text) an invitation to adopt (with regard to those represented illocutionary performances) an attitude of making believe *p*, with respect to at least some states of affairs explicitly or implicitly stated in the text by recognizing the operation on the text of certain pragmatic, nonlinguistic social and literary norms that govern normal operations within the linguistic text of semantic and pragmatic rules in such a way that the reader (in the light of these nonlinguistic norms) appropriately suspends some of the normal functions (for example, referring) of these linguistic rules.

REAPPLYING THE THEORY: FICTIONALITY AND COGNITION

In this concluding section I return to my examples in order to isolate several issues that underlie the status of their discourse as fictional or nonfictional. I show how basic disagreements have suggested the need to think twice about our habitual understandings of the oppositions between knowledge and belief, truth and falsity, the real and the fictive.

Recall part of the Kant text, the one in which the speaker is at pains to show how the quality of the attention some readers pay to the object of a judgment of taste (say, "this story is beautiful") differs from that which some readers pay to the object of any other kind of judgment (say, "this story is moving").

> Now, where the question is whether something is beautiful, we do not want to know, whether we, or anyone else, are, or even could be, concerned in the real existence of the thing, but rather what estimate we form of it on mere contemplation (intuition or reflection). . . . All one wants to know is whether the mere representation of the object is to my liking, no matter how indifferent I may be to the real existence of the object of this representation.[27]

[27]Kant 1977:644.

On reading this text carefully one may notice that although abstract, it nevertheless exhibits at least two different sets of properties. The first set includes such elements as having an argumentative structure, manifesting a fastidiousness about distinctions, and having recourse to a technical terminology involving a high level of resolution in the analysis. The second includes such elements as having a complex voice, displaying a rhetorical force, hesitating between sometimes synonymous expressions, and cultivating the ambiguities in the play of pronouns. A question arises of whether even such a text as this one, from Kant's *Critique of Judgment* (1790), is properly construed as fictional or nonfictional. Or, we may ask in Derrida's terms," To what extent does traditional philosophical discourse . . . derive from fiction?"[28]

The usual answer to this question is that Kant's text, and philosophical texts in general, are instances of serious discourse and consequently must be construed as nonfictional. To construe the text otherwise is, in Searle's terms, to "assimilate the sense in which writing can be said to be parasitic on spoken language with the sense in which fiction, etc., are parasitic on non-fiction or standard discourse. But these are quite different. In the case of the distinction between fiction and non-fiction, the relation is one of logical dependency. One could not have the concept of fiction without the concept of serious discourse."[29]

This answer, however, turns on certain assumptions, many of which we have already challenged. Notice here that someone may point out the unexamined opposition between serious and nonserious discourse. And indeed Derrida writes that "one could with equal legitimacy reverse the order of dependence. This order is not a one-way street (*à sens unique*) (how can the serious be defined as postulated without reference to the non-serious, even if the latter is held to be simply external to it?) and everything that claims to base itself upon such a conception disqualifies itself immediately."[30] But this point itself turns on one's accepting the legitimacy of Derrida's characteristic play with oppositions, and Searle for one rejects this kind of move.[31]

It may not be possible to resolve this kind of disagreement. But before conceding such a point, we need to recognize that the controversy here about the fictional and the nonfictional turns on different interpretations of what is meant by "serious discourse." Whether a text can be said to be fictional, I suggest, depends not only on the series of considerations we have been exploring in revising the standard theory, but also reverts

[28]Derrida 1977b:217.
[29]Searle 1977:207. See also R. Rorty 1977:679–81 and R. Rorty 1978:142–43.
[30]Derrida 1977b:248.
[31]Searle 1983:76–77. Cf. Hirsch 1983.

in part to a question as to just how we are to understand the implication that serious discourse makes truth claims.

Consider the next part of the Hegel text, the one in which the speaker is concerned to show why the figure of the connoisseur has come to replace the person of taste.

> For when great passions and the movement of a profound soul are re-vealed, there is no longer any question of the finer distinctions of taste and its pedantic preoccupation with individual details. It [a profound soul] feels genius striding over such ground, and, retreating before its power, finds the place too hot for itself and knows not what to do with itself.
>
> For this reason the study of works of art has given up keeping in view merely the education of taste and proposing only to exhibit taste. The connoisseur has taken the place of the man of taste or the judge of artistic taste.[32]

Less abstract than the former one, this text when reread exhibits a balance of both argumentative and expressive features; consequently, to catego-rize the text as either fictional or nonfictional discourse is more difficult than in our first case. Moreover, the text makes at least one basic assertion for which it provides some justification, namely, the claim that the con-noisseur has replaced the person of taste. The question arises whether such a claim can be understood as true or false. And a strategy begins to take shape. For if the claim can be appraised as true or false, then sufficient warrant seems to be in hand for construing the text as "serious discourse" and hence as an instance of the nonfictional.

The usual answer here is: yes, the text does make a claim; the claim can be assessed as true or false; and in fact, because times have changed since Hegel delivered his Berlin lectures in the 1820s, the claim is obviously false in just the way Searle means when he writes that "Derrida has a distressing penchant for saying things that are obviously false."[33]

But such a verdict is not uncontroversial. Derrida replies: "whenever I hear the words 'it's true,' 'it's false,' 'it's evident' 'evidently this or that,' or 'in a fairly obvious way,'[34] I become suspicious. This is especially so when an adverb, apparently redundant, is used to reinforce the decla-ration. . . . the notion of evidence, together with its entire system of as-sociated values (presence, truth, immediate intuition, assured certitude, etc.), is precisely what *Sec* [his paper "Signature Event Context"][35] is calling into question."[36]

---

[32]Hegel 1979:34.
[33]Searle 1977:203.
[34]Ibid., 204.
[35]Derrida 1977a.
[36]Derrida 1977b:175–76.

This reply, however, seems to assume what it is trying to refute, namely, that some reliable argumentative basis for distinguishing between true and false claims is available. If this basis is neither the evidence nor the other matters mentioned here, nonetheless Derrida implies that there is at least some basis. But that view is exactly what is in question. Searle goes after this point in a review[37] when he writes that "on the question of truth, Jonathan Culler wants to have it both ways. . . . saying that truth is a kind of fiction and that 'truth is both what can be demonstrated within an accepted framework and what simply is the case, whether or not anyone could believe it or validate it.' "[38] Polemics being what they are, however, this criticism is attacked in turn as a misrepresentation[39] only to be reaffirmed in even stronger terms. A "purely textual analysis of the works" he has cited, Searle replies, would show that deconstructionists such as Derrida are not as one of their defenders claims "almost obsessively occupied with truth."[40] "Authors who are concerned with discovering the truth are concerned with evidence and reasons, with consistency and inconsistency, with logical consequences, explanatory adequacy, verification and testability."[41]

But surely this is a special version of truth. Moreover, it is only one of a variety of versions which have been explored in the history of philosophy from Plato to Nietzsche. And besides being traditionally controversial, this narrow version of truth is newly controversial today. Hence it cannot be accepted as presented here, adverbially, as "obviously" supported by a firm consensus, an orthodoxy by which any philosopher today who claims competence is to be judged.

Texts that make truth claims, then, cannot be judged simply as fictional texts when the kind of truth at issue in such texts turns out to be unrecognizable on Searle's view of truth.[42] In short, the current view of Hegel's text and philosophical texts generally as nonfictional cannot be assumed to be correct without better arguments. For just as in the case of Kant's text where the issue was how to construe the sense of the predicate "serious discourse," so too here where the issue is one of parsing the proposition "this text makes a truth claim," recent controversies about poststructuralism confront us with the likelihood of our current proposals turning out to beg the question: whether a text can be said to make a truth claim, I suggest, reverts to a still prior question—whether the text in question is cognitive.

[37]Searle 1983:77.
[38]Culler 1982:181, 154; emphasis omitted.
[39]Mackey 1983:47.
[40]Searle means Mackey 1983.
[41]Searle 1984:48.
[42]See Danto 1983a and Mackey 1983.

Consider, then, one of the texts we began with, a text in which the speaker reflects on the transformation of certain understandings of life through the experience of art.

> ... it is only in the midst of this world that a new transfiguring illusion becomes necessary in order to keep the animated world of individuation alive. If we could imagine dissonance become man—and what else is man—this dissonance, to be able to live, would need a splendid illusion that would cover dissonance with a veil of beauty. This is the true artistic aim of Apollo in whose name we comprehend all those countless illusions of the beauty of mere appearance that at every moment make life worth living at all and prompt the desire to live on in order to experience the next moment.
>
> Of this foundation of all existence—the Dionysian basic ground of the world—not one whit more may enter the consciousness of the human individual than can be overcome again by this Apollinian power of transfiguration.[43]

More complicated than our previous ones, this text displays a pervasive metaphorical character that is reinforced by striking images and harmonious cadences. Moreover, in a highly figured way, this text would seem to be urging a particularly strong claim about the transfiguring powers of art. But as to whether or not we construe the text as fictional, and regardless of whether we take the text to be making a truth claim, the prior question arises of whether metaphorical discourse of any sort can be a source of genuine knowledge.

If we start with Plato by taking "genuine knowledge" as justified true belief, we need to worry about what will count as justification. And if we go on to construe justification with the Cartesian tradition as the metaphysically indubitable certainties of self-consciousness, then we soon go astray. For, as Searle writes, "we have come to believe that this general search for these sorts of formulations is misguided. . . . we can't in the traditional sense found language and knowledge on 'sense data' because our sense data are already infused with our linguistic and social practices." Searle goes on to criticize Derrida for holding the belief "that unless there are foundations something is lost or threatened or undermined or put in question. . . . that without foundations we are left with nothing but the free play of signifiers."[44]

But the reply to this charge is already on hand. For it will not do to force poststructuralist views about knowledge into the peculiarly Anglo-American "no-no" called "foundationalism." The issue of foundationalism, far from being clear in continental philosophical practice, is not even

[43]Nietzsche 1967:143.
[44]Searle 1983:78–79.

settled in Anglo-American work.[45] Why, then, assume that Derrida's so-called antifoundationalism leads to nothing else than a pantextualism, the free play of signifiers? In the aftermath of such debate, knowledge may better be understood as closer to interpretation than to explanation.

But what of the second matter here, the nature of the metaphorical? On one view,[46] truth of metaphor is taken as sliding "treacheously from a metaphorical characterization of philosophy to a characterization of philosophy as metaphorical. It contends fallaciously that a non-metaphorical analysis of metaphor is logically excluded by the fact that metaphor itself is a metaphor."[47] If this is right, a metaphorical text might still be a genuine source of knowledge.

But this description has been challenged as an oversimplification. A more accurate description of this view is "that a general theory of metaphor (a 'metaphorology') is impossible because all the terms in which the theory is stated would themselves be metaphorical and subject to the logic of metaphor. The theory, that is, would not and could never be a metalanguage of metaphor since it would be written in that language and contaminated by its errant logic."[48] So if this view is right, then a metaphorical text cannot be a genuine source of knowledge. What undermines this second formulation, however, is distinguishing between the term "metaphor" and the concept of metaphor. "The term 'metaphor' is indeed a metaphor. . . . But it does not follow that the concept of metaphor is metaphorical. . . . So we may give a non-metaphorical analysis of the concept, even if we may use metaphorical terms, without a fatal circularity."[49] Consequently, we are left with the first formulation, the view, namely, that a metaphorical text—say, Nietszche's 1874 edition of *The Birth of Tragedy* and philosophical texts generally—despite difficulties with reference, may be cognitive; that is, genuine sources of knowledge where knowledge is to be understood in larger, more interpretive terms such as understanding and enlightenment rather than in the traditional terms of explanation or confirmation.

Consider, then, Derrida's remark that "the task is to consider philosophy also as 'a literary genre.' "

> A truth is then prescribed: to study the philosophical text in its formal structure, in its rhetorical organization, in the specificity and diversity of its textual types, in its models of exposition and proclamation—beyond what were previously called genres—and also in the space of its *mises en scène*, in a syntax which would be not only the articulations of its signifieds,

---

[45]Mackey 1983:48.
[46]Derrida 1982.
[47]Danto 1983a:1036.
[48]Mackey 1983:1279; emphasis omitted.
[49]Danto 1983b:1374.

its reference to Being and to truth, but also to the handling of its proceedings and of everything invested in them. In a word, the task is to
consider philosophy also as a particular literary genre.[50]

How are we to take such a view?

Some would argue that once we construe philosophical texts as literary
and go on to take the "literary text" as nothing more than the play of
signifiers, then what initially prompted us to take up such books and
read—namely, their claims to tell the truth—simply evaporates. But we
may understand Derrida's remark differently. One philosopher writes:

> Derrida does not think that philosophy is a literary genre in the sense that
> there is a genre of texts (called "literature") of which philosophical works
> (along with novels, lyrics, epics, etc.) are species. On the contrary he has
> argued that it is impossible to distinguish and clearly demonstrate different
> genres of writing. What we ordinarily recognize as philosophy and what
> we ordinarily call literature are linked by their common submission to the
> conditions of writing. . . . It does not follow, therefore, . . . that to read phi-
> losophy as literature is to discount its concern with truth, or that the
> interest of a philosophical text evaporates once its claim to tell the truth
> has been disturbed by deconstructive analysis. It is indeed just that claim
> to tell the truth and the preoccupation with truth which are most inter-
> esting to a deconstructive reader of philosophical texts.[51]

My concern has been to suggest instead that current questions of
speech-act theory and genre which may arise about such texts as the
philosophical ones we have looked at lead back to questions about
whether such texts are fictional or nonfictional. A reconstruction of a
speech-act account of this distinction is persuasive. But this distinction is
currently based on a prior set of considerations about whether a text can
be properly construed as making truth claims, and about what is called
"seriousness." However, since the sense of truth most often evoked in
talk about truth claims is the narrow sense of truth as truth-functional,
the issue of seriousness leads to the problem of how the cognitive character of a text is to be understood. Here again we currently find a disagreement between those who would interpret cognitivity strongly in terms
of a text being a source of knowledge as justified true belief, and those
who would insist on the weaker but richer view of a text's cognitive
character as its capacity to be a source of insight or enlightenment. This
latter view comes to the notion that any philosophical text can be taken
to address the truth: regardless of its genre, it may be serious work, and
this sometimes results in the enhancement of perception, the deepening
of self-understanding, and the small, progressive, and incessant trans-

[50]Cf. Danto 1983a:1036.
[51]Mackey 1983:1280.

formations of our habitual and unreflective dealings with a so-called real world. But these are larger issues, and they require sustained attention in their own right. I turn to some of them in the next two chapters.

Appendix 1A   Genre as a Criterion of Fictionality

The standard account of fictionality I have constructed here, some might argue, is seriously flawed in omitting altogether the notion of "genre." Without complementing the speech-act analysis with a relevant discussion of genre, we wind up with an account of fictionality which is either overingenious or simply counterintuitive. The account is overingenious because it depends on what seems to be a continuing and probably unending series of technical amendments designed to obviate an equally inexhaustible supply of counterexamples. And the account is counterintuitive because it works straight against the grain of our habitual practices of initially categorizing most if not all texts in terms of some loose sense for kinds, sorts, and types—in short for genres.

We need to present this objection more fully:

> To account for fictional discourse, we need not postulate a separate but equal set of linguistic rules; we need only postulate one rule—the pretense-of-reporting rule. The rule knowledge required to focus or interpret fictional discourse is identical with that required for non-fictional with the exception of this one rule. Let's call this rule a genre rule to distinguish it from grammatical, propositional-act, and illocutionary-act rules. . . . fictional and non-fictional discourse share the grammatical and speech-set rules of the language.[52]

This view, when cast into the form of an objection to the standard account of fictionality, cannot be sidestepped with dismissive remarks about inappropriateness. For the objection already incorporates many of exactly those features of the standard account which I have been relying on for my construction. The objection in fact is an internal one, phrased with the help of the central terms of the theory it challenges, and hence quite robust. But can this objection overturn the standard account? I do not believe so.

Granted that the central term in the objection is vague, can we obviate the objection by applying critical pressure to the peculiar indeterminacy in the way the vague notion is used? For notice that this basic objection not only includes distinctions between broad and narrow genres, discrete and overlapping ones, genres and subgenres, but even coincident genres.

[52]Brown and Steinmann 1978:152, 157.

"Sonnets," this account reads in another place, "can be either fictional or non-fictional discourse. Wordsworth's are fictional; Elizabeth Barrett Browning's non-fictional; Shakespeare's in doubt. The genre rules that constitute sonnets—specifying phonological, semantic, and graphic features—are neutral to fictionality."[53] Such a generous view of genre has its liabilities, but we need not analyze them here. For our critics may appeal to some principle of charity in alleging that, given the occasion, the theory of genre their objection turns on in principle could be sufficiently detailed. Of course charity can turn into license, but, obligingly, we may say that in this case it does not.

What may allow an effective reply to this basic objection is focusing critical attention on neither vagueness in its central term nor indeterminacy in the uses of that notion but on the incoherence of its cardinal feature—"the pretense-of-reporting rule."

We know roughly what this curious expression refers to—namely, the recent view that fictional storytellers, unlike nonfictional ones, are engaged in pretense. Instead of describing, reporting, asserting, evaluating, judging, and criticizing, writers of fiction are merely pretending to describe, report, assert, evaluate, judge, and criticize. Thus, when we read a text that includes an apparently genuine description but which we already know antecedently is a fictional text, we are to construe that putative description as a pretended one only. For the claim is that sentences constituting those putative descriptions are in fact to be understood as prefixed with some such phrase as "in the fiction such and such" or "in the novel such and such." Further, this prefixing must itself be understood against the so-called background beliefs operative in a culture at a certain time. Thus, the prefixing plus the background beliefs are the prerequisites for the pretense on which the genre of this text turns.

This view of fictional discourse as pretended discourse is not a naive one. A number of important works in recent years have made use of refined versions of this notion. But despite its sophistication, the appeal to such a view in support of objections to the standard account of fictionality is threatened with incoherence. The problem lies in the conjunction of a questionable account of pretense with an open-end use of the term "rule." For the basic objection turns on the expression "the pretense-of-reporting rule." We can leave the narrowness of this formulation—why just reporting and not asserting, affirming, denying?—without comment. But we cannot leave unremarked the suggestion of equivocation here in the use of the word "rule." For if this objection is to work, we must make room for grammatical rules, utterance-act rules, propositional-act rules, illocutionary-act rules, sets of linguistic rules, and

[53]Ibid., 153. For several of the many technical issues here, see Seuren 1985 and Forbes 1987.

the pretense-of-reporting rule, which we are told is also to be called "genre rule." One needs to know whether all these rules are, or indeed can be, rules in the same sense. The question becomes all the more crucial when we note that this objection already explicitly includes a distinction between at least two kinds of rules, regulative and constitutive ones.

Our critical question here, moreover, is not uncharitable. It arises from linking talk about grammatical rules to talk about propositional rules. Such rules exist. But we know that they are different in at least three respects—these rules not only pertain to different kinds of things and incorporate different contents, but they are said to be rules in arguably different senses of the word "rule." If, however, the suggestion of equivocation arises with respect to how the concept of rules is to be understood in this familiar and standard distinction, the suggestion of equivocation arises even more strongly in the unfamiliar and deviant talk about a pretense-of-reporting rule. In linking discussion of rules with a controversial account of pretending, the talk here is unfamiliar. And it is deviant in that the proponents of this objection resort to stipulation in categorizing this rule—"Let's call this rule a genre rule," they write.

I suggest, then, that this serious objection to the standard account of fictionality is nonetheless ineffective because it allows good grounds for doubting its coherence. The notion of genre is clearly central for any account of fictionality, and presumably a standard account must eventually make some room for some such notion. But unless more cogent reasons than the ones adduced here can be brought forward in its support, the objection is not a substantive one.

Recall that we have constructed a standard account of what makes some texts fictional. We have seen that this view does not seem able to account for the putative nonfictional character of some representative philosophical texts. And we have investigated and finally found unacceptable a fundamental objection to the standard account. We are left therefore with several alternatives.

We may on the one hand construe philosophical texts as counterexamples to the negation of the standard account. The consequence is that we persist in taking philosophical texts as nonfictional on some as yet to be explained intuitive basis but not on the basis of the present theory of fictionality. This calls for further revision of the standard account so that virtually all counterexamples of this sort will be obviated. We may on the other hand construe the philosophical tests as subsumable under the standard account. The consequence, then, is that we begin to read at least some philosophical texts with an eye to their fictional components. Accordingly, the task is to take up the much more immediate job of revising our traditional and still largely intuitive accounts of what is the nature of a philosophical text. Other alternatives of course can be formulated, but already faced with these two, I will pursue the first.

Appendix 1B   Saying, Showing, and Speaking-of

Can a different explanation—and a simpler one than Strawson's—of pre-conventional communication be provided? I suggest that a modified doctrine of "showing" (*zeigen*) may accomplish in a simple and less mysterious way than Strawson's genetic analytic account the explanatory task facing the communication theorists and thereby helps fill out the background assumption of a revised speech-act theory. I limit myself here to arranging a confrontation between one of Strawson's formal semantists, the early Wittgenstein, and someone who usually is not associated with theorists of communication, the later Heidegger.

Recall briefly the doctrine of showing in Wittgenstein.[54] For the Wittgenstein of the *Tractatus*, to say something is to describe something. But to describe something is to formulate empirical propositions. Thus, the totality of what can be said is coextensive with what the natural sciences can verify because this totality is equivalent to anything that can be formulated empirically. But replacing saying with describing implies two results. On the one hand, what can be said is clearly stipulated as what can be described. On the other hand, what cannot be said is just as clearly indicated by what cannot be described. But if what cannot be said is nothing other than what cannot be described, what can we do with what cannot be described? Wittgenstein answers: what cannot be described is what is capable of being neither true nor false, that is, what is not capable of being formulated empirically. For the Wittgenstein of the *Tractatus* the decisive move for the distinction between what can be said and what can only be shown is to see if a proposition can or cannot be compared with reality. Such a demonstration raises the question of the relationship between the limits of language and the limits of the world. What can be said is situated within the limits of the two; what cannot be said is beyond those limits. To speak of something outside the world is to formulate something nonsensical, to try to utter a proposition about something beyond language. That about which one cannot speak cannot be said and that which cannot be said is what can be shown.

We have, then, three kinds of propositions—empirical propositions, which can be true or false; logical propositions, which can only be true or only false; and philosophical propositions, which can be neither true nor false. Empirical propositions can be true or false because they can be compared with reality. Logical propositions can only be true or only false because they are either tautologies or contradictions. Philosophical propositions can be neither true nor false because they can neither be compared with reality nor conceived as tautologies or contradictions. Thus, empirical propositions say what can be said; logical propositions don't say anything

[54]Wittgenstein 1961. For the transformation in this doctrine, see Pears 1987:193.

but show "the formal-logical properties of language and of the world"; philosophical propositions try to say what can only be shown. In other words, empirical propositions have a meaning (are *sinnvoll*), logical propositions without being nonsense have no meaning (are *sinnlos*), and philosophical propositions are nonsense (*unsinnig*).

Recall now the characterization Heidegger has proposed of two contemporary interpretations of language, as a concept and as an experience—the scientific-technical concept of language and the speculative-hermeneutic experience of language. The latter Heidegger claims for himself; the former he ascribes to Carnap. Here is Heidegger's presentation of the matter: "the first named position [Carnap] wants to put all thinking and all language even that of philosophy under the dominance of a sign system such as can be constructed by technology and logic, that is to say to fix these as an instrument of science. The other position [Heidegger] arises from the question of what is the thing which we can have an experience of for the thinking of philosophy and how this thing (being as being) can be said."[55] Heidegger raises the question of whether in a general fashion it makes sense to speak of a thinking and a language that do not objectify.

Heidegger holds that thinking is not necessarily objectifying in the sense that it would posit something in the realm of scientific representation. Nor is language necessarily objectifying in the sense that it would transform the content of thinking into quantifiable sounds. Certain ways of thinking and speaking are not objectifying in the sense that they do not represent things as objects. To think and to speak are not necessarily to objectify except in the realm of scientific and technological presentations where things must be calculated and require a causal explanation in terms of empirical propositions.

What is suggested in Heidegger's allusion to a nonobjectifying language is the distinction between "speaking about something" and "speaking of something." Two discussions in *On the Way to Language* can be helpful with regard to this distinction: the first referring to language's signal character; the second, to the distinction just mentioned.[56] In these passages Heidegger defends at least the following theses. There is a distinction between language and the essence of language: the first can be objectified, the second cannot. To speak about language (in our terminology, discourse about the fictional work) implies an objectifying language, whereas to speak of language does not. One cannot speak about the essence of language because the essence of language cannot be objectified; one can only speak of the essence of language. One can also signal to the essence of language. Heidegger in effect wants to distinguish

[55]Heidegger 1970:39.
[56]Heidegger 1959:114–19, 150–54.

between the sign character of language and its signal character. The first objectifies; the second need not. Because the essence of language is understood (in a very obscure way) as being in some sense a manifestation of being, discourse that speaks about the essence of language must make way for discourse that speaks *of* this essence.

There is a difficulty in Wittgenstein's doctrine of showing concerning the role attributed to definition. Once we admit that "saying" holds the place of "describing," then "showing" can pertinently be understood as the negation of "describing." But what other reasons besides these pragmatic ones would allow preferring this definition to others or to any whatsoever? No reasons are given. The later Heidegger would hold that the concept of logic implied in this strategy corresponds to only one of the interpretations of the ambiguous Greek word *logos*.[57] This interpretation of logic leads us to believe that thinking consists above all in asserting something about something else. Consequently, we understand thinking essentially in terms of propositional thinking. Heidegger asks what are the reasons for letting logic decide how "thinking" must be understood. In short, the cornerstone of Wittgenstein's doctrine of showing, the stipulated meaning of "saying," depends on an interpretation, strained without necessity, of "saying" as "asserting." Speaking of "saying" and, more precisely, not of "saying" but of "describing"—this won't do.

Nevertheless, the Heideggerian doctrine in turn is not free of confusions. One of the difficulties of this doctrine concerns its coherence. Even if we are capable of overcoming the formidable terminological difficulties, the problem of knowing what kind of a reasonable evaluation of Heidegger's thesis is possible continually comes up. What makes such an evaluation of Heidegger's claims here about nonobjectifying thinking so difficult is his repeated insistence on the fact that "evaluation," to the degree that this term implies a logical evaluation or even, more weakly, an argumentative appraisal, is a term already situated inside the traditional theory whose presuppositions Heidegger would like to criticize. In short, the interest in Heideggerian doctrine of a nonobjectifying language, the critique of a historical and univocal interpretation of logic, is continually and, as it is formulated, necessarily threatened with circularity. Speaking in circles, whether hermeneutic or otherwise—this won't do either.

Is it possible to retain some form of a doctrine of showing without making use of stipulation? Can the force of the Heideggerian critique of logic be maintained inside the same theory without becoming incoherent?

[57]Heidegger 1961.

If it can, then the Heideggerian distinctions between the sign and the signal character of language, between speaking about and speaking of, between objectifying and nonobjectifying language, deserve our attention insofar as they represent a possible alternative to the explanation Strawson gives of preconventional communication.[58]

[58] Anthony Cascardi's constructive comments on an earlier and shorter version of this chapter were very helpful. I thank also Philip Hanson and Ronald Moore for similar comments.

2

Literary Truths

Works of literature are able . . . to suggest hypotheses about
human behaviour, human motivation, human action, and
sometimes about the social structure.
—John Hospers

. . . the experience of the work of art always fundamentally
surpasses every subjective horizon of interpretation.
—Hans-Georg Gadamer

[The] chief function of literature is to show the possible and
necessary connections between the qualitative endowment of
objects . . . and values and to enable man to enter into a direct commerce with values by acting on his emotional life.
—Roman Ingarden

Here is a poem, a dramatic monologue by Posthumus from Act II of
Shakespeare's *Cymbeline*.

> Is there no way for men to be, but women
> Must be half-workers? We are all bastards; all,
> And that most venerable man which I
> Did call my father was I know not where
> When I was stamp'd; some coiner with his tools
> Made me a counterfeit; yet my mother seem'd
> The Dian of that time; so doth my wife
> The nonpareil of this. O! vengeance, vengeance;
> Me of my lawful pleasure she restrain'd
> And pray'd me oft forbearance; did it with
> A pudency so rosy the sweet view on't
> Might well have warm'd old Saturn; that I thought her
> As chaste as unsunn'd snow. O! all the devils!

On reading such a text carefully we sometimes find ourselves asking
different kinds of question. What kind of text is this? How does this poetic
statement differ from other kinds of literary statements? Are such fictional
statements ever true or false? How are we to describe the content of this

text? Are there procedures available for interpreting this text in an un-ambiguous way? How are we to evaluate the success or failure of this work? How can we assess the propriety of a particular performance of this monologue? What does this text mean? And most central to our present concerns, what would allow us rightly to hold that such a text exhibits literary truths?

These questions are not idle ones, as George Steiner's magisterial anal-ysis of the many difficulties in this text has amply demonstrated.[1] We find here lexical problems (the term "pudency"), syntactic difficulties ("and pray'd me oft forebearance"), semantic problems ("chaste as un-sunn'd snow"), rhetorical issues ("O! vengeance, vengeance"), textual problems (what was the original version of these lines?), performance problems (is the conventional Elizabethan presentation of such mono-logues normative in any faithful production of the text?), and more.

Shakespeare's monologue, then, and—to multiply the genres for what follows—such texts as the choral ode in Sophocles' *Antigone*, or Dante's geometrical vision at the end of the *Paradiso*, or the hunt scene in Tolstoy's *War and Peace*, raise a variety of issues which require some sorting.

We do well to notice here initially what Beardsley has referred to as "three different levels of question."[2] There are, first, "particular questions about particular works" (13). Here, for example, someone may well ask whether Shakespeare's Sonnet 116 is a misleading example of the form we know as Shakespearean sonnet, or whether the hunt scene in *War and Peace* is, properly speaking, an instance of pastoral. Questions of this sort are those for the practitioners of criticism. "They do not require theoretical reflection, but demand true information and interpretive skill" (13).

Other questions may be asked of these works at a more general level. Thus, someone may inquire whether all tragedy requires explicit gener-alization as in Sophocles; or whether the epic can only be understood as a rhymed poem as in Dante or also as allowing realization in prose as in Tolstoy's epic novel; or whether the Shakespearean monologue is but an instance of the lyric and not a genre in its own right. Questions of this sort insist on systematic knowledge of the arts, the kind of knowledge we have come to expect of a theorist of the arts or, in short, of an aesthe-tician in the broad sense.

Finally, still other questions may be raised about such texts at an even more general level in those cases where the texts themselves—say, Pope's *Essay on Man* or Boileau's *Art poétique*—deploy a certain range of critical terms in their own right. Thus, someone may ask whether the critical term "unity" is not used equivocally in Pope's essay, or what are the

[1]Steiner 1975:chap. 7.
[2]Beardsley 1966:13.

assumptions about mind in Sophocles' use of the term "hamartia," or whether Dante's understanding of harmony is logically consistent with Aquinas's interpretation of Aristotle's physics. These questions, although clearly involving some attempt at systematic inquiry, are usually understood as more than just aesthetic concerns; in fact, they are taken as philosophical concerns above all. We have, then, critical, aesthetic, and philosophical questions as instances of at least some but not all of the many kinds of issues which literary texts raise in a preeminent way.

But this division is not yet very clear. We ought, then, to make explicit briefly the last two of these kinds of questions.

It is not only linguists, rhetoricians, literary critics, textual editors, translators, actors, men and women of letters, and so on who turn to literary texts, but philosophers as well. The logic of fictional sentences, for example, in literary artworks is of interest to formal semanticists and philosophers of logic. The kinds of entities whose descriptions one finds in such literary artworks as, for instance, the *ficciones* of Borges, together with the conditions and criteria that govern their identity, are of continuing interest to ontologists. The nature of judgments that both fictional characters and author's *personae* or authors themselves express in such literary artworks as, for example, the plays of Molière remains a fruitful area of inquiry for epistemologists. And the peculiar features of particular literary plots—think of the novels of Dostoevski or George Eliot or Flaubert or James—attract the interest of some specialists in moral philosophy and even in the philosophy of religion. Here, then, are several of the many examples that could be cited, and at much greater length, in support of the claims that literary artworks invite the serious attention of philosophers.

The interests of philosophers of art, however (or aestheticians—and I will use the latter term hereafter as a shorter expression for the former), are somewhat more difficult to make precise. For even when we artificially narrow the sense of the word "aesthetics" to include philosophical issues only, it is not immediately evident that there is any further set of questions for the aesthetician to investigate than those we have already noted as topics of interest for the logician, the ontologist, the epistemologist, and so on. The independence of aesthetics as a philosopher's discipline, in short, is controversial. For whatever questions would seem to be grist for the mills of aesthetics, the frequent claim is, turn out after some grinding to be the stuff of epistemology or moral philosophy.

One countermove to this reductive strategy is particularly prominent in the specialized journals. However much analysis is undertaken, the counterclaim goes, there is at least one set of questions about objects, perceptions, judgments, predicates, values, and criteria which is not reducible to the actual concerns of other traditional branches of philosophy. And this set of questions concerns aesthetic objects, aesthetic perceptions, aesthetic judgments, aesthetic predicates, aesthetic values, aesthetic criteria.

With this dispute in mind, then, we may proceed as follows. There is at least one philosophical question that some of the texts cited or others like them may be taken as raising. And this is a question about aesthetic truth.

LITERARY TRUTHS

In one of the most consequential reflections on the problems of literary aesthetics, *The Apology for Poetry*, Sir Philip Sidney wrote that poets never lie because they never affirm anything.

> Nowe for ye Poett hee nothing affirmes and therefore never lyeth, for as I take it; To lye is to affirme that to be true which is false. So as yet other Artists and especially the Historian affirming many things cann in the Clowdy knowledge of mankinde hardly escape from many; But the poett as I saide before never affirmeth . . . and therefore though he recount things not true, yet because he telleth them not for true, he lyeth not.[3]

Sidney's own affirmation has continued to exercise philosophers and literary critics even today. For his comment raises more than one issue.[4] Do some artworks provide us with what may properly be called aesthetic truths, or is talk of truth in this domain finally nothing more than another species of figurative speech? If we may speak properly of not just truths, and aesthetic truths, but of literary truths, then just what analysis of truths as such can sufficiently warrant this talk? More simply, what are literary truths, how are they presented in literary artworks, how do we as readers come to know such truths, and exactly what are literary truths true of?

In this chapter I address only one of these questions, the nature of literary truths. Do some literary artworks present us with a set of truths about, say, persons, truths that may properly be called aesthetic truths in general and literary truths in particular? This is the issue we now need to bring into sharper focus with the help of a contrast. I examine two different contemporary accounts of literary truths, an analytic account and a hermeneutic one, before I conclude by showing how several common features in this set of philosophical disagreements invite further inquiry.

---

[3]Sidney 1969:31.

[4]Some evidence of the difficulties here is available in recent work on the application of formal hermeneutics to literary texts. See Gabriel 1975, Aschenbrenner 1968, Mellor 1968, and Pavel and Wood 1979.

AN ANALYTIC PERSPECTIVE

I begin with a rough characterization of some analytic views about truths in literature. Although I shall not rely exclusively on their works alone, I shall refer most often to Weitz, Mandelbaum, Beardsley, Hospers, and Purtill, whose work in this area is representative.[5] The view I present, however, is a construction and not attributable to any one thinker alone.

Many analytic philosophers who are interested in the literary work of art often begin with a familiar observation. Literary works of art consist of different kinds of sentences about different kinds of things. Moreover, some of these sentences often purport to be communicating truths about many important matters.

Scrutinizing any classic work of fiction—say, *War and Peace*—is usually sufficient to see that this observation is correct. Literary works of art such as *War and Peace* consist of many different kinds of sentences. There are, to keep our list short, statements, accounts, questions, exclamations, commands, curses, prayers. Moreover, each of these items appears in more than one guise. For we have foreign language expressions, idiolect, slang, broken utterances, incomplete sayings, and more. There is great variety both of kinds of sentences and of variants these sentences assume. Examination of literary works and linguistic analysis of such works provides a welter of additional data for those who wish to itemize further.

If the kinds of sentences in literary works are numerous, then, the matters these sentences deal with are even more extensive. Even when we confine ourselves to statements alone, we find all kinds of topics in evidence. Literary statements, for example, often propound putative truths about those features of the world which the natural sciences are accustomed to describing. We can read claims being made about the nature of society, culture, and human institutions in a vein we have come to expect more often in the social sciences. Truths are offered about historical events and human actions in a way historians most often formulate such matters. Literary statements are made, too, about the nature of mind, about human ideals, about even such important but surely obscure matters as individual destiny.

With these vague but noncontroversial observations in hand analytic philosophers proceed to sharpen their concerns by operating several exclusions. The point of interest is not, initially at any rate, understood as a set of questions about the values we catch sight of when dealing sympathetically with literary works of art. The accent falls, rather, on truths. Moreover, the concern is not with truths of any great stature, in the way, for example, that didactic theories of art (so important to Plato in several periods of his thought) focus narrowly on the presence or absence in

[5]Weitz 1935, Hospers 1946, Beardsley 1958, Mandelbaum 1965, and Hospers 1960.

literary artworks of "great truths." Nor, finally, is the analytic philosopher usually concerned with symbolized truths of the sort readers encounter in, say, Kafka's work—putative truths about the world which they are not able to formulate in nonfigurative terms. Of course there are important questions, and indeed philosophical ones, which concern values, great truths, and symbolic truths. And some might even hold that at least paradigmatic cases of successful literary artworks provide privileged access to such matters. But for the most part analytic philosophers are almost always concerned with what they like to refer to as the everyday garden variety of commonsense truths, not the *pâté de grives* and the *canard à l'orange* but the peas and carrots on the philosophical menu. The accent, then, falls squarely on the question of whether some sentences in some literary works can be said to deal with truths at all, and if so how?

Before we look at the usual response to this question three distinctions of unequal importance should be noted. We need to distinguish first between sentences within the literary work and sentences about such a work. The distinction is of course commonplace, as we said in Chapter 1. Yet it is one we need to make explicit if we wish to avoid slipping from talk about truths that sentences within literary works refer to and truths that sentences within literary-critical works refer to. This second variety can be extensive in its own right once we begin to reflect on critical practice. But the expectations we bring to works of literary criticism are very different indeed from those we bring to literary works of art. Sometimes, it is true, these expectations overlap, as in those cases where works of literary criticism would seem to have aesthetic pretensions of their own quite apart from the artworks they purport to be reflections on. Yet in general, and however difficult any anatomy of these sets of expectations might prove, the fact of such difference is plain enough.

A second distinction some analytic philosophers continue to find useful is a more slippery one, that between propositions and predications. Despite almost a hundred years of work in modern philosophy of logic, propositions remain elusive entities that appear to many philosophers as at best only half real. Propositions, some would argue, are not themselves linguistic entities, although, if they are to be found at all, they are to be found only in the company of sentences. "Predication," on the other hand, is a technical term in the context of this discussion. The relevant sense here is almost exclusively confined to the kinds of issues philosophers struggle with when they raise questions about saying and showing. This sense has been construed as "each distinguishable respect in which a discourse or part of a discourse may be said to be true or false."[6] Thus, a statement that says one thing and suggests another is taken here to make two predications. An example might go like this. "Peter is not the

[6]Beardsley 1958:404.

worst player in the tennis tournament," which says that at least one player is worse than Peter and suggests further that Peter is at any rate a pretty bad bet. Now, the truths in literature which philosophers are concerned with are not those that assume a propositional form but those that are expressed in the predications occurring in many of the sentences that make up the literary work.

A third and final distinction we need to note turns on a contrast between the kinds of interest analytic philosophers have with the sentences in a literary work and the interest the literary critic has.

The literary critic, we might say with Beardsley, is largely concerned with three tasks. The first is that of explication, the attempt, that is, "to determine the contextual meaning of a group of words . . . given the standard meanings of the words plus information about their ranges of connotation." The second is that of elucidation in the sense of determining "parts of the world of the work, such as character and motives, that are not explicitly reported in it, given the events and states of affairs that are reported plus relevant empirical generalizations." And the third is interpretation in the sense of determining not the thesis of a work, that is, "its doctrine or ideological content," but the themes of the work, that is, "something named by an abstract noun or phrase," such as, say, the tragic character of poverty (401–3).

Philosophers, by contrast, are usually concerned mainly with what can properly be termed true or false in the literary work. This may well turn out to be the thesis the critic has been able to isolate with the help of his different training, skills, and sensibility. The philosopher, however, will go on to ask his or her characteristic questions about such theses, questions about the world, for example, or how such truths are presented whether by statement or assertion, or what kind of truth or falsity such statements can be properly said to exhibit.

Each of these distinctions raises questions in its own right. But these questions need not occupy us here. Rather, we have to note, now that the starting point, the issue, and the relevant distinctions are in mind, just what answer the philosophers are wont to provide to their own question.

One way to get a clearer idea of the answer is to cast the initial question in a more general form to see what positions have been taken in its regard. The problem here is not about fictional discourse in general, which we have already discussed above; the problem, rather, is how fictional statements differ from nonfictional ones. At least five kinds of responses are worthwhile recalling here briefly.[7]

1. The first view holds that fiction is not true, whereas nonfiction is true. Yet there is a difficulty here with saying just how we are using the

---

[7]See ibid., 419–20.

vague word "true." The main problem with this view, however, is that many fictional works contain true statements (for example, *War and Peace*), whereas many nonfictional works contain false statements (for example, *Principia Mathematica*).

2. A second view holds that fictional works consist of sentences that are neither true nor false. But the same kind of consideration that proved fatal to the first view proves fatal to the second as well. For some non-fictional works contain sentences that are neither true nor false (commands, say, in programmed logic texts), and some fictional works contain sentences that are either true or false (census figures for small Pennsylvania towns in the 1920s in John O'Hara novels).

3. A third view holds that all declarative sentences in fictional works are disguised imperatives of the form "suppose that" or "let us pretend that," whereas no such disguised imperatives are on the loose in non-fictional works. When we reflect on the variety of uses to which declarative sentences are put, however, this view appears overly ingenuous.

4. A fourth view locates the differences between fictional and nonfictional works in readers' attitudes rather than in the sentences of the work. The attitude of a reader who takes up *War and Peace* to determine Tolstoy's philosophy of history is different from the attitude of a reader who takes up *War and Peace* to enjoy a novel. But this view, like the preceding one, also seems too simple. As Beardsley puts it, "you do not have to ignore the truth-value of a discourse for it to be literature, and ignoring the truth-value of the *Principia* does not make it fiction" (420).

5. A fifth view turns on a distinction between uttering a sentence and asserting one. A journalist may, for example, utter a sentence in reporting certain views about the Canadian constitution. But one is both uttering and asserting such a sentence when one utters the sentence in such a way as to communicate to one's listeners that one believes the sentence is true. Fictional works, then, are construed to include truths of utterance only, whereas nonfictional ones include truths of utterance and truths of assertion. It is not difficult, however, as the journals in philosophy show, to raise important doubts as to the well-foundedness of such a distinction without even multiplying those doubts by considering the legitimacy of its application to literary works.

With these five general views as background, I turn to the usual response given to a narrower question, that of how putative truths found in literary texts differ from truths found in nonliterary ones. The most commonly held response to this question goes as follows.

Truths in literary works differ from truths in nonliterary works in the way that suggested truths, the truths of predications, differ from asserted truths, the truths of propositions. But how are truths suggested in literary works? Literary works do not suggest truths either in the sense that these truths are intended by the author or in the sense that these truths are graspable by the audience. Thus, neither writers' intentions nor readers' responses do sufficient justice to the work itself. "We want to be able to say," John Hospers writes, "that something is implied [suggested] even though the author may not intend it and be quite unaware of it, and even though the audience [reader] may be so imperceptive as not to grasp it."[8]

But just what kinds of truths are implied in this large sense of implication as suggestion?

"Works of literature," Hospers continues, "are able . . . to suggest hypotheses about human behaviour, human motivation, human action, and sometimes about the social structure. . . . These works may suggest or intimate (say without saying) numerous propositions predications in our terminology . . . about the world, about the subject matter of the work itself. And since some of these suggested propositions are doubtless true, we have here surely an important sense of truth in literature." (213).

A HERMENEUTIC PERSPECTIVE

An alternative approach to the problem of literary artworks and putative truths is one I will characterize simply as a hermeneutic approach.[9] It is important to recall that neither here nor earlier is there any attempt to represent any one particular position as such. Rather, the concern is with sketching the main features of a general position, most of whose elements a certain group of thinkers would characteristically find to be important in the light of their own individual views.

Hermeneutic thinkers concerned with questions about truths and literary artworks have a different point of departure than their analytic colleagues. Instead of remarking on the curious fact that many statements appearing in literary works of art are similar and yet different in important ways from those that occur in nonliterary texts, hermeneutic thinkers are struck, for example, by the way temporality and history are represented in such texts, by the play of language and silence in literary texts, and especially by a peculiar expectation of literary artworks as of all art. This expectation might be put as follows. Hermeneutic philosophers are less concerned to analyze the truth conditions of different kinds of sentences, whether literary or nonliterary, than they are intrigued by the possibility that artworks may provide access to truths that are otherwise unavailable. The starting point here, then, if we confine ourselves to questions about

[8]Hospers in Margolis 1962:203.
[9]The major text here is Gadamer 1975.

literature and truths, is not an observation but, roughly speaking, an assumption.

We need to try to get clearer, however, about what the issue here may be. Hermeneutic philosophers are not characteristically concerned with whether or not a certain class of sentences can be said to be true or false on some analyzed sense of those cardinal terms. Rather, a general assumption has already been made before the literary artwork is approached, general in that it accompanies hermeneutic reflection not just on literary artworks but on artworks of every kind. The assumption, as I understand it, comes to something like this: artworks present truths about many things; literary artworks present truths especially about persons (characters) and about their actions (plots).

The point, then, is that whether artworks present truths at all is not at issue for the hermeneutic thinker. Rather, what invites his or her reflection is, granted that artworks present truths, just what are these truths about and how do artworks present such truths? Most interesting is what I referred to above as an assumption. For work on these questions is characteristically in the service of a larger interest, the question of whether some artworks present some truths about persons and actions which are not available anywhere else, so that their peculiar linguistic medium is taken to be in some as yet unclarified sense a privileged site for the manifestation of such occult truths. The issue here, then, does not turn on the similarity between literary and nonliterary texts (both comprise sentences), but on the dissimilarity between a class of putative truths accessible in literary artworks preeminently and the inaccessibility of such a class elsewhere.

If these, or something much like them, are the starting point and the main issue of a hermeneutic reflection on literary artworks, what is the further context that we need to make our initial formulation of the question more understandable? We especially need to appreciate the polemical character of hermeneutic thinking on the nature of aesthetics.

Hermeneutic reflection, in proposing for investigation what seems to be an intriguing property of literary artworks which is not found to the same degree in other artworks or indeed outside the realm of art, is self-consciously trying to contest certain consequences of what is taken to be an established scientific world view. Consequently, the issue this view calls to our attention is to be understood inside a critical understanding of the history of modern aesthetics. Aesthetics, this larger claim goes, has been understood up to the present as a progressive and largely helpful subordination of a philosophical discipline to one of a number of possible interpretations of science. Aesthetics, thus, has come to function as an investigation of particular kinds of objects with the help of a methodology extrapolated from the models of modern mathematics and physics. More specifically, whatever kinds of truths are taken to be aesthetic truths are as such almost all construed further in terms of concepts derived from our contemporary understandings of the nature of science as an intelligible discipline and our understandings of the truths that science is concerned to formulate.

So, in locating the issue in terms of some hypothetical feature of artworks alone, the hermeneutic view is indirectly contesting the models we habitually work with in delimiting certain questions as problems in aesthetics, say, rather than as problems in ontology. And this view is also contesting indirectly the models we habitually bring to bear on questions pertaining to the nature of truths. In short, part of the background here includes a polemic against a construal of the separate domains of philosophy after the model of mathematical understandings of modern science and a construal of truths in artworks on the model of truth-functional analyses of scientific truths. Questioning the understanding of truths in literature which much analytic philosophy presents, then, involves questioning the understanding of modern aesthetics as a philosophical discipline.

But even supposing that such a polemic were largely if not in all its details justified, what does the hermeneutic view propose?

This position draws attention to the kinds of indirect knowledge which have traditionally been associated with humanistic traditions. Gadamer, for example, holds that the humanities have preserved until recent times a different, looser, more open-ended, one might even say more contextual understanding of truth than the natural sciences have. This understanding, so the story goes, is still operative in the early Dilthey until the struggles with psychologism finally move him beyond the perduring insights of his neglected masterpiece, the biography of Schleiermacher. With important qualifications, a similar understanding is to be found also in parts of Collingwood's work; for example, in his treatment of the logic of question and answer to which Gadamer refers explicitly. Still, we must persist in asking what the positive element in this different understanding of truth looks like.

One important element in this account is the contention that, whatever characterization we settle on for those nonobjective, nonverifiable, nonscientific truths in literature, we must situate those truths neither in the sentences of the work nor in those about the work. Rather, these truths are to be identified within the understanding of the texts. And such an understanding may assume, as the case of dramatic production clearly indicates, more than a sentential form only.

But doesn't this further contention bring back into play all the versions of intentionalism, whether centered on authors or performers or audiences, which both analytic and hermeneutic philosophers have been so ingenious in disqualifying? This is not clear. In fact, it would be necessary to look much more closely at just what intentionalism is before trying to judge this matter intelligently. What should be noted for now, however, is the characteristic way in which the hermeneutic thinker responds to such a query." The experience of the work of art always fundamentally surpasses every subjective horizon of interpretation," Gadamer writes. Moreover, his own work in large part aims to "show that understanding is never subjective behaviour toward a given 'object,' but towards its effective history—the history of its influence; in other words understanding belongs to the being of that which is understood" (xix, xxi).

Most of this may be the case. The persistent problem is finding persuasive reasons, and reasons of a sort that analytic and not just hermeneutic philosophers would accept, for justifying such a view. We have, at least in the remarks above, no such arguments but assertions only. They may be true, and then again they may not be. What we require from the hermeneutic philosopher, however, and precisely here, is less assertion and more argument. But this final point requires more elaboration.

Notice both how important the point at issue here is and how the hermeneutic thinker retorts. The point at issue of course is how we are to know what stands for or against the kind of suggestive but hardly rigorous reflections put forward so far. How are we to evaluate such reflections? And if we do not settle on a solution to this puzzle, then exactly why need we try to look further into the nature of truths in literature than analytic philosophers are already doing? At least we know what can count as answers to the questions they are asking. And we know what form such answers should take even if these answers are not yet all in hand.

The hermeneutic thinker characteristically replies to this cardinal objection in some such terms as these. To meet the conditions analytic philosophers impose on putative aesthetic theories about truths and literature would be inconsistent with the critique of a one-sided view of scientific truth. To put hermeneutic reflection, then, into such an acceptable form would be to practice just the kind of powerful but overly narrow kind of thinking which these reflections have been designed to question.[10] Perhaps not all the issues we have to raise about truths in literature can be poured into the mold of problems seeking solutions. Some of these issues we may not yet be able to get into proper question form.

So much, then, for the starting point, the focus, the contexts, and the point at issue of a second set of views about literary truths.

---

[10]See McCormick 1976.

A CONTRAST: TRUTH AS CONCEPT OR EVENT?

Let us pursue further at least one basic opposition between these two perspectives.

If the characteristic form for the questions many analytic philosophers bring to literary texts is something like "Just how do truths in literature differ from truths elsewhere?" what if any question characterizes the other approach? With the polemical context still in mind, I think we can put the hermeneutic question something like this: "Just what if any truths make themselves manifest in the understanding of literary works of art and not elsewhere?"

Here again we require some background.

Putting our question this way stresses the idea, now more familiar since careful critical reflection on Roman Ingarden's work has begun, that the literary work of art is in some important sense a processlike phenomenon.[11] An aesthetic object, this story goes, is constituted in the interaction between the stratified structure of the literary work of art and the active understanding of its readers. The claim, then, is that the work of art is a kind of event, in fact an ontological event in the sense that such an event brings about the appearance of one species of objects, the aesthetic object, makes this appearance manifest to the sympathetic understanding of a reader, and makes available in this phenomenon access to truths about persons and actions. It is capital here to recognize the primacy of the artwork over the imagination. For if there is a way out of the impasses of psychologism which continue to threaten hermeneutic theories of aesthetic truths, then such an issue cannot be found in the direction of subjectivity alone, no matter how deeply we pursue the archaeology of knowledge. Husserl's greatest achievements in phenomenology itself and not just in the theory of phenomenology, his endless studies on temporality, have demonstrated this point. And Husserl, as the tortured drafts of his intersubjectivity materials show unequivocally,[12] came to understand the point of his interminable beginnings, a lesson Heidegger learned early on. That is why, while insisting on the understanding of the literary work of art as that area in which there comes to presence whatever truths literature yields, Gadamer writes: "Literature as an art-form can be understood only from the ontology of the work of art, and not from the aesthetic experience that occurs in the course of that reading" (143).

But what, more precisely, is it that such understanding is active upon? And what is it in the literary work of art that makes such presences possible?

[11]See the primary and secondary bibliographies in McCormick 1986a:181–261.
[12]See McCormick 1976.

Both the hermeneutic and the analytic philosopher here appeals to the peculiar role language plays in literature. For the hermeneutic philosopher, however, language is no longer viewed as simply a means of communication and therefore an entity to be understood in terms of either sophisticated mathematical theories like Shannon's or imaginative structuralist theories like Jakobson's or metaphorical self-referential theories like Derrida's. Nor is literary language to be construed simply as a means of expression and therefore to be subjected to all the puzzles of expression theories or art. Rather, language in the literary work is listened to with something like the attention we see at work in Heidegger's mediations on Trakl's color symbolisms or George's formalisms or most notably Hölderlin's lyric memorializings: that is, language on the hermeneutic view is habitually understood not in the sense of a formal system but in the obscure and almost mystical sense of a speaking event, a verbal happening. The text speaks or, as Heidegger never tires of saying in *On the Way to Language* in some of his most carefully deployed tautologies, "Language speaks . . . the essence of language is the language of essence."

This is part of what lies behind some of the cryptic statements in Gadamer's work about cultivation, common sense, taste, and tact as modes of indirect knowledge, about inexplicitness and inexpressibility (34–36). "All encounter with the language of art," he writes, "is an encounter with a still unfinished process and is itself part of this process." The controlling idea is that the peculiar kind of speaking that goes on in the literary work of art is a domain, a site, a *topos* where we are summoned, as Heidegger likes to say, by the unarticulated possibilities of a world breaking through the language of the text of our understanding. This kind of language, the claim here goes, may make available to us truths that are otherwise inaccessible.

Again, I think we need to say plainly that this kind of talk is for many of us philosophically unsettling. What should be noted, however, is the primacy, in such unusual talk about language as speaking, of an experience with language rather than of a concept of language. If we are ever to come to critical terms with the central oppositions between analytical and hermeneutic approaches to truths in literature, as I think we must, we need to recognize this central opposition between a concept of language and an experience of language. The former is a difficult enough affair; but the latter refers us exasperatingly to time, to history, to—for one example only—the mysteriously privileged speaking of language which characterized the ritual of Greek tragic drama in Athens.

One final point should be made. With this focus on the process character of the literary work of art as an event and the speaking of language in the active understanding of such a work, clearly the accent in the hermeneutic view falls on some as yet implicit account of experience. Dilthey of course worked long and hard at developing a more comprehensive

account of experience than the empirical account that continued to preoccupy him even after his reading of Kant.[13] And Husserl too, in a different
vein, looked toward reconstructing a view of experience that would be
up to the measure of what he called "the life world." Regardless of the
different problems each of these attempts foundered on, a common and
enduring feature of both was the stress on time and history. The objectivities of science were to be set aside, or got around, or even transcended
in the vital interest of situating things and events anew at the center of
a history of understanding. So the hermeneutic approach characteristically
stresses origins while skirting biographical fallacies, and stresses traditions while sidestepping historicisms. "If it is acknowledged," Gadamer
writes, "that the work of art is not a timeless object of aesthetic experience,
but belongs to the world that endorses it with significance, it would follow
that the true significance of the work of art can be understood only in
terms of its origin and genesis in that world" (148).

But does this text give us access to truths that are otherwise inaccessible?
To the contrary. It would seem that, without forcing all truths into the
form of sentences, we still can notice that the truths to which the hermeneutic approach directs us seem more like old chestnuts than novel
revelations. What could be more familiar than the cycle of seasons, the
cycle of childbearing, the cycle of birth and death, the cycle even of our
knowledge and our ignorance?

We have to recall here the early contrast between a concept of truth
and an experience of truth. Granted that we are not at all clear about just
how the term "experience of truth" is to be reconstructed, we do understand nonetheless that truths in the second sense are more happenings
than mental constructs. So in asking what truths this text gives us access
to, we need to reflect on the possibility that such a text does not so much
afford us insight into novel concepts but, the claim is, occasionally brings
about some kind of event of understanding.

Our initial problems, then, return, but now in a different form. For we
are pressed to ask how we are to know when such events come about,
how we are to characterize such events, and most important, what such
events, if there are any, have to do with if not concepts then, to use the
recommended phrase, experiences of truth.

Neither the analytic nor the hermeneutic thinker provides an unambiguous response to such difficulties. Each merely again raises the doubt
that this kind of difficulty about the nature of literary truths—namely,
the tortured relations between their contents and their understanding—
allows no consistent solution without a reexamination of the paradigms
within which we do philosophy. Let us turn, then, to sketching an al-

[13]See McCormick 1975.

ternative account that draws on some of the regional clarity that distinguishes much analytic work while focusing on some of the difficult issues that preoccupy hermeneutic thinkers.

LITERARY TRUTHS AND QUASI-JUDGMENTS

In *The Literary Work of Art*, where he replies to the criticisms brought against his work by K. Hamburger in *Die Logik der Dichtung*,[14] Roman Ingarden presents a central formulation of his prespective on the nature of literary truths. The key passage is:

> ... do literary works of art (fictional poems) constitute pure judgments (pure "reality statements" in Hamburger's terminology) or not? It seems to me beyond doubt that Hamburger must say: No, in no case. Poetry is not composed of judgments. Fine. Then I ask: What, then, are those propositions that are components of poetry? In a general sense, they are predicative sentences. . . . Are they then pure "assumptions" in Meinong's sense? Or are they somewhat "neutralized" affirmative propositions? Both seem false to me. . . . There must be something else, therefore. In my opinion it is precisely the "quasi-judgments."[15]

In short, if there are such things as literary truths, Ingarden holds, then these truths depend on the existence of a peculiar class of judgments called literary judgments or quasi-judgments.

But his formulation poses at least three tasks for anyone who would evaluate Ingarden's view both sympathetically and critically.[16] The first is describing the nature of quasi-judgments, the second articulating the connections between quasi-judgments and predicative sentences, and finally stating succinctly the consequences for a theory of literary truths. I look at each of these issues in turn.

In the conclusion to the first volume of the 1966 edition of his *Studia z estetyki*,[17] Ingarden provided some important later reflections on the theme of literary truths, which had already occupied him in both *The Literary Work of Art* and *The Cognition of the Literary Work of Art*.[18] He examines there, among other things, the nature of judging. When properly performed, judging is judging seriously. And "judging 'seriously,'" he writes, "is the primary and proper sense of judging performed with full conviction when the judging subject discharges himself fully in the act of judgment without any reflective distance from himself . . . and without

---

[14]Hamburger 1957.
[15]Ingarden 1973a:180–81, cited hereafter as *LWA*.
[16]See Ingarden 1985.
[17]Ingarden 1966:415–64.
[18]Ingarden 1973b, cited hereafter as *CLWA*; and Ingarden 1946.

any reservation regarding either the judging itself or the object of this judgment."[19] Judging, then, is preeminently a nonreflexive kind of activity (the exception, which Ingarden explicitly mentions in a passage I have omitted, being when judging is directed to one's own self).

But granted that the act of judgment is performed in a certain way, a second element must also be present if we are to speak of judging in the proper and primary sense. Later in the same essay Ingarden makes explicit the ontological status of those matters with which proper judgments are concerned. Thus, he writes, "judgment arises only where a sentence predicating a certain state of affairs 'places' that state of affairs in the real world or in some other world existentially independent of the act of judgment" (179). Proper or genuine judgment, then, is both "serious" in the sense of being sincere and not primarily reflexive, and objectively oriented in the sense of predicating something of an actual referent.

Ingarden is anxious to distinguish these genuine judgments from quasi-judgments. This distinction, however, is difficult to engineer because, unlike the formal languages of mathematical logic, at least in some of the early work done during this century in such treaties as the *Principia Mathematica*, no special signs mark the occurrence of quasi-judgments in either colloquial or literary languages. Ingarden refers, in both *The Literary Work of Art* and *The Cognition of the Literary Work of Art*, to Russell's use of the assertion sign to distinguish between genuine judgments or theses of the system and pure affirmative propositions or "assumptions" (Meinong's *Annahmen*) which share with genuine judgments a peculiar form but lack their peculiar function (namely, assertion).[20] Ingarden claims that quasi-judgments are neither genuine judgments nor pure affirmative propositions, and this claim is difficult to make without becoming deeply involved in logical, epistemological, and ontological issues all at once.[21]

Put in summary form, however, Ingarden's case runs as follows. Quasi-judgments cannot, on the one hand, be genuine judgments because on this interpretation the existential status of the referents of such judgments would be that of actual objects instead of that of intentional objects. And this, as is shown by reflection on the variety of imaginary entities and states of affairs which literary works present, would contradict our experiences of literary works. But quasi-judgments cannot, on the other hand, be pure affirmative propositions either because on that interpretation the existential status of the referents of such judgments would lack both verisimilitude and above all credibility, and this too would run counter to our experiences of literary works.

Of these two claims, that quasi-judgments are neither genuine nor

---

[19]Ingarden 1973c [translation of Ingarden 1966:415–64]:167. Hereafter cited as "TIL."
[20]*LWA*, 179, *CLWA*, 64.
[21]"TIL," 166–67.

merely pure affirmative propositions, the second is more puzzling. Ingarden did, however, extend this earlier account in the later essay already mentioned. The key idea there is an inference from his treatment of pure affirmative propositions. For if such propositions lack the assertive function, then they also make no belief claims. Sentences expressing quasi-judgments, Ingarden writes, cannot be "Meinongian assumptions," pure affirmative propositions, "that is, sentences completely devoid of assertive power and *therefore* not conveying any belief regarding the reality of what they designate. For if they were 'assumptions,' objects presented in literature would have been deprived of all character of real existence, and, although they would as regards their properties perhaps resemble real [actual] objects, they would not have been able to pretend to be such objects and would not have imposed themselves as real. All artistic illusion would then become impossible."[22]

But what, then, are quasi-judgments?

Quasi-judgments are modified genuine judgments. The modification is of a double sort. First, the mental acts that result in quasi-judgments are not serious in the sense in which they make no reference to independently existing actual objects or to actual states of affairs. "I perform the sentence-forming act," Ingarden explains, "but at the same time I behave as though I were judging that I was not doing this seriously. . . . I take no responsibility. I do not intend to submit what I am reading to an examination, I do not look for arguments for or against the assumption that what the sentences say is or was true. I do not . . . assume that they claim a right to truth or even that they designate a certain state of affairs in the real world" (169). And second, the basis of a quasi-judgment is not "the receptive cognition of objects" but mental acts only and these of a peculiar kind. These mental acts are intentional acts that aim not at achieving an accommodation (or even a correspondence) to what exists antecedently, but at a "progress beyond the world already given, and sometimes liberation from it and the creation of an apparently new world" (170). Quasi-judgments, then, are neither properly serious nor primarily oriented to the world.

These two qualifications provide us with a general view of how genuine judgments are modified. They do not, however, particularize because the modification can be manifold depending on whether the quasi-judgment in an individual case is more like the genuine judgment than the pure affirmative proposition or vice versa. Some quasi-judgments seem closer to pure affirmative propositions, as in the case of Maeterlinck's symbolist dramas in *Les Aveugles* or *Pelléas et Mélisande*, where no claim to historical verisimilitude is made at all. Other quasi-judgments occupy, we might say, the middle ground between the two extreme positions, as in the case

[22]"TIL," 202–3; my emphasis.

of Biedermeier novels, where no historical claims are made strictly speaking but where nonetheless "the represented objectivities" do refer in some loose sense to a real world. Finally, still other quasi-judgments seem closest to genuine judgments, as in Schiller's trilogy *Wallenstein*, where the represented objectivities are presented in as faithful a manner as possible in the light of scholarly historical accounts of the same facts and states of affairs. The relative intermediate status, then, of quasi-judgments seems to be a function of whether or not, and if so then to what degree, the reader of the literary work refers the contents of the purely intentional correlate of his intentions to independently existing actual objects or states of affairs. In short, quasi-judgments and the idea of reference to a world is also difficult to accept without further qualification. For Ingarden here speaks mysteriously, in what seems a deliberate echo of post-Kantian idealism, of "placing" (the quotation marks are Ingarden's) or positioning an intended state of affairs in the spatio-temporal world. But surely when we first think of something or other and then, in a subsequent reflection, think about this something's existence or nonexistence, we may be performing a mental act of far more ordinary and simple epistemological status than "placing" the intentional content of the first act by the mediacy of a second act in the actual world. Why not a simpler, less figurative, and less psychologistic account here, and not just of "reference to the world" but of seriousness and reflexive distance as well?

But if the description of the first term ("genuine judgments") with which Ingarden wishes to contrast quasi-judgments is misleading, the description of the second term ("pure affirmative propositions") is very hard to make much sense of at all. The problem here is not finally with the reference to Meinong's account of assumption, although in its own right this account is both extensive and complicated. At least the reference to "assumptions" gives a general view of what Ingarden has in mind when speaking of "pure affirmative propositions." And this general idea is clarified by the further reference to Russell's not unproblematic talk, in the context of the *Principia*, of "assertions." The difficulty here, rather, is with a contrast between quasi-judgments and pure affirmative propositions. In other words, the contrast is poorly calibrated since the notion of proposition remains, although for a shrinking minority of philosophers who still hold for the existence of such entities instead of plumping for sentences *tout court*, a controversial one. Even were we to translate talk of propositions here into talk of sentences, however, Ingarden gives us no help as to just how such a translation would proceed in such a way as to respect at least the major lines of his own comprehensive ontology. Finally, a closely related difficulty here has to do with the unspecified ontological status of the contents of preaffirmative propositions. Do these contents have the same status as that of any intentional correlate whatsoever, or do they, as Ingarden's remarks seem to suggest, have a special status? If so, then what specifically is that status?

One major difficulty with Ingarden's account is clear: Ingarden cannot elucidate the nature of quasi-judgments with the sole help of a double contrast so long as the description of each term in that contrast remains either misleading or virtually unintelligible. But this difficulty is one of detail only.

THE NOTION OF LITERARY TRUTH

The poet Sidney's affirmation that the poet never lies because "hee noth-ing affirmes" raises, I have tried to show, a number of confusing issues about the nature of aesthetic truths in general and literary truths in par-ticular. I have been concerned to illustrate and then to clarify by contrast at least some of the central elements these issues involve. The implicit suggestion is that the fact of contemporary philosophical disagreement about the nature of these details invites renewed inquiry. Before that investigation can be pursued in a thematic fashion, however, it is nec-essary to win some critical distance on such contemporary formulations of the problem literary truths by examining the historical contexts and interpretations that thoroughly condition these formulations, even if they do not determine them. I have tried to make a start here by calling at-tention to the views of Ingarden.

Throughout my description of Ingarden's account I have been con-cerned to point out both positive features and problematic ones. These comments, however, have been restricted to individual details; we might now step further back.

To begin with, it is difficult to see how Ingarden's account of literary truths, for all its inventiveness and subtlety, can be accepted. For the central concept in this account is that of the quasi-judgment. And this concept itself is spelled out only with reference to a problematic account of genuine judgments and an even more problematic account of so-called pure affirmative propositions. Moreover, the discussion Ingarden con-secrates to the kinds of sentences and so-called sentential contexts in which quasi-judgments are expressed requires a number of precisions as well (see Appendix 2A, "Quasi-Judgments and Predicative Sentences"). Nonetheless, when we go through Ingarden's account of literary truths more critically there do not seem to be, at least in the materials we have examined, grounds for any in-principle objections to this account. Pro-vided that the relevant detail in Ingarden's discussion, that is, of both quasi-judgments and sentences, can be adequately reconstructed, then his account of literary truth can be proposed as a coherent whole.

But there is still one fundamental issue that may not be amenable to such generous and sympathetic efforts and hence may include grounds for an in-principle objection to the account.

The question to be answered is whether Ingarden's account of literary truth entails the concept of *the aesthetic*, particularly in its guise as "the aesthetic attitude" or as "aesthetic experience." In one of the central and late texts already referred to, when discussing the peculiar kind of sentences in literary works, Ingarden writes: "the nature of these sentences is not easy to describe precisely. It is connected with the aesthetic attitude with which we read literary works and specifically with the special way in which as a result the reader regards predicating sentences."[23] And toward the end of the same text, when Ingarden is discussing the relations between literary artworks and values, he writes with respect to these values: "There experience is made possible by, among other things, the aesthetic attitude in which the work of art places its consumer" (201–2). And finally, we need to recall in this context much of the continuing dispute in aesthetics generally and especially in the evaluation of Ingarden's aesthetics about the putative existence of aesthetic objects. For besides the aesthetic attitude and aesthetic experience, Ingarden's view of literary truths involves, even if it does not entail a commitment to, aesthetic objects. But to the degree that Ingarden's theory of literary truths necessarily involves the concept of the aesthetic, that is, to the degree that this theory cannot be detailed without appealing to such a concept, then this theory seems flawed in principle. For—it is one of the few things aesthetics has managed to demonstrate at least in the mid-twentieth century—aesthetic experience theories cannot finally resist determined criticism.

But this objection would require extensive clarification in its own right as well as careful rereading of Ingarden's fuller treatment of the concept of the aesthetic. And this is beside our present purpose.

These problems notwithstanding, it is appropriate to end this discussion of literary truths (see, however, Appendix 2B, "Literary Truths and Metaphysical Qualities") with a final citation from Ingarden's work in which he makes a rare attempt to summarize the kernel of his views: "The function of art in general and of literature in particular is not to teach man by means of judgments what the real world is like, and in performing its task it does not have to resort to judgments in the strict sense. Its chief function is to show the possible and necessary connections between the qualitative endowment of objects, and of man in particular, and values and to enable man to enter into a direct commerce with values by acting

[23]"TIL," 165–66.

upon his emotional life" (203). Such a claim, however, requires attending to questions not just about discourse and truth—the subjects of the first two chapters—but about knowledge and value, to which I now turn.

Appendix 2A   Quasi-Judgments and Predicative Sentences

Ingarden's elusive treatment of quasi-judgments hesitates somewhat between formulations that rely on judgments and formulations that rely on sentences. Can we remove this hesitation by scrutinizing Ingarden's later discussion for clarity about the kinds of sentences he has in mind when talking of quasi-judgments?

The starting point for reflection on this issue must be the analytical observation that literary works are composed of a great variety of sentences, only some of which are the declarative sentences that expose judgments. Moreover, literary works contain predicating sentences that perform different functions. Part of Ingarden's task is to sketch this variety in more detail.

The declarative sentences at issue here, Ingarden holds, are usually singular statements, whether those that refer to discrete particulars such as individual persons, or those that refer to higher-order particulars such as the referents of class nouns like "company" or "regiment." In either case, these statements function as means for the construction of the work's fictional world, what Ingarden calls "the presented quasi-reality," even though, he adds, "they themselves do not belong to it" (174). In addition to these singular predicating sentences, there are plural predicating sentences, singular and general sentences of the type either "some S are P" or "every S is a P," and finally general predicating sentences, which achieve what Ingarden calls "gnomic generalization"—sentences, that is, which "do not refer directly to any particulars presented in the work" (175).[24]

Since we need to have this set of distinctions clearly in view it will be useful to summarize schematically the four basic kinds of predicating sentences discussed so far, together with their respective objects:

1. singular predicating sentences, which refer to individuals or classes;
2. plural predicating sentences, which refer to the same kind of objects as (1);
3. singular predicating sentences of the form "some S are P" and plural

---

[24]Ingarden 1930a and 1930b.

predicating sentences of the form "every *S* is a *P*," both of which
refer to individuals or classes; and
4. gnomic generalizations, which refer to particulars only indirectly.

Before bringing his discussion to a point, Ingarden adds a second element. If we are to determine more exactly just what are the relations
between quasi-judgments and sentences, Ingarden thinks we must take
into account more than just the structure of the particular sentence concerned. We must, that is, consider the context of the sentence as well,
"its background and the function it plays in the totality." Consequently,
and with this principle in mind, Ingarden goes on to deploy those sets
of sentences with contexts: (a) "sentences clearly quoted in the text and
uttered by one of the characters presented in the work"; (b) "sentences
appearing in lyrical works"; and (c) "sentences appearing in the works
of a borderline character" (176). Examples of each type described here
are provided. Thus, for (a), consider such sentences as Aeneas's general
judgment in the *Aeneid*, "en Priamus, sunt etiam sua praemia laudi, /
sunt lacrimae rerum et mentem mortalem tangunt, / solve mutus"; for
(b), consider such sentences as du Bellay's lyric "hereureux qui comme
Ulysse a fait un beau voyage"; and for (c), consider such sentences as
Goethe's line in *Hermann und Dorothea*, "Doch Homeride zu sein, auch
nur als letzter, ist schön" (176).

Finally, against this double typology—four kinds of sentences and three
kinds of sentential contexts—Ingarden defines the major relationship between sentences and quasi-judgments. Quasi-judgments are thus not just
modified genuine judgments expressed in predicating sentences in literary works, but specifically those judgments expressed in sentences of
type 1 which appear in *no* contexts like (1), that is, "singular statements
that are neither quoted nor uttered by any of the characters presented in
the work and that apply to objects presented in the work" (178).

Ingarden notes specifically that such sentences may be construed as
authorial utterances only at the price of serious ambiguity. For the author
may speak inside his or her role as author-poet about the world of represented objectivities, or outside that role about the independent actual
world. But here, the question of just whose utterances these sentences
are is not beside the point. In fact Ingarden's reformulation of the question
brings him to the heart of his discussion: "Is it that, when the author
utters directly within the realm of his poetic work certain judgments in
the strict sense of the word about some extra-artistic reality, he abandons
his poetic role, or is it that, by uttering them, he not only retains his role
but such utterance also constitutes the effective fulfillment of his role?"
(177–78). And, of course, behind this formulation is an operative distinction assumed throughout between the author of a work and what Ingarden calls "the lyrical subject" of a work (184).

But what about sentences of type 1 which appear in lyrical contexts or borderline contexts?

Ingarden claims that, in the case of lyrical works, as long as the distinction is preserved between author and lyrical subject, then predicating sentences of the lyrical subject, given the other requisite conditions as well, are in fact instances of quasi-judgments. And in the case of borderline texts such as Goethe's sentences from the literary preface to *Hermann und Dorothea*, which is often printed separately as an elegy, Ingarden claims that such sentences have a "double aspect," which requires "a similar duality in the reader's attitude" (196). But if the first case is reasonably straightforward, the second is complicated and requires more discussion than our present purposes allow.

So much, then, for at least the central relations between quasi-judgments and predicating sentences.

Again, just as in the first part of Ingarden's analysis of quasi-judgments, there is much of substance here. We need only notice the unusual and penetrating way Ingarden makes the familiar distinction here between author and lyrical subject, or the careful discussion of the status and kinds of authorial comment in literary works, or the useful remarks about the nature of borderline cases, a topic Ingarden discusses further in an extraordinary analysis of Plato's *Symposium* (197ff.). And again, here too we need to enter further particular reservations.

The analysis of sentences Ingarden provides us with leaves much to be desired. This remains the case even when we note his very restricted purposes, the generally dated quality of his extensive discussion of the "stratum of linguistic sound formations" in *The Literary Work of Art* (which requires extensive revision in the light of developments in empirical linguistics since the early thirties, when this material was first published), and even when we exclude his unsatisfactory treatment of terms. For Ingarden does not make clear what distinction, if any, he wishes to introduce between declarative and predicative sentences. Moreover, his account wavers between talk of particular and general sentences. And of course Ingarden makes no mention here of the problematic yet important cases of negatives, conditionals, interrogatives, and (important for his account) both the distinction between and the kinds of direct and indirect discourse.

A more complicated problem arises when Ingarden proceeds to talk of sentences plus their contexts. The immediate difficulty is that we are not able to determine just what the context of the relevant sentences includes and what it excludes; we do not know, from Ingarden's account, just where to draw the line.

Much more important is the subsequent problem with the tripartite division of sentences and contexts. Why three kinds and not two or four or however many? Ingarden provides us with no justification. Moreover, scrutinizing the actual divisions he proposes seems to compound our initial puzzlement. Is the distinction here effected in terms of genre, type 1 being fiction, type 2 being the lyric? If so, then what happens to the third type? Is the distinction, then, between fiction (types 1 and 2) and nonfiction (type 3)? If so, why specify type 3 as a borderline case instead of just nonfiction? Ingarden does not answer.

These difficulties with both Ingarden's account of sentences and his typology of sentential contexts are not without consequences. For when he arrives at specifying the nature of the sentences in which quasi-judgments are expressed, his account is necessarily uneven. We find again a lack of definiteness in his switching between talk of sentences and this time not propositions but statements. Moreover, the negative reference to the first type of sentential context is especially weak because no attention has been paid to the distinction between direct and indirect discourse. Finally, the unspecified notion of context is made to do too heavy a job when left undetermined. The result is a description of a class of literary sentences, normally those in which putative literary truths are supposedly expressed, which far from enhancing our understanding of the cardinal concept of quasi-judgments actually impedes that understanding by its surprising incompleteness.

Appendix 2B   Literary Truths and Metaphysical Qualities

The central difficulty for Ingarden in his account of the nature of literary truths is the tension between the modified character of judgments and the persistent claim that literary artworks have something to do with reality. Thus, the question about literary truths "arises, on the one hand, from the assertion . . . that no sentence in a literary work of art is a 'judgment' in the true sense of the word, and, on the other hand, from the . . . assertion that the poet seeks to give 'reality' in his work."[25] If, however, we are clearer about Ingarden's views on quasi-judgments, the new idea here of "reality" needs some sorting out before we can grasp clearly enough the opposition between these two assertions.

Ingarden provides us immediately with four different senses of the cardinal term "reality." (1) The strictest sense of the term refers to "a determinate relationship between a true predicative proposition and an objectively existing state of affairs selected by its meaning content" (300). This idea of "reality" would at first seem to be the idea required by a traditional correspondence theory of truth. But such an interpretation would be premature, as is demonstrated by Ingarden's further talk here

[25]LWA, 300.

of the proposition being characterized by "a relative quasi-feature," a topic already detailed at length in chapter six of Ingarden's *Essentiale Fragen.*[26] (2) A second sense of the term "reality" is the figurative sense in which the judicative proposition itself, rather than the relationship between the proposition and the world, is called a "truth." (3) The third sense is that in which a true judicative proposition's intentional correlate is described as its "truth." (4) And the final sense of "reality" is that in which he speaks of "the appertaining objectively existing state of affairs."[27]

It is clear from this enumeration, however, that Ingarden's discussion is once again overly loose. For each of the four senses just distinguished is to be understood as a gloss not so much on the term "reality" as on the term "reality as truth," or, more simply, as "senses" of the word "truth," a not uncontroversial view. Moreover, no one of these senses does justice to the idea of literary truth. For as Ingarden himself points out, senses 1 to 3, in that they all refer to genuine or proper judicative propositions, cannot be relevant to a discussion of the quasi-judgments that characterize the literary work. And sense 4 is also irrelevant because, as Ingarden repeatedly insists, "objectively existing states of affairs in no way constitute an element of a literary work" (301). In short, whatever sense might be found for the expression "literary truth," it is in no way to be found as the content of a true proposition (cf. 303).

But if these senses are, without exception, inappropriate, in what senses may we speak of literary truths? Ingarden suggests four.

(5) To begin with, we have the sense of "literary truth" as truth by reproduction of represented objectivities, a sense of truth which is operative in contexts where we speak of a literary work being a "good copy" of something or other as in, but only in, the case of historical novels. In this sense, what is spoken of as true is what is well represented. Ingarden specifies: "we then call 'true' a represented objectivity engaged in the function of reproduction (or the sentences effecting its constitution) if it is the truest reproduction of an appropriately reproduced real objectivity" (301). (6) A further sense of literary truth is that of objective consistency. In this sense, once an author has determined the kind of entity he or she is dealing with—say, a character or an event—then the author is bound to observe in subsequent dealings with the same entity the identity conditions and criteria that determine that entity. In addition, the relevant empirical laws that may govern actual entities of the given intentional type must also be observed, together with what Ingarden obscurely calls "the a priori essential laws of the given ontic region" in which this entity is specifiable (302). It should be noted that senses 5 and 6 are not to be

[26]Ingarden 1925 and 1924.
[27]*LWA*, 301. For this discussion see also Ingarden 1987.

understood as conditions for the existence of a literary work, but only as senses of the term "literary truth." For Ingarden is aware that many literary works do not exhibit a concern for either verisimilitude or consistency.

(7) Still another sense of "literary truth" is the notion of truth as the presence of "metaphysical qualities." Ingarden has in mind here a variety of matters I will touch on briefly below. For now the main point to note is that some literary works are "true" despite the lack of either a representative function or a concern with objective consistency. In these works situations are, if not represented, at least presented, and indeed with or without their proper metaphysical qualities. When these qualities are present, Ingarden claims, we speak in this sense of literary truths.

(8) A final sense of "literary truth" becomes clear in Ingarden's discussion of the related term of the "idea" of a literary work. Here we speak of "literary truth" not just in the sense of a given metaphysical quality but in the larger sense of the presence or "manifestation" of that metaphysical quality together "with the total situation in which it is manifested." Ingarden tries to put this nuance more exactly. The "literary truth" of a work in the sense of the "idea" of a work "is based on the essential connection, brought to intuitive self-givenness, that exists between a determinate represented life-situation . . . and a metaphysical quality that manifest itself in that life-situation and draws its unique colouration from its contents" (304). This connection cannot be grasped in a purely conceptual way, Ingarden says. But when grasped this connection allows one to understand the literary work in its most fundamental unity.

In sum, we may for Ingarden speak properly of "literary truths" in none of senses 1 through 4, and in any of senses 5 through 8.

But we need now to make explicit more fully just what Ingarden would seem to have in mind by his talk of "metaphysical qualities."

The topic is a central one for Ingarden the ontologist, and thus a very extensive subject. The relevant materials for our purposes, however, can be found in sections 48 and 49 of *The Literary Work of Art*. Before trying to discern the most important features of metaphysical qualities, it is worth citing their evocative description in Ingarden's own words.

> Life goes by—if one may say so—senselessly, gray and meaningless. . . .
> And then comes a day—like a grace—when perhaps for reasons that are unremarkable and unnoticed, and usually also concealed, an 'event' occurs which envelops us and our surroundings in just such an indescribable atmosphere. Whatever the particular quality of this atmosphere, whether it is frightening or enchanting to distraction, it distinguishes itself like a shining, colourful splendor from the everyday grayness of the days, and it makes of the given event life's culmination point, regardless of whether the basis for it is the shock of a brutal and wicked murder or the spiritual

ecstasy of union with God. These "metaphysical" qualities—as we would like to call them—which reveal themselves from time to time are what make life worth living, and, whether we wish it or not, a secret longing for their concrete revelation lives in us and drives us in all our affairs and days. Their revelation constitutes the summit and the very depths of existence. . . . When we see them, the depths and primal sources of existence, to which we are usually blind and which we hardly sense in our daily lives, are "revealed," as Heidegger would say, to our mind's eye. But they not only reveal themselves to us; in looking at and in realizing them, we enter into primal existence. We do not merely see manifested in them that which is otherwise mysterious; instead, they are the primal element itself in one of its forms. But they can be fully shown to us only when they become reality. . . . They are high points which throw a shadow on the rest of our lives; that is, they evoke radical transformation in the existence which is immersed in them, regardless of whether they bring with them deliverance or damnation. (291–92)

Ingarden holds that metaphysical qualities are not "properties" of objects. Nor are they "features" of mental states. Rather, he calls them "simple or 'derived' qualities (essences)" in the sense of these slippery terms which he detailed in *Essentiale Fragen*. Examples are such things as—and here is Ingarden's own list—"the sublime, the tragic, the dreadful, the shocking, the inexplicable, the demonic, the holy, the sinful, the sorrowful, the indescribable brightness of good fortune, as well as the grotesque, the charming, the light, the peaceful" (290–91).

These qualities do not occur often. But when they do they have a positive value in the context of a life. Moreover, metaphysical qualities are not graspable—and here we recall the sense of "literary truth" as the idea of a work—by conceptual means only. In fact Ingarden goes further here and holds that such qualities are not graspable by any purely rational means in the way he says mathematical theories are comprehended. Rather, metaphysical qualities, as it were, let themselves be "seen in the determinate situations in which they arise" (292). To be grasped such qualities must be perceived by someone who is in the situation within which these qualities make themselves manifest. When perceived, metaphysical qualities exhibit a "deeper sense" to life, but such a perception cannot be forced. In some sense they conceal themselves. "And it is precisely when we are awaiting and desiring their realization and the opportunity to behold them that they do not appear" (193). Yet, says Ingarden, all persons secretly long to lose themselves in contemplation of such qualities. And this secret aspiration is what lies at the basis of both philosophical understanding and artistic creativity.

In the literary artwork, metaphysical qualities when present are exhibited by represented or presented objective situations. Indeed, Ingarden claims that a literary artwork on the one hand culminates in the manifestations of metaphysical qualities, and on the other achieves its individuality in terms of how it manifests these qualities. Such qualities are concretized in literary artworks although they are realized only in actual life situations that these concretizations simulate. Because of this simulation there is a close relation between their concretization and their realization; because of the distance between the two, however, metaphysical qualities may be contemplated in literary artworks where they most often may only be lived through in reality. Distance also accounts for the fact that realizations of metaphysical qualities transform lives more often than their concretizations do, a point Ingarden relates to Aristotle's doctrine of *catharsis*. The concretizations of such qualities allow of degrees so that literary works sometimes may only prepare such a concretization without fulfilling it, or present a concretization without any preparation at all. But the most important idea here in this talk of the manifestation of metaphysical qualities and the modes of this manifestation is the link with the larger topic of values. "The manifested metaphysical quality," Ingarden writes, "as well as the manner of its manifestations in the concretization of a literary work of art, constitute an aesthetic value" (298).

Here, then, is a fuller sense of literary truths as the presence of metaphysical qualities in literary works or as the idea of metaphysical qualities.

3

Moral Knowledge
and Fiction

This playing with words, this hiding of a secret, had a great
fascination for Anna, as it has for all women.
—Leo Tolstoy

No universal factual statements in literature can be in any
way informative or revelatory.
—Peter Mew

Our idea of anything is our idea of its sensible effects.
—Charles Sanders Peirce

Helen reads *Anna Karenina* at last and says, "I really learned something
about myself." You read *Hamlet* and later write down a few notes about
the nature of anxiety. I read one of Czeslaw Milosz's poems and discover
connections between nineteenth-century Polish history and the 1970
strikes at Gdańsk. We agree that we have actually come to know something just because we have read some literature.

These situations are variations on a familiar yet puzzling issue. Many
persons do, as we have just seen in Chapter 2, seem to come to know
important truths about a great variety of things in their dealings with
literature. Yet, the question of truth aside, how can fictions be a source
of significant knowledge?

Consider a description of a crucial passage in *Anna Karenina*:

Vronsky is riding Frou-Frou, his favorite mare, in a steeplechase. He is a
superb rider, accustomed to winning. "He felt," Tolstoy writes, "that the
mare was at her very last reserve of strength," yet he was sure that she
had enough left for one more leap, one last ditch.

"She flew over it like a bird," Tolstoy tells us, "but at the same instant,

Vronsky, to his horror, felt that he had failed to keep up with the mare's pace, that he had, he did not know how, made a fearful, unpardonable mistake in recovering his seat in the saddle. All at once his position had shifted and he knew something awful had happened."

Frou-Frou fell. "She fluttered on the ground at his feet like a shot bird. The clumsy movement made by Vronsky had broken her back." Looking down at Frou-Frou's "exquisite eyes," her "speaking eyes," Vronsky calls her his "poor thing" and cries out, "What have I done?"

What he has done is to break Anna's back too. His "clumsy movement" was in encouraging her to leave her husband when she was already at the limit of her strength. While she was making the leap to love him, Vronsky "shifted his position" and asked her to do more than she could. Though he was in control, he did not keep pace with Anna, did not sense what she needed.

The gorgeousness and the cruelty of the image perfectly expresses Tolstoy's ambivalence towards sexual freedom. No matter how well you ride an illicit passion, you can't win. Life breaks our backs, shoots our birds.

Anna was a deeply social woman, in the best sense. She drew her strength from her world. It was her element. To be a heroine, one must first be connected, perhaps even conventional. In an unstructured society, there are no heroics, only gestures. For Vronsky, society was merely a series of gestures, an officer's uniform, a shape for his vanity.[1]

This text, a critical comment about a novel, suggests that some fictions can be sources not just of any kind of knowledge, but specifically of moral knowledge, sources of what are right standards for judging actions to be morally good or bad. For this critic it seems that the conventional structure of certain societies is such that Vronsky and Anna's love affair can be rightly judged as a morally bad act by appeal to commonly accepted norms in such societies. Tolstoy of course does not say anything of the kind. He writes simply that Vronsky "had failed to keep up with the mare's pace, that he had made a fearful, unpardonable mistake in recovering his seat in the saddle." The critic, however, construes this passage metaphorically as an "illicit passion."

Now, even when we allow for a rough distinction between a critical experience of Tolstoy's novel and a literary one, some readers might ask whether the critic has interpreted this passage correctly. Others on reading of Vronsky and Anna's "illicit passion" might ask whether such an experience is always morally wrong. And still others might ask more generally whether, and if so then how, a fiction could be a source of any moral knowledge at all.

The last question is the subject of this chapter. I construe "moral knowledge" for the most part as justified true beliefs about right standards for judging human actions to be morally good or bad. This formulation of course is not uncontroversial, but it is a useful simplification. "Moral

[1]Broyard 1981:39. Tolstoy 1965:211, hereafter cited as Tolstoy.

knowledge," then, is knowledge about moral principles, about statements of those peculiar features of at least some particular situations to which appeal can be made as to a moral reason. Two examples may help clarify the sense of moral knowledge I have in mind. "Lying is wrong" is a moral principle in the sense that it "suggests that the fact that a statement is known to be false is a reason for not making it." Similarly, "adultery is wrong" is a moral principle in the sense that "it is a reason for his or her refraining from sexual intercourse with any person who is not his or her spouse." In short, moral knowledge as I use the term is knowledge of moral principles.[2]

We will find it useful first to review several distinctions about literature and kinds of knowledge with the aim of reformulating this question more precisely. In the second section we will examine an interesting response to this question. In the light of our critical reflection on this theory we can then try in the third section to articulate a more satisfying view of our own.

FICTION, KNOWLEDGE, AND MORAL TRUTHS

A sensible beginning is to take over from Ryle the familiar distinction between two kinds of knowledge, knowing-that and knowing-how. The first, we remember, is the one Plato discusses in the *Theaetetus* as "justified true belief" or what some would call "propositional knowledge," whereas the second kind of knowledge may be glossed as "not having a belief but having a skill, an ability to perform in certain ways."[3] Knowing-that and knowing-how are clearly different since a person may in a certain domain have one kind of knowledge and not the other. However, knowing-that and knowing-how are also clearly related since there is a logical and temporal priority in some domains—for instance, knowing foreign languages, such that knowing-that can be transformed into knowing-how. Knowing-that in the sense of knowing that something is the case in Japanese grammar can be transformed into knowing how to speak Japanese, and conversely, knowing how to speak Japanese can be transformed into knowing that something is the case in Japanese grammar.

Next, we should distinguish between literary discourse and nonliterary discourse. The difference, we may say here by contrast with the protracted discussion of a related distinction in Chapter 1, turns not on the kinds of sentences but on the ways we take these sentences.[4] "In all other speech

---

[2]Griffiths 1967:177.
[3]See Ryle 1949, Russell 1911, and Steinmann 1973:901.
[4]Champigny 1970, Müller in Langer 1958, Ohmann 1971, B. H. Smith 1970, and Steinmann 1971.

acts," a philosophical critic has observed, "the noun phrases (with few exceptions) refer to something, and the writer or speaker must assume responsibility for the satisfaction of certain conditions. . . . In literature, the noun phrases need not, though they may refer to something, and the writer need not assume this responsibility."[5]

Consider the simplest case, that of nonliterary discourse. In what ways can nonliterary discourse be a source of knowledge, first in the sense of knowing-that and then in the sense of knowing-how? In three ways at least. First, nonliterary discourse can be a source of knowing-that by making statements that are true, are believed to be true, and are believed to be true for good reasons. Second, nonliterary discourse can also be a source of knowing-that by expressing attitudes, emotions, and values of the writer. But these expressions must be sincere, understood to be sincere, and understood to be sincere for good reasons. Finally, nonliterary discourse can be a source of knowing-that by betraying some belief or emotion, that is, by unintentionally revealing something about its writer or speaker—for instance, by a slip of the tongue.

Some critics would extend this analysis to literary discourse.

Literature is not a source of knowing-that in the first way, the statement way, since a condition for counting a discourse as making a statement, this view holds, "is that (with few exceptions) its noun phrases refer to something; and obviously the noun phrases in literature do not."[6] In those cases, moreover, where the noun phrases in literature do refer to something, a further condition is lacking; namely, evidence for supposing that the writer in fact assumes responsibility for the satisfaction of other conditions besides reference, for example, the sincerity condition to the effect that the writer believes what he or she asserts to be the case.

Nor is literature a source of knowing-that in the second way, the expression way, since, the argument goes, "if the noun phrases in a sentence refer to nothing there is . . . nothing for the sentence to make a statement about. Nor is there, by the same token, anything for it to express attitudes towards or emotions or feelings about."[7]

Literature, however, may be a potential source of knowing-that in the third way, the betrayal way, if some prominent critics are correct in claiming that literary works may betray facts, at least about their authors.[8] But this claim is highly controversial and in fact often denied.[9] The issue turns on which principles are used in making the inferences from literary discourse to biographical facts. If these principles are linguistic rules only, then the inference is of a semantic nature; whereas if these principles are

[5]Steinmann 1973:904–5.
[6]Ibid., 904.
[7]Ibid., 906.
[8]See Spurgeon 1935 and Tillyard 1930.
[9]See Wellek and Warren 1949 and Wimsatt 1954.

both linguistic rules and psychological laws, then the inference is of a psychological nature. Semantic inference here is construed as necessarily invalid because "the rules of use that constitute the speech act that we call literature seem to be such that we cannot take literature either to make statements or to express the writer's attitudes, emotions, or feel-ings."[10] Psychological inference, on the other hand, is construed as not necessarily invalid and therefore as possible, because "there seems to be nothing in the nature of literature as a speech act to prevent the writer from betraying, and us from inferring, things about him."[11]

So much, then—with much interesting detail omitted, together with the criticisms of speech-act theory we looked at in Chapter 1—for one recent representative view of literature and cognitivity. A literary work, say, *Anna Karenina*, may be cognitive in at least two senses: first, the work may be a potential source of knowing-that by allowing psychological but not semantic inference to some biographical facts about its author; and second, a literary work may be a potential source of knowing-how by allowing the reader to acquire, whether directly or indirectly, an ability to perform certain skills.

If we assume for the sake of our subsequent discussion about moral knowledge and fictions not so much the adequacy of this account as its context and terminology, what qualifications seem called for? I suggest three.

First, we may narrow our focus to questions about cognitivity in the sense of knowing-that rather than in the sense of knowing-how. Although some instances of knowing-how seem to have a fullness that so far resists a completely satisfying translation into knowing-that, still in most cases knowing-that does retain a logical and (less often) temporal priority.

Second, we should focus our attention in what follows on actual rather than on potential sources of knowing-that. Otherwise, our concern with moral knowledge and fiction would be quickly exposed to banalization. Anything, the intuitive response might go, can be a potential source of moral knowledge. So why bother with exploring the issue further?

Finally, of the three ways of knowing-that discussed here—the state-ment way, the expression way, and the betrayal way—the first and not the remaining two should be our central if perhaps not our final concern. For the statement is the primary way in which knowing-that is commu-nicated and understood.

This representative view of literature and cognitivity—let us call it the standard view—is persuasive. But even when qualified, it is not without difficulties. I point out six such difficulties.

First, the distinction between literary and nonliterary discourse seems

[10]Steinmann 1973:909.
[11]Ibid., 909.

question begging. For we are not clear just how this distinction is to be made without appealing to some of the uses to which it is immediately put. Recall our earlier discussion of fictional versus nonfictional discourse. What complicates the task of drawing the present distinction is that often no differences between statements occurring in literary works and those in nonliterary ones are observable. Tolstoy, for instance, in novels such as *War and Peace*, uses material from the Comte de Ségur's historical memoirs, *La Campagne de Russie*, of his service as one of Napoleon's marshals.

Second, the reference condition raises problems. For it seems to be false that no noun phrases in literary works refer to anything. In *Anna Karenina*, the proper name "Vronsky" refers to one of Tolstoy's characters in his novel, to Anna's lover, and so on. The difficulty, then, is not as the standard version would have it with lack of reference, but with the nature of fictional reference. The standard version overlooks this difficulty.

Third, a problem also arises with the formulation of the sincerity condition. The claim that readers lack evidence of the author's willingness to assume responsibility for this condition also seems false. Many passages in *The Brothers Karamazov*, for example, clearly show that Dostoevski believes what he asserts to be the case. (His letters confirm this, although the novels do not require such support.) Again, the problem is not that the sincerity condition is never satisfied. Rather, we need to explain in those cases where it is satisfied, how it is satisfied, and just how it could be satisfied. The standard version does not see that this matter requires explanation.

Fourth, the claim that literature cannot be a source of knowledge in the expression way seems false too. For just as in the case of reference, so too in the matter of expression, the noun phrases seem to express attitudes, feelings, emotions, and so on about something quite definite, namely, fictional entities and fictional states of affairs. The problem is again not the absence of any objects for expression, but how literary statements can express something genuine about fictional subjects, a problem I explore more thoroughly in the next chapter. Moreover, literature may be construed as a source of knowledge in the expression way if we take the noun phrases to be referring sometimes to the attitudes and feelings of the author.

Fifth, the notion of knowledge as betrayal needs a much more careful analysis than what we find in the standard version. We require an examination of what we may call "literary implication," inferences from fictional texts to actual states of affairs. We may find some use in the distinction here between semantic and psychological inference. But surely the distinction as it stands is too narrowly construed. For other types of inference as well as other types of suggestion must also be inventoried.

Finally, the distinction between direct and indirect kinds of knowledge also requires much closer attention. The issue here is not necessarily how direct knowledge differs from implied knowledge. Rather, it concerns the more basic distinction between knowledge and belief, between kinds of knowledge, and so on.

The standard version of the cognitivity issue thus requires closer examination. Construing the cognitivity of literature in terms of some elements of literary works being genuine sources of moral knowledge that something is the case faces serious difficulties about the nature of literary discourse, reference, sincerity, expression, implication, and kinds of knowledge.

In what follows, then, the question of fiction and moral knowledge which concerns us is the question of whether some sentences of some fictional works are actual sources of direct moral knowledge-that. More concretely, the question is whether or not some fictional works are morally cognitive in the sense of being genuine sources of knowledge that certain features of some situations, when formulated as propositions, function as moral principles for judging particular human actions to be morally good or morally bad.

How, then, can Tolstoy's novel be morally cognitive in this sense?

With the present reformulation of our initial question in hand, I now consider one thoughtful response to this question.

FICTIONS AND HYPOTHESES

One influential answer to the question we glimpsed in Chapter 2 goes like this: literary works do not assert moral truths; they suggest moral truths.

But how do literary works suggest moral truths? They do not suggest moral truths in the sense that authors intend to suggest certain truths, or in the sense that particular readers actually grasp these truths. Thus, neither writers' intentions nor readers' responses do sufficient justice to the work itself. "We want to be able to say," John Hospers wrote in an article (1960) that attracted philosophers to a problem I. A. Richards had discussed much earlier in *Science and Poetry* (1926), "that something is true even though the author may not intend it and be quite unaware of it, and even though the audience may be so imperceptive as not to grasp it."[12]

But how are moral truths implied in this large sense of implication as suggestion? "Works of literature," Hospers continues, "are able...to suggest hypotheses about human behaviour, human motivation, human action, and sometimes about the social structure.... These works may

---

[12]Hospers 1960:40.

suggest or intimate (say without saying) numerous propositions . . . about the world, about the subject matter of the work itself. And since some of these suggested propositions are doubtless true, we have here surely an important sense of truth in literature."[13]

One substantive criticism of this theory comes from Peter Mew, who thinks that the formulation of this theory turns on the notion of universal factual statements. Here is an instance of such a statement from *Anna Karenina*: "This playing with words, this hiding of a secret had a great fascination for Anna, as it has for all women."[14] What is the central claim of this criticism? The claim is "that no universal factual statements in literature can be in any way informative or revelatory."[15] And what is the main argument for this claim? Basically, that whatever truth such statements may contain incidentally cannot be informative because "authors of literary works do not employ the scientific techniques necessary for the establishing of facts."[16]

The difficulty with this view, Mew thinks, is the mistaken construal of all facts as scientific facts only and all factual statements as the prerogative of scientific discourse only. He rightly objects to the exaggerations in such a view. Mew points out related difficulties in the theory's assumptions about the role of universal statements in scientific discourse and the construal of universal factual statements in literature as inductive generalizations. Making use of the Tolstoy example, he is able to undermine the essential requirement of such a view, the need for controlled observation inside some kind of a scientific research program. Finally, Mew claims that Hospers ignores the possibility of construing the subject matter of universal factual statements in literature not as empirical truths but as hypotheses.

This criticism is helpful because it raises the possibility of considering putative literary truths as something other than just empirical truths.[17] Moral truths can be discussed as well. But we should note also that Hospers in fact does not ignore the hypothesis idea. What this critic has to offer is not a new idea but a development; Mew extends Hospers's notion of treating implicit statements in literature as hypotheses to treating explicit statements as hypotheses also.[18]

According to the amended version, then, the theory should read something like this: many but not all highly general factual statements in literary works, although not offered as such, may be usefully taken as hypothesis-like statements, that is, statements analogous to those put forward in the

---

[13]Ibid., 45.
[14]Tolstoy, 319.
[15]Mew 1973:335.
[16]Ibid., 329.
[17]Scriven 1954.
[18]This development leads to a denial of the original "antitruth" theory.

sciences as statements that are not commonly accepted as true and are not obviously false either. Literary hypotheses, however, unlike scientific ones, have no explanatory functions.[19]

Here is an illustration of the theory. "In Jane Austen's novel *Emma*, the narrator remarks: 'Human nature is so well disposed towards those who are in interesting situations that a young person who either marries or dies is sure of being kindly spoken of.' I think the most natural and fruitful way to respond to this statement," the critic writes, "would be to see how it accorded with one's own experiences; in short to treat it as a hypothesis to be confirmed or falsified by one's own experiences."[20] I return to this comment in the last section of this chapter.

Thus, the usual response to our question of how fictions can be sources of moral knowledge, once modified along these lines, seems persuasive.[21] But at least one further element needs to be added. For we need to specify the nature of the kind of implication involved in deriving moral knowledge from fictional works.

Consider several interpretations of this implication. First, the kind of "implication" at issue here—"literary implication," we may say— cannot be interpreted strictly as logical implication since, as one recent paper has argued, "the relation we are looking for is not one which holds between the work and every proposition whatsoever, simply by virtue of the fact that the work is fiction."[22]

Second, literary implication cannot be stated as a truth-table tautology because such an interpretation would be both too narrow ("most of the associated claims in which we are interested are not tautological consequences of the works with which they are associated") and too broad (many of the tautological consequences do not interest us at all).[23]

Third, literary implication cannot be interpreted as entailment in any strict sense for reasons similar to those brought against the second interpretation.

Fourth, literary implication cannot be interpreted as inductive inference either because the link between the explicit reports or reflections and the alleged implicit ones is supported by too few cases.

Fifth, expanding the previous interpretations to include inductive inferences plus what has been described as ordinary commonplaces about the world won't do either because many such commonplaces seem out

[19]Mew 1973:331–34.
[20]Ibid., 333. Mew cites Austen 1966:143.
[21]See Mew 1973:336. Note that although many novelists (recall Balzac) make such universal statements, these statements are far less important than the fictional world in which they arise. To what degree do these statements interest us as readers once we abstract from their fictional contexts? (I owe this point to Sven Linnér.)
[22]Sirridge 1975:460.
[23]Ibid.

of place in particular fictional contexts, and because we do not know how to decide on just which commonplaces in a particular case should be relied on.[24]

Finally, interpreting literary implication counterfactually seems to be no good either. The basis of a counterfactual analysis is the observation that, even though many of the explicit reports and reflections that can be articulated are the antecedents of a literary implication, the consequents are taken to follow anyway. But far too often the antecedents in such counterfactuals are neither explicit reports nor reflections from which the consequent may be said to arise as an implication. Moreover, when this is not the case, the relevant antecedents in the counterfactuals lack direct textual support.

But if the reasons urged against the first five interpretations of literary implication are tolerably convincing, those urged against the counterfactual interpretation seem unpersuasive. For it may well be possible to find an example in some other literary work where some species of a so-called explicit report both is actually stated in the text in counterfactual form and is supported from what is in the text. Perhaps we do need to look at counterfactuals more closely.

Consider the view to which I alluded in Chapter 1, that storytellers are engaged in pretending.[25]

The gist of this view is that descriptions in fictional works are taken as "abbreviations for longer sentences beginning with an operator 'In such and such a fiction. . . . ' Such a phrase is an intensional operator that may be prefixed to a sentence Q to form a new sentence. But then the prefixed operator may be dropped by way of abbreviation, leaving us with what sounds like the original sentence Q but differs from it in sense."[26] A problem arises here, however. For any particular description in a literary work may be ambiguous in that inspection does not make clear whether the sentence in question is or is not to be taken as an abbreviation for a sentence with the appropriate prefix.

Where, then, do counterfactuals come in?

What is true in the literary work is what would be true in that work were the descriptions recounted there to be told not as fiction but as known fact. When we tell a story, the idea is, we do many different things. One thing we do in some fiction is describe. But describing in fiction is making suppositions that are contrary to fact. These suppositions may and most often do include factual premises. But these premises are used in a modified way; they are not used with a complete freedom but

[24]See ibid., nn. 12, 18, and 19.
[25]D. Lewis 1978.
[26]Ibid., 37–39.

with just so much freedom as we require to be inside the possible world that would make our suppositions true. But further attention must be paid to the background of the pretense here, to the condition that as few changes as possible should be made in the actual world when telling our usual stories.[27]

We have, then, the claim that truths in fiction consist of counterfactual statements, explicit contents plus a background. And the further suggestion is that this background be construed not as the constantly changing contents of our own generally prevalent beliefs, but as the more stable contents "of the beliefs that generally prevailed in the community where the fiction originated."[28] These beliefs must be shared, held by most members of the community; in short, they must be overt, generally prevailing beliefs.[29]

This leaves us with two sets of worlds rather than any number whatsoever, "the worlds where the fiction is told as known fact, and the collective belief worlds of the community of origin. The first set gives the content of the fiction; the second gives the background of relevant beliefs."[30] Our initial formulation of the counterfactual interpretation, then, must be expanded. What is true in the literary work is what would be true in that work "according to the overt beliefs of the community" were the descriptions recounted there to be told not as fiction but as known fact. More concretely, what is morally true in *Anna Karenina*—say, that Vronsky's actions are morally wrong—is what would be true according to the overt beliefs of Vronsky's community were what is recounted in the novel told not as fiction but as known fact.

Now, what are we to make of this theory? Despite many difficulties here—for example, a narrow and shallow conception of "literary truth"— several good suggestions are in evidence and we should bring these together.

The notion that literary discourse involves pretense of some sort does coincide with most of our intuitions about these matters. Spelling out the nature of this pretense, however, in terms of prefixing and counterfactuality is strained because of the implicit-explicit distinction, the distinction roughly between what the text actually says and what it may be taken to show.

Moreover, the idea of transworld identity, although comprising a number of features that raise difficult questions in ontology and the philosophy of logic, seems to correspond to our intuitions here also. Some like to

[27]Ibid., 40.
[28]Ibid., 44.
[29]Ibid.
[30]Ibid.

talk, for example, of the "world of Tolstoy" or of "Proust's world" as a peculiar kind of domain that, although very much like the everyday world, is nonetheless different in important ways.

Further, the notion of overt and generally available background beliefs of a community is the kind of context to which one would like to appeal in order to situate more largely the overly constricted approach of a particular semantic theory.[31]

Finally, the emphasis not so much on the mental acts that may or may not accompany the sentences to be found in the literary works, the author's pretense in writing them, of our counterfactual suppositions in reading them, but on how sentences in literary works actually affect their readers is also suggestive. "It is the work of fiction itself, the story it tells, not the reliability of the author, which determines the effect the work has on our beliefs."[32]

We may say, then, that fictional works are morally cognitive in the sense that they may be sources of genuine moral knowledge. Literary works such as *Anna Karenina* may suggest moral knowledge in that they imply that appeals to some features of human situations may function as appeals to a moral principle by allowing counterfactual suppositions to arise in the course of readings. Here, then, is one interesting response to our initial question, a response we must now examine.

FICTIONS AND MORAL BELIEFS

In this final section I propose an alternative account of moral truths in fictions. This account involves a theory of the contents of literary works, including what can be inferred from the work, a functional rather than a representative view of the literary work, and finally, a weaker version of the standard interpretation of literary cognitivity.

The Contents of the Literary Work

One way of describing the cognitive character of literary works is to argue that these works include propositions that are usually associated with the moral or theme of the work. It is for these propositions and not just for any proposition whatsoever a literary artwork may include that the phrase "the propositional content of a work" has been advanced. The general problem here is how the propositional content of a literary work is to be specified. And any propositional theory of truth in literature may be taken as a putative solution to this problem.

[31]See Gabriel 1975.
[32]Sirridge 1975:470.

Recently, several versions of a propositional theory have been proposed and critically examined.[33] The first version is put as follows: "the propositional content of a work of fiction consists of whatever is present explicitly in the work and is true or false."[34] The key phrase "whatever is present explicitly" is construed further as whatever sentences in the work are properly described as "explicit reports."[35] In other words, explicit reports are "sentences of the work which outside the work of fiction would normally be used to state a fact."[36] Explicit reports need, however, to be distinguished from explicit reflections that are sentences of the work "in which the narrator ostensibly states an opinion about the events of his narrative or generalizes on them."[37] This clarification yields an amended version of the first theory, which now runs: "the propositional content of a work of fiction consists of all and only the reports and reflections of the work."[38] But this version is unsatisfactory because it is too narrow, in the sense that it excludes far too much. For it excludes from the propositional content of a work all those many putative truths that can be taken legitimately as following from the work even though they are not explicitly articulated in actual sentences of the work.

To keep the parallel with the terminology so far, we may go on to use Beardsley's other terms to cover the further types of truths referred to here. Thus, the work is taken to include both explicit reports and reflections and implicit reports and reflections. This more comprehensive second version of the propositional theory may be put as follows: "The propositional content of a work of fiction is constituted by all and only (i) those true or false reports and reflections which are explicit in the work, and (ii) those reports and reflections which are implied by the explicit reports and reflections."[39] But this version is also unsatisfactory because we still lack an agreed upon procedure for determining what the relevant construal of the implication relationship should be. Although six candidates have been examined—logical implication, truth-table tautology, entailment, inductive inference, inductive inference plus commonplaces about the world, and counterfactuality—the conclusion some philosophers draw is "that there is no well analyzed sense of 'imply' in which these propositions can be said to be implied by the work with which they are commonly associated."[40]

This conclusion, however, is shortsighted. For we may pick up an echo

---

[33]See Pollard 1977 and Sirridge 1970. The basic paper is still Sirridge 1977.
[34]Sirridge 1975:457.
[35]Beardsley 1958:409–10.
[36]Sirridge 1975:457.
[37]Ibid., 457–58.
[38]Ibid., 458.
[39]Ibid., 459.
[40]Ibid., 462.

here of the earlier talk about hypothesislike statements and analyze literary implication by considering a seventh candidate, Peirce's notion of abduction.

Here is an informal description of abductive implication. Part of its interest is the way it improves on talks of hypotheses. Briefly, the claim is that statements occurring in fictional works such as *Anna Karenina* may be said to imply abductively the truth these works express, although they cannot be said to imply those truths either inductively or deductively. Abduction, or we may say inference to the best explanation, is the kind of inference which scientists often use when articulating a hypothesis. The logical form of abductive implication is the following: "Considerations C are absurd. But if the hypothesis H were true, C would be a matter of course. Hence, there is reason to suspect that H is true."[41] Notice, however, that the hypothesis in question cannot be considered confirmed. For in affirming the consequent, the reasoning here would be fallacious. Nonetheless, "if the hypothesis does deductively imply the condition observed, then it must be considered to have some degree of epistemic warrant."[42] (See Appendix 3A, "The Paradox of Abduction.")

When we say, then, that Tolstoy's *Anna Karenina*, although it does not include the statement "Vronsky's affair is to be judged a morally bad act," nonetheless abductively implies this statement, we mean that the hypothesis that this statement is true is the best explanation of what happens—of what happens to Vronsky and Anna in the world of Tolstoy's novel. Thus, a reader may use the kind of inference a scientist uses. But whereas the scientist applies this procedure in order to explain the actual world, the reader applies it in order to understand a fictional world.

If we make use of Peirce's notion, then, we may settle initially for a third version of the propositional theory: the propositional content of a work of fiction is constituted by all and only (i) those true or false reports and reflections that are explicit in the work, and (ii) those reports and reflections that are implied in Peirce's sense of abduction by the explicit reports and reflections.

Two further elements, however, must now be added to this account, both of which arise out of a criticism of the counterfactual theory: a functional rather than a representative view of the literary work and talk of beliefs rather than of truths.

A Functional View of the Literary Work

Recall the general outline of the counterfactual theory. There are truths of various sorts about our world, our histories, ourselves. Some of these are moral truths, truths about the moral quality of human actions and

---

[41]See Schick 1982. Schick cites Peirce 1955:151.
[42]Schick 1982.

about the criteria for making such judgments. We normally come to know these truths through our observations, our experiences, our reflections. We come to know that something or other is the case, that p. Occasionally, this story goes, we can also come to know something by inferring from fictional texts that p. In order, however, to account for the puzzle of how a fictional text can be a source of genuine knowledge, we need to understand the relevant sentences of these texts in a peculiar way. We are, in short, to understand these sentences as implying something about a possible world.

On this account what it is we come to know may be understood as something represented in the text in the way some literary critics were accustomed to think of "meanings" being present in the text and in the way some philosophers were accustomed to think of "representation."[43] Tolstoy, we might say in an exaggerated way, knows already, among the many things he knows before penning his passage, that Vronsky's affair is to be judged an illicit passion. And to communicate this idea he represents this putative knowledge in the imaginary details of his fictional text. Readers discover this moral truth when they are brought to reflect on just what moral truths the text incorporates. And the condition for their reflection is adopting with regard to the text a counterfactual attitude. Readers can discern a particular moral truth the text conceals by asking what would be morally true were what is implied by the text in its fictional world to be implied in the actual world.

But even when we eliminate from this description the exaggerations we have allowed in order to highlight its major features, serious difficulties persist. The hinge on which these difficulties turns, I suggest, is a fundamental and mistaken view about literature and cognitivity. A literary work, we may argue, is best regarded not so much as a finished product that includes among its many elements "truths"—whether moral, empirical, or otherwise—but as a dynamic process whose major elements are incomplete until the text is read. One of these elements is the work's capacity to generate the adoption of cognitive attitudes in some of its readers. The point is that whatever cognitive elements a literary work may properly be said to be sources of are not to be found already in the finished product (a book) but can sometimes be generated in a particular performance of the work (a reading).

This second element in our theory, a revised account of the idea of a fictional work, needs a word or two of elaboration.

Recall one of Roman Ingarden's major tenets, the view that the literary work presents "schematized aspects," possibilities that the reader "concretizes."[44] The text, thus, is seen as having a double character. The author's text is the artistic pole, whereas the reader's concretization of

[43]See R. Rorty 1980.
[44]See Ingarden 1947.

this text in a particular reading is the aesthetic pole. The literary artwork is not to be identified with either the author's text or the reader's text, but only with some kind of "virtual entity" understandable perhaps as sets of possibilities which the author composes one way, the reader disposes in another, and which intersect in a reading. Whatever cognitive elements we may conclude the literary work is a source of are not, then, to be found prior to the reader's own activity.

More recently, some of these views have developed further.[45] Some critics want to talk about the text as a "structured indicator" that organizes a potential effect.[46] This potential in the reading process can be understood as soliciting the reader's perceptual and imaginative participation in the text.[47] When successful, the solicitation initiates on the part of the reader a particular and unique performance of the text. Thus, two structures are at issue here, that which governs the organization of the text's possible effects and that which governs the organization of the reader's particular responses.[48] The potential of the text is realized in the response of the reader. The fictional is thus not to be understood by contrast with the actual, which is an assumption behind the counterfactual theory. This representational view is challenged by a functional view in which the fictional is understood as linked to reality in terms of communication.[49] Consequently, literary truths are not what would be true in the real world, but what in fact may be true in the actual world.

But when we talk of the reader's constructive response to the solicitations of the text, we still need to satisfy which reader. Is the reader the historical reader? If so, then which historical reader? The one we can reconstruct from extant documents, or the one we can construct from what we know about the reader's own time, or the one we can extrapolate from the author's text as the role the author intended the reader to play? Or is the reader in question here, like the text, some kind of fiction too, another fiction, an ideal reader of some sort? If so, then how are we to interpret this reader? As a "superreader,"[50] or as an intended reader,[51] or as an implied reader?[52]

If we follow a recent argument, we will have to recognize the implied reader as a role the text offers, a construct that embodies all the predispositions required for the text to work its effect, "a network of response-inviting structures which impel the reader to grasp the text."[53] But such

[45]Iser 1978.
[46]Ibid., 9.
[47]Ibid., 18.
[48]Ibid., 21.
[49]Ibid., 53.
[50]Riffaterre 1978.
[51]Wolff 1971.
[52]Iser 1978:34–35.
[53]Ibid., 34.

a suggestion still needs further precision if we are to have available an intersubjective basis for appraising a particular reading.[54] In short, whatever reader we finally argue for will have to be seen not just in ideal terms but also in real enough terms to allow talk of consensus, community, convention, and culture. The overt beliefs of a community, then, as in the earlier discussion of the counterfactual theory, must be brought in again. On such a view, "the cognitive element" of a literary work would not be what is true in the actual world, but what is taken to be true by a community of readers. And literature would be cognitive in the sense that it can suggest, that is, generate, such truths in a community.

The abductive implication, then, from the passage in *Anna Karenina* that Vronsky's affair is morally wrong, and similar explicit and implied statements in other literary works, can be taken not just as something morally true counterfactually but as something morally true in the real world. More generally, Tolstoy's novel may be called morally cognitive insofar as it is a source of knowledge that something is the case in the sense that at least some of its passages are so structured that they can solicit the adoption on the part of a community of readers of morally cognitive stances.

Cognitivity in Literature

I turn now to the question of whether a fictional work can properly be described as morally cognitive in the sense that it can be a genuine source of moral knowledge.

Recall first the initial distinction that the standard account of the cognitivity issue takes over from Ryle, the distinction between knowing-that and knowing-how. This distinction in fact goes back to Russell, who proposed, however, a second distinction, which Ryle neglected and the standard account overlooks. The second distinction is between knowing truths and knowing things.

When I know a truth, I know that p is the case. But when I know the constellations, for example, I know simply Sagittarius and Ursa Major and Scorpio; I know neither that p, nor that q either. Knowing things is different from knowing truths, even though knowing things can be transformed into knowing truths. If I know Ursa Major, I may also know that stars a, b, and c have sufficient magnitude to be observed under certain climatic conditions, in certain seasons, from a certain hemisphere, and that they can suggest a particular outline in the night sky. But knowing Ursa Major does not entail knowing that p, q, and r are the case. Cognitivity, then, even when interpreted in terms of knowledge, need not commit us to the view that literature is a source of knowing truths with the concomitant problem of explaining the nature of such putative truths.

[54]For the intersubjective basis, see Fish 1980.

More simply, we may hold that some literary works may be sources of knowing things, not truths.

But this interpretation of cognitivity is still too strong. For now instead of having to explain the nature of literary truths, we are committed to explaining the nature of the literary entities. And the difficulties with this task, as Meinong's fascinating but ultimately unsuccessful attempts to delineate such an ontology have shown, are almost as formidable as those that complicate any attempt to elaborate a theory of literary truths.

Thus, whether we think about "knowledge" epistemologically in terms of truths or ontologically in terms of entities, serious difficulties arise in both cases from traditional and still current understanding of knowledge as justified true belief. In the first case, the problem is how to attach sufficient content to the notion of "true" when we are dealing with statements occurring in literary works or abductively implied from such statements; in the second, the problem is how to parse the notion of "justification" in such a way as to make sense of reference to fictional entities. Of course, this traditional concept of knowledge has often been put into question since Plato's discussion—each of the three terms in the concept has occasioned serious criticism. But most philosophers today agree that these criticisms have not yet been answered.[55] So changing the traditional definition of knowledge does not provide a way around these difficulties because we have no sufficient agreement yet on what a more satisfactory account of knowledge would look like. But if these difficulties persist, then we really cannot continue to interpret the cognitivity issue in terms of knowledge at all.

These difficulties, however, need no longer arise, I suggest, if we construe cognitivity in literature more weakly in terms of belief.

The epistemological problem need not arise. For a belief may be true or false but need not be, since beliefs may be incomplete, or confused, or contradictory. And the ontological problem need not arise either. For beliefs may be neither true nor false. Moreover, even if true, a belief may perfectly well lack justification and merely happen to be true, or may in fact be justified but not knowable as such, or be justified and not yet known as such. In those cases of beliefs that happen to be true, justification for their truth is rightly sought outside the literary work. But as we have noted, many beliefs in fact do not even happen to be true. So either the justification problem does not arise, or it arises in such a way that it allows of solution along traditional lines.[56]

My suggestion, then, is that the cognitivity issue concerns the question of whether literary works can be sources not of knowledge but of beliefs

[55]See, e.g., Quinton 1967.
[56]See Firth 1981. Several other important issues here are treated in Baier 1985 and Shepard and Cooper 1986.

of whatever kind about the actual world on the part of a community of readers. Some of these beliefs may be moral beliefs. These beliefs, further, may be novel in the sense that prior to the experience of reading certain literary works the community did not entertain such beliefs. But in no case can we conclusively argue either that the truth of these beliefs or the justification of the truth is to be found in the literary work itself or in the communities' experiences of the literary work. I would add, but not develop here, that whatever justification and truth some of these beliefs may exhibit derives not just from analysis of sentences that articulate these beliefs in the text, but also and perhaps especially from larger entities, call them typical pictures of life, which these sentences present and which some readers recognize. (See Appendix 3B, "Moral Obligations and Ethical Responsiveness.")

We may conclude by recalling the passage we began with, in which Vronsky has just urged his favorite mare into one last leap in the steeplechase. "She flew over it like a bird," we remember reading, "but at the same instant, Vronsky, to his horror, felt that he had failed to keep up with the mare's pace, that he had, he did not know how, made a fearful, unpardonable mistake in recovering his seat in the saddle. All at once his position had shifted and he knew something awful had happened."

My concern in this chapter has been to raise several critical questions about the claim that sentences like these in literary works such as *Anna Karenina* can be construed as morally cognitive in the sense of being sources of genuine moral knowledge. Recall that Tolstoy himself does not assert explicitly that Vronsky's affair is rightly judged as a morally bad action. Rather, some of his critics have argued that his text suggests this viewpoint. More specifically, the text is said to be complexly organized— metaphorically, rhetorically, and so on—in such a way as to allow valid implications by its readers about the moral quality of actual as opposed to fictional acts of adultery. But this view, I have argued here, even when supported with an ingenious counterfactual theory, relies on an erroneous conception of the literary artwork as merely representative, leaves unexplained the nature of literary implication, and is committed to an overly strong view of cognitivity and literature.

Some literary works, I have urged to the contrary, may be cognitive in the sense that they are functional entities that may allow abductive implications from fictional worlds to the actual world, but only if we construe the cognitive dimension of these works as sources of beliefs on the part of a community of readers rather than as sources of truths for individuals only.[57]

---

[57]Note, however, Sven Linnér's qualification that bringing the reader onto the scene is not without difficulties. "Let us assume one brilliant critic who interprets a certain text a

Some fictions may indeed be cognitive; some passages such as the one I have worried about may indeed be sources of genuine moral beliefs about actual and not just fictional human actions; some moral fictions may even be cardinal components of any reflective person's attempt to articulate a satisfactory moral viewpoint. But we do the power, the suggestion, the cognitive force of fiction a disservice if we construe that force too strongly in terms of moral knowledge when moral beliefs are so much more adequate. Part of that force derives from some connections to which we must now turn, namely, those between fictions and feelings.

Appendix 3A   The Paradox of Abduction

This central element in my view needs some comment. Gilles Granger writes: "This 'paradox of abduction' has little relationship with your own use of abduction in moral knowledge. Nevertheless, it might help pointing out how irreducible it is to a mere logico-mathematical scheme.

"Let a be a surprising fact, h a hypothesis making it a 'matter of course.' I'll try to translate the inference in terms of probability.

"Let $P(a)$ be the probability of a, a priori; $P(a/h)$ the probability of a if h; $(P(a/\text{not} -h)$ the probability of a if not $-h$.

1. We have

$$P(a) = P(a/h) \cdot P(h) + P(a/\text{not} -h) \cdot (1 - P(h)) \tag{1}$$

"$P(h)$ is the probability of h, which ought to be great when $P(a/h)$ is great, even if $P(a)$ is a priori very low (according to the abduction inference).

But we calculate from (1):

$$P(h) = \frac{P(a) - P(a/\text{not} -h)}{P(a/h) - P(a/\text{not} -h)} \tag{2}$$

"From (2) all we can infer is that, if $P(a)$ is low, and $P(a/h)$ is high (which entails $P(a/\text{not}-h)$ negligible), $P(h)$ will be *low* ... which is a conclusion contrary to the abduction inference.

2. Try another interpretation. Let $P(h/a)$ be the probability of h if a. The Bayes theorem gives:

certain way. He is the first to do it, until later on people accept his reading. For a time at least his interpretation is highly individual. On the other hand, he uses the language and culture of his times: he stands for the best possible reading in that particular community. By my admittedly fictitious example I wish to indicate that the relation between the individual reader and the community is probably still more complex than appears in your paper" (private communication).

$$P(h/a) = \frac{P(h) \cdot P(a/h)}{P(a)}$$

"Now, the probability of h if a is high if $P(a)$ is low and $P(a/h)$ is high, which is the very abduction conclusion.

"Obviously, this last model conveys the meaning of the abduction inference more adequately, since the required probability is the probability attributed to h *after* a has been observed. However, the first interpretation has been possible on account of the vagueness of the notion corresponding to $P(a)$ and $P(h)$. This would support the conclusion that the abduction procedure is, in fact, rather a *pragmatic* inference than a logical one. It involves a number of *presuppositions*. Peirce's comments purport to a similar opinion (*Collected Papers*, 5.189).

"All the same, I would like to say—as an afterthought—that my word 'paradox' is too strong." (Letter to the author, 15 January 1983)

Appendix 3B: Moral Obligation and Ethical Responsiveness

Of the many kinds of obligation, what we usually call moral obligation—if we agree to follow, as I will here, one recent account—is one kind only even though it involves both general and particular obligations.[58] General obligations or duties include such practices as keeping promises, whereas particular obligations include, say, one's returning good service to those who have rendered them. The main idea behind the notion of moral obligation is practical. Confronted with a certain kind of experience, the moral agent must deliberate. And on the grounds of moral reasons, the moral agent must settle on a conclusion about whether or not one is under an obligation to act in a particular way with respect to the particular situation in question. The accent in this understanding of moral obligation falls strongly on the nature of moral obligation as a practical conclusion. This central character of moral obligation accounts for its several features: that a moral obligation is an obligation to act; that what the agent is obliged to do must be in the agent's power; that unlike ordinary obligations, moral obligations are subject to an agglomeration principle (whereby I am obliged to do both X and Y if I am obliged to do X and obliged to do Y); that moral obligation is inescapable; that failure to observe one's moral obligations results in such first-person reactions as remorse or guilt or self-reproach and such third-person ones as blame between persons; that

[58]Williams 1985. Subsequent references are given in the text. See the important criticisms of McDowell 1986.

moral obligation is categorical in the Kantian sense that, whether one accepts the moral perspective or not, being a responsible agent entails living within the moral system. In short, what counts as a moral obligation seems to be on this description whatever course of action there is most moral reason to take on a given occasion (178–79).

This sketchy account omits a number of important distinctions that require detailed treatment—for example, the distinction between moral obligations of justice and other moral obligations, or between being inside or being outside a moral system, or between *a* moral system and *the* moral system. But the sketch is sufficient to exhibit, some believe, a serious deficiency in such a set of views. This failing consists in the tendency to reduce all ethical consideration to questions of moral obligation. Such a tendency, however, is clearly mistaken. For it overlooks the fact that conflicts between one's moral obligations can be resolved without incurring either self-reproach or blame. I may resolve the conflict between keeping my promise to visit my mother and accompanying an injured bicyclist to the hospital without having to maintain only that one obligation supersedes another. There need be no general obligation here that overrides that promise to visit my mother. The key insight is that our ethical experience is such that some courses of action are decidable morally as possible rather than as necessary ones. Some moral actions I need not have to perform; I merely may perform them. The problem in a moral system as opposed to a more nuanced ethical orientation is that moral obligation comes to be both an unavoidable necessity and a totalitarian force that gradually imposes itself on the entire range of actions available to me as a deliberative, responsible subject.

The alternative to this traditional description is to view moral obligation as only one of several central ethical considerations. Grasping this alternative involves seeing several points about the vague yet essential notion of importance. First, persons do have this notion, for persons do find a difference between what is trivial and what is not. Second, the notion of importance is a relative one, for things are found to be more or less important with respect to certain considerations. Third, although we do have a notion of something being important simply, this notion is extremely vague and is not implied by the fact that something can be found to be relatively important. Fourth, to call something important is not just to assign something a high deliberative priority, for something may be important for a particular person or group and yet that person or group need not allow this matter to outweigh most other considerations: the matter may remain beyond the scope of the person's or group's power—they may not be able to do anything about it.

On the utilitarian view of morality, what is important is not moral deliberation but that welfare be maximized, whereas on the Kantian view what is important is not the amount of welfare but that moral motivation be given this primary role in the description of morality. But each view is deficient here. For the utilitarian view leaves open the essential question as to just what moral considerations should be included in moral deliberation, whereas the Kantian view leaves empty the content of moral considerations. Moreover, conciliation between such conflicting views is difficult in that more than just the nature of morality opposes them. Yet if we reconsider moral obligation something that directly connects both the notions of deliberative priority and importance, we arrive at a basic notion of persons requiring something they can rely on. An ethical life is one that fosters the end that some things, such as not being murdered or enjoying freedom of expression, can be relied on. For leading an ethical life can "instill a disposition to give the relevant considerations a high deliberative priority—in the most serious of these matters, a virtually absolute priority, so that certain causes of action must come first, while others are ruled out from the beginning" (185).

A moral obligation, thus, is a set of considerations "that are given deliberative priority in order to secure reliability" (185); that is, "a state of affairs in which people can reasonably expect others to behave in some ways and not in other ways" (187), a state to which correspond certain rights. Such obligations are of several sorts: negative, which serve certain fundamental, important interests by specifying what one should not do; and positive, which stress what is important and immediate. The latter focus on people's vital interests by recognizing that the occurrence of emergencies involves immediacy—rescuing someone. Further, the notion of immediacy must not be construed narrowly in terms of physical nearness but much more broadly in terms of rationality and imagination. Returning to our previous example, we may then say that breaking my promise to visit my mother in order to accompany an injured person to the hospital is ethically justifiable not because within a particular system one moral obligation can be taken to supersede another, but because within an ethical perspective one ethical consideration is important and immediate enough on this occasion to outweigh a particular moral obligation. Thus, the conclusion of my deliberation here is not so much a moral obligation as an ethical consideration. Consequently, some ethical actions need not be either morally obligatory or even matters of moral obligation, for in involving fundamental matters of importance and sometimes of immediacy they are more than obligations and they may be foregone without either guilt or blame. Moreover, the agent who concludes to act in such cases may recognize that the demand he finds himself ethically not compelled to respond to may not present itself that way to others.

Some cases of practical necessity on this account, then (cases where one simply must do something), involve, *pace* Kant, a conditional element in that the agent concludes to do a certain thing just because of a desire the agent does not merely happen to have but had to have in order essentially to be the person he or she is. Some ethical actions, then, are not "absolutely unconditioned by any desire" (189), as Kant demanded in consequence of his view that the noumenal self was dispensed from the laws of causality. On the contrary, an ethical consideration can present itself as a moral and indeed objective demand without being inextricably linked with some moral foundation in objective moral law which I must reverence; it can present itself, in other words, as a conclusion of practical necessity which arises not from without but from within the shared ethical life of the moral agent.

At the basis, then, of this alternative account of moral obligation is a vision of morality as one version only, a peculiarly Western vision of the various ramifications of the ethical in human lives (196). More specifically, this view would urge on us a revisionary and not just a traditional understanding of moral obligation as one kind only of various ethical considerations, of ethical practical necessity as larger than merely moral obligation, and of the ethical life as much larger than the narrow contrasts between the obligatory and the arbitrary, the voluntary and involuntary, theory and practice, the rational and irrational, perhaps even the just and the unjust. What makes the ethical life worthwhile, the examined life worth living, is not the pursuit of the community of reasonable persons, which is an illusion, but the everyday, concrete practices of individual communities that differ profoundly in their social and historical beings. What counts on this vision are individuals and groups with their particular dispositions, characters, and histories living meaningful, ethical lives within social structures they themselves are continually working to render more transparent, if never totally explicit. But this vision is beyond philosophy. "How truthfulness to an existing self or society is to be combined with reflection, self-understanding, and criticism is a question that philosophy, itself, cannot answer. It is the kind of question that has to be answered through reflective living" (200).[59]

---

[59]For written comments on an earlier version of these materials I am grateful to my colleagues Hilliard Aronovitch, Keith Arnold, Ina Ferris, and Andrew Lugg.

4
Fictions and Feelings

> We weep for the misfortune of a hero to whom we are attached. In the same instant we comfort ourselves by reflecting that it is nothing but a fiction.
>
> —J. B. Dubos

> The fiction of tragedy softens the passion, by an infusion of a new feeling, not merely by weakening or diminishing the sorrow.
>
> —David Hume

> Not even one's own pain weighs so heavy as the pain one feels with someone, for someone, a pain intensified by the imagination and prolonged by a hundred echoes.
>
> —Milan Kundera

In Milan Kundera's *Unbearable Lightness of Being*, when Tomas discovered that his friend Tereza had opened his desk to read his intimate correspondence with his mistress, Tomas loved Tereza all the more. But how could he, we might ask? Tereza violated Tomas's right to privacy. It would be reasonable for Tomas to be angry with Tereza. But he is not; he loves her even more. Consider the passage in detail.

> By revealing to Tomas her dream about jabbing needles under her fingernails, Tereza unwittingly revealed that she had gone through his desk. If Tereza had been any other woman, Tomas would never have spoken to her again. Aware of that, Tereza said to him, "Throw me out!" But instead of throwing her out he seized her hand and kissed the tips of her fingers, because at that moment he himself felt the pain under her fingernails as surely as if the nerves of her fingers led straight to his own brain . . . , because compassion was Tomas's fate (or curse), he felt that he himself had knelt before the open desk drawer, unable to tear his eyes from . . . his mistress' letter. He understood Tereza and not only was he incapable of being angry with her, he loved her all the more.[1]

---

[1] Kundera 1984:20–21, cited hereafter in text.

This kind of situation—one we know in life and not just in literature—may well strike some readers as strangely moving. For one central suggestion here is that a person may come to know another's particular affective state of mind with such immediacy, such certainty, and such completeness that the assertion of one's own legitimate feelings of distress ("I'm furious with you!") may yield to an affirmation of the supervening importance of the other person ("I love you more than myself!"). But some of us have settled, for good reasons we think, on remaining chary of construing knowledge of another person's state of mind, whether affecting or not, in terms of immediacy, certainty, and completeness. Such knowledge, we insist, is always and perhaps necessarily indirect, hesitant, and partial. Milan Kundera would have us reconsider. Some instances of understanding, his novel suggests but does not assert, are compassionate. And when compassion is construed as feeling-with in contrast to suffering-with someone, then compassionate understanding is said to be "an act of emotional telepathy" (21). But how could the plight of fictional characters properly be said to affect nonfictional persons?

THREE VIEWS

Recently, a number of papers have appeared which have tried to formulate what exactly is problematic about our apparent emotional involvement with fictional works.[2]

The problem is the product of the usual connections we insist on between sincere beliefs and genuine emotions.[3] In reading fictional works such as Kundera's *The Unbearable Lightness of Being* we know that the characters and events we are reading about do not exist. And since these beliefs are in some sense prerequisites for responding genuinely to what we are reading, knowing that these characters and events are fictional entails that we also sincerely believe that they are fictional. Accordingly, the question arises as to how someone can be genuinely moved by sincerely believing in the existence of certain states of affairs he or she knows not to exist. More generally, how can fictions be proper objects for genuine feelings?[4]

One philosopher puts the matter even more strongly:

---

[2]Redford and Weston 1975, Radford 1977, Paskins 1977, Walton 1978a and 1978b, Schaper 1978, Rosebury 1979, Novitz 1980, Mounce 1980, Skulsky 1980, Lamarque 1981, Eaton 1982, Iseminger 1983, Charlton 1984, Lord 1984, Redden 1984.

[3]Radford 1977:68.

[4]Radford and Weston 1975:82. See also the important recent work of Gordon 1987, de Sousa 1987, and Stocker 1987.

We know of at least some characters in fiction that their counterparts in real life do not exist and never have existed, and that the events in which they are caught up never occurred. And so we must have beliefs to that effect . . . , yet we are, at least sometimes, genuinely moved by these characters and what happens to them, and so it appears . . . we must hold beliefs that certain people are caught up in certain events—beliefs which are as a matter of fact false. So . . . it seems that either we are committed to holding contradictory beliefs about characters and events in fiction or we must deny that we can, logically, be moved by fictional events or characters.[5]

When articulated in this form, the problem of how to account for some fictions genuinely moving some readers may seem insoluble. For as long as we subscribe to the two underlying assumptions here, that genuine knowing involves believing and that genuine feeling presupposes believing—and these are reasonable views—the quandary appears inescapable. More disconcerting still, the problem is not easily ignored, for we can hardly deny—not only because of others' accounts of their reading but from our own experience—the claim that the reader is genuinely moved. Moreover, the problem is not easily solved. One philosopher, after thoroughly scrutinizing six different prospective solutions, soberly concludes that readers who think themselves genuinely moved in reading fictional works are involved in inconsistency and incoherence.[6] Yet however serious-minded, such a conclusion remains counterintuitive. How, then, are we to resolve the apparent paradox of disbelieving that fictional states of affairs exist and yet behaving as if we did believe that they existed? Here is one account.

> 1. When we say that we are genuinely moved by a fictional work such as *The Unbearable Lightness of Being*, we mean that we sincerely believe (a) that the work we are reading is fictional, (b) that certain states of affairs occurring in the work are not fictional, and (c) that this second belief and not the first is the actual basis of our emotional response.[7]

Notice that this view turns on the apparent conflict between two sets of beliefs, those that are the bases of what we know, and those that are the bases of what we feel. But notice also that this view purports to distinguish between two orders of belief. And it is this second distinction, the claim here is, that enables one to see that the two sets of beliefs are not in contradiction. Rather, one set is consequent upon the other.

But the position is unsatisfactory: it does not actually solve the problem

---

[5]Schaper 1978:3.
[6]Radford 1977:78.
[7]After Schaper 1978:39.

of how we can be genuinely moved by works of fiction. The difficulty lies in effecting the distinction between those two sets of beliefs where one is taken as the logical contradictory of the other.[8] The first set of beliefs is about a particular state "of affairs occurring in a fictional context, whereas the second set concerns a particular state of affairs occurring in a nonfictional context. The first says, "I believe this story never actually happened," whereas the second says, "I believe this story actually happened." But although these sentences are contradictories, the beliefs are not. Hence the need for postulating different orders of belief is not sufficiently motivated.

This objection to the first attempt at solving our problem with fictional feelings has been summarized as follows:

> ... how can a belief which resembles a belief that p is the case, to the extent that it shares with it the power to make possible an emotional response ... be simultaneously a belief that p is the content of a fictional statement or representation axiomatically devoid of existential substance ...? Only, it is clear, if we can find a belief having the force of a belief that p is the case ... which yet does not contain an existence assertion and is therefore disqualified ("by some awareness of acknowledgement of the origin of its object in an artistic statement or representation"). (124)

And postulating different orders of belief does not guarantee us any such find at all. We are then left with our initial problem.

Here is a second attempt to solve that problem.

> 2.   When we say that we are genuinely moved by a fictional work such as *The Unbearable Lightness of Being*, we mean that we sincerely believe (a) that the work we are reading is fictional, (b) that certain states of affairs occurring in the work are not fictional, and (c) that the actual basis for our emotional response is the meanings of the text. (120–21)

This formulation does not assume the task of distinguishing between different orders of beliefs, some about actual things and some about fictional things. What undermined that task, we recall, was the constraint that some genuine beliefs be uncommitted to the existence of their own contents.[9] But such a belief reduces to a belief plus something that is not a belief, namely, a claim that the contents of the belief existed. By contrast, the present formulation appears against a different background, the view that whatever the contents of the belief may be, if the belief is sincere

---

[8]Rosebury 1979:122. Further references in the text are to this piece until otherwise indicated.
[9]Kueng 1984:143–56.

then the belief must involve a commitment to the existence of its own contents.[10]

But though arguably an improvement on its predecessor, this formulation still incorporates a serious problem of its own making. For in trying to account for the nature of sincere beliefs, the second version introduces a curiosity as the object of a reader's belief.

The difficulty lies neither with the nature nor the contents of a text as the object of a reader's beliefs but with the specification of the object as textual meaning. The assumption on this account is that something is already there in the text—its meaning—which the reader can discover. Once brought into the light of the reader's consciousness, the text's meaning can shine forth splendidly in its pristine glory just as it existed previously either in the author's mind or in the text itself. Prior to any activity on the part of the reader, the meaning is taken as already there.

Such a view, however, runs counter both to our usual experiences as readers of literary works and to several familiar concerns in the philosophy of language. Readers do not so much find a meaning buried in a text but, as I argued in the previous chapter, ceaselessly interpret the significance of particular textual features. This fact is what accounts in part for our repeated satisfaction with rereading some fictional works. Similarly, in the philosophy of language we cannot usually construe meaning as something independent of certain multiple, varied, and particular uses of language. A meaning is not something to be discovered behind or under the patterns of language uses, but something we gradually articulate by invoking our own linguistic competence in dealing with the uses of language a writer sets working before us.

So neither distinguishing first-order from second-order beliefs nor construing the objects of readers' beliefs as real meanings in the fictional texts solves the problem of how we can properly be said to be genuinely moved by fictional work.

Nevertheless, I find the insistence in the first version on belief rather than knowledge helpful. For it exonerates us from having to construe the cognitivity of literature in what are, I have suggested, inappropriately strong terms. Further, I also find helpful the shift in the second version from talking about beliefs to talking about the contents of beliefs. For such a precision reminds us of the ambiguities that bothered even Kant in the use of mental terms such as judgment or belief where each can be construed as either a mental act, or the object of a mental act, or the contents of a mental act. Consider, then, one further version.[11]

---

[10]Rosebury 1979:127. See further Margolis 1977:919 and 1983:179–203.
[11]After Lamarque 1981:302. For a different prospective, see Peacocke 1986.

3. When we say we are genuinely moved by a fictional work such
   as *The Unbearable Lightness of Being*, we mean (a) that we respond
   emotionally to the contents of sincere beliefs in our own minds
   and (b) that these contents arise from but are not identical with
   the senses of fictional sentences.

This formulation recognizes that sincere beliefs involve a commitment to the existence of their contents. Moreover, these contents are
located in the reader's mind rather than identified with features in fictional texts. So neither the nature of beliefs nor the need for true beliefs to be based on actual rather than fictional situations is violated.
But in order to take the critical measure of this third formulation we
require more detail.

The cardinal distinctions in the background here concern the objects of
those mental acts we call beliefs. Distinguish first between unique states
of consciousness, which are the objects of one person's beliefs, and representations, which are the objects of someone else's beliefs. The former
are private, unrepeatable, and cannot be fully communicated; whereas
the latter, because they include specifiable contents, are potentially public,
repeatable, and can be communicated more fully. The object of our beliefs
on this third formulation, thus, are those repeatable contents of the representations of our beliefs, and not those private states of consciousness
which may or may not accompany those contents.

The second background distinction now appears. Some of these contents may be characterized further as "propositional" in the sense that
the thought—that Tereza is thinking of making herself suffer more—has
a content that is identifiable under a propositional description. Other
belief contents may be called "predicative" in the sense that the thought—
the suffering of Tereza—has a content identifiable under a predicative
description.

Distinguish finally between a thought-content and a belief. "Strictly
speaking," one philosopher writes,

> a thought-content, even if identified under a propositional description, is
> not assessable as true or false. Certainly the very same propositional con-
> tent could be incorporated in a judgement or assertion and as such have
> a truth value. But as an identifying property of a thought the proposition-
> al description involves neither judgement nor assertion. . . . A thought-
> content is different from a belief. Belief is a psychological attitude held in
> relation to a propositional content. It is one among many attitudes, in-
> cluding dislike, rejection, remembering, and contemplating, that we might
> assume with respect to the contents of some of our thoughts. (293–4)

With these three distinctions in hand we may now return to the view
we are considering, that is, what moves us in fictional works such as *The
Unbearable Lightness of Being* are not the beliefs we entertain about real

objects, fictional objects, or mental objects but the contents of our own thoughts, the contents of our thoughts of Tereza's suffering. And just as some things may frighten us even though we know that nothing actual corresponds to such things, so too the contents of our thoughts of Tereza's suffering can genuinely move us without there being anything actual that corresponds to these contents.

On this third formulation, then, our problem now seems solved. For we are not moved by something we know does not exist. What genuinely moves us, rather, are our actual thoughts about something that does not exist. The objects of our feelings are not beliefs but thought-contents. We respond emotionally, then, to thought-contents and not to beliefs at all.

THREE DIFFICULTIES

This current view of how we can be genuinely moved by fictions involves, even in the qualified form I have presented here, at least three serious deficiencies.

One difficulty is with reference, with specifying the interpretation of reference as denotation only, a point I investigate in some detail in Chapter 7. Perhaps we can see this point more clearly if we describe just what it is that is taken to determine the thought-contents that are said to move us genuinely.

What specifies these contents are the senses of fictional sentences in the work *The Unbearable Lightness of Being*, that is, the modes of presentation of the referents of fictional expressions within a story (298). And these senses, unlike the senses of nonfictional sentences, are taken to be neither true nor false. We have, then, a parallel between the truth-functional values of assertions and beliefs on the one hand and the lack of such values in the senses of fictional sentences and thought-contents on the other.

But the key expression here, "fictional sentence," still needs a gloss. "A sentence is fictional," this view continues, "not in virtue of semantic features of its content but in virtue of pragmatic features of its use . . . (i.e., the illocutionary force of its utterance). Thus a fictional use of a sentence is defined in terms of a writer's (illocutionary) intentions and the conventions of story telling" (296).

This account relies on a theory we have already looked at critically in Chapter 1. We confront here the familiar view that a speaker intends to perform a particular speech act of one sort or another, whereas a writer of fiction only pretends to perform such an act. "A storyteller pretends to be reporting events that actually happened and the conversation of people who actually exist."[12] The one twist here is that storytelling, unlike lying, is pretending without the intention to deceive, a storytelling more like charades than perjury.

The consequences of this fuller account are important. Works of fiction do not, properly speaking, refer at all because fictional sentences, while making sense, do not have any truth values; hence, they lack reference. The writer of fiction not only pretends to describe and to assert; he or she pretends to refer because the nature of fictional sentences is such that he or she cannot refer. The writer of a nonfictional work in using nonfictional sentences intends to refer; by contrast, the writer of a fictional work only pretends to refer. Reference is not denied within the fictional world within a story. But no possibility exists of "reference outside the story in the real world." We may legitimately refer when we retell a story to someone else or when we tell someone about a story, but we may not legitimately refer in simply telling a story. External reference is suspended; in fact, "suspended reference" is a euphemism for "blocked reference," for external reference in this view is as effectively blocked as traffic through a closed border crossing into Kundera's Czechoslovakia.

But such a view, I hope to show later, construes external reference too narrowly on the model of one kind of reference only.[13] Further, this view fails to account for the experience many writers and readers report, the independent and apparently actual existence of something like what the senses of some fictional sentences would seem to refer to.

A second serious deficiency on this view of fictional feelings is the related interpretation of truth in terms of the truth-value of assertions only. For on this view the cognitive force of fictional works is seriously put in question. In fact, we are back with Sir Philip Sidney's eloquent claim that "the Poett . . . never affirmeth . . . and therefore though he recount things not true, yet because he telleth them not for true, he lyeth not."

Recall that what moves us genuinely is said to be thought-contents and not belief-contents. The strategy, of course, is to divorce thought-contents from truth-values so that we can dissipate the paradox of being genuinely moved by something we know does not exist. And the controlling idea is

> to show that when we fear and pity fictional characters our emotions are directed at real, albeit psychological, objects. We do not have to postulate either that the emotions are fictional or that they are directed irrationally at nothing at all. Nor do we have to postulate beliefs which we know to be false in order to explain the emotions. We have, on the one hand, the

[12]Ibid., 297.
[13]See Evans 1982.

notion of a thought-content which can be the proper object of emotion. On the other hand, we have the propositional contents of fictional sentences in which through the mediation of suspended illocutionary intentions . . . the senses of the fictional names replace the fictional references. (300)

For all the sophistication of this account, a difficulty arises again from our own mundane experiences as readers of fictional works. For even when this view makes some room for the varieties of imaginative activity we readers exercise on our texts, it refuses categorically to recognize that some of this interaction with the text has to do with truth and falsity. For often we do respond to texts in terms of their truth, their truth to our own experience. This kind of truth is of course not the truth of correspondence. For what we are responding to may allow of no unambiguous counterpart to what we may have in mind. Rather, readers sometimes check the truth of a fictional work in terms of its being true to their lives, plausible in the richness of its suggestions, fruitful in the discoveries it seems to allow, and powerful in the changes it may indicate for the trajectory of a life.

Our theorist may quickly retort that whatever truth to life a fictional work may be said to have, it surely cannot be said to have such truth in the same sense in which genuine nonfictional assertions may be said to have truth-value. But we may concede this point with impunity. For the issue here is more fundamental than just which sense of truth an account finally relies on—truth as truth-value or truth as truth to life. The issue turns, rather, on the controversial move of stipulating—for that is what this account does—the sense of literary truth as truth-value without providing any sustained argument. Yet without such argument, why should we accept the stipulations? And even with some such argument eventually in hand, why should we accept the stipulation only? Hence, just as with reference as denotation so too with truth as truth-value, the current account would urge on us an overly narrow interpretation.

One final difficulty with this view is its susceptibility to an arguably overly generous interpretation of the fictional world as a possible world.

Recall once again several salient features of this account. The initial paradox, the claim goes, is dissipated. For this account purports to show that we now understand "how we can know something is fictional but still take it seriously without having to believe or even half-believe it. We can reflect on, and can be moved by, a thought independently of accepting it as true . . . although it incorporates a *de dicto* account of fictional characters, it acknowledges the pull of *de re* accounts; fictions comprise sets of ideas, many having correlates in reality, and these ideas invite an imaginative supplementation and exploration" (302).

We may be tempted to agree that such a view does do away with the puzzle that troubles us. But regardless of how cogent we find the earlier difficulties with reference and with truth, the final cost also includes an unacceptable hesitation among different ways of understanding the fictional world. This view, we note, does acknowledge that some (if not all) elements in fictional worlds may have nonfictional counterparts. And the view recognizes, too, that the objects of our emotional responses may sometimes be merely fictional states of affairs and other times the actual contents of real thoughts in our minds. But we are never clear enough just how the fictional world is to be understood, both with respect to the actual world we are living in, to the virtual worlds we often take ourselves to be on the verge of, and to any number of possible worlds we could choose to realize or not.

This matter touches once again on the larger issue of the cognitive status we accord to fictional worlds. If we follow the drift of the current view, the status of the fictional world is pretty much left open. Consequently, arguing that such worlds are merely possible is just as good an interpretation as plumping for some version of fictional worlds as actual. The problem most basically depends on the inveterate mental habit of taking the fictional as the opposite of the actual. The inevitable consequence is that whatever status a fictional world may have, it certainly cannot be accorded the kind of ontological warrant we reserve for the nitty-gritty. Fictional works, like works of art generally, slide once again into the unenviable position within our lives of being nothing more than elegant distractions, self-indulgent fantasies.

But this lack of precision, I hold, is too generous in the sense that it leaves fictional worlds open to too large an array of ontological interpretations. And most of these interpretations, as we know from the recent attempts to use possible-worlds analyses to enlighten us about fiction, wind up ascribing to fictional worlds far less substance than their roles in our lives seems to demand. We need, I argue in Chapter 7, an account of fictional worlds which accommodates their variety but constrains their indefinite proliferation, a view, in short, which distinguishes fictional worlds from both possible worlds and actual ones. The present view blinks this requirement.

I turn now to developing several suggestions for an alternative account of feelings and fictions which would preserve the cardinal insights here without including the central deficiencies.

REFERENCE, TRUTH, AND WORLD

What resources, then, are available for a more adequate account of how readers may properly be said to be genuinely moved by fictional works? My suggestion is that we look more closely at several reflections in recent continental philosophy, specifically in Paul Ricoeur's discussion of Goodman's work, which I alluded to in Chapter 1.[14]

To begin with, for Goodman, "We 'make' the world by construing symbol systems... which are numerous and equally legitimate: descriptive theories, perceptions, novels, paintings, musical scores, etc."[15] Unlike Cassirer's views, Goodman's involve no hierarchical system. No one symbol system—science's or otherwise—is to be privileged over another.

Next, "each of these ways of world-making is a world-version rather than a version of the world in the sense that there is no world in itself before or beneath these versions" (108). The crucial move here is once again a radicalization of Cassirer's view. The dissolution of substance into function is carried one step further to the claim that there exists no unique world in terms of which one function could ever be construed as exactly the same as another. Thus, the relativism here is as radical as the pluralism.

And finally, "world versions other than scientific ones are neither true nor false. And yet some may be said to be right and others wrong. There must be therefore criteria to assign or to deny rightness to non-descriptive world versions" (109).

We touch here on something very similar to one of the central claims in the current account of fictional feelings, the restriction of truth to the domain of assertions and the concomitant claim that assertions in works of fiction, because they are not genuine assertions, are neither true nor false. More fundamental, however, is the view that, even within such restrictions, truth cannot be tested by comparison with something called "the world." Truth here remains truth-functional.

To summarize, Goodman's central thesis may be put in terms of a gradual expansion of the sphere of reference. Goodman's categorization "proceeds by way of a succession of extensions of the sphere of referentiality: (1) Starting from descriptions (verbal symbols), (2) adding metaphorical to literal description, (3) then conjoining depiction, non-verbal symbol, to description, (4) then adding metaphorical to literal depiction to complete the field of denotation, (5) then complementing denotation by exemplification and expression" (110–11).

Now, Ricoeur's description of this view of world-making, I suggest, may be read as providing us with elements of an alternative account of fictional feelings as well as the closely related notions of fictional beliefs and fictional worlds.[16]

First, why not work toward a fuller and less restrictive notion of ref-

[14]Ricoeur 1980 and Goodman 1984.
[15]Cited in Ricoeur 1980:107. Further references in the text are to this piece.
[16]Cf. Ricoeur 1979 and Goodman 1984. (Strictly speaking, for Goodman not all of these qualify as symbol systems.)

erence than the one to which the current view of fictional feelings is committed? For the point here is that not only denotation but also exemplification and expression involve reference. (See Appendix 4A, "A Taxonomy of Reference.") Of course the entire notion of nondenotational reference needs careful elaboration. For surely the talk here of exemplification and expression is too elliptical even when we parse these terms in the larger context of the semantics Goodman deploys in *Languages of Art*.[17] Nonetheless, the distinction between the reference of denotation and that of exemplification and expression is not altogether obscure, especially if we take this distinction at least initially as on the same level as that between kinds of saying and kinds of showing. But Ricoeur himself has provided a more suggestive construal of these kinds of reference in his notion of productive reference.

"Because fictions do not refer in a 'reproductive way' to reality as already given," he writes, "they may refer in a 'productive' way to reality as intimated by the fiction. . . . Because it has no previous referent, [fiction] may refer in a productive way to reality, and even *increase* reality."[18] Of course this notion of productive reference is very bold. And Ricoeur himself concedes that making such a notion coherent entails shifting from linguistic frameworks to perceptual ones and linking fiction more closely to world. Nonetheless, when coupled with elements in his discussion of metaphor as semantic innovation, Ricoeur's notion of productive reference is arguably an alternative to the restrictive notion of reference as denotational only. Such a notation allows us to talk of fiction not as representing worlds but as renaming worlds, reconstructing new stories, and finally redescribing the real, as rendering a world. More recently, Ricoeur suggests that talk of reference in fictional contexts should yield to talk of configuration and refiguration.[19]

Thus:

4. Fictional feelings that some works of fiction such as *The Unbearable Lightness of Being* may arouse may be taken as both the intensional referents of the various uses of language in fictional discourses and as the extensional referents of the contents of reader's emotions.

What moves us in Kundera's novel is that Tereza's sufferings make reference to the actual sufferings of our families, our friends, and ourselves.

Second, this discussion of rethinking reference in fictional contexts raises a similar possibility of disassociating the notion of truth from the domain of assertions and statements, the domain of truth-functions. The matter here is perhaps more delicate. But Ricoeur has noticed that in

[17]Goodman 1976.
[18]Ricoeur 1980:126–27. See also Ricoeur 1979:123–41.
[19]Ricoeur 1983–85:vol. 1.

Goodman's system, when we are dealing with predicates as categories, rational appraisal involves the notion of rightness of categorization. And when we are dealing with an entire system of categories—that is, a categorical system—rational appraisal involves fitness in exemplification, or right projectability, or simply considerations of whatever the categorical system can do. But once one recognizes the possibility of construing the referential function more largely than in terms of denotation, and once one notices the curious criteria mentioned here of "rightness" and "fitness," then it seems that even within Goodman's own work some larger sense of truth than the truth of statements is not absent.

Again, this criticism of Goodman is the reflection of a long series of discussions of different notions of truth which stretch across Ricoeur's work as a whole. One of his most fruitful observations, I think, arises from his repeated returns to Aristotle and to the *Nicomachean Ethics* and the discussion there in Book VI of practical knowledge. What is striking on Ricoeur's rereadings is not the particular interpretations he provides of practical knowledge but how he takes the distinction between *phronesis* and *nous*, between practical and theoretical knowledge. The key insight is that Aristotle presents two accounts of *nous* and not one. So theoretical knowledge is understood not just as knowledge of principles with practical knowledge taken as knowledge of how to apply those principles. Rather, theoretical knowledge itself is of two kinds: knowledge of rules but also knowledge of just which situations can accommodate the application of rules.[20] Knowledge, then, can be taken not just as knowledge of rules and knowledge of how to apply such rules, but more richly as involving the capacity to recognize certain situations as precisely those in which something like rules may well be applicable. The kind of truth one may be said to know on this interpretation of knowledge may be formulated as the truth of statements. But there is always a shortfall in such formulations because the kind of truth at issue here is not reducible to the truth of statements. I take Ricoeur's reflections here as opening up a second path to the interpretation of fictional feelings, this time leading to the underlying notion of fictional beliefs as being true to life and not just as being truth-functional.

> 5. Fictional beliefs, which are connected with the fictional feelings some works of fiction such as *The Unbearable Lightness of Being* may arouse, may be taken as beliefs about what is true to life, which communities of readers come to entertain in their understanding of fictional works.

Part of what we come to believe in reading Kundera's novel is that some actions that resemble, say, Tomas's compassion are morally significant.

A third and final suggestion as to how we may deal more adequately with

---

[20]I owe this point to discussion with D. Carr and D. Devereux.

fictional feelings may be found in Ricoeur's discussion of Goodman's ontology.

Ricoeur calls attention to a curious asymmetry in Goodman's expressions "world-versions" and "versions of a world" on the one hand and "chimera-versions" and "versions of a chimera" on the other. He suspects that Goodman's inconsistent attempts to do away with the world by talking of world-versions is finally no more than an artifice of language. "The irreducible difference," Ricoeur writes, "between world-versions and versions of the world arises from the connection that no version exhausts that which requires to be, literally or metaphorically, described, depicted, exemplified, or expressed. Otherwise why, throughout cultural changes, would men and women have wanted or needed to make new kinds of versions of the known kinds again and again?"[21]

Ricoeur's suggestion here is that we need to pay much closer attention to the repeated attempts of writers of fiction continually to render a world. What stands behind these attempts, he says, is not so much the world Goodman rejects or even the plurality of worlds he advocates. Rather, we can entertain the notion of a world that, though never reducible to any one world-version or even to classes of such versions, remains nevertheless always ineluctably part of a particular world-version. It is this notion of a world which may do better justice to the perceptual inexhaustibility of world, "the interplay between all the perceptual fields, the movement of attention which dilates and contracts alternately and the indefinite flight of the perceptual horizon" (117–18). And it is this notion of a world as well which addresses the opacity of the world, its unrelenting resistance to our repeated scrutiny. In short, world-versions are versions of a world as a horizon.

With such a notion of world as horizon, we may be better able to deal with the difficulties of making out the distinctions I alluded to earlier between fictional worlds and possible worlds on the one hand and fictional worlds and actual ones on the other. How to make out that larger sense of a world as horizon on some less encumbered terms than those of either a Heidegger or a Husserl, Ricoeur doesn't say. But following the lead of those thinkers, he often looks back to the Greek distinctions between reality and appearance and tries to sort this talk of world as horizon in another, may we say "originary," vocabulary.

Thus:

6. Fictional worlds, which are connected with the fictional feeling some works of fiction such as *The Unbearable Lightness of Being* may arouse, may be taken as neither possible or actual worlds independent of some descriptions, but as virtual worlds that can only exist with world-versions whose horizons always surpass their articulation in particular versions of a world.

Part of what we come to be at home with in the fictional world of *The Unbearable Lightness of Being* is nothing more than a horizon of a virtual world we already inhabit.

[21]Ricoeur 1980:117–18.

Here, then, are three suggestions taken from other contexts and yet perhaps indicative of other resources in contemporary philosophy for furthering our reflections on problems with fictions. We have thus a notion of reference as productive rather than strictly denotational; of truth as what I have loosely called truth to life rather than truth as truth-functional and of world as horizon rather than world as merely modal, whether possible or actual. Each remains to be articulated in the more richly detailed contexts of specific concerns with literature and philosophy. But it seems already clear in anticipation how each may well present a serious alternative to the corresponding notions in the current account we have so far of fictional feelings. In the next three chapters of this book I explore these suggestions more thoroughly by relying closely on case studies from lyrical poetry while trying to draw on the relevant reflections from both contemporary analytic and hermeneutic philosophy.

But let us return to our story.

Seven years after Tomas carried Tereza's heavy suitcase into his flat in Prague, and seven months after they had found a place as exiles in Zurich, Tereza decided to return to Prague. And for five days after Tereza left him, Tomas told himself he was "sick with compassion."

> Don't think about her! Don't think about her! He said to himself, "I'm sick with compassion. It's good that she's gone and that I'll never see her again, though it's not Tereza I need to be free of—it's that sickness, compassion, which I thought I was immune to until she infected me with it."
> On Saturday and Sunday, he felt the sweet lightness of being rise up to him out of the depths of the future he had never known. The tons of steel of the Russian tanks were nothing compared with it. For there is nothing heavier than compassion. Not even one's own pain weighs so heavy as the pain one feels with someone, for someone, a pain intensified by the imagination and prolonged by a hundred echoes.[22]

How can such a fiction be called genuinely instructive? Because some communities of readers come to believe, rightly, that a loving like Tomas's may lead to actual and intolerable suffering. How can such a fiction be called genuinely moving? Because some communities of readers come to feel a genuine grief that a leaving like Tereza's is virtually their own. In responding imaginately to fiction we judge Tomas and ourselves, we feel for Tereza and ourselves. But such imaginative responses, whether on the part of individuals or communities, are all species of action. How, then, are we to understand the larger issues involved in the relations between fictions and actions? I look at some of those issues in the following chapters, where I rely on much closer readings of fictional texts than we have required so far.

[22]Kundera 1984.

Appendix 4A   A Taxonomy of Reference

Goodman's view of reference is not only very general; it is also very broad in the interest of being as fully extensional as possible. A context, we are told, is extensional if and only if intersubstitutability *salva veritate* obtains, that is, "if and only if substitution of coreferential expressions for its terms preserves the truth values of the original sentences";[23] otherwise the context is intensional. Goodman's idea is to exclude such intentional notions as sense, content, features, properties, and to reinterpret extensionally such usually intensional contexts as the mental, the modal, and the fictional. His grounds are that no satisfactory intensional semantics for a natural language is yet available, that the basic notions of such a semantics appear to be inexorably obscure, and that intensional notions appear to allow no way of individuating their objects. Of course sometimes it is impossible to decide whether two expressions are co-referential, particularly in the case of so-called semantically dense symbol systems, that is, those that provide for "infinitely many compliance classes so ordered that between any two there is a third."[24] But undecidability, the claim goes, does not tell fatally against such an understanding of a fully extensional theory of reference. Goodman does not eschew the difficult cases by restricting the scope of a language and excluding them from consideration; rather, he tries to incorporate them into his view even if he does not always succeed. Thus, Goodman subscribes to the view that "the reference of a term depends not on its use in a single sentence or on its use in a sentence in a context, but rather on its role in a language."[25]

Because the term "reference" is primitive Goodman prefers to illustrate kinds of reference rather than to elaborate a definition of reference. Briefly and with some oversimplification he distinguishes between elementary, literal, and nonliteral reference on the one hand and complex reference on the other. Each includes subspecies.

Elementary literal reference includes mainly but not exclusively kinds of denotational reference—verbal, notational, pictorial, and quotational—and a kind of nondenotational reference called exemplification. Verbal denotation includes all those cases in which a verbal symbol (a term, a phrase, or a predicate) stands for one thing, as in the practices of naming, predication, and description, which can involve different degrees of generality, vagueness, ambiguity, and temporal and contextual variation. Strictly speaking, sentences do not verbally denote for Goodman because he rejects the consequences of such a view, namely, what he takes to be reification of truth-values, the identification of the denotation of all true

[23]Elgin 1984:6.
[24]See Goodman 1976:153 and Elgin 1984:chap. 6.
[25]Elgin 1984:9.

statements despite differences in topic, and the neglect of nondeclarative sentences.[26] A notational symbol (say, a symbol in the Labanotation dance system) denotes differently than a verbal symbol in that the former but not the latter is both semantically and syntactically distinct and unambiguous. No character in a notation may denote the things another character denotes. Pictorial denotation (depiction and representation, whether particular or general of different sorts) differs from both its verbal and notational cousins in that only pictorial symbols are taken to function in a symbol system that is both syntactically and semantically dense and replete (that is, one that includes significant variations in many respects). Quotational denotation is distinctive in that the relationship here between a symbol and what it denotes is nonreferential—"what is quoted must be included within the quoting symbol." Finally, besides these denotational kinds of reference, we have a nondenotational kind called exemplification. This involves how a symbol or label applies to, refers back to, the label itself or to some of its elements (for example, the denoted refers back to the denoted instead of vice versa in the case of denotational reference). An example: a tailor's swatch exemplifies some of its elements.

Elementary nonliteral reference includes such species as figurative and fictive denotation, and metaphorical and expressive reference. Thus, a symbol may refer and indeed denote something factually but not literally by consisting of a figurative expression; another symbol may refer and denote something by consisting of a fictive expression. Still other symbols such as metaphorical expressions may refer and denote by applying a resorted schema of labels. Metaphor here is understood as arising "by transferring a schema of labels for sorting a given realm to the sorting of another realm" while being guided by the antecedent sorting (61). Finally, some symbols such as expressive expressions may metaphorically denote in a distinctive way, that is, by being placed within but not being coextensive with metaphorical exemplification in the way that some sounds of a symphony may express by metaphorically exemplifying some feelings it metaphorically, rather than literally, possesses.

Besides these kinds of elementary literal and nonliteral references Goodman claims that there are varieties of complex references as well, that is, varieties of reference which include more than one link in a referential chain. One central case is remote reference. The key idea here has to do with denotational level, with how denotation can obtain at more than one level in a denotational hierarchy variously organized. Say we have a hierarchy that from bottom up runs from labels with null denotation to those with pictorial denotation and so on. We find that some labels, for example "word," occur at more than one level. Thus, the strata of denotation are at times more like intersecting layers than superimposed

---

[26]Goodman 1984:55–56. Further references to this work are given in the text.

levels. What we also find is that one label refers to another at different locations in the hierarchy not by any one species of reference but by two or more, say, by a complex of denotation and exemplification (62–63). Further, any label in the referential chain is more or less remote from any other label in terms of a certain number of links in the referential chain at issue, whether its direction is up or down. More precisely, Goodman suggests that referential remoteness be construed with respect to the beginnings of a referential chain. Thus, "the referential remoteness of an element in a chain is the number of links to that element from the beginning of the chain" (63).

Goodman thinks this notion of referential remoteness is often more interesting than the notion of denotational level. He cites the case of literacy, where "an element that does not denote anything and is not even a null label . . . may yet occur in a referential chain anywhere from top to bottom" (63).[27] Referential remoteness, however, must also be expanded to include the kinds of displacement which occur when the metaphorical application of a term is understood against the background of its literal application. Thus, in cases like "Peter is a mouse" the label "mouse" stands at different degrees of remoteness to its literal and metaphorical denotation. Citing Goodman, "'mouse' denotes mice, which exemplify some such level as 'timid,' which also denotes and is exemplified by the person in question. Here 'mouse,' though only one referential step away from the mice it denotes literally, is three away from the man it denotes metaphorically" (64).

Another kind of complex reference besides the direct and indirect operations of referential chains is allusion, a term often used loosely. Here Goodman proposes a choice: either we leave the term to vary according to our transient purposes—now referring to any kind of complex denotation, or another occasion applying it more narrowly "to include references via any chain that passes more than once through any one level" (66)—or we can regiment the term to apply ambiguously to a particular kind of reference we are anxious to pick out in a systematic account of complex reference; for example, as referring very narrowly to any symbol's referring "to something at the same level in the denotation hierarchy . . . via a chain passing through one or more levels" (65–66). Perhaps, more sensibly, we can use the term "allusion" to refer to "the way a metaphor recalls the objects in the literal extension of a term"—it alludes to them.[28]

This gives us a brief survey of Goodman's latest attempt not to define "reference," which he insists on taking as a primitive term, but to exhibit how the term is to be understood by considering its species and subspe-

[27]For excellent examples, see Elgin 1984:143–52.
[28]Ibid., 146. See also Elgin and Scheffler 1987. Contrast these views with MacCormac 1986.

cies—from elementary literal reference (including denotational and nondenotational) to elementary nonliteral reference, to the complications, iterations, and proliferations of complex reference across denotational and nondenotational levels and layers.

Several features about this view of reference need highlighting briefly. Notice that Goodman's starting point is merely formal. That is, he does not begin with an uninterpreted calculus, a certain number of factors in the environment of natural speakers, and proceed to try to work out the correct interpretation of the language.[29] Rather, he begins with the observation that many expressions actually refer; in other words, he begins with an interpreted system and proceeds to try to work out how these observations can be explained. Thus, Goodman's major concern is not to understand how a language has come to have a certain structure or how a speaker of a language has knowledge of that language's structure or even how it is that speakers refer when they perform certain speech acts. For Goodman, rather, expressions refer, not speakers, and it is the actual structure of a language at a particular time, not its history or the knowledge speakers have of that structure, which focuses the speaker's interests. The task, then, is to account first for how language refers, not how speakers have in the past or actually now succeed in the present in doing so; to articulate reasonable interpretations of *that* structure rather than to reconstruct the intention that produced it—it is a conceptual geography, then, and not a conceptual history.

We need not pursue the details of Goodman's brand of nominalism and his various disagreements with Quine and others on varieties of nominalism and the nature of individuals. We should not overlook, however, Goodman's construing individuals in a larger sense than usual. We are to recognize a vast variety of individuals since Goodman's nominalism "admits only individuals," yet also anything to be taken as an individual—that is, bars the composition of different entities out of the same elements" (52). Finally, Goodman claims against Frege that only expressions or terms denote, whereas sentences, for a variety of reasons, do not properly speaking denote at all. So far, then, we have a restrictive notion of verbal denotation as involving terms and not sentences and including actual objects only and not possible ones, and a correspondingly expansive notion of individuals as including all different kinds of actual objects.

Granted that several matters require fuller treatment here, still an already evident major difficulty centers on how different utterances are to be identified and interpreted as instances of a single term. For many situations consist of expressions that allow of more than one syntactic and semantic interpretation. And depending on the particular referential framework and antecedent philosophical commitments one brings to the

[29]See ibid., 10–18.

interpretation of a sentence, the sentence will be parsed variously. Goodman has worked out a whole series of reflections for "disambiguating"
terms in such a way that the character of certain syntactically equivalent
marks can be specified, even if only by an appeal to controversial features
or, failing that, by stipulation. This syntactic task of spelling out just which
conditions enable us to take different utterances as instances of a single
character and the related semantic task of settling the conditions that
determine that different expressions are instances of the same referent
covers a variety of issues involving alphabets, orthography, different
kinds of vagueness, and ambiguity, literal and metaphorical interpretations of characters, indexical expressions, personal indicator expressions,
spatial and temporal indicators, and so on. Similarly, Goodman has
worked just as extensively on determining the conditions that enable one
to identify predicates and the objects in their extension.

In general, Goodman's position can be summarized as follows: "The
dependence of our systems of kinds on our theories, and the dependence
of these in turn on our interests, values, technology, and the like, make
questionable at best the thesis that our predicates pick out real properties
or natural kinds whose existence, extension, and metaphysical status are
independent of any contribution of ours" (35). Thus, Goodman's theory
of denotation involves, besides an insistence on actual individuals rather
than possibilities and classes, a strong emphasis on the dependence of
both syntactic and semantic identification and interpretation of terms and
predicates on antecedent interests, choices, purposes, and projects, some
of which are incompatible with others.

Terms and predicates, however, usually attract our interest not as isolated items but as part and parcel of larger groupings of objects of different
sorts. Goodman proposes here, as elsewhere, a terminology. Groups of
such terms and predicates Goodman calls *schemes*, the groups of objects
they sort *realms*, and when realms instead of objects are sorted, the group
is called a *system*.

Here, too, a variety of problems requires consideration. One basic problem has to do with how the interpretation of such expressions as "is
identical to" or "is the same as" is determined with respect to a system
that uses them. Such interpretations are not to be settled, as for Quine
and others, by appealing to a special system but with respect to the system
itself. Further, how is it that some systems that differ are closely related?
For Goodman such a result follows from the fact that different realms can
be organized by the same scheme and that different schemes can organize
the same realm. "A system involves a term in a network of labels that
organizes, sorts, or classifies the items in a domain in terms of the types
of diversity that the system is prepared to recognize. And a system sus-
tains continuity of reference from one use of a sign to another by determining criteria for the reidentification of individuals and for the

classification of diverse individuals as instances of the same kind."[30] A system, moreover, is not a language but rather a technical term in a semantic theory such as Goodman's.

And it must be recognized that almost any body of discourse can be systematized plausibly in more than one way. What we have here, then, on the level of system is a reflection of what we have already found on the level of terms and predicates, a radical pluralism but one that is said to be subject to a series of strong constraints.

[30]Ibid., 41.

5
Actions and Poetic Fictions

All action is symbolically mediated.

—Paul Ricoeur

Desiring is a species of preferring . . . and its role in action is
to form or generate intentions.

—Richard Brand

We must be still and still moving.

—T. S. Eliot

Poetry and Action

An Action from Poetry

Consider one of the many enigmatic passages in T. S. Eliot's *Four Quartets*, a section from Part III of "East Coker" which begins "I said to my soul, be still, and wait without hope."[1] Part of the difficulty many readers have with understanding such discourse is not only its distance from our own secular culture rooted in a century of unprecedented horrors—recall Samuel Beckett's effective parodies of Eliot's visions and values—but also its frequent use of paradox. One of these paradoxes has to do with action, with the suggestion that not acting, waiting, can in some sense be an action, a philosophical or a spiritual passage of sorts.

The passage that presents this paradox begins with a repetition of an earlier line, "I said to my soul, be still, and wait," which is an echo of other poems in *Four Quartets* (for example, "Dry Salvages," Part III, or "Little Gidding," Part I), Eliot's earlier work (sections 1 and 2, for example, of "Ash Wednesday"), and many passages in Hebrew religious poetry (for example, Psalms 27, 37, 45, 46, 53, 54, 62).[2] Here the repetition serves to focus our attention on the phrase long enough for an ambiguity to

---

[1]Eliot 1959:24–25. Further reference are to this edition of *Four Quartets*.
[2]Hay 1982:174.

appear: "be still" as "do not speak" and "be still" as "do not move." In the light of the later expression in the same passage, "so the darkness shall be light, and the stillness the dancing," the second of these readings—"be still" as "do not move"—seems the more plausible. Thus, the passage begins with an account of a kind of movement that is not a movement, a notion that is formulated at the end of the last section of "East Coker" in the phrase "we must be still and still moving."

Throughout this passage Eliot provides some clarification of this paradoxical notion of a moving stillness by linking the general idea of such a movement to a peculiar type of action he calls "waiting"—"I said to my soul, be still, and wait." This action is peculiar in that waiting is usually not taken to be an action at all. Here, however, it seems linked with effecting a particular kind of passage from one state of being to another. Thus, just as the beginning of this text presents us with a movement that is not a movement but a moving stillness, so we find here also an action that is not an action but an efficacious waiting, a waiting that brings something to pass. The first is the image of the second.

These puzzling notions recur often in Eliot's poetry. But before looking at their occurrence here in the light of several variations elsewhere, we need to bring the central image into sharper focus. When Eliot left the philosophy department in Emerson Hall at Harvard in the summer of 1914, after three years of doctoral studies, including two as a teaching assistant and one as president of the graduate student philosophical society, he had almost completed his dissertation on F. H. Bradley even though he would not defend it until 1916. His teachers in the philosophy department saw him as a future academic and awarded him a travel fellowship to spend the academic year 1914–15 at Oxford reading Aristotle with Joachim after working on his German during a summer at Marburg. The war cut short his summer, but it was neither the war nor his Aristotle studies that led Eliot away from philosophy; rather, despite the sessions with Russell, one of his Harvard teachers now back in England, it was the involvement with two new friends—Ezra Pound and the woman Eliot married two months after meeting her that fall, Vivienne Haigh-Wood. Yet Aristotle continued to interest Eliot, and it is in the *De Anima* (III.10) that we can find the main source of the central image in the text we are considering.

Aristotle presents an image for the way the good both moves desire and attracts desire in the unmoved center of a wheel imparting movement to the wheel's rim. "For everything is moved by pushing and pulling," Aristotle writes. "Hence just as in the case of a wheel, so here there must be a point which remains at rest, and from that point the movement must originate."[3] Eliot uses other passages from Aristotle elsewhere, so we

[3]G. Smith 1974:188.

need not hesitate unduly in taking such a text as a source for the basic image behind Eliot's figure in "East Coker" of an efficacious waiting as a moving stillness. The wheel image recurs in other places in Eliot's work, notably in Becket's opening speech in *Murder in the Cathedral* with the added suggestion (taken not from Western but from Eastern philosophy and especially from the Sanskrit and Pali texts of the Veda and the Upanisads, which Eliot studied for almost two years while at Harvard) that all human beings are caught up in the endless pattern of *samsara* or illusion. But here, where action is at issue, the central image is Aristotelian even though the idea of action it is used to particularize is not.

This primary notion of a species of action which is more like nonacting than acting, stillness than movement, is quickly complicated, however, by other suggestions in related passages. One nuance arises from Eliot's theme of motionless moments, of moments that no longer move in time but are suspended in time, of epiphanies and moments of fullness. These moments can be found throughout his poetry—the rock pool and the silences between waves in the early poetry, the still pool and the light-filled water in the late poetry, and the moments with the hyacinth girl or in the rose garden. All are caught up in the enigmatic figure of *La figlia che piangia*. Another complication comes from Eliot's repeated meditations on the interaction of time with eternity at "the still point." Here, however, the emphasis is not directly on action but on a theology and philosophy of history which owes much to Augustine and to Hegel.

In each of these two closely related cases—the timeless moments and the moments of interaction—the accent does not fall on action as it does in the first case, for action here is not an issue. Nonetheless, these other passages serve to enrich the background of the primary notion of an efficacious nonaction even though they should not be confused with that notion.

The text I have cited from "East Coker" has many parallels in *Four Quartets*, in "Ash Wednesday," and in the poetic drama *Murder in the Cathedral*. Several of these passages require some attention, however brief. "Ash Wednesday" (1930),[4] for example, opens with a passage that anticipates an element in the present text: "Because I do not hope to turn again. Because I do not hope. Because I do not hope to turn" (section 1). And the last part (section 6) uses the same lines, substituting, however, "Although" for "Because." But the context is different from what seems to set the scene in "East Coker," Part III, and whereas "Ash Wednesday" echoes the brief mention of hope, the main business of "East Coker," Part III, is not with hope at all but with finding the figure for an efficacious waiting. This is true also of

[4]Eliot 1970. Further references are to this edition of *Selected Poems*, hereafter cited as *SP*.

the related passage in *Four Quartets* itself, for example, in "Dry Salvages," Part II: "Having hoped for the wrong things or dreaded the wrong things, is not in question." Similar remarks apply to the gloss from "Little Gidding," Part I, on the line "Wait without thought" and from "Dry Salvages," Part V, "the wild thyme unseen."

Much more important is "Burnt Norton," Part II, where the notion of a moving stillness is centered in the figure of the stillness in the dancing. Without trying to interpret this passage as a whole, we can at least observe the linking of two themes, that of efficacious waiting and that of the intersection of time with eternity—the image of the still point in the dance, which enables the dancer to move in measure, and the very important negative characterization of what the moment in time involves: action and suffering, inner and outer compulsion. The passage from "Burnt Norton," Part II, suggests that the paradoxical notion of an efficacious nonaction involves a tension between activity and passivity, between action and suffering. And it is this tension that calls to mind a concrete example of the peculiar kind of action the lines from "East Coker" figure, a waiting that is at the same time a doing, Eliot's dramatization of the key moment in the story of Thomas à Becket.

Eliot's *Murder in the Cathedral* (1935),[5] like other related poetic dramas such as Sophocles' *Oedipus at Colonus* or Milton's *Samson Agonistes*, is only in part about suffering, reenactment, and reconciliation through death. Moreover, as in the case of "East Coker" we are again dealing with a text that poses difficulties for interpretation, to the degree that the explicit religious concerns in this play are not easy late in the twentieth century for everyone to approach dispassionately. In fact, the play expressly tries to address such difficulties at the very end when the knights who have murdered the archbishop present, as self-appointed judges, their verdict to the audience: "Suicide while of Unsound Mind" (90). The play, however, need not be read as centrally about the religious consciousness of Becket and the tensions between spiritual and secular power; more generally it can be seen as centered on the understanding of action and suffering. In this perspective, as one of Eliot's most thoughtful commentators writes, Part I "presents the motif of suffering through Becket's decision not to act; and Part II presents the motif of action through Becket's suffering and acts of others."[6] The problem is how to articulate the relation between action and suffering in a way that does justice to the complexities of what Becket is dramatically represented as doing. And it is this problem I would like to examine in more detail.

---

[5]Eliot 1968. Further references are to this edition of *Murder in the Cathedral*, hereafter cited as *MC*.

[6]G. Smith 1974:182.

A Dramatic Presentation of Waiting as an Action

What is to be gained from turning to a case of action in poetry is the richness of the example, from which philosophical reflection can only hope to benefit. It is necessary, then, to consider the case in more detail. Eliot's *Murder in the Cathedral* begins with a choral meditation on waiting, a notion isolated as a cardinal element in "East Coker," Part III, as well. The old women of Canterbury are discovered before the cathedral in December in the year 1170. "Here let us stand, close by the Cathedral. Here let us wait," go the play's first words. And further on in the same opening choral passage the women chant: "The New Year waits, destiny waits for the coming." The martyrs and saints are said to wait and the poor as well, for whom "there is no action."

This opening choral ode is doubly important, for it both announces waiting as a central theme of the play and exhibits the usual understanding of waiting as a backdrop against which another understanding is to be viewed. The usual construal of waiting is, as here, in terms of a state of affairs, something static that is "no action" at all. But the "waiting" the play will go on to dramatize will be a more dynamic thing, more like a course of events which both flows from and completes certain mental acts Becket will effect. Such acts, however, as the play will show, become possible only after Becket overcomes temptations of sensuality, secular power, and betrayal of his country, and the much more subtle and un-expected temptation of spiritual pride. This last temptation is the desire to be a martyr, and it leads to the final impasse Becket must circumvent, a dilemma that turns on his awareness of the danger of spiritual pride. "Can I neither act nor suffer without perdition?" he cries out in wrestling with the last of the tempters.

Before we can appreciate how Becket resolves this dilemma, we need to note how the key relation between action and suffering is formulated in the play. Just as with the repetition in "East Coker," Part III, "I said to my soul, be still, and let the dark come upon you," "I said to my soul, be still, and wait," so too a key passage is repeated prominently. The first words Becket utters in the play, when he admonishes his priests to let the poor women be, and the final words his last tempter quotes back at him in the spiritual climax of the drama are the same except for one phrase.

> They know and do not know, what it is to act or suffer
> They know and do not know, that action is suffering
> And suffering is action. Neither does the agent suffer
> Nor the patient act. But both are fixed
> In an eternal action, an eternal patience,
> To which all must consent that it may be willed
> And which all must suffer that they may will it,

> That the pattern may subsist, for the pattern is the
>   action
> And the suffering, that the wheel may turn and still
> Be forever still. (22)

And the passage can be plausibly linked with the continuation of the passage from "East Coker" considered earlier in this chapter, beginning "you say I am repeating / Something I have said before."

The themes of knowing and not knowing, a pattern in the intersection of time and eternity, and the earlier image of the wheel moving at the rim and still at its centerpoint are familiar. What is new is the talk of a willing that is a consenting. However obscure, a connection seems to be suggested here between an action that is passive, a willing that is not a wanting but a consenting, and a waiting that is an action, an efficacious waiting.

The center of the drama turns, I believe, on the idea that Becket must learn how neither to save himself nor to sacrifice himself. He must try neither to escape ("he should still have easily escaped; he could have kept himself from us long enough to allow our righteous anger to cool," says the Fourth Knight) nor to actively seek martyrdom; rather, he must learn how to act in not acting, how to enact a kind of waiting. Both acting and suffering are fixed in an eternal action, a pattern to which all must consent. This is something Becket knows and does not know, says the Fourth Tempter, repeating to Becket his own words and thereby fulfilling his task of telling Becket only what he knows (39). Later, in the sermon Becket preaches on Christmas morning, this acting and suffering are said to be involved in a larger reality. For the pattern comprises being born and dying, beginning and ending, the sorrowful reenactment of a death and the joyful celebration of a birth in the same mysterious action that is Becket's Mass (51). Becket must learn, in the words of "Little Gidding," "to make an end."

The sermon includes the key insight that enables Becket to resolve his dilemma, the insight that spells out the till now cryptic and repeated doctrine of consent to a pattern. A Christian martyrdom, Becket tells the people, is not "the effect of a man's will to become a Saint, as a man by willing and contriving may become a ruler of men. A martyrdom is always the design of God . . . never the design of man; for the true martyr is he who has become the instrument of God, who has lost his will in the will of God, and who no longer desires anything for himself, not even the glory of being a martyr" (53). This passage echoes "our peace in His will" at the end of "Ash Wednesday," itself an echo of Dante, and anticipates the talk of "purification of the motive" at the end of "Little Gidding," Part III.

To win through to this insight Becket is shown as having understood that the last temptation is to do the right thing for the wrong reason. He thereby escapes from the fate that would otherwise have overtaken him, the terrifying loss Eliot describes in passages in the play and elsewhere about "the void," "the horror of the effortless journey, to the empty land / Which is no land, only emptiness, absence, the Void" (77, cf. 20) and to which Eliot alludes in his echoes of Conrad in the earlier poetry. The insight here seems to be the one formulated in Eliot's poetic pageant, *The Rock*, where the choruses repeat: "*Make perfect your will . . .* make perfect your will"[7] (*SP*, 109). And in Part II of *Murder in the Cathedral*, Becket will say in trying to calm his frightened priests who want him to save himself and thereby save them as well: "All my life / I have waited. Death will come only when I am worthy; / And if I am worthy, there is no danger. / I have therefore only to make perfect my will" (75).

Becket's peculiar action, his waiting, is finally the action Eliot described in "Dry Salvages," Part III, as "the one action (and the time of death is every moment) / Which shall fructify in the lives of others" because it is through this action that the suffering poor women of Canterbury are brought to realize, however vaguely and obscurely through hints and guesses, that their own suffering is part of the same pattern that has included Becket's. Becket's action is intended to encompass the spectators as well. For in Eliot's view the essence of tragedy is to be found in its ritualistic and communal dimensions and thereby involves participation by a community and the recreation and reaffirmation of its identity.[8] The play ends with another choral ode, which now, unlike the opening ode, is no longer an expression of a paralyzed inactivity but is a psalm, a song of praise, thanks, and contrition. Becket's action has fructified in the lives of these women in opening their eyes to a spiritual vision of all experience. He has achieved a consummation of his life in a martyr's death, a consummation he has learned not to forgo through inaction nor actively to avoid nor actively to desire but to affirm in an efficacious waiting, in the still movement of the danger, in a moment of neither action nor inaction.

In the context, then, of other meditations on the enigmatic action of waiting in *Four Quartets* and "Ash Wednesday" and especially of the dramatic example of such an action as we find it represented in *Murder in the Cathedral*, we can return to the passage we started with from "East Coker": "I said to myself, be still, and wait."

How are we to understand this waiting, this peculiar kind of active inaction or inactive action? The basic problem here is understanding the implicit claim throughout that Becket's waiting, just like the unfamiliar doctrine from "East Coker" which it dramatically illustrates, is, however,

[7]Eliot 1970:109.
[8]Moody 1977.

peculiar and however unlike the Wittgensteinian paradigm of raising one's arm, indeed an action.

In what follows I look first at a recent analytic account of action and then at a recent hermeneutic account in search of conceptual resources for articulating the nature of Becket's waiting action as an instance of the puzzling adage "be still, and wait." In the final section I go on to suggest why accounting for actions like Becket's requires a more comprehensive view of action than either account presents.

Describing Actions Naturalistically

A Critical Summary

Richard Brand's aim in his book *Intending and Acting*,[9] which pulls together several decades of work in analytic philosophy of action, is to provide a naturalized theory of intentional action which will integrate conceptual analysis with scientific work in cognitive and motivational psychology. (See Appendix 5A, "Action, Immediate Intending, Cognition, and Conation," for an extended exposition of the many important details in Brand's theory.) Brand begins with the conceptual background of action theory and argues first that "actions are the proximate effects of a specific type of mental event he calls an immediate intention" (46), and second that intentional action is planned action. Next, actions and intentions are analyzed as events and events as particulars. Further, Brand argues that "Intention is a mental attitude with a content, . . . the objects of attitudes are properties and that all attitudes are at their cores self-referential" (47). A commonsense psychological account of the attitudes of believing, desiring, and intending is then described and criticized. Finally, Brand argues that intentional action involves two complex elements, a *cognitive* component that includes guidance and monitoring elements a well as representational ones, and a *conative* component that includes a motivational system and what is called a production set. In the first case a scientific transformation of the commonsense view is presented, but in the second, despite the use of computational models, the transformation of the folk psychological view is taken to be programmatic only.

With this initial orientation in mind and with details available in Appendix 5A, I will formulate in a summary fashion four stages of this account as prospective descriptions of the action of Thomas Becket in *Murder in the Cathedral*: the initial description of action, the discussion of intending and believing as well as of intending and desiring, the char-

---

[9]Brand 1984. Contrast Tuomela 1984, Gustafson 1986, and Dennett 1987.

acterization of intentional action and cognition, and finally intentional action and conation.

Thus, in terms of the first stage of the analysis in the first section of Appendix 5A, "Action and Intentional Actions," schematically presented here, we may say:

B1. Thomas acts
   a. in bringing about an event, and acts intentionally in doing so according to a plan.
   b. Thomas's action is a causal sequence, initiated by a nonactional mental event (say, choosing to wait), which is its proximate cause, and completed in overt behavior (say, standing at the cathedral altar), which is its proximate effect.
   c. Thomas's action is intentional in that, although not explicitly planned, it is part of a pattern of planned activity (say, Thomas attempts to act in such a way as to make perfect his will), incorporating both focal points and unforeseeable eventualities.
   d. Thomas's intentional action, more specifically, is the proximate effect of the innate antecedent mental event called an immediate intending (Thomas's intentional act flows from his immediate intention to wait).

Several elements in this initial account need highlighting. Notice first the focus on a sharply limited set of concerns. The aim is to provide a naturalized philosophical theory not of all human action but of intentional action in particular, and of intentional action not in all aspects but especially in its cognitive and conative aspects. One central consequence is that this account excludes from consideration the affective influences on action. Although an important place is reserved for desire, many other important affective influences on action are set aside.

Second, the initial distinction here between events and actions is admittedly stipulative in part. But granted the reasonableness of such a practice at the outset of the inquiry, we need a fuller description of the relations between these terms if we are to make sufficient sense of the crucial notion in the version offered of the causal theory, namely, nonactional antecedent events as the proximate cause of action. In this light the exclusion of terms like "act" and "activity" from the account seems shortsighted.

Third, perhaps it is only in the context of the limitations on the scope of this account that it makes sense to talk of "the fundamental problem in philosophical action theory" as specifying the proximate cause of action. The account may come to be seen as overdetermined by the narrowness of such a claim. And finally, it must remain highly controversial whether Brand is justified in claiming, without sustained argument, that action theory is ontologically neutral with respect not just to the mind-body problem (this seems correct) but to the nature of causality and the ontological status of mental events as well. For these last two matters are deeply implicated in any account of human action, a point we need to investigate shortly. Moreover, the author points out that a satisfactory definition of action depends on specifying both the "attitude-type" of the antecedent mental event and the "context" of that event, and this task cannot be accomplished without both presenting an ontology and urging it on one's readers as more than simply neutral. Thus, four items in this initial stage need monitoring—the limitation of scope, the working terminology, the centrality of the question the account is designed to answer, and the supposedly neutral status of the ontological commitments the account adopts.

We can summarize and illustrate the second stage of the naturalistic account in the second section of Appendix 5A, "Immediate Intending as the Proximate Cause of Action," by returning to our example:

B2. Thomas acts, and
   a. his action includes a cognitive component, namely, a complex representation for the monitoring and guidance of his bodily movement (say, the patterned perception, feedback, and correction of Thomas's resolute stance by the altar as the murderous knights approach).
   b. Further, this component is not to be identified with either Thomas's beliefs of whatever sort or his desires of whatever sort, or some combination of the two, but with his immediate intending to wait (understood on a servomechanistic model as a self-correcting movement).
   c. However, Thomas's immediate intention to wait arises out of a background of dispositional beliefs and comparative preferences (such as his dispositional beliefs in theological providence and his favoring the performance of some actions over others).

Now, the initial distinctions in these first steps toward describing the cognitive features of the intention as the proximate cause of action, the temporal distinctions between prospective and immediate intentions, and between occurrent and dispositional intentions, are cardinal ones. Brand stresses the role of immediate and occurrent intentions. But he leaves the other kinds of intention without sufficient commentary and does not seem to recognize that the temporal basis of the distinctions requires further reflection. Second, the attempt to eliminate belief in the main cognitive context of intention is only partly successful. For the description of belief that is criticized here is borrowed from a vague folk psychological conception, thereby preempting the claim of other accounts of belief such as anthropological, social, or psychoanalytical ones, which may be stronger candidates. Moreover, the kind of cognitive candidates Brand is willing to accept seem overdetermined by his naturalism, which as he himself points out in a later discussion of conation is not always adequate. Why overlook the credentials of a notion of belief which is neither folk psychological nor scientific psychological, especially since both may share common bases in cognitive structures?

Third, although more successful than the exclusion of belief, the attempt to exclude desire from the cognitive content of intention is not entirely persuasive either. Some of the arguments (for example, those against the notion of desire as a species of intending) remain controversial, and the interpretation of other arguments (for example, those of Aristotle and Hume) are in important respects speculative. Why not keep the account open to an understanding of desire which is more descriptive precisely in the empirical and scientific psychological vein that is favored for belief? Such a move would protect the account from adopting prematurely a somewhat tendentious description of desire as a "pro-attitude," a notion Brand himself has already criticized in another context when discussing Davidson. In short, it is not evident that both belief and desire, under some perspicuous description, are definitively to be rejected as interpretation of the contents of even immediate intention, not to speak of the more interesting case of prospective intention.

In the third stage of the analysis (see section three of Appendix 5A, "Intention, Cognition, and Action") the relation between intention and cognition is discussed more positively. Returning to our example again we may say:

B3. Thomas acts, and
   a. the cognitive complex of his action as intentional, in scientific rather than in folk psychologistic terms, is a complex representation of a storied activity
   b. in which Thomas self-awaredly plays a leading role, which allows for substitution, improvisation, and interruption.
   c. More specifically, this complex representation is a set of abstract, hierarchically ordered, scene-length chunks that guide and monitor Thomas's action to its completion.

But just as in the discussions of believing and desiring versus intending as the basic cognitive component in the understanding of the proximate cause of action, so too in this further attempt to provide a naturalized account of intention several difficulties arise. The discussion of both neobehaviorist views and script theory is helpful. But in the key case of script theory at least two cautions are in order. First, the cognitive component of the intention to act is taken as a preconceived master complex representation. Although this complex includes a reasonably detailed account of memory, the essential imaginative component that is especially important for prospective intention is not well understood scientifically. Moreover, the talk here of a "preconceived" representation is far too elliptical. And second, the further discussion of a revised script theory, which adds the notion of future planned activity represented in a special kind of story, raises additional difficulties. For here the revised units of analysis, the "separable scene-length chunks," is presented without sufficient discussion of just how the "separations" are actually effected. Moreover, the nature of the story included in the master representation is not explicated in detail—what of the temporal structures here? In both cases, despite the sophisticated responses to various objections from the standpoint of cognitive psychology, a basic difficulty remains with any merely computational model of intention as the cognitive component of action—namely, the lack of a scientifically acceptable account not only of the formal idea of central processes but of the more resistant notions of plan formation and planned activity. And any such account must not leave unaddressed the role of imagination by focusing too narrowly on memory alone.

The fourth and final stage of the naturalistic account, namely, the discussion of intention and conation in section four of Appendix 5A, "Immediate Intention, Conation, and Motivated Action," may be summarized in the light of our example as follows:

B4. Thomas acts, and
   a. the conative complex of his action is a production system for the master representation of a planned activity; this transmits the motivation of the ongoing enactment of that plan to the activation of bodily moment.
   b. Further, Thomas's selection of a production system and his initiation of his action flows from his motivational system, which itself may well be a kind of innate response system sensitized to environmental conditions and situational uses.

Here, as earlier in the account of a computational model for understanding the complex cognitive component of action, the discussion of a computational model for the complex conative element is enlightening. But though the criticism here of relatively sophisticated neobehaviorist views is instructive, again we need to notice at least three controversial points.

In discussing the adaptive control theory as a production system, the controversial distinction between consciously accessible and not consciously accessible knowledge goes unchallenged. The problem of course lies with an unexplicated account of "consciousness." And yet without at least some discussion of this notion, the nature of talk about "calling forth a production set" remains obscure. Second, the interesting limitation of adaptive control theory to the transmission of motivation rather than its inclusion of plan selection and motivation as well depends on a successful explanation of just what motivation comes to. And here Brand concedes that his own reliance on extrapolation from ethological claims about innate response systems in rats remains speculative. Accordingly, the utility even of a restricted appeal to a production-system account remains speculative as well. Finally, we touch here on the aims of the naturalistic account. The presupposition is that, unlike the complex cognitive component of intention as the proximate cause of action, the complex conative component cannot be given a complete scientific account. But this is misleading. For as we have seen with the case of unexplained plan formation, the cognitive component itself must be completely transformed. Some transformation is possible, as Brand ably shows; but complete transformation in either case is yet to be achieved. Thus, however, praiseworthy in aim and execution, the ideal of a naturalized theory of action still remains an ideal. The point here is that some important philosophical interest must remain attached to the intermediate stage (which Brand thinks must now be left behind) of attempting an account of action which is neither folk psychologistic nor scientific in the overly strong sense of this approach.

Descriptive Gaps in the Naturalistic Account

When we look back through the naturalistic account of action, we find working definitions of action and intentional action together with descriptions of their complex cognitive and conative components. Action is to be defined not as a mere doing nor as a mere knowing that one is doing something but as an event understandable in the context of a particular version of the causal theory. Thus, informally:

> *Action* is a type of event which results from some proximate and appropriate antecedent nonactional mental event that cannot be identified merely as a conjunction of believing and desiring.

And similarly:

> *Intentional action* is an action whose mental antecedent consists of an immediate intending that involves both complex cognitive and a complex conative element, and which proximately causes that action.

Since not all but most specifically human action is taken to be intentional action, the fundamental problem is to provide a scientific psychological account of the cognitive and conative complexes. Accordingly:

> *The cognitive complex* of immediate intentions as the proximate cause of intentional action is taken as, first, the preconceived master representation of a planned activity in the form of an agent's having a mental story in the plans, scripts, and scenes in which that agent ascribes him or herself with self-awareness the primary role; and second, the agent's guidance and monitoring through perceptual feedback and correction of that activity throughout its not completely foreseeable course to completion.

And similarly:

> *The conative complex* of intentional action as a proximate cause of such action is taken to involve, first, with respect to plan selection, a largely speculative motivational system that initiates action by interaction with memory on the occasion of environmental stimuli; and second, with respect to plan enactment, the operation of production-set motor schemata that guide bodily behavior.

The criticisms developed thus far remain largely within the idiom in which this analytic account is developed, and they are of a sort that philosophical analysis on its own can generate. What is more germane to the overall theme we are pursuing here—the relation between fictions and philosophies—is a further kind of criticism. For we can observe more directly now how some of the peculiarities of many subtle and important human actions set before us above all in fictions, like Becket's waiting, are seen obscurely on this account if at all. When we return to the poetic representation of at least Becket's action, what we find does not seem to be appropriately described in terms of an exclusively naturalistic version of complex cognitive and conative components of the proximate causes of Becket's action.

Recall that the expression "Becket's action" is ambiguous in that it can be interpreted in various ways. In the light of several critical readings of Eliot's work, however, we have narrowed the range of these interpretations and then proposed that "Becket's action" be construed as "Becket's deciding to wait," which is neither to save himself from great danger nor to seek martyrdom. More specifically, "Becket's action" is plausibly to be taken as "Becket's deciding to wait on what is to happen." This fuller expression is what I have in mind in using the shorter forms "Becket's action" and "waiting."

We need to recall a second point now, namely, that Becket's action can be situated in more than one conceptual framework. This is not obvious. Becket, after all, is taken to be a saint, and thus the most plausible framework here is surely the Christian one. But such a view betrays an inattention to the language in which Becket's action is represented and to

Eliot's poetry in general. Thus, someone may wish to argue that Becket's action is to be understood as the decision to renounce his own will in assenting to God's design that the fallen world be redeemed through participation in the mysterious and saving acts of Christ's sufferings. But one could also argue that Becket's action is a symbolic act whereby the victory of fertility over sterility, spring light over winter darkness in the solstice, and the agony of the dying god, are achieved in the communal and ritual killing of a sacrificial scapegoat, the *pharmakos*. And one could just as well argue that Becket's action is a purification of his existence through self-surrender to fate in light of the goal of achieving release from the cycle of birth, death, and rebirth.

Thus, although the Christian interpretation of Becket's action is the most plausible one, a close analysis of Eliot's poetic diction, imagery, and symbolism would allow of mythic and Hindu interpretations too. The Christian interpretation is, then, neither the only one nor the only plausible one. Both of these initial reminders—the specification of Becket's action and its openness to more than a Christian interpretation—need to be kept in view if we are to respond attentively to some of the suggestiveness in the poetic presentation of action.

In this context we need now to focus on four aspects of Becket's action which, though they do not obviate sophisticated causal analysis on computational models, both intimate their final inappropriateness and invite an account of human action in other than merely causal, componential, and computational terms alone. First, Becket's action arises, as we have seen, out of an unusual dilemma—whether he acts or does not act Becket thinks he will violate his own ideal of personal fulfillment: if he acts prudently by avoiding mortal danger he loses the opportunity to witness before his community to certain values he holds to be transcendent, namely, the primacy of the spiritual order; yet if he does not act, he risks failing to witness before his community to other values he also holds to be transcendent, namely, spiritual humility. In the first case he risks sacrificing the primacy of the spiritual to the interest of self-preservation, whereas in the second he risks sacrificing humility to the proud impulse to be a martyr. Whether he acts or not Becket can only fail. Yet Becket acts and succeeds. The first elusive feature, then, of Becket's action is that it arises unexpectedly from a spiritual dilemma it succeeds in resolving.

Second, Becket's action here is neither the self-directed performance of an action nor the self-serving forbearance to act, but the decision to wait on what is to happen. As such, this act is both an enactment of what has gone before, an instance of a ritual repetition through memory, and an anticipation of what is to come, a prophetic gesture in a charged social space. The gap here between the antecedent mental event and the actual effect in waiting is not to be characterized just in terms of a gap between remote and proximate causes in a causal process; it must take into account such opaque elements as self-doubt, temptation, weakness, and so on—what Eliot calls "the shadow between motive and act." Describing the shadow as a causal gap is inappropriate because such a description leaves out too many relevant features. Thus the second elusive aspect is the nature of the relation between proximate and remote antecedents to acts of a symbolic and ritual sort.

Further, Becket's act, at least on the language of the play and the related poems, seems to involve certain curious prerequisites if not conditions. Becket, in order to act in waiting, needs to attain what is described here and elsewhere as a state of personal dispossession, an emptiness, an attitude toward his own action—"proffering one's deeds to oblivion" in the language of "Ash Wednesday" and, in that of the *Selected Poems*, "seeking the good deeds that lead to obscurity" (108), or "the one right action that will fructify in the lives of others." In short, a prerequisite is detachment, but detachment understood in a special way. Eliot described this state of mind partly in the lines quoted earlier from "East Coker" as well as in the lines from another section of *Four Quartets*, "Burnt Norton," which I will look at more closely further on. Accordingly, a third elusive feature of Becket's action is the nature of its prerequisite, which a merely analytic account of causal antecedents, whether remote or proximate, leaves without comment.

But if this curious state of mind called detachment is a prerequisite for Becket's act, the actual features of that act seem just as puzzling. Becket is represented as having to act in such a way as not to perform an action, all the while being occupied in acting, and to renounce not the act but its fruits. Becket is to incorporate what Eliot's Harvard teacher Irving Babbitt called "the will to refrain." His act is to be a renunciation, a sacrificial act, an enactment that both reenacts what is past and creates a possibility for future acts of community.

What follows on such an act of renunciation are not so much results as consequences—both at the individual and communal levels. Thus, Becket's act is to yield a release not from a cyclic existence but from suffering, a reconciliation among those who are caught up in its circle, a fruitfulness in subsequent stages of communal activity. Here the public dimension of action is not to be understood by opposition to the private but as a communal feature of certain acts that allow a community to participate in some action, and thereby to recreate and to reaffirm its identity while opening itself outward through subsequent activity of its own toward world and cosmos.

Here, then, are four elusive features of actions like Becket's which do not seem to receive an appropriate description, if any, in terms of representative analytic accounts of human action—their source in dilemmas rather than strategies, their peculiar links to past and future action through reenactment and prophetic witness, their dependence on selfless states of mind, and their promise of both individual and communal liberation. Such features, however, do not simply call for still further revisions in a naturalized causal theory of action; they seem to put into question in different and perhaps still obscure ways the appropriateness of the entire idiom of such accounts. Consider, then, an alternative account.

Describing Actions Phenomenologically

A Critical Summary

A representative hermeneutic analysis of action is to be found in the work of Paul Ricoeur, especially in a central chapter in his recent *Temps et récit* as well as in an earlier monograph, "Le discours de l'action."[10] I articulate the central elements in this account in a summary presentation of four stages: the triple structure of action, the conceptual network of talk about action, a protracted reflection on causes and reasons, and a discussion of the explanation and interpretation of action. (See Appendix 5B, "Action, Imagination, Discourse, and Causes," for an extended exposition.)

Although Ricoeur's hermeneutic account of action is extensive and complex, its salient features can be represented not unfairly in the four somewhat schematic analyses that follow. We need now to look briefly but critically at each.

The first phase of the hermeneutic analysis (see section one of Appendix 5B, "Action, Imagination, and Discourse") involves the semantic, symbolic, and temporal structures of action. When speaking of "the structural traits of action" Ricoeur calls attention not so much to a concept of action as to a particular conceptual network. For Ricoeur, the crucial significations of the word "action" are largely a function of its interrelations with the ways closely related words are used. An action, we are told, is "what someone does."[11] What someone does, however, implies anticipated goals. Action also involves explanatory reasons. Further, action is always interaction with others, whether positive or negative. And finally, actions have issues or consequences. Such outcomes are often not willed; they are the results of complex causal chains not all of whose results can be foreseen. In short, agents do something, in the light of motives and goals, in the practical contexts of various constraints, in cooperation or conflict with others. Thus, the concept of action is to be understood as one element only in a dynamic conceptual network.

[10]Ricoeur 1983–85 and 1981.
[11]Ricoeur1983–85, 1:88. Further references to this work are to volume and page number.

The second major element of this account of action is the idea that before it is recounted in a narrative all action is symbolically mediated: action is "already articulated in signs, in rules, in norms" (1.91ff.). As a result, the accent falls on the public rather than the psychological character of the symbolic mediations of action and also the specifically structured features of symbolic groups. Action thus is always part of a structured, public, and cultural whole. This rich symbolic mediation of action is in fact what enables the meaning of an action to be interpreted.

Besides semantic and symbolic structures, action involves temporal structures as well. Just as the conceptual network in which the term "action" is situated involves implicit symbolic mediations of action inside a culture, so these mediations themselves involve implicit temporal structures. There is also a correlation between some action categories and individual temporal structure. Effective action, for instance, can be understood as involving a unification of the three temporal dimensions of past, present, and future in a triple present (following earlier analyses of Augustine). But the main point involves distinguishing the abstract moment of the present from what Ricoeur calls the existential moment. The latter is the relevant aspect of the intratemporality of action. Action is always within a symbolic domain, which involves an existential rather than an abstract temporality.

If we turn with this discussion in mind to the particular literary case we are using as a touchstone for theories of human action—namely, the representation of the puzzling instance of action performed by Thomas Becket in *Murder in the Cathedral*—we may rearticulate this first discussion informally as follows:

R1. Thomas acts in that he
    a. both does and undergoes something;
    b. in a motivated, goal-oriented manner both circumscribed with restraints and issuing in consequences (whether anticipated or unforseeable);
    c. in the context of symbolic cultural mediations of a public and interactional nature; and
    d. at a time that is to be understood not merely as an abstract temporal instant but "existentially."

This notion of action has several important weaknesses. First, while taking some pains to spell out the elements that make up the "conceptual network" in which "action" is to be understood, Ricoeur neither specifies whether this list is complete nor distinguishes between central and peripheral notions, or between necessary and sufficient conditions of action. Further, in his discussion of the symbolic structures of action, it is not clear enough just how we are to take the important claim that all action is necessarily articulated, mediated, and interpreted in symbols. For example, in the crucial case of articulation is the meaning that, necessarily, action is first corporeal gesture before it is conceptually formed, or merely that there is no action properly speaking without antecedent conceptualization, or if neither of them exactly what? Finally, the reflections on the temporal structures of action do not provide sufficient room for the abstract notion of the present moment while attempting to develop this aspect by construing it, in a largely metaphorical way, as "existential."

Still, whatever the fate of these initial objections, the hermeneutic analysis makes several striking points. "Action" is not to be understood, especially in its broader sense, which involves the notion of suffering, by remaining within the limits of a strictly conceptual analysis. For the cultural contexts of action require attention to "symbolic" dimensions as well. Moreover, if action is understood to involve "symbolic" articulation, its interpretation must also be "symbolic." The problematic expression here, "symbolic," may be used in different ways when we pass from articulation to interpretation. But Ricoeur thinks formal interpretation, although necessary, is finally insufficient because he holds that at least some "symbolic" features of the articulation of action are resistant to formal analysis. Furthermore, the metaphorical characterization of the temporal moment in which action takes place is, however puzzling, suggestive nonetheless. For it points to at least one area where formalization may require supplementation, and it opens up an important space for the roles of memory (past) and imagination (future) in the analysis of action. Finally, it is argued that because some actions allow of assessment as good or bad, some actions are to be understood as involving degrees of value and thereby require for their interpretation not just criteria but also norms within a culture.

Consider again the case of Thomas's central action in *Murder in the Cathedral*, this time from the more detailed position in a second hermeneutic discussion (see section two of Appendix 5B, "Action, Intention, and Reason") of the elements in the conceptual pattern involved in talk of action. Thus:

R2.   Thomas acts in that he
    a. exercises a certain capacity of which he need not have any prior knowledge,
    b. within a motivational context that includes certain dispositional forces he does not so much exercise as undergo;
    c. in so doing he makes an imaginative selection from a repertoire of basic actions,

    d. in the articulating of a project in propositional and discursive forms as well as predicative ones,

    e. in such a way as to include both the diverse influences of dispositional forces on the articulation of reasons, motives, and intentions, and

    f. with the recognition that this understanding may well require interpretation as well as explanation.

And Thomas acts intentionally in that he

    g. exercises this capacity to act by being able to declare and assume responsibility for the hierarchy of reasons for this act, a hierarchy that arises from the dispositions of his character.

But just as in the first discussion we find here a peculiar complexity in the account of what it would mean to say that Thomas acts. Moreover, we are not sure whether this description is meant to replace the conceptual description in the first account, to supplement it, or merely to overlap that account.

And again certain difficulties are evident. Thus, if we now have the claim that within the series of elements which make up the conceptual network of our uses of "action" three are particularly important, we find a certain redundancy in the first. Does Ricoeur mean that the three key elements in his conceptual description of "action" are action, intention, and motive? Or are they rather agent, intention, and motive? Surely the latter. But then we still lack an explicit account of agent which would parallel that of intention and motive. Similarly, the point of the discussion of Hart and his critics is not plain enough. Are we to understand that an act is intentional when it is an event for which an agent may be held responsible? Or is an intentional act, rather, one whose proximate immediate cause is a hierarchy of reasons? Finally, the notion that an act arises out of a context of motives, no one of which may be parsed in terms of causes or reasons, is obscure, particularly when the idea is added that part of the relevant context for action includes dispositional forces. What sense does it make to call such forces—for example, the force of desire—a motive rather than a cause or a reason?

Still, this discussion's stress on the role of imagination in all of the capacity, the intention, and the project of action is suggestive because it attracts critical attention to the need for a fuller account of planning in the analysis of action. Moreover, the programmatic notion here of an analysis of action that would include, besides the predicates, both action propositions or sentences and action "discourse" or ends-means strategies in decision making averts an overly narrow reading of what Ricoeur has in mind when he describes the conceptual pattern of "action." It becomes clearer also how to construe the broad sense of action as what someone both does and undergoes, namely, as involving effects on intention, reasons, and motives of dispositional forces. And seizing upon an implicit phenomenology of "I can," Ricoeur parses the notion of capacity in terms of an accessible repertoire of basic acts. Finally, the idea that connecting intentions with motives is analogous to interpreting texts by appeal to contexts is not misleading in that the analogy suggests that the analysis of intention may require interpretive understanding and not just causal explanation.

With the example of Thomas's action once again in mind, consider a third stage in the hermeneutic account (see section three of Appendix 5B) "Action and Speech Acts"):

R3. Thomas "acts intentionally" in that he

a. exercises certain capacities in such a way as to fulfill both essential and inessential conditions of having the intention to act,

b. intentions that include among others both verbal and mental expressions of that intention;

c. moreover, the mental expression itself includes a voluntary component in being an intending *that*, a trying, and a doing; and

d. a mental expression of the intending assumes the form of a command or decree addressed to oneself in the first person to initiate and to carry through to completion a plan.

Here, too, we need to win some critical distance. Thus, we are not told whether the verbal or the mental expression of an intention or both is an essential or an inessential condition for action. Further, the talk here of a conative element in acting intentionally, although extremely important, remains too sketchy. And the perhaps equally important notion of the role of first-person analyses in understanding intentional action remains slight as well.

But the effort here to focus more sharply on the nature of intentional action does lead to several important ideas. Thus, the notion that understanding an intention to act involves attending as well to some inessential and not just essential features of intentional action reinforces the earlier claims about dispositional forces. Moreover, however inchoative, the distinction between verbal and nonverbal expressions of intention opens up room in the analysis of intentional action for the theme of the lived body. Furthermore, the emphasis on first-person self-addressed commands or injunctions invites more detailed analysis of the ineliminable self-referential character of intentional action. And finally the renewed insistence on agent capacity suggests that a satisfactory account of intentional action requires attention to more than both a cognitive and conative element.

Turn, then, finally to the fourth stage of the discussion (see section four of Appendix 5B, "Actions, Causes, and Reasons"):

R4. Thomas acts in that
   a. he exercises a capacity that cannot be reduced either to a merely causal antecedent or to a mere desire, but
   b. in exercising that capacity Thomas at the same time passively undergoes certain dispositions to desire which arise out of the lived experience of his body as being his own, especially as the locus of motivational forces and drives; further,
   c. in deciding to exercise that capacity while undergoing such constraints, Thomas traverses degrees of deliberation in settling on the specific ends his project articulates; and
   d. in carrying through the exercise of this capacity Thomas intervenes in natural courses by setting in motion the operation of the closed system his exercise has isolated, thereby making rather than letting things happen.

This final stage in the discussion, just like the others, fills out our previous understanding of this account, especially in linking motivational forces to the *corps propre*, in making room for ends in the context of projects, and in providing still further arguments for the irreducibility of agent capacities. Moreover, we find here an important distinction overlooked so far between noncausal antecedents of intentional action (such as wanting and desiring) versus merely causal ones. It is suggested also that computational models of intentional action may have the serious defect of excluding ends from the understanding of intentional action, especially the role of ends in the nature of projects. Moreover, the discussion of von Wright opens up the possibility of an analysis of intentional action where capacity rather than causality is taken as primitive. And finally, Ricoeur mentions in passing that for him at least the fundamental problem for a philosophical theory of human action is not orchestrating talk of reasons and causes as antecedents for action, but understanding the interaction of capacities versus dispositions in intending to act.

But this final installment in Ricoeur's ongoing discussion of action, which now stretches from his three-volume phenomenology of the will in 1950 to his 1986 Gifford lectures, leaves a number of previous difficulties unresolved while raising new difficulties in its own right. However, rather than pursuing this account any further we do better to turn our attention, as we did with the rival account, to certain descriptive gaps.

Descriptive Gaps in the Phenomenological Account

If we now look back through the hermeneutic account of action, we might summarize these views along the following lines:

> *An action* is what an agent both does and undergoes.
> a. As an activity, action is an exercise without any requisite prior knowledge of certain capacities that cannot be reduced either to their antecedent causes or to mere desires.
> b. As a passivity, action is the issue of certain dispositions, and motivational fields that include motives, forces, and especially desires arising out of the agent's lived experiences of his or her own body precisely as a *corps propre*.
>
> *An intentional action* is one that fulfills both essential and non-essential conditions for the agent to have an intention to act.
> a. Forming an intention to act involves imaginative selection from a repertoire of basic actions, and the propositional and discursive articulation of derived actions or action strategies in a project.
> b. In deciding to act intentionally the agent traverses degrees of deliberation before settling on the specific ends the action project then incorporates.
> c. Acting intentionally involves not just a verbal but also a mental expression of the intention to act. The latter has the form of a first-person, self-addressed command to initiate, carry out, and complete what is intended, and includes as well a voluntary component.
> d. Completing an intentional act involves making rather than letting things happen. The agent carries through the exercise of his or her capacity to act by intervening in natural courses of events and thereby setting in motion the operation of a closed system this activity has already isolated.
>
> *Representing* an intentional act involves a necessary symbolic articulation of action at the different levels of concepts, social practices, and cultural conventions. All action is mediated symbolically.
>
> *The explanation*, understanding, and interpretation of action must include the systematic articulation of the conceptual network in which the term "action" is situated. It must also include the interpretive readings of the symbolic mediations of action, and metaphysical reflections on the "existential" and not merely formal character of the temporal instant in which action takes place, a gathering of the past and the future in a lived now.

Again, the criticisms of this account articulated in the last section remain largely within the very terms in which the hermeneutic view is presented. And again, these terms keep us from seeing still other aspects of actions like Becket's than those I called attention to earlier in discussing the analytic account. For when we return to the fuller poetic description of Becket's action in the play and the related poetry, we find certain features that even so comprehensive a hermeneutic account as Ricoeur's is not able to describe within an appropriate idiom. To the four features of Becket's action which seem inappropriately described in the idiom of a naturalized analytic account, then, I add four others to which the idiom of a hermeneutic account does not seem adequate either.

The first of these additional features is the paradoxical character of Becket's action, which is both an action and not an action but an undergoing, a willing and not a willing but a consenting. Becket's action, we may say, involves both the passive action and the willed consent of an enacting, a waiting neither for something nor to do something but rather on what may or may not eventualize. But this paradoxical feature of Becket's action is not appropriately captured in the hermeneutic reminder of passivities in action, motivational fields, and affective influences because this vocabulary, even though it can accommodate dialectic, cannot hold both aspects of Becket's action in suspension simultaneously. The elusive feature here, then, is the specific kinds of paradox Becket's action involves.

A second remarkable feature of Becket's action is its presentation as an action that arises not out of an ignorance that is remediable but out of an invincible not knowing. Becket must act in the light of ends he scarcely comprehends—to overcome temptation, to bear witness, to accomplish a spiritual metamorphosis. But more seriously, he must act according to a pattern and according to a design without ever being able to know either. Unlike the dancer who in following the measured movement of his or her partner accomplishes the design of the ballet without knowing its fuller pattern, Becket must conform to a figure he does not know and can never know. Talk of a cognitive component in action as "complex" is not an instructive way of talking about such a feature.

A third obscure feature of Becket's act is its temporal specification. Although the hermeneutic account takes a step beyond the merely formal talk of a temporal instant in analytic description and tries to incorporate a richly existential account of the temporalization of action, the hermeneutic discussion does not capture the specific peculiarities in the time of Becket's act. For this act is said to be not in time at all. It is, rather, situated in a "critical moment" in the etymological sense of a moment of judgment which takes place "always, now, and here" (MC, 61), a time described as "too late / For action, too soon for contrition" (73); it is a time seeming to lack duration, where "we wait, and the time is short / But waiting is long" (58). Becket characterizes the time of his act when he says "out of time my decision is taken" (79). In short, the time of Becket's action is not time in some usual sense at all, but an intersection of time and eternity, a timeless gathering of historical, mythical, and cosmic times.

Finally, still another feature of Becket's action needs attention, and again it is one that a hermeneutic account does not capture appropriately. Becket acts, we have noted, for a variety of obscure but very cogent ends. One of the goals of Becket's action is to make an end, a theme that reverberates in other descriptions found elsewhere in Eliot's poetry. Here to make an end is neither to die nor to learn how to die. It is rather to act in such a way that one will be—of all things—worthy to die."All my life / I have waited. Death will come only when I am worthy" (75), we remember Becket saying. Being worthy here, however, is not the result of the agent's effort but the transforming effect on the agent of the advent of death. Moreover, the particularly enigmatic element here is the further suggestion that Becket is to act, that is, to make an end, in such a way that his end makes him worthy, transforms his being in transforming his beginnings—"in my end is my beginning." We have, then, another reflection of the earlier view that Becket's act must be a response to something he must wait upon, a response that if adequate both changes his present status (he is rendered worthy to die) and mysteriously and retroactively transforms his beginnings. Even the phenomenological descriptions of action which unwind from the uses of dialectic in the hermeneutic account leave this centrally important peculiarity of acting to make an end just as unrepresented as the other three features—the specific paradox of Becket's action, an action without knowledge, and an action at a moment of timeless gatherings.

Intentional Actions and Philosophical Idioms

In this final section I move away from the dramatic particulars of Becket's puzzling action in *Murder in the Cathedral* and return to our starting point with a poetic generality in the text from "East Coker." Our initial move was to illustrate what seemed to be the point of that text in the details of an extended example that dramatized certain enigmatic features in Becket's decision to wait on what might eventualize. We then made a long detour by way of two representative contemporary accounts of human action with the aim of identifying and then drawing on both analytic and hermeneutic conceptual resources for understanding such complicated cases of putative intentional actions like Becket's. However rich each of these contrasted accounts proved, neither by itself nor both together spoke pointedly enough to what the poetic texts present. My point is not that Becket's action is a counterexample to these accounts, although

I think this is true in many respects. Rather, my aim is to show how the poetic representation here of a peculiar kind of action is not a representation of what action is but a presentation of what action might be. More specifically, I suggest that many of the peculiarities of Becket's action are puzzling not because they are only incompletely describable on analytic or hermeneutic terms but because they can work such an effect on readers and audiences that the very terms in which both analytic and hermeneutic accounts present human action seem strongly inappropriate. In short, the poetic representation of Becket's action I will be taking as an invitation to consider new idioms for circumventing old impasses. These idioms in turn may allow those who would explore them to bring into focus some cardinal aspects of some human action which cannot be discerned clearly on either of the vocabularies we have been scrutinizing.

In what follows I suggest, in a more pragmatic than demonstrative way, that several general features of Becket's action are probably features of an important class of human actions, and perhaps even of many human actions altogether. My point is that critically entertaining such a possibility, a possibility arising out of the very rich detail in poetic representations of action rather than out of philosophical arguments as such, requires changing the usual idiom of both analytic and hermeneutic reflections on action.

In "East Coker," Part III, immediately following the passage we begin with—"I said to my soul, be still, and wait"—is one of the few but extremely important extended citations from other works to which Eliot wanted to call attention. Thus, just as with his protracted reference to Juliana of Norwich's *Cloud of Unknowing*, the *Bhagavad Gita*, and Sir Thomas Elyot's *The Gouverneur*, Eliot here cites with some variations part of a passage from John of the Cross's *Ascent of Mount Carmel*. Here the reader will need to recall the passage that begins, "You say I am repeating / Something I have said before."

Now, these are difficult sayings to understand. And whatever sense we manage to make of them in the restricted context of filling out the background of Becket's waiting, these sayings could hardly be taken to apply as such to central features of intentional action. Yet I think these peculiar lines, together with those that immediately precede them, do present a challenging suggestion about at least some features of intentional action which much contemporary philosophical theory continues to overlook. Most of these features can be indicated generally after the example of the poetic presentation not so much as motivational systems or individual desires, or as causal and volitional elements of action, or even as cognitive and conative aspects of proximate and immediate intentions, but more generally as negativities. However, to capture some of the detail required here to show any philosophical interest such an overly general description might include, we need to recall now, in the context of these more general presentations in Eliot's poetry, just where the analytic and hermeneutic descriptions appear unsatisfactory.

Thus, on the analytic account we may say generally that actions such as deciding to wait are intentional in that those events called proximate effects issue from antecedent nonactional events called proximate causes or immediate intendings. These immediate intendings in turn are mental spatio-temporal particulars called attitudes, which take properties as their objects. The cognitive complex of intending as an attitude is a master-storied representation of waiting as a planned activity together with a guidance and self-correcting monitoring system; its conative complex is a motivational operation of a production set through the completion of the activity.

We have already seen how a much fuller exposition of this view does not accommodate central features of Becket's decision to wait. The point now is to see that the summary description leaves virtually no room for several important features of intentional action in general, namely, the features I have alluded to abstractly as negativities. With Eliot's poetic texts now taking the place of the more restricted dramatic portrait, we may perhaps indicate four general features of many intentional actions this account either does not describe or simply overlooks.

Analytic accounts such as Brand's sophisticated causal naturalism make no room first for the suggestion in these poetic texts that much intentional action involves not so much a cognitive element as a lack of knowledge. Some agents, that is, seem to act intentionally yet without, strictly speaking, knowing what they are doing. Second, some intentional actions arise not from interest but from disinterestedness. Third, some intentional actions seem to be directed without regard for consequence. And finally, some such action does not seem properly describable just in terms of continuous causal agency in that these actions are more like letting go, surrendering, succumbing—uninitiated actions. Here, then, are four negative features that are important aspects of some intentional actions and yet go largely unaddressed in many analytic accounts: intentionally acting without knowledge, without interest, without consideration of consequences, and with a movement of release rather than one of initiative.

Instead of a naturalized causal account, a sophisticated hermeneutic version of human action such as we find in Ricoeur's account is more of a reflective and dialectical description centered on volition. Thus, again, on such a hermeneutic view deciding to wait is an intentional action in that while comprising both passive and active elements, it satisfies essential conditions (including passage through stages of deliberation about ends, mental and verbal expression, imaginative variations on possible action strategies, first-person self-addressed injunctions, and unexplained volitional components that initiate intentional action), it necessarily involves symbolic mediation and requires for its articulation as part of a conceptual pattern interpretive and teleological understanding as well as causal explanation.

Again, we have seen how this account does not satisfactorily describe certain features of Becket's action. But further, we can now claim that it leaves out more general features of many intentional actions. For when we reread Eliot's text with such a description before us, the suggestion arises that some intentional action may well involve no fulfillment of intention at all. Rather, the immediate intendings of some agent may well undergo transformation instead of fulfillment. Further, some intentional action may not be properly describable as satisfying essential conditions, since talk of essences even in the eidetic idiom of phenomenology involves a commitment to invariant contents that many intentions may not involve. Third, the hermeneutic account awards a central place to talk about the self whether in terms of capacities of the self, self-addressed injunctions, or deliberations of a self. But the suggestion here is that some intentional action may well be independent of talk about the self, at least in such a transcendental idiom, requiring in its stead another idiom for making sense of selfless frames of mind, of selfless agents. And finally, the hermeneutic account complements the analytic view with its insistence on the role of passivity in the nature of action. But again this point is not so much invalid—for many actions do involve such a component—as lacking purchase on what seems to be an important feature of many intentional actions, namely, the *active* consent to certain passivities that are not merely undergone, as the hermeneutic account would have it, but in some sense assumed. Thus, four more possible features of much intentional action come into view: its active passivities, its nondependence on a transcendental self, its nonessential contents, and its frequent nonfulfilled character.

The suggestion, then, in thinking twice about certain poetic representations not of what action is but of what it might be, comes to a series of negativities which neither the naturalized idiom of analytic causal accounts nor the transcendental idiom of reflexive volitional accounts seems to be able to capture adequately.

Return then, briefly to Eliot's text for the suggestions of several positive features of intentional action. These features are closely related to the kind of phenomenon one of Eliot's commentators has isolated in the play of opposites at the opening of "Little Gidding": "midwinter spring," "cold that is the heart's heart," and an epithet that echoes in Wallace Stevens, "the unimaginable / Zero summer."[12] "These co-existing opposites are not like the paradoxes of the *via negativa* ('Our only health is the disease'), and they are very different from the intensifying negatives of the sestina

[12]Eliot 1970:41.

('the withering of withered flowers'). Their effect is to hold in tension opposing qualities, without resolving or reconciling them, and in such a way that the negative intensifies the positive. Thus the stress falls upon 'spring'; and 'Zero' carries the mind to 'a summer beyond sense.' This is neither negation nor transcendence, but an intensification of what is actual, or an expansion of the actual towards the ideal."[13]

In our context, the suggestion is that some intentional action may be viewed as neither inaction nor action but as the intensification of certain enacted negativities such as the ones just pointed out. For example, Thomas is neither agent nor patient but an actively motionless instrument of a supposed providential pattern that in him reaches out to his historical community and, through dramatic reenactment in fiction, to Eliot's community of playgoers in 1934 and to his spectators and readers thereafter.

More generally, in the context of the poetic presentations of action we may say that, besides the negativities that a more adequate account of intentional action needs to address, there are as well certain positive features of such action which these negativities intensify. We can catch sight of some of these by recalling other texts from the poetry. Two passages deserve renewed attention here.

Consider first the beginning of "Little Gidding," Part III, I rewrote as prose in Chapter 2. This passage raises the suggestion that a satisfactory positive description of intentional action must include some account of at least three elements. First, some intentional action is deeply implicated in a complex mental state, a state of detachment we may perhaps call evenness of mind, equanimity. Here, some intentional action requires such equanimity for its execution. Second, some intentional action also includes certain neglected central features that are closely linked with the transformation of its own accompanying awareness from a self-centered state to a selfless one, a selfless consciousness. And finally, this evenness of mind, together with a movement toward selflessness in some intentional action, issues preeminently in an ethical domain of values that are neither individual and private nor public and social but in both actual and symbolic senses communal and participatory, a very general if not universal solidarity.

The second passage, part of which we have also seen earlier, is from very early in *Four Quartets*, a text composed not long after *Murder in the Cathedral*—"Burnt Norton," Part III. This passage, like the first, involves many aspects that cannot engage us here. One aspect, however, is its suggestiveness with respect to three further positive features of many intentional actions much current philosophical theory seems to overlook. A striking feature is the accent again on stillness. The suggestion for us is that besides a conative complex a less inappropriate description of much

[13]Moody 1977.

intentional action needs to be attentive to what I have been describing as a certain release, a letting go, a moment of neither action nor inaction. Further, we find in this passage a strong reinforcement of the earlier suggestion that talk about the cognitive complex of intentional action needs renewed scrutiny in the light of some intentional action arising not from knowledge but from at best a quasi-cognitive background—"I cannot say . . . I cannot say"—which issues nonetheless in a kind of epistemological courage, an acting without knowing enough. Finally, the passage brings together some of the paradoxical comments about the temporal character of intentional action. Here the suggestion is that neither the formal analytic nor the informal existential analysis of time can do justice to some temporal peculiarities of intentional action, its involvement through memory and imagination with past and future but more its apparent intersection with timeless states where history is caught up in what one is tempted to call perduring cosmological puzzles. Rather, the temporal character of some intentional action would seem to involve suspended rather than continuous moments—moments, as Eliot says, out of time, whatever these could be, where time becomes a balance of infinite motions.

The rich detail, then—not just of Eliot's concrete and dramatic representation in *Murder in the Cathedral* of Thomas à Becket's quasi-historical action of deciding to wait but especially of his lyrical yet abstract presentation in *Four Quartets* of what action might be—suggests the need for a wider consideration of certain negative and positive features of many intentional actions to which neither current analytic nor hermeneutic reflection does sufficient justice. Further, the need cannot be met merely by reworking these accounts to make them more comprehensive, because each is articulated in an idiom that illumines important aspects of intentional action only at the cost of occluding certain of its cardinal features. Rather, we require here, if not a new idiom that is neither just naturalistic and causal nor just volitional and reflexive, at least an idiom that is capable of articulating some of what this rich poetry metaphorically suggests to us. Most important, such an idiom, I suspect, would require an extended critical analysis of the alternative ontologies at work here in the perplexing but challenging light of poetic fictions. (See a sketch only in Appendix 5C, "Actions, Intentions, Events, and Properties.") On the evidence of the preliminary analyses here, taking the critical measure of such a suggestion seems to require an ontology richly imaginative enough to deal with situational complexes comprising both states of affairs and courses of events as invariants, and individuals, properties and relations, and location as uniformities, but allowing strangely of intermittencies and uniformities that accommodate incongruities. Or perhaps we require an idiom for aimless projects, empty intentions, ineffectual causes, fruitless actions, and inconsequential results—in short, an idiom for many of what are still among our most important intentional actions. It is this "our" and the nature of the subject and its fictions to which I now turn, once again with the help of another extended case study of poetic fictions.

Appendix 5A   Action, Immediate Intending, Cognition, and Conation

ACTION AND INTENTIONAL ACTION

Brand first proposes an initial distinction between what people do and what happens to them—each is taken to be an instance of an event and each is called an action rather than an act in a partially stipulative way. Second, an agent performs some actions (say, Becket raises his arm in the cathedral) while knowing what he is doing without observation, whereas an agent performs other actions (say, Becket raises his arm in the cathedral to ward off a sword blow) not knowing what he is doing without observation. This Wittgensteinian distinction is already familiar in a looser version in Ricoeur's use of Anscombe. What is fresh here is the gloss on "observation." Observation is not required to know what one is doing when what one is doing involves bodily movement or mental movement only. Observation, however, is required to know what one is doing when, besides movement, action also includes the bodily movement's causal consequences.[14]

The actions an agent can perform while knowing what he or she is doing without observation are said to be intentional actions, whereas their counterparts are called nonintentional. Intentional actions include the element of "an action being planned prior to execution," whereas nonintentional actions lack this element. Nonintentional actions include various kinds, some of which overlap. Thus we have actions that may be rote, habitual, automatic, routine, involuntary, mistaken, accidental, responsible, and so on. Brand is mainly concerned, however, with the first two kinds. In short:

> B1.   An action is a type of event, and an intentional action is a planned
>   action.

More specifically, Brand argues that "it is highly plausible that a human action is associated with a sequence of causally related events" (6) regardless of whether the action is a bodily event like Becket's raising his

[14]Brand 1984:5. Further references are given in the text.

arm or a mental event like Becket's deciding to wait, and regardless of whether the event is simple, like these actions, or complex, like Becket raising his arm to signal the priest. The problem for Brand is to identify the action with a specific part of the causal sequence. Is the action the entire causal sequence, or the initial event in the causal sequence, or the "bodily or mental effect of the antecedent mental event" (6)? Although other variations are possible, the major responses (with a necessary temporal specification here omitted) can be put under five rough headings.

The first theory, that action is the entire causal sequence—call it the volitional theory (VT)—reduces action to "causally related nonactional events" thus translating action sentences into nonaction ones. The only ontological categories required are persons, events, and relations. Historically, this view is ascribable (where "volition" equals nonactional mental event) to Mill (1872) and Austin (1873) in the nineteenth century as well as to Hart (1968) and Thomson (1977) in recent work. More formally, where S ranges over persons, A over event types, B over types of behavior including some nonactions, and where ME stands for some unspecified nonactional mental event such as a wanting plus a believing, and MA for some unspecified mental action such as a willing, the volitional theory reads (7; with some small changes):

VT S's A-ing is an action if and only if there is an ME of S such that:
  i. ME caused S's B-ing,
  ii. ME is appropriate to S's A-ing, and
  iii. S's B-ing is associated with S's A-ing.

The second theory—call it the mental action theory (MAT)—can be ascribed to Berkeley (1713) where a "volition" refers to a mental action, Prichard (1949), and more recently to Aune (1979), Davis (1979), and Hornsby (1980). Here an action is "the cause of certain types of behaviour" (9). More formally:

MAT S's A-ing is an action if and only if there is a MA of S such that:
  i. MA caused S's B-ing, and
  ii. S's B-ing is associated with S's A-ing.

The third theory—call it the causal theory (CAT)—can be found in Hobbes, Locke, and Hume, and more recently in a large set of views deriving mainly from Davidson (1963) and most clearly illustrated in Goldman (1970). Here an action is "the effect of certain types of (mental) behaviour" (9). More formally:

CAT *S*'s *A*-ing is an action if and only if there is an *ME* of *S* such that:
   i. *ME* caused *S*'s *A*-ing, and
   ii. *ME* is appropriate to *S*'s *A*-ing.

A fourth theory, which is a variant of the third—call it the agency theory (AT)—also identifies the action as an effect; the cause, however, is taken not as a mental event as in (CAT) but as an agent or substantial self. Historically, the view can be ascribed to Reid and arguably to Berkeley, while more recent proponents include Chisholm (1976a) and R. Taylor (1966, 1974). More formally, letting *S* range over the self as substantial agent:

AT *S*'s *A*-ing is an action if and only if there is an *ME* of *SA* such that:
   i. *SA* causes *S*'s *A*-ing, and
   ii. *SA* is appropriate to *S*'s *A*-ing.

A final theory for our purposes—call it the social action theory (SAT)—identifies the action with rule-governed behavior within a social context (Melden 1956), and one for which responsibility can be ascribed to an agent (Hart 1948–49). More formally, letting *RGB* range over rule-governed behavior and *SC* over social contexts:

SAT *S*'s *A*-ing is an action if and only if there is an *SC* of *S* such that:
   i. *RGB* in *SC* causes *S*'s *A*-ing;
   ii. *RGB* is not viciously circular, and
   iii. *SC* is appropriate to *S*'s *A*-ing.

Each of these theories, however, faces difficulties. The volitional theory's apparent ontological economy—its reductive claim— does not resist scrutiny and therefore cannot be a serious rival to at least the mental action theory and the two kinds of causal theories. The mental action theory, however, is counterintuitive (it violates ordinary intuition about ascription of moral responsibility) and still lacks a persuasive account of willing as "the mental action that initiates the causal sequence" (15). The agency theory, in turn, has a similar problem with providing a persuasive account of just what it could mean for an agent to be a substance having causal-like relations to the events that are its behavior, and how an agent can be caused to act without being necessitated to act. And the social action theory is too narrow in that some actions do not seem to require a social context (Geach 1960) and seem to involve vicious circularity (Kripke 1982) in appealing to rule following (which is arguably already in action) in defining action. The details of these analyses persuade Brand to favor some version of the causal theory as the most plausible one and the most consistent with what he takes to be a convincing detailed picture of human action (Thalberg 1977). Accordingly:

B2. "an action is a causal sequence
a. which in the cases of bodily action includes overt behaviour, and
b. which was in turn initiated by a non-actional mental event of a specified sort." (16)

Although most persuasive, the theory faces difficulties of its own. The main problem is causal deviance, whether in the form of a problem about the connection between the antecedent mental event and the initiation of a neurobiological causal chain linked to overt behavior ("antecedential waywardness") or in the form of a problem about unintended consequences of the activity, which has begun appropriately ("consequential waywardness"). The first concerns the definition of action, the second that of intentional action (17–18).

Antecedential waywardness cannot be left to the special sciences because, besides the details of causal series, an account of what is a normal or characteristic causal series is also required. And such an account requires not just a view about statistical prevalence but also a criterion for normalcy. But this kind of criterion can arise only from the conceptual analysis of action, from philosophical reflection. Solving the first problem involves defining action in such a way that no "causal space" can intervene between the antecedent mental event and the inception of the causal chain leading to behavior. Accordingly, the notion of a proximate cause is introduced. Thus, one event remotely causes another when the first causes the second and there are causally intervening events, whereas one event proximately causes another when the first continuously causes the second and there are no intervening events. Formally, where e ranges over events:

"S's A-ing during t is a continuous causal chain . . . if and only if there is a chain of casually related events, $e_1, e_2, \ldots e_n$ such that:
i. S's A-ing during t is identical with this causal chain and
ii. there is no S^*, distinct from S, non-actional mental event ME^*, and duration t^*, where $t^* \geq t$, such that S^*'s having ME^* during t^* is identical with e_i, an event in the causal chain." (22)

This formulation, for all its prolixity, leads nonetheless to a useful articulation of the notion of proximate cause:

"ME proximately causes S's A-ing during t, where S's A-ing during t is a continuous causal chain." (22)

And with the notion of proximate cause in hand, the causal theory in Brand's version (CAT-B) can be more fully formulated as a schema in such a way as to obviate the problem of antecedential waywardness:

CAT-B S's A-ing during t is an action if and only if there is a nonactional mental event ME of S such that:

   i. ME proximately causes S's A-ing during t, and
   ii. ME is appropriate to S's A-ing during t. (20,27)

This schema in turn leads to a definition of the concept of action which both specifies the mental antecedent ME and provides the conditions of appropriateness. Specifying the mental antecedent, that is, the nonactional antecedent mental event, involves specifying the antecedent's "attitude type," whereas specifying the conditions of appropriation involves specifying "the content of the mental antecedent" (20). Thus, facing the issue of antecedential waywardness leads to a reformulation of the causal theory with the help of the notion of proximate causation, and this formulation leads to a clearer idea of what a definition of action must include. Accordingly:

B3. An action is an event "proximately caused by a non-actional mental event of a certain sort." (33)

Facing the second problem, consequential waywardness, involves articulating more clearly not the notion of action but that of intentional action, an action performed in following a plan. An "action plan" is first described as an ordered set that includes various dependency relations among action types in that one action type is causally necessary, or causally sufficient, or conventional for another and which both causal and conventional relations can hold among proposed actions (26–27). Intentional action is then defined accordingly:

"S's A-ing during t is an intentional action if and only if
   i. S's A-ing during t is an action; and
   ii. S has an action plan P to A during t such that his A-ing is included in P and he follows P in A-ing." (25)

Since, however, some intentional actions do not figure explicitly in a preconceived plan but are merely part of a pattern of intentional activity involving representations of focal actions in a plan, this initial definition needs to be broadened so as to make room for improvised actions within planned activity. Thus, the definition of intentional should also include within the notion of planned action some room for substituting one action for another, for improvising some action, and even for interrupting part of the action. After formalizing each of these Brand summarizes: "an action retains its status as intentional provided only that it is part of an action plan even if that plan is not instantiated in the manner originally conceived" (29). These qualifications when put together allow Brand to claim that the problem of consequential waywardness is thereby obviated.

> B4. An action is intentional if it is "either explicitly planned or part of a pattern of planned activity" (25) which may incorporate both focal points and unforeseeable eventualities.

Brand now turns to the task of specifying the nature of the proximate cause of action where "action" is understood in the context of his formulations of the causal theory and where it is assumed that, if not all action, certainly "a great deal" of human action is intentional.

IMMEDIATE INTENDING AS THE PROXIMATE CAUSE OF ACTION

Brand first reviews recent discussions of the proximate cause of action. One of the most important (Davidson 1963) is a version of the causal theory which identifies the antecedent to action as "a complex mental event" specified in terms of a pro-attitude. Davidson includes here "desires, wantings, urges, promptings, and a great variety of moral views, aesthetic principles, economic prejudices, social conventions and public and private goals and values" (68), plus "a belief" (34). The notion of "pro-attitude," however, has been criticized as too general and providing not the proximate cause but its "mental background" only. The antecedent to action, however, can be taken as an intention to perform an action here and now (Sellars 1973), what Brand calls "immediate intending." This is an improvement because it is less general. But it is still not specific enough to court as the proximate cause of action because it does not specify "what properties mental events of this type have" (35). In fact Brand argues that the fundamental problem of action theory is to specify the properties of the one event type that proximately causes action whether mental or physical.

In the idea that immediate intending initiates action, intention is taken controversially as a primitive from which other mental events can be analyzed, and intention sentences are understood also controversially as requiring no special logic. But even when these claims are accepted provisionally we have no more than an account of intentions in terms of relational properties instead of one in terms of what Brand calls structural or internal properties. What is required, Brand thinks, is "some property of the intention itself" or "properties immediate intention has in virtue of which it alone proximately causes action" (38–39).

To overcome this problem it might be claimed that mental events such as intending cannot be characterized "structurally" but relationally only, that is, functionally in terms of the roles they play in the acquisition and use of thought and language. If functionalism is the view that "mental events are to be characterized in terms of their actual and counterfactual causal relations to input events, output events, and other mental events" (41; after Block 1980 and Fodor 1981), then we must distinguish between folk psychological functionalism and scientific psychological functionalism on the one hand, and between surface and depth functionalism on the other. Only scientific psychological functionalism has recourse to computational theories, which Brand holds to be the best available scientific psychological theory today, and only depth functionalism includes the idea that causal relations are only part and not all of what is knowable about mental events. Each of these is more plausible than its counterpart. But the view in question is neither scientific nor depth functionalistic and hence for Brand remains "insufficiently informative" (41).

Brand criticizes what he calls the underlying difficulty with folk psychological and surface functionalist accounts of intention, namely, the claim that "a theory of action is dependent on a general account of the nature of mental events" (42). Brand rejects this claim. So far as a theory of events is concerned, Brand thinks that action theory is "on the whole" neutral, that is, not logically committed both with respect to the ontological status of mental events and to the relations between mental events and physical events. Thus, whether functional roles can finally explain mental events and whether the relationship between mental events and brain events is to be captured in, say, a token-token identity theory whereby every particular mental event is identified with some particular physical event action theory leaves open. Action theory can proceed without resolving such problems, just as it can proceed without providing a final account of the nature of causation.

Having argued the need for a more internal account of the nature of immediate intending than available in the literature, Brand now advances his own hypothesis. The proximate cause of action is immediate intending, which is construed as a complex mental event consisting of both cognitive and conative elements, "a representation of the future course of action and the motivation to undertake that course" (46). Thus:

> B5. An action is the proximate effect of a specific type of proximate antecedent mental event called an immediate intending whose internal properties include cognitive and conative complexes.

INTENTION, COGNITION, AND ACTION

With an initial description of action in place, together with a discussion of both intending and believing and intending and desiring, Brand now moves to transform the cognitive feature he takes as common to all action whether intentional or not, namely, the "guidance and monitoring of ongoing activity" (173), from a folk psychological to a scientific concept. His approach, however, is not to advocate specific scientific theories but, by using a case study method, to propose certain necessary conceptual perspectives for a philosophical theory of action. Accordingly, he examines critically a series of prominent psychological theories.

The first of these is "the ideo-motor theory" (Greenwald 1970 and Goldman 1976), a theory that defines the cognitive component of immediate intention as memory or response images that store information about action types and guide ongoing activity. On this theory, the intention does not stop when action begins but continues until action terminates. Further, of the two elements here, guidance and monitoring, the first is taken to be primary since monitoring depends on guidance but not vice versa. Finally, unlike William James's view (1890), which it resembles, the ideo-motor theory construes response images as necessary but not sufficient for action, thus leaving room for the eventual role of noncognitive features. Brand points out difficulties with this theory—a tension in the description of response images as both particular (events) and yet abstract (functional classes), the exact nature of the function of response images, and especially the scope of the theory that accounts for some actions but not for others. Even in the most plausible cases such as highly routinized sequential actions like knotting a necktie, other mechanisms than the ones the ideo-motor theory includes are required. And in simple cases such as shopping for food a single response image is not involved at all. So the ideo-motor theory is judged to be largely implausible.

A second theory, more abstract than the learning theoretic approach based on a mechanical model behind the ideo-motor theory, is called "the program theory of guidance" (see Miller, Galanter, and Pribram 1960). This theory relies on a computational approach based on a computer model. Specifically, the theory tries to provide a scientific functional account of output systems. On this view the cognitive component of immediate intention is to be understood in terms of Test-Operate-Test-Exit (TOTE) units, which can be arranged hierarchically to control a sequence (or "plan"), stored, and selected for execution. An example: "Suppose that I grasp a nail. Then my action consists of the following: I locate my hand and the nail in the perceptual field (Test); I close my finger around the nail (Operate); I again locate my hand and the nail in my perceptual field (Test); and I terminate my activity (Exit)" (180). Thus, to act is to execute a plan, and to perform a particular act is to choose among a set of programs, with the help of the valences or positive values of future activities (Lewin 1935, 1938), a particular plan for execution.

Despite some clear attractions, this computational model includes several difficulties. The program theory assumes wrongly that persons are always acting and hence the theory fails to distinguish nonactional activities like sleeping from actional ones like speaking. Moreover, key terms like "plan" and "value" remain at a folk psychologistic level. Further, the basic unit of analysis, the TOTE, is not depth functionalistic since it can be analyzed into more elementary phases. The model also fails to explain some overlearned actions like reciting the alphabet which require appeal either to ideo-motor mechanisms or to serial-chaining mechanisms. Further, the model is "viciously regressive" in that one stage of its explanatory unit for action—namely, "Operate"—is itself an action. And finally, the model fails to account for how action is initiated—it lacks a motivational component. Some of these difficulties disappear if the program theory is interpreted not as a theory of action but as a theory only of the guidance and monitoring of action. Thus Brand provides a brief description of some recent work (Rumelhart and Norman 1982) which corrects and extends the earlier account of simple activities like hammering a nail to complex ones like skilled typing by appealing to parallel processing and to higher-level functions than servomechanisms.

These two theories focus on the common cognitive element in the antecedent of action, "the neo-behaviourist learning theoretic concept of a response image and the computational idea of an abstract structural hierarchy of servomechanisms" (201). A final theory, the script theory (Schank and Abelson 1977,[15] Schank 1982), focuses on the common cognitive feature in the antecedent to intentional action. Briefly, this feature is taken to be the notion of "scripts and plans," a notion developed in work on artificial intelligence and the representation of stereotypic situations (Abelson 1981) involving event-sequences.

Although the script theory aims at providing a theory of how narratives are understood, Brand takes this theory in terms of human action in general. Thus, the folk notion of "following a plan" is to be transformed into the scientific notion of "having a representation." More formally:

> "(S) S's A-ing is an intentional action *only if S* has a representation for understanding a story in which he plays, with self awareness, the lead role and in which he performs an action of type *A*."
> (204)

The unit of analysis in this theory is the script, a complex routine, "a predetermined, stereotyped sequence of action that defines a well known situation" (204; citing SAB, 42). Scripts originate in less elaborate general forms called "plans." Although specific, they allow of different variations called "tracks," and scripts also are divided into "scenes" where variations are called "scenarios"—for example, the scenario of reading the menu versus that of asking the waiter's advice in the coffee shop as opposed

---

[15]Schank and Abelson 1977, hereafter cited as SAB.

to the hotel dining room track of the restaurant script in the plan of getting something to eat. Plans themselves, "although the operative representation when the activity is not sufficiently practical to be routinized" (211), are subordinated to three basic "long-range predispositions to act in certain ways": role themes, interpersonal themes, and life themes (205; SAB 131ff.). Acting intentionally on this model involves both memory of certain events that precede the present and imagining a future activity "within the constraints of a plan" (208). In both cases representation is involved. Thus, the distinctive cognitive feature of the antecedent to the immediate intention to act is complex representation.

Brand underlines difficulties in this theory with a view toward reformulation. One problem is that the theory does not specify that the intentional agent "thinks of himself in a first-person, self-referential way" (210), a feature the hypothesis (S) requires. Yet some scripted and planned activity is self-referential, so the theory should specify some mechanism to account for the feature if the theory is to have broad theoretical appeal. Another problem is that this theory does not include any discussion of its ontological commitments presumably to propositions that, if the theory is taken to include intentions, would for Brand have to be recast as a commitment to properties he favors as the objects of attitudes like intention. A further difficulty arises from the theory's failure to discriminate between kinds of goals (representations of prospective intentions for action) an agent can propose to him or herself—state goals (to be someone) versus action goals (to do something) on the one hand, and on the other instrumental versus terminal goals (213). Moreover, the theory is too narrow in that it cannot account for some actions being intentional by virtue of their "being included in a pattern of activity without being preconceived" (215) as, for example, in the cases of substituted or improvised actions.

In the light of these difficulties Brand proposes his revision:

> "(S*) 'S's A-ing is intentional if and only if;
>   i. S's A-ing is an action; and
>   ii. *either* S has a representation for understanding a story in which he plays, with self-awareness, the lead role and in which he performs an action of type A, *or* S's A-ing satisfies" versions of what Brand calls the substitutivity principle, the improvisation principle, and the interruption principle. (216–17)

With these revisions Brand claims that "an action . . . is intentional if it is a preconceived part of some story, no matter whether the story unfolds as represented" (217). Moreover, after a critical discussion of the artificial language the theory relies on for coding its information, Brand adds that the existence of "the cognitive structures hypothesized by script theory are independent of claims about the presentational languages used to encode information within these structures" (220; see Minsky 1975 and Hayes 1980).

The script theory, however, has also evolved since its first presentation, and in a final section Brand reflects on recent revisions to the key notions of scripts and plans. Rather than construing the elementary or atomic constituent representations of scripts and plans implausibly as "isomorphic to events in the world," a revised theory substitutes for that interpretation the idea that they are "representations of basic event types" which proceed not by specification of necessary and sufficient conditions but by family resemblance (222–23). Similarly, instead of taking the molecular constituents to be unified wholes (scripts) consisting of temporally ordered parts (scenes), experiments have shown that a revised theory should, rather, substitute the notion of "separable abstract scene-length chunks that can be ordered hierarchically" (235). Still, the details of these revisions do not require any changes in the scientific notion of a "plan," which Brand substitutes for the folk notion.

This substitution may not be possible since no satisfactory account is yet available for the key element in the theory, namely, central processing, which includes both memory and plan formation (229). Nevertheless, the cognitive component of immediate intention differs in an important way from central processes such as the fixation of a belief in that the first and not the second is "modular"; in other words, it is "domain specific" and its operations are mandatory, fast, "associated with fixed neural architecture, and . . . informationally encapsulated" (Fodor 1983). Thus, central processes have global properties that resist analysis, whereas modular systems do not. But to the degree that the cognitive component of prospective intention involves plan formation, which in turn is linked to central processes, the difficulty in explaining central process affects the task of scientifically explaining intentional action. But perhaps this objection can be overcome by some revised versions of the script theory of plan formation. Such plan formation (planning to do something), then, although less amenable to scientific explanation than, say, vision, is certainly more amenable than, say, practical reasoning (deciding to do something; 232–33).

In summary, the distinctive cognitive feature of intentional action is "the subject's having a representation of a story in which he performs this type of action" (235). This representation is not so much a matter of particular scenes and general scripts but of hierarchically ordered abstract scene-length chunks, that is, generalized scenes constructed into master representations with the help of contextual information and scripts as particular scene-length units (227–29). Thus, the cognitive component of the proximate cause of action is complex, for it involves both the monitoring and guidance of ongoing activity and, in the case of intentional action, the master representation of planned future activity. What remains to be added is the noncognitive component. Fortunately, given the present disarray in motivational psychology, Brand's account here is less extensive than his discussion of the cognitive component.

5A.4 IMMEDIATE INTENTION, CONATION, AND MOTIVATED ACTION

Like the cognitive component of the proximate cause of action, the conative component that alone can initiate action is also complex, involving a feature common to all action and further features common to all intentional action. However, unlike the transformation of the folk concept of the cognitive component into a scientific one, a complete transformation here is not yet possible. For the key discipline, motivational psychology, does not yet have a tenable scientific theory available for such a transformation.

Brand begins with a presentation of the folk psychological view of conation, namely, the view that an agent performs an action only when moved or motivated to do so by some antecedent mental event that has conative properties (238). The basis of such a view is intuition. Folk psychology here has to explain both the initiation of nonintentional and intentional action as well as, for the latter case, the conative properties that initiate plan selection and those that result in following a plan. Moreover, following a plan must be kept distinct for acting according to a plan out of mere luck. To follow a plan the agent "must instantiate an hierarchical structure of action types, *and* he must be aware, in some sense, of what he is doing" (240). Brand now turns to consider several proposed explanations of conative properties, first neobehaviorist theories and then a computational one.

According to drive theory, response to stimuli determines motivated features of behavior. This theory is a modified or neobehaviorist rather than a radical or classical behaviorist view in that it makes room for more than mechanistic elements (Hull 1943). Thus, the stimulus-response (S-R) motivation is seen to arise from a combination of the habits and drives of the agent, where habit is a learned action type and drive is what activates behavior. "Drive . . . provides the energy for behaviour (action) and habit determines the direction" (234). Later (Hull 1951) the notion of incentive was added to this account to explain motivation arising from sources other than mere "tissue deficiency" or homeostatic imbalances. Drive was used to explain the conative aspect of immediate intention, whereas habit was linked with the cognitive aspect. However, experimental evidence has shown that each of the four properties of drive— being rooted in biologic needs, contributing only to the energizing and not to the directionof behavior, being nonspecific (not divisible into types), and drive reduction being the basis of reinforcement—is chimerical. Further, the attempt to substitute incentive for drive has not succeeded (Spence 1956), partly because conceptual difficulties can be added to these empirical ones, for example, the ontological problem of linking properties of physiological states such as drive and incentive to properties of mental states such as having an immediate intention, and the fact that the conceptual framework of drive theory derives from nonhuman behavior (rats) and hence omits the distinction between intentional and nonintentional action. Thus, drive theory cannot adequately explain the conative features of human action.

Unlike drive theory, which focused on mechanistic aspects of motivation using S-R sequences as units of analysis, expectancy theory (Tolman 1932, 1952) stresses its cognitive aspects and uses larger-scale units (molar behavior such as eating in a restaurant) as units of analysis. This theory distinguishes antecedent physiological conditions (drives) from "dispositions to undertake consummatory behaviour" (needs) and elaborates a series of relations between the two. Moreover, expectancy theory awards a central place for beliefs and values and makes room for a series of selections in the motivational process. Thus, two elements generate responses—belief or expectancy (a cognitive one) and values or valence (a motivational one). Brand summarizes the theory as follows: "a subject's immediate physiological condition and envîronment, together with standing conditions such as genetic makeup, age, and so on, cause the arousal of needs. These needs contribute to the formation of a belief (expectancy)-value matrix, in which the subject weighs his beliefs (expectations) about what he can do and the values he places on each type of action. As a result of this process the subject restructures his thought about the available options. The process continues until he narrows the field to one. Thereupon, he acts" (250).

But once again there are problems. The key notion of "motivational construct called the valence of an *expectandum*" is not satisfactorily explained, for on the most plausible interpretation valence is a disguised notion of preference, and preference, Brand claims, cannot initiate action (254). Moreover, whatever the interest of the emphasis on molar units as basic, expectancy theory overemphasizes the cognitive element in action. Further, the neobehaviorist background to expectancy theory as well as to drive theory—that is, the assumption that no mental events exist and that all intervening elements between motivation and action can be operationally defined in terms of observed behavior—is no longer taken as a plausible basis for a scientific psychology. Consequently, Brand moves to a third kind of theory based on computational rather than mechanistic or cognitive frameworks, the theory of production systems.

The conative element can be partly explained, if not completely, by various production systems theories. One of these, adaptive control theory (Anderson 1976, 1983), Brand considers in detail. This theory comprises "a series of conditional rules that codify procedural knowledge," that is, knowledge of how to do something as opposed to declarative knowledge or knowledge of a proposition (256). Production theories hold that declarative knowledge is stored in a network of propositional representations and is consciously accessible, whereas procedural knowledge is stored in a list of production rules for the action in question, a production system, and is not consciously accessible. Global central processes are involved in both. But if those that are connected to declarative knowledge seem resistant to analysis, by contrast those central processes involved in procedural knowledge do seem analyzable.

Three features of a production system are especially noteworthy. Such a system interacts with memory—that is, both declarative and production memory are linked with active or working memory. But such a system, as a set of translation rules for putting information into a workable form for motor systems, neither produces information (the input system) nor yields action (the output system) but interfaces with both. Finally, a production system is not self-starting. The nature of production systems in general, and these features in particular, lead to the conclusion that production systems, though irrelevant both to plan selection and to the source of motivation, nonetheless do explain "the transmission of motivation. . . . in general, there is no explanation of the selection of production sets" (260). In short, a production theory system explains plan following, but leaves plan selection, the onset of motivation, "the lead antecedent," unexplained.

Brand now summarizes. "Scripts" or "large-chunked centrally located schemata" are stored in declarative memory. "A script is selected by means of a motivational system. . . . Each scene, or each segment of a scene, calls forth a production set stored in production memory. Production sets interact with working memory, which results in the activation of motor schemata. These motor schemata guide bodily movement" (261–62) with the help of peripheral schemata. We have, then, scripts (or "patterns for recognizing sets of features"), motor schemata, and peripheral schemata, together with memory and production sets (or "models for skills") and the mysterious "motivational system." More simply, production sets here are viewed as intermediate structures between scripts and motor schemata.

Brand finally turns to several proposals about the nature of motivational systems based on generalizations from studies on animal learning (Masterson and Crawford 1982). The crucial work is an ethological analysis of the natural rather than laboratory behavior of rats, which, when wary of danger, first ready an entire set of avoidance responses and then, depending on environmental cues, activate one member of this set. The extrapolation to human behavior proceeds on the assumption that "persons have innate motivation systems" (256) which include but also extend beyond the innate response system of rats. Appropriate environmental conditions prime "one or more" of these motivation systems. "Intentional cues serve then to activate a type of response. Selection is based on past reinforcement. Sometimes a motivational system directly leads to action . . . provides satisfaction of the lead antecedent in a production set. This is motivated non-intentional action. Sometimes, however, motivational systems yield an output that filters through as stored, large-chunked schema. This is motivated intentional action" (265–66). This comes to the view, more simply, that environmental stimuli generate motivation by operating on activated innate and species-typical response sets (266). Conceding that such an account faces problems in its own right—providing a formalism that will lead to the construction of a model, and the difficulty in describing and categorizing many human actions that seem to be classifiable under an indefinite number of headings ("the plasticity of human action")—Brand concludes that his proposal can only be properly evaluated in the actual attempt to construct working models (268).

Appendix 5B   Action, Imagination, Discourse, and Causes

ACTION, IMAGINATION, AND DISCOURSE

Ricoeur's recent account of action is not his only one. For besides his three-volume thesis on the phenomenology of the will (1950), two other discussions from the mid–1970s which he refers to explicitly in *Time and Narrative* also require attention.

In his article "L'imagination dans le discours et dans l'action" (1976), Ricoeur provides a summary account of action under the adage "no action without imagination" (217). In this context "imagination" is used generally although not uncritically, as Ricoeur's preliminary treatment of four uses of the term indicates (208–10). The main points, however, concern the role of the Kantian notion of *productive imagination* with respect to three elements of action.

Ricoeur distinguishes among three levels: that of the project for action, the motivation for action, and the capacity for action. The project, and what Ricoeur specifies as the "objective" of noematic content of the project, involves "a certain schematization of the network of ends and means," a schema of what the agent wants to do. Consequently, the schema is oriented toward the future. Further, action involves a motivational process that may consist in the organization of a variety of different elements such as "desires . . . ethical norms . . . professional rules, social customs, or strongly personal values" (217). And finally, action also includes the notion of capacity or power, the idea of actually being able to carry out what I have both planned and intended to do (218). In each of these three elements imagination is at work, whether in anticipating alternative action schemes, in providing scenarios where different motives can be compared, or in working imaginative variations on how I can exercise the power to act of which I am immediately certain.

What is still missing, however, is a more detailed analysis of human action which would fill out the summary discussion Ricoeur relies on in *Time and Narrative*. Ricoeur tries to provide this fuller account in his monograph "Le discours de l'action" (1977), in which he organizes his discussion around three different tasks: a conceptual description of action, a reflection on the propositions that express action, and an analysis of certain arguments involved in an action strategy.

The first task turns on the now familiar claim from *Time and Narrative* that "action" is implicated in an extensive network of concepts. This network is taken here to include "intention, goal, reason for acting, motive, desire, preference, choice, agent, and responsibility" (5). These notions are seen to be essentially nonempirical concepts and categories that arise within a public domain of ordinary talk about action and not just within a private realm of intuitions about the lived experience of individual persons. Ricoeur follows in the wake of much ordinary-language reflection on the later Wittgensteinian themes of the *Investigations* (1953; notably pars. 611–60) and stresses the distinction of actions and reason as opposed to movements and causes.

The second task relies mainly on a reading of speech-act theory to articulate the structures of the propositions in which ordinary-language concepts of action are embedded. Thus, the actions in question here are centrally those in which the agent is a speaker who does something precisely in and by saying something. The concept of intention at issue in the analysis of action is one an agent declares or can declare in the first person (8). Here Ricoeur underlines not so much the classification of performatives in Austin (1962) as Searle's work on illocutionary acts (1969). Nonetheless, he explicitly keeps a certain critical distance from both the particular conceptual analyses to be found in early ordinary-language philosophy and the "propositional analyses" in speech-act theory.

The "properly discursive character" of action, Ricoeur says, appears when the play of question and answer, whence talk about action arises ("what did you do? I did . . . "), is understood to comprise the action strategies of ends and means (10). This discursive domain is larger than either the conceptual or the propositional, for it includes the concatenation of means and ends in making decisions. In this area Ricoeur examines the logic of action to determine whether a certain lived understanding of action is prior to the role of action in decision theory or vice versa.

ACTION, INTENTION, AND REASON

Ricoeur, then, sees talk about action as involving three levels of analysis: the "conceptual, the propositional, and the discursive" (10). He equates the first two with the "syntax" of action and the third with the "semantics" of action (86). This tripartite schema differs from the later one in *Time and Narrative*, where action is said to exhibit semantic, symbolic, and temporal structures. But the two triads are closely related. For what we find in this earlier and fuller account is a description that in large measure underlies the later discussion. We have an interest, then, in looking at this earlier account more closely. Consider first Ricoeur's discussion of the cardinal notions of action, intention, and reason.

An *action* is to be distinguished from a movement or event (as in Melden 1961), for an action is something I do, whereas a movement is something that happens, an observable event. The phenomenon of kinesthetic sensations does not undermine this distinction: Ricoeur, with Austin, holds these and their relations to movement to be just as fanciful as the relations of "sense data" to perception. Actions are prior to such movements in the way objects are prior to sense data. Nor do desires underlie action, for the relevant desires are taken here as desires to act. Thus, action depends on no observation of any internal phantom states, on no prior knowledge, for example, of how to raise my arm; when I raise my arm I exercise a capacity rather than apply any knowledge gained from the inner observation of sensations. My action is not a verifiable assertion but a kind of event known without observation (Anscombe 1963) and involving practical not theoretical knowledge.

Ricoeur adds to these initial points Danto's distinction between basic or immediate and derived or mediated actions, which he carries over into his discussion in *Time and Narrative*. Danto's distinction between two kinds of action derives from the epistemological difference between two kinds of knowledge (Chisholm 1976a). Ricoeur raises the question of whether this distinction is not easier to make in epistemology than in action theory. And he claims that the distinction in action theory itself is based on a logical argument that turns on the impossibility of an infinite regress. Yet he notices that the logical argument itself rests on "an implicit phenomenology" of "I can" (30)—an agent's capacity to act consists in a repertoire of basic actions. Here "capacity" or "power" seems to function in the realm of action in the way that "evidence" functions in the epistemological realm.

Ricoeur's second cardinal notion is *intention*. He is aware that linguistic analyses of action resist any attempts either to identify a metaphysical mental antecedent to physical movement or to formulate some "final cause" (31). The linguistic strategy is, rather, to link intention to some characteristic of a public rather than private fact by scrutinizing the putatively cardinal uses of the word "intention" in ordinary language. Following Anscombe, Ricoeur recalls the differences among three expressions: "I intend to do something or other," "I did this intentionally," and "This was done with such and such an intention." The last two are to be preferred on the grounds that they obviate appeals to private entities. Further, with respect to the second use, "calling an action intentional . . . involves excluding explanation in terms of a cause" in the play of question and answer in a language game and appealing rather to reasons (33–34). Finally, the third sentence involves the notion of "intention in which" and introduces a strategic element into the understanding of action, and thereby an order of action with a hierarchy of intentions.

A closer relation exists of course between agent and intention (51–58). An intention can be said to bear the mark of a person, a characteristic that comes into play when an action is imputed to someone (51). Ricoeur reviews some of Hart's work on ascribing responsibility and focuses on ascribable actions in the context of legal propositions as defeasible ones— that is, actions that can be abrogated or invalidated. In the juridical realm, too, the intentional character of an action is not a matter of some particular mental state but of certain public facts, whether the clauses of a contract or the observable elements of a particular deed. Throughout a series of discussions of Hart's work Ricoeur seizes on the repeated connection made between action and its subject and, with Aristotle, adopts the view that action arises out of *hexis* or dispositions and habits (55).

The final key notion is that of *reason as motive*. Ricoeur insists, with many analytic philosophers, on the difference between the relation between motive and intention on the one side and that between cause and effect on the other. A motive is an answer to the question "What are you doing?" says Ricoeur, whereas an intention is an answer to the question "Why are you doing that?" (40). Yet Ricoeur resists the move to reduce all talk of motive and intention to talk of reasons to do something. At the same time he insists on the logical difference between the relations of causality (external and contingent) and that of motivation as a willing (internal and noncontingent). He urges that motivation be understood as an interpretation, "a way of characterizing, of considering as, of placing an action in the light of such and such an idea" (41).

Ricoeur sees a kinship between this analytic reflection on motive and the hermeneutic reflection on interpretation. For action, he says, "can be treated as a text and its interpretation through motives as a reading— reattaching an intention to a set of motives is like interpreting a part of a text by its context" (41). Motivation makes action intelligible. Yet much analytic work overlooks a basic aspect of motivation, namely, the force of desire. Ricoeur refuses to follow the analysis of desire in terms of wanting and willing (Melden) and prefers instead the close conjunction of desire with meaning (Anscombe), where desire is something we "make sense of." However legitimate the attempt to restore desire to the domain of practical reason, that domain cannot be constructed in terms of action only; it must also comprise passivity and the "undergoing of force" (44). Consequently, Ricoeur keeps open the idea that at least in some cases the opposition between reasons and causes is too simple. One of these cases is that in which to desire is to be disposed to do something, and here "neither the notion of cause as constant antecedent nor motive as reasons for" provides an adequate account (45). For Ricoeur such motivational factors as dispositional force can explain some events without requiring an appeal to causal antecedents, just as certain kinds of teleological explanations can explain actions by looking to ends rather than to causes (C. Taylor 1964).

Ricoeur summarizes his views as follows: "we say of someone that he has 'done' something (a) if he is a remarkable cause (in particular in the case of complex actions); (b) if he is the identifiable author (in simple or complex agency); and (c) if the action can be imputed to him (if the action is virtually blameable or praisable)" (58). More particularly, the key notions of action, intention, and reason are understood as arising out of the conversational and hence public give and take of "question and answer." The intention of an action is taken to be mainly "the non-constrained but coordinated and reflective way in which an action is performed (I did it intentionally) or the hierarchy of things to be done to arrive at a desired result (I did this with the intention to).[16] A reason as a motive is largely an explanation one provides to oneself or others of why one has done something. The "why" here, however, is often but not always to be construed as a reason and not as an antecedent cause, where "reason" is taken broadly enough to include such dispositions as beliefs or desires constituting a context for action. And action is seen to be centrally linked with the notion of an agent as a basic particular possessing a certain capacity or power and describable with a proper name or a personal pronoun. Identifying the agent is sometimes difficult in cases of complex actions such as collective ones.[17] But Ricoeur insists "we are committed by the language game of action to seek the meaning of action in the intersection of questions and answers bearing on intentions . . . motives, and the agents of action" (S, 34–35).

[16]Ricoeur 1981:31. Cited hereafter as S.
[17]Ricoeur 1977. Cited hereafter as SA.

ACTION AND SPEECH ACTS

Besides this conceptual network centered on the notion of action comprising the three cardinal notions of agent, intention, and reason as motive, Ricoeur is also concerned with the role of these concepts in certain propositions, especially as these propositions are treated in the speech-act theory of Austin and Searle. Ricoeur calls attention to a certain "oscillation" in Austin's earlier analysis of illocutionary acts into an initial and presumably basic opposition between constative and performative, and then his later opposition between locutionary and illocutionary. The relation between these two distinctions Ricoeur finds problematic, especially in the light of related work in the French tradition by Benveniste (1966a, 1966b) on the diversity of what Austin first calls the performative and on the proliferation of kinds of illocutions.

Ricoeur then focuses on the notion of wanting or willing (*vouloir*) and points out that when taken as intentional action, wanting can arguably be classified in all five of Austin's illocutionary kinds—verdictives, exercitives, promissives, comportmentatives, and expositives. Thus, wanting in its evaluative character is a kind of verdict, a verdict of approval. In exhibiting a kind of power or capacity, wanting is also a kind of decree, a decision favoring a certain cause of action. Moreover, in wanting to perform some action, the speaker imposes on him or herself a certain obligation: wanting thus involves a kind of commitment. To the degree that action always involves a certain social behavior vis-à-vis other persons, wanting is also a kind of taking account of others. Finally, in wanting to do something, the agent can justify his or her action by rendering an account of it: thus, wanting is seen to imply the possibility of exposing a point of view.

Ricoeur finds this fivefold aspect of wanting both revealing and, in the looseness of the distinctions and the apparent impossibility of establishing a complete empirical enumeration, disconcerting as well. But his own standpoint here is also somewhat unstable. For in trying to exhibit his claim that wanting seems to be equally an instance of all five illocutionary kinds, he both leaves an important ambiguity unresolved (wanting versus willing) and slips repeatedly from talk about wanting (*vouloir*) to talk about "intentional action" (*vouloir ou de l'action intentionelle*, 68) and to the "will" (69), without specifying whether he takes these expressions as synonymous or, if not, just how their differences are to be understood.

Turning to a more systematic analysis in Searle, Ricoeur recognizes the goal of constructing certain ideal models of illocutionary acts with the help of a metalanguage. And he endorses the view that illocutionary acts are governed by constitutive rather than regulative rules and that not all instances of such acts are to be taken as equally central. Each illocutionary type for Searle is seen to be governed by an essential condition, one that is necessary and sufficient. But talk of essence recalls Husserl's doctrine of the intuition of essences, an eidetic rather than psychological doctrine that Ricoeur thinks must finally depend on semantic analysis to bridge the gap between fact and essence. Conversely, a linguistic analysis that centers on "essential conditions" such as those Searle tabulates in *Speech Acts* (65–67) must involve something like a phenomenological doctrine on the intuition of essences (72).

For Ricoeur, the correlation between essential and nonessential conditions in Searle's theory is interesting because the conjunction of these conditions, as he understands the matter, "constitutes the 'semantic rules' for the use of any illocutionary force whatever" (73). Ricoeur follows Searle closely in the articulation of these conditions and correlations while looking carefully at the recurrence in these analyses of talk about verbal and mental intentions. Thus, he stresses in Searle the repeated links between intention on the one hand and belief and desire or wanting on the other. For carrying out an illocutionary act requires the verbal expression of some mental states. This distinction between verbal and mental intention is the basis for his claim that a correlation between the semantic and the psychological is necessary. The absence of such a correlation makes any merely linguistic analysis of the intentional incomplete.

"Intention," however, is used variously, and Ricoeur notices that Searle is attentive to Grice's reflections (1969) on the expression "having the intention to," specifically the distinction between natural and nonnatural meaning. Intention and meaning are to be linked not in terms of a Fregean view about objective meaning but in terms of intersubjective meaning— I intend that my intention *to* be recognized by my interlocutor is an intention *that*. Intention thus is taken to involve essential, mental, and recognitional conditions (75).

Even after Searle's more systematic treatment of illocutionary acts, however, Ricoeur remains concerned about the problem first raised with respect to Austin, namely, the possibility of an incomplete enumeration. On his view the same problem recurs in Searle in that the connections between essential and inessential conditions remain unsystematic, the essential condition is not always explicit, and some conditions overlap with the result that the basic illocutionary acts cannot be definitively specified.

These difficulties lead Ricoeur to focus more narrowly on the connections between the semantic and the psychological in questions about mental intentions as expressed in certain classes of verbs. Here the key expressions are p and "believing that p" as well as p and "wanting that p" or "intending that p" (77). Both "believing" and "willing" or "intending" are seen as particular instances of the more general expression "judging." Drawing on Geach and Kenny, Ricoeur stresses that judgment is not, as with Frege and Russell, the grasping of an entity, a meaning, but the mastery of a use (78), and that, as the logic of quotation shows, a psychological proposition "can be considered as a metaphorical use of a citation" (78). Thus, the terms in an object language may at times be replaced with the ideas for these terms.

This analysis suggests a strategy for reinterpreting Searle's talk about a sincerity condition for illocutionary propositions. Ricoeur (following Kenny) goes on to construe the psychological status of intending as willing as a "command addressed to oneself" (79) in which the "volition" may involve the notion of a wish, or of a command, or simply what he calls a "volitive intention." This analysis receives some confirmation in Benveniste's discussion of the triple division among pronouns, which arguably corresponds to this tripartite analysis of intention. Accordingly, wishing is taken as "intending that you," and voluntary intention is "intending that I." Willing becomes "a command given to oneself" (80).

These analyses lead Ricoeur back to the claim that the sincerity condition in Searle's theory needs to be reinterpreted with the help of such philosophical psychologies as one may find in Geach and Kenny. In this way the private realm of "lived experience" is brought back within the domain of a linguistic analysis of willing or intending. Ricoeur goes on to argue that in willing or intending "the illocution is indiscernible from the locution—what one does in saying something is at the same time what one does by the fact that one acts, for one does it with respect to oneself" (82). Pursuing this suggestion further into considerations about inchoative verbs, Ricoeur claims that "every intention is a forcing oneself to act so that . . . exhorting oneself to obtain the result that . . . an intention can be described in terms of the action it initiates and that action in turn can be described in terms of the result it pursues. Thus, the result in which the performance ends also characterizes the intention which 'promises' or 'commands' the action" (83). More summarily, he concludes: "what we call in ordinary language an intention is . . . the initiation of doing something in such a way that something else comes about. . . . voluntary intention is analyzable into: (1) an intending that (mental act), (2) a beginning to do or trying, and (3) a doing in such a way as" (83–84).

Ricoeur's rereadings here of Austin and Searle, however we choose to criticize his understanding of certain details in this far from simple story, bring us a step farther in understanding his view of action. We find here two important glosses. First, "intention" is now seen to involve at least three basic components. The idea that intention involves both essential and nonessential conditions allows Ricoeur to allude to the Husserlian question of how such conditions are apprehended. The tantalizing response is by "intuition," where "intuition" is to be taken not in a psychologistic, introspective sense but in what Husserl calls an eidetic and

descriptive one. Moreover, the distinction between verbal and mental
expressions of intention allows Ricoeur to recall his concern with supplementing the conceptual analysis of the "lived experience" of action.
And the stress on conversational implications of discourse about action
opens the discussion not just to the recognition of intentions but to what
Ricoeur called earlier the interactional context of action. Most important,
however, is the narrowing of the focus on action to the idea of the mental
conditions for acting intentionally—what Ricoeur goes on to describe
mysteriously as "volitive intention."

Actions, Causes, and Reasons

Besides the triple structure of action, the conceptual network operative
in talk about action, and an attempt to reinterpret the theory of speech
acts in terms of what he calls loosely a "semantics of intention," Ricoeur's
account of action also involves a sustained reflection on causes and
reasons.

Like many contemporary philosophers Ricoeur finds that the Humean
notion of causality cannot do justice to the agent's capacity or power to
act. For Ricoeur just as for R. Taylor (1966) causality is a primitive philosophical notion that can be explicated only by reference to synonyms
and to its place in a pattern of concepts. What strikes Ricoeur in the
attempt to show that causality is an irreducible notion is the role of the
primitive assertion of capacity, "I can." This first-person possibility is
precisely what cannot be reduced to any kind of logical, epistemological,
or physical possibility. Further, this notion of personal or subjective capacity, despite certain recent work, cannot be reduced either, Ricoeur
thinks, to the idea of a causal antecedent or to wanting, for such a putative
event remains fatally unobservable, numerically without limit (every
movement would require one), and subject to an infinite regression.

Ricoeur, however, disassociates the two cases of causal antecedents
and antecedent wantings or desires. He calls attention to an important
difference between intention and desires in that the latter often comprise
not just action but, once again, certain passivities, events the agent undergoes. Moreover, Ricoeur thinks that much analytic philosophy of action
overlooks the diverse phenomena of passivity. One reason for this over-
sight is the lack of a correlative analysis of the body not as an object but
as "my own body" (le corps propre), as a "lived body."

Further, the notion of agent causality as a primitive is linked with the
idea of agency as a way of describing the relation between an agent and
his or her action on the one hand, and the agent's capacity for action on
the other. The notion of capacity and intention are taken here to be
correlative in the sense that an intention to do something is in my case

always my intention, referring thus to my capacity to act. Hence agent causality is understood as already implied in the notion of intention itself. Causal explanation of certain movements thus reach an end when they are traced back to the body of the agent ("the match lit the fire," "my hand lit the match"). Ricoeur, however, is still critical of the arguments adduced in favor of this position on the same grounds as earlier—"what this kind of analysis basically lacks," he writes, "is the consideration of passivity as distinct from both physical causality and human activity. Activity has two opposites, not just movement as event but passivity precisely as mine" (90). The analysis of the difference between physical causality and human activity thus is incomplete, Ricoeur thinks, without an analysis of the relation between human activity and human passivity, especially passivity with respect to desires, the passivity that is linked to the body as a lived objectivity.

Besides these notions of agent causality and the correlations between intention and capacity, motives too are given a further discussion. Thus, the action of an agent is to be understood not just with respect to the agent's capacity but also as a function of his or her motives. Here also Ricoeur insists on interpreting motives not just as reasons contrasted with physical causes but as involving certain passivities. Otherwise, he claims, the difference between intentions and causes seems to collapse. What is required is a distinction between capacities (*pouvoir de*) and dispositions (*disposition à*), a relation Ricoeur takes to be "the ultimate difficulty in the theory of action" (92). Only with such a distinction, which would turn on an analysis of desire as something that is both a cause and a motive, can a theory of action make room for psychoanalytic notions. Desire here would be linked to motive through its connections with motivational fields, and to causes through its separation from such fields to the degree that no systematic evaluation of motives takes place. Desire here is a force and not just a reason or a cause.

In this area especially the analysis of action must extend to mental acts. In moving from physical to mental acts Ricoeur turns from talk of causality and motivation to a particular kind of motivation—namely, deliberation, "motivation insofar as it is an act itself" (94). But just as in the case of R. Taylor's analyses of motivation and desire, so too with deliberation Ricoeur finds once again no discussion of another species of passivity, inner constraint. The analysis of deliberation fails to take account of the degrees, the intermediate stages, which range from one extreme where action is impossible (no alternatives for action) to the other where action is inevitable (no alternatives but action).

Ricoeur now turns to a consideration of two attempts, by C. Taylor and von Wright, to find some alternative between causal and teleological explanations, a species of explanation which is more complex and yet more primitive as well in that it both precedes and accompanies the development of modern scientific explanation in Galileo. For Taylor, this historical dimension to the understanding of explanation is often missing in the analytic approaches to the explanation of action. In the course of protracted consideration of Taylor's views Ricoeur underlines the connection Taylor sees between teleological explanation and ordinary language and with the appeal to the notion of desire between explanation in terms of antecedents and explanation in terms of ends. This notion of ends, like that of "project," is threatened by the substitution of talk of programming for talk of desire and project. Ricoeur is also attentive to Taylor's idea that intentionality introduces a kind "of backwards reference to some center of responsibility whence action procedes" (102) to a conscious interior, and to Taylor's extensive criticisms of certain empiricist assumptions in the explanation of action. What he retains from Taylor's discussion is not so much the analysis of the logical form of teleological explanation or the analysis of how ordinary language implies certain uses of teleology or even the critique of reductive strategies in empiricist accounts of action. It is, rather, the insistence on an ineliminable mental component in the explanation of the agent as conscious subject. But this element requires a further reflection on the differences between explanation and understanding, a task Ricoeur takes up with a final reading, this time of von Wright, whose work in part reacts to Taylor's.

Ricoeur expounds von Wright's ideas on the epistemological validity of the idea of causality (modern scientific thought does not succeed in replacing this idea completely with the idea of function), and his explanatory model of action, which isolates a fragment of world history in order to construct a closed system. Taking a decision involves setting in motion such constructed systems in that such an action constitutes an intervention in nature, thereby producing certain changes in initial states that otherwise would remain unchanged, and then observing passively their further development. For von Wright, "intentional interference in the course of nature is the paradigm of 'doing something'. To accomplish an act is to produce the initial state of a system, thus setting a system in motion" (106–7). Two notions come together in the idea of intervention— the capacity to do something, and that a sequence of events (which we make happen) constitutes a closed system. For von Wright the causal relation holds between the result of an action and its consequences, and not between an action and its results and "only in this sense is the concept of action conceptually prior to that of cause" (197). Hence action can be included in the notion of causality—what is primitive is not the notion of causality but that of capacity, the capacity to set in motion initial states of a system.

For von Wright, Taylor's discussion of teleological explanation requires the introduction of a further element into the overly simple opposition between strictly causal and strictly teleological explanations that simulate teleological explanations in the way homeostatic mechanisms do without adding anything to the causal element, and that of quasi-causal explanations that are, as in the case of irresistible desires, disguised teleological explanations. This more nuanced view is, von Wright thinks, to be substituted for Taylor's idea especially of purely teleological explanation as "interiorised in the consciousness of the agent in the form of an intention to act" (109). One key reason that both *kinds* of explanation are compatible is that each has a different *explanadum*: natural events on the one hand, actions already interpreted as intentional on the other. In the former, when I observe I let things happen, whereas in the latter, when I act I make things happen.

Von Wright's analysis combines logical techniques with ordinary-language analysis without overlooking an appeal to "the lived experience" of intentionality. What Ricoeur retains is von Wright's demonstration of a juncture between the experience on explanation and understanding, where "we intervene in the course of things in exercising our own capacities which at the same time are both what we are able to do and what we know how to do" (112).

To summarize, in this last stage of his analysis of action—reflections on the discourse of action in the context of decision, explanation, and understanding—Ricoeur repeats some of his earlier points and adds several fresh notions as well. We find him again stressing the importance of the subject of action, the irreducible agent in agent causality, as well as the now familiar call for a fuller discussion of passivity as part of action broadly understood, and the insistence on the cardinal role of agent capacity in a satisfactory analysis of action.

What is new is the introduction of the notion of the lived body as a resource for describing that dimension in the capacity of the agent which merely causal analyses cannot reach. What is at issue here is not so much the passive element in action but "passivity as mine." Further, Ricoeur is now more explicit about one of these passivities, what he earlier called the dispositional force of desire. He distinguishes between the agent's capacity for desire and the agent's disposition to desire. In the one case we are talking about desire as a cause and in the other of desire as a reason. Yet when it combines both aspects, desire may also be taken as motive and thereby linked to the play of psychoanalytic elements in motivational fields. Finally, Ricoeur underlines the role of ends in the projects of agents, an element that till now has been absent. Ends, moreover, require for their understanding a closer look not at the logic of decision making but at the idea that making a decision involves not just acting but making things happen by initiating changes in the neutral course of events, which then, through causal chains, run their course as closed systems. Acting here is the domain of deciding, of not letting things happen but making things happen.

Appendix 5C Actions, Intentions, Events, and Properties

EVENTS AS SPATIO-TEMPORAL PARTICULARS

The hermeneutic account generally tries to integrate descriptions of action in different analytic accounts and, by moving to a reflexive level, complement those descriptions with the results of eidetic investigations in a phenomenological vein. Thus, the analytic descriptions are taken to the basic. In this appendix I look at the ontology one of these descriptions involves and, in criticizing that ontology briefly, suggest still further features of action which the conjunction of these accounts cannot treat appropriately either. Thus, just as I tried to show how each account separately leaves out some important features of action, I now proceed on the assumption that a conjunction of these theories, if ever manageable, would on Ricoeur's usual practice include at least an analytic ontology such as Brand's whatever other elements his own phenomenological hermeneutic would add. But whatever the fate of its possible supplements, the ontology in the analytic account we have been examining is already extensive enough to exclude the possibility of accounting appropriately for certain further features of Becket's action.

Since actions and intentions are both taken to be events, one physical and the other mental, some account of the nature of events is required if Brand's analytic theory is to exhibit its ontological commitments. Brand provides this account early in his work when he argues generally that events are very much like objects in being particulars, whereas intentions are self-referential attitudes with contents whose objects are properties. Thus, two claims are worked out, events as spatio-temporal particulars and properties as the objects of mental attitudes.

Brand begins with an informal picture of certain parallels he thinks hold between linguistic and ontological items. Thus, he pairs singular terms with particulars, predicates with properties, and sentences with propositions. Under particulars he includes physical objects, nonpersonal animate objects, persons, numbers, and sets; under properties the attributes of objects; and under propositions the "abstract bearers of truth and falsity whose structure reflects relationship between particulars and properties."[18] Although this picture is admittedly controversial, Brand takes it as a "plausible working hypothesis."

Brand next points out that the place of events in this picture is not clear since some have argued that events are propositional (Chisholm 1976b), others that actions as events are properties of persons (Goldman 1970), or property exemplifications of concrete particulars (Kim 1970), and still others that events are concrete particulars (Davidson 1967). Brand chooses

[18]Brand 1984: 52. Further references are given in the text.

to place events in the category of particulars and goes on to provide his reasons.

Parsimony is not one of them. For some events recur, and in order to account for the recurrence of concrete particulars, which strictly speaking can occur only once, types must be introduced and types are properties. Further, "in order to account for persons having certain types of mental attitudes," certain objects must be added from the proposition category (53). Nor is the apparent advantage of being able to parse event sentences in extensional first-order logic a good reason for particularism since some event sentences involving adverbial modification are resistant to this kind of analysis. Nor finally is the fact that particularism corresponds with commonsense views of events a good reason either since common sense is often erroneous. But Brand's main reason for particularism is the similarities he argues for between physical objects as particulars and events.

These similarities include using definite and indefinite descriptions, proper names, and so on for both physical objects and events. Moreover, just as the parts of physical objects are physical objects, the parts of events are events. And just as some complex physical objects when dismantled become "scattered objects," so some complex events when dismantled become "scattered events." Finally, like physical objects, events occupy spatio-temporal regions (however difficult it may be to identify such regions exactly) and are not strictly repeatable, even though, unlike physical objects, events do not completely occupy the region in which they exist. This final point for Brand is the crucial difference between physical objects and events and the basis for his claim that they are ontologically independent. "Some events do not involve physical objects and some physical objects exist for a time without being involved in an event" (58).

With this initial description in hand Brand now moves to clarify the nature of events more formally by providing identity conditions that specify their properties. Abstracting from true statements of identity conditions for sets being identical (just in case they have the same members) and for physical objects being identical (just in case they occupy the same spatio-temporal regions), Brand proposes a form for the statement of identity conditions where K ranges over ontological kinds, that is, things that without being universal allow of instances and whose instances are necessarily of an ontological kind (Lombard 1979):

(IC) $(x)(y)$ (if x and y are K's, then $x=y$ if and only if Fxy).

Here the dyadic property F, which is a property of pairs of objects belonging to the same ontological kind K, can be read as "having the same members" or "occupying the same spatio-temporal region" (59). Unlike their close cousins, true identifying conditions that are evidential statements in epistemological and pragmatic contexts either for determining the number of a certain kind of object or "for reidentifying a single, enduring object of a kind," true identity conditions are infallible in the sense that they allow no genuine counterinstances. Identity conditions are a formulation of an object's ontological kind, whereas identifying conditions are a formulation of "a criterion for making judgements about sameness and difference for a kind of object" (60). Identity conditions, then, do not define "identity"; rather, they specify "conceptually significant properties of ontological types" (61). But determining adequate identity conditions for an ontological kind is a substantial issue since "no algorithm exists for determining F given a K" (62–65).

In the light of five constraints he articulates for statements of identity conditions generally and in the light of statements of identity conditions for physical objects, Brand proposes the following formulation (B) for events (where e and f range over events, r over spatio-temporal regions, and O = "occupies"):

(B) $(e)(f)$ [if e and f are events, then $e = f$ if and only if $\Box$ $(r)(eOr \equiv fOr)$].

Thus, the identity conditions for events "consist in *necessary* spatio-temporal coincidence" although they also allow the "occurrence of distinct events in one spatio-temporal region" (65–66). The kind of necessity here Brand thinks is difficult to specify exactly, but he interprets it not as physical but as logical necessity.

Brand now contrasts his proposal with a similar one, (D), which formulated identity conditions for events in terms of sameness of causes and effects. Thus, where C = "causes" and g and h range over events:

(D) For any e and any f, if e and f are events, then $e = f$ if and only if $(g)(gCe \equiv gCf)$ and (h) $(eCh \equiv fCh)$ (67).

In both cases the identity conditions for events do not state internal properties but external ones, and they leave open the question of whether events have internal structures. But (B) is arguably superior to (D) in that it is not open to the charge of vicious circularity on the grounds that causes and effects are themselves events.

Another alternative, (K), is to formulate the identity conditions for events in terms of property exemplification (Kim 1970, 1973, 1976), a view that is addressed to a supposedly uniform internal rather than external structure of events. Formally,

(K1) For any e, if e is an event, then there is a physical object x, a property F, and a duration t, such that $e = [x,F,t]$;

(K2) for any $[x,F,t]$ and $[y,G,t']$, if $[x,F,t]$ and $[y,G,t']$ are events, then $[x,F,t] = [y,g,t']$ if and only if $x = y$ and $F = G$ and $t = t'$ (70).

Thus, what guarantees identity is sameness of constituent physical objects, properties, and times or durations. But Brand finds difficulties here also—formal ones with the interpretation of brackets including ordered triples and hence abstract rather than concrete particulars, and substantive ones about (K1) and (K2) presupposing identity conditions for physical objects, properties, and durations where those for properties are extremely difficult to articulate. Moreover, this formulation commits one to the mistaken view that all events include physical objects. Finally, no criterion is provided for determining the range of F, that is, for those properties that constitute events. Accordingly, Brand rejects the property exemplification view just as well as the causal one in favor of his own view of the identity conditions for events being necessary spatio-temporal coincidence.

Brand now moves to supplement the syntactic schema (B) with a semantic criterion for what can be appropriately substituted for the variables e and f in (B) to yield "true event-identity sentences" (73). He first stipulates a complete canonical event description as "a singular term of the form

$$x's\ F\text{-ing occupies } r$$

or some tensed or colloquial variant of it, where 'x' is replaced by a name or definite description of a physical object (including a person), 'r' by a name or other referring expression of a spatio-temporal region, and where 'F' is a predicate expression. An instance . . . is 'Nixon resigning on January 20, 1973 in the oval office' " (73). Two qualifications in the interests of simplicity are: the criterion is not fully general, and event descriptions not referring to physical objects are ignored. Brand next investigates several metalinguistic renderings of this criterion and, with the help of some discussion in philosophy of logic (Kripke 1972 on rigid designators and Kaplan 1978 on functions that rigidify contained singular terms), settles on a metalinguistic formulation of his canonical event description:

> For any two canonical event descriptions α and β, if α^+ and β^+ are rigid, then $\ulcorner \alpha = \beta \urcorner$ is true if and only if $\ulcorner \Box(r)\ (\alpha^+ Or \equiv \beta^+ Or \urcorner$ is true (75).

This results in the first sentence being true just in case the second one is true—"Nixon resigning = the 37th President's resigning" is true just in case "Necessarily, for every spatio-temporal region r, (Nixon's resigning)$^+$ occupies r if and only if (the 37th President's resigning)$^+$ occupies r" (74–75).

Finally, Brand argues that his semantical criterion is applicable to mental events as well as to physical ones. The difficulty here arises from the requirement to specify not temporal but spatio-temporal locations for mental events. After scrutinizing four hypotheses about the spatial location of mental events, Brand concludes that "all events, including mental ones are spatio-temporal, that identity conditions for events are to be given in terms of necessary spatio-temporal coincidence, and that his theory (B) of event identity conditions as necessary spatio-temporal co-incidence provides truth conditions for many event-identity sentences including some that contain descriptions referring to mental events" (83).

This account of events seems to progress smoothly from the presentation of an initial ontological picture, the location of events within that picture, the justification of this move, the specification of a syntactic form for identity conditions for events and its semantic criterion together with critical attention to alternatives, and finally the discussion of an objection. But we need to raise at least three questions about the satisfactoriness of this account.

First, how successful is Brand's discussion of the major objection that his semantical criterion, which relies centrally on spatio-temporal location, cannot accommodate mental events? Can mental events (ME's) be located spatio-temporally, as this theory requires? Brand considers four hypotheses: (H1) ME's "do not have spatial locations"; (H2) for any person S, the spatial location of a mental event of S is identical with the spatial location of some *brain event* of S; (H3) . . . is identical with the spatial location of S's *body*; and (H4) . . . is identical with the spatial location of S (81). After working through these views Brand claims that, even though (H4) is the most attractive, no decision is required because each allows one to accommodate mental events. Accordingly, Brand concludes that "all events, including mental ones, are spatio-temporal, that identity conditions for events are to be given in terms of necessary spatio-temporal coincidence and . . . his canonical event description provides truth conditions for many event identity sentences, including some that contain descriptions referring to mental events" (83). But this account, in claiming that the canonical event description applies to some sentences only, is on its own terms insufficiently general. Whatever the fates of (H1) to (H4) and however controversial Brand's claim that his ontology requires no decisions, the charge of insufficient generality cannot be finessed.

Second, the main argument Brand provides in support of his interpretation of events as particulars is unpersuasive. For despite the parallels he lists between physical objects as particulars and events, the argument's reliance on the idea of "scattered events" and its assumption that spatio-temporal regions for all events can be identified do not inspire confidence. In both cases we are dealing with speculation. Brand's own qualifications in the careful statement of his conclusions above reinforce doubts about whether such regions can be identified for all events, especially mental ones. And the basis for the doctrine of "scattered events"—namely, Goodman's nominalistic views about "scattered objects"—remains highly controversial.

Both of these difficulties derive from Brand's commitment to a certain understanding of particulars inside an ontological framework. But as Brand recognizes, other frameworks than the one he uses are available, for example, the understanding of particulars from a situationalist perspective. In this alternative picture reality consists of situations, and situations consist both of invariants—whether static (states of affairs) or dynamic (events)—and uniformities (individuals, properties and relations, and locations). Individuals are real things, uniformities persisting through some courses of events, having properties, and standing in relations. Properties are uniformities of things, relations are uniformities between objects at some times and at some places, and locations are uniformities in which different things at different times happen at some places. Here particulars are individuals. In Brand's framework particulars are not just individuals but, paradigmatically, "physical objects . . . persons and other animate objects . . . sets and numbers (if they exist)" (52). And, we now know, all events must be added to this list, including all mental events. Without arguing the details of these constructed ontologies we need to note here that Brand has built into his category of "particulars" a range of entities that differ considerably among themselves—some concrete and some not, some spatio-temporal and some not. And it is this inflation that leads to a basic vagueness in his claim that all events are to be construed as particulars. We need to know on Brand's framework what kind of particulars, whereas on an uninflated alternative framework we already know.

PROPERTIES AS OBJECTS OF MENTAL ATTITUDES

Besides an account of all events, including mental ones, as spatio-temporal particulars, Brand's ontology also includes an account of the objects of some mental events. The mental events that take objects Brand calls "attitudes." From the perspective of action the most important of these attitudes are believing, desiring, and intending. Each is construed as irreducibly distinct. And each takes as its objects not particulars but properties. Thus, "all attitudes, including attitudes about oneself, physical objects, other persons, and abstract object, can be analyzed in terms of attitudes that take properties as objects" (85).

Kinds of attitudes can be distinguished either by construing the objects of putative attitudes as different and the attitudes as the same, or by construing the objects as the same and the attitudes as different. Brand labels the first case "attitude assimilationism" and the second "object assimilationism." Thus, believing (B), desiring (D), and intending (I) can be taken as having different objects while being of the same type of attitude to these objects, or as being different attitudes toward the same objects. In the latter case the objects are usually taken to be propositions named by "that" clauses, and the attitudes are called propositional attitudes and are expressed by attitude verbs. Further, in object assimilationism, propositions are taken orthodoxly on the Fregean view to be "abstract (nonspatial) . . . structured in some way that corresponds to or matches declarative sentences . . . bearers of truth and falsity . . . and person-independent and context-independent" (87). But his understanding of propositions remains controversial and object assimilationism has been strongly challenged.

Brand takes up one version of attitude assimilationism (Castañeda 1975, 1976, 1980) according to which B-objects are ontologically different from D- and I-objects. On this view B-objects are orthodox propositions, but D- and I-objects are objects of practical attitudes called "practitions." Practitions differ syntactically from propositions in not mirroring the structure of declarative sentences where something other than a copula links the subject to the verb. And they differ semantically in being neither true nor false but either legitimate or illegitimate depending on whether or not the practition "is required in the context of the agent's hierarchy of ends and the ends of other persons he considers important" (88). Further, practitions are of three irreducible kinds—first person, second person, and third person. But behind these views are what Brand calls "the Fregean Presupposition," the view that thought is isomorphic to natural language at least with respect to primary structural features. This presupposition generates the view that "features of mental attitudes . . . can be derived from features of ascriptions of mental attitudes" (89).

What invites an alternative to the traditional view of object assimilationism is not so much controversies about the existence of propositions but the fact that the traditional views cannot accommodate the self-referentiality of certain attitudes. Arguing from a series of examples, Brand shows that some objects of action attitudes can be parsed if at all as propositional functions only and not as propositions. Moreover, the proposed revisions to the propositional object assimilation theory involve serious difficulties in their own right. Finally, even the attitude assimilationist alternative has a related difficulty with the self-referentiality of intending. The point, then, is that even if attitude assimilationism is to be preferred to its rival on the grounds that not all objects of attitudes can be construed as propositions, the practition version of assimilationist theory cannot be accepted as is because of the unresolved problem it faces with the self-referentiality of all intendings.

But the practition theory's explanation of the initiation of action is also problematic. According to the theory, "fully endorsing a first-person practition as opposed to a first-person proposition is, under propitious circumstances, sufficient for action. . . . the conative feature of action initiation . . . is having an attitude of fully endorsing toward a special type of object" (95). Brand, however, refutes this view by showing that it involves three claims that cannot all be consistently maintained, namely, that believing and intending are both species of one kind of attitude called fully endorsing, but that intending initiates action whereas believing does not. Thus, if object assimilationism cannot account for self-referentiality, attitude assimilationism cannot account for the initiation of action.

Consequently, Brand moves to consider a less parsimonious view. This holds that both the objects and the attitudes are different. More specifically, Brand sees this view as a nonassimilationist view committed to assimilating objects not as propositions but as properties—property object assimilationism. Thus in the sentence (P),"Peter believes that he is married," the object of Peter's belief, although apparently a proposition, is actually a primitive self-ascribed property; thus (P) should be rewritten as (P'), "Peter self-ascribes the property of being married" (97; cf. Lewis 1979 and Chisholm 1979, 1981). Brand's theory claims to solve the problem of self-referentiality by locating self-referentiality "in the attitude itself" rather than in the objects of the attitude (98). Believing, desiring, and intending are taken to involve essential reference to the agent subject. Thus "P intends to eat dinner" is to be rewritten as "P set himself to acquire the property of eating dinner," and "P desires to eat dinner" as "P self-favours acquiring the property of eating dinner" (98). Self-ascription of a property (believing), setting oneself to acquire a property (desiring) are part of the respective attitudes and are taken as primitives. Moreover, this account can be extended to include complex cases of multiple, reiterated, and multiple plus reiterated self-reference.

Brand now expands the theory from one of self-reference (*de se* attitudes) to one of other reference (*de re* and *de dicto* attitudes). Two ways of proceeding are available—take other referentiality as primary and reduce *de se* attitude to *de re* ones, or take self-referential as primary and reduce *de re* attitudes to *de se* ones. After close consideration of various examples, Brand argues that within the limits of Fregean semantics, which do not allow for propositional-like objects that are person and context dependent, "there appears to be no way to make the uniqueness of first-person cases in which there is self-awareness" (103; 274). Thus, he turns to the task of elucidating *de re* attitudes in terms of *de se* attitudes. He proceeds to argue that in the case of believing and desiring, "a person attributes a property to something else when he attributes to himself the complex property" (103). After providing a formal statement of this view both for the case of a person ascribing to another a property (believing) and for that of a person favoring another acquiring a property (desiring), Brand adopts the convention of restricting "believes that" and "desires that" to *de dicto* attitudes and "believes of" and "desires of" to *de re* attitudes. "*De re* belief is, essentially, ascribing a property to an object that is selectively considered (that is actively attended to). *De dicto* belief is a special case of *de re* belief: it is ascribing a property to a proposition, through the intermediate step of selectively considering a sentence in one's representational language that expresses the proposition" (118). And similarly for *de re* and *de dicto* desire. With this in hand Brand refines his analysis in the course of considering a number of problem cases that lead him through a discussion of different kinds of *de re* attitudes, as well as recent work in the conceptual bases of cognitive psychology. We need not track these complications, however. For our purposes Brand's summary nicely catches the major point he has argued for in his theory of property object assimilationism:

   i)   Natural language and thought are structurally similar. . . .

   ii)   Belief sentences (ascriptions of belief) and beliefs (what occurs in the head) are structurally similar. (from i)
   iii) Some belief sentences are irreducibly first person. . . .
   iv)   Some beliefs are irreducibly self-referential. (from ii and iii)
   v)   All belief sentences can be translated into first persons ones.
   vi)   All beliefs can be analyzed in terms of self-referential ones. (from ii and v) (118)

As for the premises, (i) is assumed, (iii) is justified by showing that first-person reference cannot be eliminated from certain sentences without denying the meaning, and (v) is justified by taking irreducible self-referential belief as primitive. Brand claims that a parallel argument can be made for desire.

This second discussion of ontology is more complicated and extensive than the first. However, the main claims stand out reasonably well. In particular, three such claims require a closer look.

First, Brand's proposal is that those attitudes that take properties as objects include three basic ones—believing, desiring, and intending. In short, intending is a type of mental event which takes properties as its objects. Brand is persuasive in arguing for the irreducibility of intending to either believing or desiring or their conjunction. And his argument in support of taking the objects of intending as properties is perspicuous and impressive. But the larger claim here—namely, that all intendings take propositions as their objects; that intending, believing, and desiring are basic attitudes; and that all attitudes are to be understood as mental events that take objects—goes largely unjustified. This lack of justification is a serious problem especially for the last of these claims. For this claim is already tributary to the earlier claim—a controversial one—that all events are to be understood as objectlike particulars. Thus, since the earlier claim is controversial the present one is too, and hence whatever the fate of the first two unargued claims here, at least the third needs explicit support.

A second difficulty with the property object assimilationist view of intending is the way in which the problem of self-referentiality is solved. Brand wants to build self-referentiality into the internal structure of intending as a mental attitude. This is fair enough. But simply claiming that "setting oneself to acquire a property" is to be taken as primitive for intending doesn't do the job. We still need a fuller analysis of how exactly this is to be done. And such an analysis involves providing a description of the agent if not as substance (a view Brand has explicitly challenged), at least—to use his own expression—the agent as subject. This gap in the discussion is closely related to a similar gap in the description of the conative complex when Brand leaves undeveloped the critical notion of consciousness in talk about being accessible or nonaccessible to consciousness. In short, on Brand's account, the problem of self-referentiality seems to be solved by decree instead of by argument.

A third difficulty in this discussion of intending as a basic attitude touches on the problem of awarding the primacy to *de se* attitudes in the treatment of *de re* and *de dicto* attitudes. An initial caution arises from the terminology here, which is technical and hence not part of the data of natural language. For as has been argued, such expressions may "cut across the grain of the phenomena in unnatural ways, generating artificial problems and constraining the space of possible solutions to the genuine puzzles that language presents."[19] A second worry concerns the introduction of the agent's attributing to him or herself not just simple properties but complex properties of standing in certain relations to other things and to other persons. Here Brand's analysis does seem to constrain the range of possible solutions in linking his discussion to a set of topics which has only a partial connection with intendings that are irreducibly first person (118) and in leaving unexamined the question of whether self-ascription of complex properties appreciably affects the earlier stipulation that referentially is part of the internal structure of intending. In fact, Brand's theory leaves entangled three matters that are related but different in important ways: the necessary self-referential character of intending as an attitude irreducible either to believing or to desiring, the self-ascription of both simple and complex properties including relations, and the primacy of *de se* attitudes in explaining *de re* and *de dicto* attitudes.

When we reflect again on the ontology that is explicitly presented as a

---

[19]Barwise and Perry 1983: xii. See also Barwise and Perry 1985, Fine 1985, and Taylor 1985.

basis for this analytic account of human action and recall our assumption that the hermeneutic account relies minimally on such an ontology in trying to put analytic description to it own dialectic uses, then it becomes necessary to confront this ontology with the example of Becket's action. When we do so, we discover at least four more features of Becket's action and those like it which such an ontology does not seem to describe appropriately.

In the case of the understanding of attitudes as mental events with objectlike particulars as their contents, Becket's intention to wait on what may come about seems to comprise an attitude that either may have no content at all or may have other contents than those describable as objectlike particulars. In fact it seems that Becket's intention includes an element that finds no place at all in the discussion so far. For that intention includes an aspiration toward the fulfillment of some kind of a spiritual ideal. Becket intends to wait, and in doing so he aspires to make perfect his will. Here, if the intention is properly describable as having aspiration as its object—and this seems awkward—then aspiration as the object of his intention is surely not to be taken as an objectlike particular but more like a state of affairs in its own right.

Considering Becket's intention from the perspective of this ontology of attitudes also overlooks a second feature. Brand argues that in the case of a distinction among *de se*, *de re*, and *de dicto* attitudes, the *de se* are best taken as primary. But in the case of Becket's intending, a curious feature undermines the proposed account here, namely, the self-sacrificial element. Becket's intending to wait includes a symbolic awareness of the sacrificial nature of his action, which is carried through in imitation of Christ's sacrificial death and in conjunction with the sacramental reenactment of that event in the Roman Catholic mass. Part of this awareness is the realization that both the primacy of his own act must lie outside himself in whatever is or is not to eventualize as well as the central consequence of that act on the members of his community rather than on himself. Thus, even if the distinctions in this ontology were to be endorsed, their respective priorities and interrelations would require rethinking.

When we turn from the ontological attitudes to that of event and the claim that all events, including mental events, are to be understood as objectlike particulars and then scrutinize Becket's action in this light, two further puzzling elements of that action come into view. Becket's mental act in deciding to wait is not satisfactorily described as an event because it involves a particularly static frame of mind which is of its essence. Becket's action here is more of a letting go than an activity, and this letting go is more of a being acted upon than the performing of an action. Thus, his decision is not described as an active assent to a pattern or design but as a consent, something that acknowledges an initiative being involved which is not one's own. Perhaps an image for this kind of action, which is more of a static state of affairs than a dynamic occurrence, can be found in Eliot's talk of a moving stillness, the still point of the turning wheel. Or, to use another image, Becket's action as a letting go is like the bow string's releasing the arrow rather than the archer doing so when, through progressive muscular fatigue, the tensed fingers of the archer's hand are opened by the pull of the bow's tensed cord. In short, calling Becket's action an event *tout court* effectively obscures our view of its peculiar character of acquiescence in a movement that originates outside the agent and yet implicates the agent in its dynamics. Becket's action is more an eventlike happening than a self-initiated event.

Finally, just as the interpretation of Becket's action as an event seems inappropriate, so too the understanding of his action as even in some revised form a quasi-event seems inappropriate too. For we need to recall that for Brand an event is neither a proposition nor a property, but an objectlike particular. The difficulty here is that Becket's peculiar intending to wait on what happens, although arguably like an event without being one, does not seem to be properly describable as any one of these three. The ontology, in short, seems too restrictive. For what is going on here seems to invite a larger scale of treatment, one, say, in terms of a situation involving a course of quasi-events or—to recall one of the theories Brand rejects (Goldman)—in terms of a property of a person where, however, both the property and the person are ontologically nonstandard. In short, the situational character of Becket's action, its conscious insertion in a series of overlapping courses of events involving spatio-temporal considerations and religious and mythic dimensions, is on Brand's reading of events as objectlike particulars simply left out.[20]

[20]Nicholas Wolterstorff's and Evan Simpson's written comments on portions of this chapter were very helpful as were discussions about Eliot with my colleague Dominic Manganiello.

6

Fictional Selves and Virtual Persons

I can always ask, "Am I about to die?" But it is not true that,
in every case, this question must have an answer, which
must be either Yes or No. In some cases this would be an
empty question.

—Derek Parfit

In order to understand the thing which is the person, or in
order to understand the product that is the person's life, we
need to understand the process that is the person's leading
his life.

—Richard Wollheim

To the flashing water say: I am.

—Rainer Maria Rilke

In a letter to one of his friends a year before he died in 1926 Rilke wrote
of the connections between his last works, the "Duino Elegies" and the
"Sonnets to Orpheus": "Elegies and Sonnets support each other constantly. And I consider it an infinite grace, *with the same breath*, I was
permitted to fill both these sails: the small rust coloured sail of the Sonnets
and the Elegies' gigantic white canvas."[1]

These poems have long interested Rilke's most accomplished readers
and translators for different reasons. One pivotal concern is clearly the
relation in Rilke's work between the figure of the angel in the Elegies and
the figure of Orpheus in the Sonnets. I begin with a distinguished recent
interpretation of that relation, that of the American poet and critic Robert

---

[1]To W. Hulewicz, 13 November 1925, trans. S. Mitchell, in Rilke 1982: 316. Further references in the text are to this edition.

Hass.[2] My concern is to call attention to one peculiar effect some poetic works can have on competent readers, what I call the presentation of certain ethical ideals; here it is the invitation to a transformation of the self. But the notion of self-transformation is obscure. Consequently, I investigate critically two recent accounts of personal identity with a view to locating conceptual resources for articulating the notion of self-transformation more clearly. With these resources in hand I return to Rilke's later poetry and offer a sketch only of the breath that filled the small rust-colored sail and the gigantic white canvas of his late poetry.

POETIC FICTION: TRANSFORMATIONS AND FUTURE SELVES

Rilke spent the winter of 1911–12 high on the coast of the Adriatic Sea at the castle of Duino. In one of the extraordinary moments of his life while walking in a furious storm, he later wrote his host, "it seemed a voice had called . . . 'Who, if I cried out, would hear me among the angels' hierarchies?' " He copied this line down and, by the evening, he had written the first of what he already knew would finally be ten elegies, the Duino Elegies.

"The angels embody the sense of absence," the critic Robert Hass comments, "which had been at the center of Rilke's willed and difficult life. They are absolute fulfillment. Or rather, absolute fulfillment if it existed, without any diminishment of intensity, completely outside us."[3] This reflection is then elaborated:

> You feel a passion for someone so intense that the memory of their smell makes you dizzy and you would gladly throw yourself down the well of that other person, if the long hurtle in the darkness would then be perfect inside you: that is the same longing for the angel. The angel is desire, if it were not desire, if it were pure being. Lived close to long enough, it turns every experience into desolation, because beauty is not what we want at those moments, death is what we want, an end to limit, an end to time. And . . . death doesn't even want us; it doesn't want us or not want us. All of this has become clear suddenly in Rilke's immensely supple syntax. He has defined and relinquished the source of a longing and regret so pure, it has sickened the roots of his life. It seems to me an act of great courage. And it enacts a spiritual loneliness so deep, so lacking in con-

[2]Hass, in Rilke 1982: xi–xliv.

[3]Cf. Rilke's comment in the letter above to Hulewicz: "The angel of the Elegies is that creature in whom the transformation of the visible into the invisible . . . already appears in its completion . . . ;that being who guarantees the recognition of a higher level of reality in the invisible" (317).

solation, that there is nothing in modern writing that can touch it. The
company it belongs to is the third act of *King Lear* and certain passages in
Dostoevsky's novels. (xxxv)

The critic is doing at least three things here: he is putting into his own
words what he thinks the speaker in this poem is saying while taking
this speaker to be Rilke himself; he is interpreting Rilke's poetry as both
a definition of a peculiar species of personal longing and an act of relinquishment which has unusual consequences; and he is judging the sense
of what he takes to be going on here in ethical terms.

In particular, the critic understands Rilke to be using the figure of the
angel as a representation of an impossible project, namely, the perfect
fulfillment of our deepest longings as human beings. This representation
"lived close to long enough" is utterly inimical to a person's vitality. For
with such a resplendent figure too much before us we are filled with such
profound regret that we lose the will to live. And even while recognizing
that death itself is a mundane phenomenon indifferent to our plight, we
want to die in order to still this infinite yearning for what is impossible
and to do away with regret.

Rilke is understood as defining a central fact about what it means to
be a human being—namely, to enact endlessly an experience of basic
incompletion—and then to relinquish the search for a complete personal
fulfillment finally seen to be impossible. But the figure that represents
the satisfaction of the infinite longing for completion remains always
present. Thus, the relinquishment results in a profound "loneliness" utterly "lacking in consolation."

Finally, the critic judges Rilke as having in this poem accomplished an
act of great spiritual courage. What the critic finds courageous is Rilke's
working so hard to define something essential in part of what it means
to be a person while at the same time relinquishing any belief in an
ineradicable hope having any substance. Rilke is courageous because he
has worked to define clearly the nature of an inalienable hope that is
finally an illusion. And because Rilke recognizes that such a work must
result in relinquishing even the hope of consolation, he must undergo a
profound spiritual desolation.

In fairness we need to underline the speculative character of at least
part of these remarks. Unfortunately, however, speculation is unavoidable because the critic is not wholly explicit about exactly what he takes
Rilke to be saying. Nor does the critic provide any detailed evidence in
favor of his reading. Moreover, the rhetorical resources the writer himself
uses—for example, his description of an intense, passionate feeling—are
evocative and consequently invite us to fill out for ourselves some of what
the critic seems to want to say.

With this caution in mind, I suggest nevertheless that part of what is going on in this reading of Rilke is an articulation of the voices of the speaker in the opening lines of Rilke's work in terms of an ethical ideal. Rilke, the suggestion here may well be, is a person who has learned how to accomplish an act of high and unusual spiritual courage, and thereby enacts a deeply lonely but authentic way of life. And most important, in praising Rilke as the speaker and in interpreting what Rilke is saying in such terms, the critic presents a certain ethical ideal to himself and perhaps to some of his readers as well. The critic, in short, evokes the possibility of himself, at some time in the future, being a person of such a sort as to be capable of a similar act of high courage. And this evocation can function for some readers as a recommendation.

But if the critic's discussions here, whatever else they may well be, are also recommendations, then exactly what is being recommended? Very generally, the critic is recommending, just the way the speaker in Rilke's "Archaic Torso of Apollo" is recommending, that the reader or implicit reader change his or her life. More specifically, acting on this recommendation means here transforming one's relationship to a peculiar and presumably defining element among others in one's being a person, that is, to one's *eros*, to one's own *conatus*, to one's being an endless striving, to silence in a perfect fulfillment the question one is always becoming to oneself. But the change must also include the realization that such a transformation in one's relationship precisely to oneself is finally to result in a transformation in one's relationship to everything else as well.[4] And perhaps it is not without interest to recall that this final transformation may well lie beyond poetry, at least in the sense in which Rilke's *Gesang ist Dasein* is said to be untranslatable, always momentary, and finally ending in a "To the flashing water say: I am."

The recommendation, then, in this poetic context, is an invitation to transform the entirety of one's relationships to every single thing that is through the process of transforming one's relation in the future to one's own present and past self. However obscure this may at first sound, Rilke's poems and their distinguished readers largely support such a view. What is not clear is what we are supposed to be changing from. What exactly is the old relationship to ourselves and through that to everything else we are recommended (not enjoined) to transform? Moreover, how are we to understand the alleged connection between self-transformation and transformation in our relationship to everything? And assuming we could agree on some rough answers to these questions, what finally are the reasons and just how good are they for construing a transformation as one that, for all its obscurities, is well worth thinking about?

[4]See Amstutz 1945: *passim*.

I now turn from this consideration of a reading of Rilke's late poetry to the task of seeing just what kind of philosophical talk about personal identity may be appropriate for such a context. My assumption is, on the evidence of this discussion so far, that some poems do succeed in presenting to some competent readers certain ethical ideals for future self-realization such as Rilke's ideal of a transformed self. And my question is ultimately: just what changes, if any, such fictional ideals for the self seem to require in our usual understanding of what is to count as a satisfactory analysis of the continuities of personal identity through time. How can a person be understood to change across time in something like the ways reading such poems suggest? On what understanding of the person can the relations of self-concern in which one may stand with respect to one's future states be characterized as rational and ethical?

PERSONS AND FUTURE SELVES: A FIRST ACCOUNT

Persons and Their Identities

One of the most comprehensive recent discussions of the nature of the person and personal identity is to be found in Derek Parfit's *Reasons and Persons*.[5] Parfit has developed his position over the last fifteen years and has now reformulated this position freshly in a major work. Further, his account develops from a thorough critical discussion of most of the central work in the field.[6] My task here is not to attempt an assessment of that work as a whole but, with a number of cautions, to try to focus on just one part, "the most absorbing and the most controversial."[7] After calling attention to the background of this account I articulate successively the aim and the gist of the account, and several salient difficulties before turning to the details of a rival view.

If this view is to be understood properly, one needs to note at the outset that it develops out of a particular reading of our times. This reading is in no way original, but it generates the particular account of the nature of the person and of personal identity at issue here. A citation from Nietzsche stands at the head of this reading: "At last the horizon appears free to us again, even granted that it is not bright; at last our ships may venture out again . . . the sea, *our sea*, lies open again; perhaps there has never yet been such an 'open sea.' "[8] Nietzsche is taken here to be referring to the need for an ethics that is free from commitments to religious

[5]Parfit 1984.
[6]Parfit documents this work in an extensive bibliography in his book.
[7]Strawson 1984.
[8]Nietzsche 1963:448.

beliefs of any kind. For such an ethics is still lacking today, this view holds, even though religion in many places has fallen on hard times. The citation from Nietzsche echoes throughout the account until at the end of a very long discussion it is expanded into a fuller statement of the background against which the account is meant to be viewed. "Belief in God, or in many gods," we read, "prevented the free development of moral reasoning. Disbelief in God, openly admitted by a majority, is a very recent event, not yet completed. Because this event is also recent, Non-Religious Ethics is at a very early stage. We cannot yet predict whether, as in Mathematics, we will all reach agreement. Since we cannot know how Ethics will develop, it is not irrational to have high hopes."[9] (The color photograph on the book jacket is the author's own, the falling of dusk on the splendor of Venice.) Now, some may want to challenge the accuracy of such a diagnosis and especially the implications the account seems to draw from this diagnosis. But this is not essential right now. More important is the need to take note of just how the account is presented—as part of an attempt to articulate a secular ethics that responds to a reading of the needs of our own times. I return to this context later.

If the context of this account is ethical, what exactly is the aim? The aim, we are told, is to provide us with good reasons for changing some of our beliefs and revising some of our theories. For the basic conviction behind this account is the view that most people's beliefs about their nature as persons and the perdurance of their identity as persons across time are false. Hence, the aim is to exhibit the unsatisfactoriness of these views and thereby motivate both changes in beliefs and revisions in theories. More specifically, the way things are requires of us a change, a deflationary move, in both our understanding of ourselves as persons and in our concern with ourselves as persons. For the basic claim in this account is that there is much less to us as persons than we think, or at least than we have good reasons for so thinking. What is required is a much more impersonal view of ourselves as entities that, far from being fundamental, exist not so much in the way individuals exist but in the way—to use the analogy of Hume's that recurs here—nations exist. In particular, the concern is to argue that "most of us should change our views about the nature of persons, and personal identity over time. The truth is here very different from what most of us believe" (450). In short, this account is designed to modify our views about the nature of persons and our related moral views as well. Central to this aim is an unusual interpretation about the nature and especially the importance of personal identity.

[9]Parfit 1984:454. Subsequent references are given in text.

What, then, is the substance of this account? Two traditional views are put into question[10]—the idea that a person is in some central sense a separately existing entity, and the idea that each person should always act in such a way as to promote his or her own self-interest.[11] Roughly speaking, for the second we are urged to substitute the idea that each person should act in such a way so as to promote the interests of others, and for the first the idea that a person is not a single determinate entity of any sort whatsoever but a more or less unified, although indeterminate, collection of continuous and/or connected experiences. We have, in short, a Humean altruism. More simply, the claim is that "the unity of a life involves no more than the various relations between the experiences in this life" (346). Persons, however, are not just series of events, actions, and thoughts; rather, they are agents and thinkers. But persons do not exist as separate entities. The key to understanding this view lies in a suggestive passage. "We deny," the author writes (in the first person plural), "that we are not just conceptually distinct from our bodies, actions, and experiences, but also separately real. We deny that a person is an entity whose existence is separate from the existence of his brain and body, and the occurrence of his experiences. And we deny that a person's continued existence is a deep further fact, that must be all or nothing, and that is different from the facts of physical and psychological continuity" (341).

In order to appreciate this view, we need to distinguish what it rejects from what it accepts. This view accepts that the lives of most human beings are properly characterized in terms of psychological and physical continuity because, physically, human beings have overlapping memories, intentions, dispositions, and traits connecting the earlier and later phases of their lives. This view, however, rejects the idea that the identity of a person requires something further than physical and psychological continuity and connectedness; namely, the perduring existence of some more fundamental and purely mental separate entity (whether a substance, a Cartesian ego, a soul, or an elusive self) which is the unique subject of that person's memories, intentions, dispositions, traits. The point is that whatever entity satisfies the physical and psychological conditions described in the account is a person. Since these conditions alone are logically sufficient for the definition of personal identity, no further conditions are required. Those who hold that still other conditions must be satisfied are not so much subscribing to an incoherent view as simply subscribing to an

[10]Letwin 1984:24.
[11]See Sen 1985.

implausible account. For much evidence stands against the truth of this alternative and little in its favor.

The present account, thus, is benignly reductionist in the sense that this view, while accepting that the person is not just a stream of events, nonetheless reduces the person to a set of experiences of physical and psychological continuities and connections whose unity is a matter of degree subject to important variations over time. Beyond such continuities and connections nothing else is either logically required for personal identity to hold nor indeed is to be found. Moreover, the psychological connectedness is precisely what matters most to us (284). Consequently, we care less, and should care less, for our remote futures than for our nearer ones (206). But what is meant by calling this account a "reductionist" one?

First, distinguish between a nonreductionist and a reductionist view. Both the nonreductionist and the reductionist hold that persons exist, are distinct from their experiences, and are distinct from their bodies and brains. The nonreductionist holds further that persons exist as separately distinct entities; this the reductionist rejects. "The existence of a person during any period," this account reads, "just consists in the existence of his brain and body, and the thinking of his thoughts, and the doing of his deeds, and the occurrence of many other physical and mental events" (275).

This distinction may help, but we still require a fuller description of the reductionist view. And this is difficult to provide (274). Further, when presented, such a description does not inspire much confidence even in those who propound it (280). Still, consider the difference between two views—the presence or absence of the belief that a fact beyond physical and psychological continuity and connectedness is required. "It is natural to believe in this further fact," this account continues, "and to believe that, compared with the continuities, it is a *deep* fact, and is the fact that really matters . . . but there is no such fact" (279).

Finally, add one further element, the claim that the conjunction of the following views is consistent. For the reductionist holds: (a) that a person "consists in the existence of a brain and body, and the occurrence of a series of interrelated physical and mental events"; (b) that a person "is *distinct* from a brain and body, and such a series of events"; (c) that although persons exist, a complete description of reality can be given "*without* claiming that persons exist" (211–12). The point of this last view is that a complete description could be given by simply describing, impersonally, particular existing states of affairs consisting of brains and bodies and interrelated physical and mental events. Here, then, is the gist of the reductionist view.

If we focus on this formulation as such, however, we run the risk of missing an essential feature in this account. For the point is not that a person is rightly described in reductionist terms but that what matters in the understanding of persons is the discussion of personal identity as the prolonging of a person's psychological continuity rather than the prolonging of his or her existence as just the person he or she happens to be, the preservation of personal identity. What really matters is "the prolonging of psychological continuity, or, more importantly, of those direct connections between phases of a mental life, the overlappings of which yield, in an ordinary life, the psychological continuity that characterizes it from beginning to end . . . this connectedness-and- continuity, though normally a feature of continued identity, is theoretically separable from it . . . it is, perhaps, of all the features of continued identity the one that matters most to us."[12] More specifically: "the rival view is that personal identity is not what matters. I claim, what matters is Relation R: psychological connectedness and/or continuity with the right kind of cause" (215, emphasis omitted; 262; 279). So much, then, for a statement of this first account. (See the first section of Appendix 6A, "The Reductive Account," for a series of criticisms.)

Future Selves and Rational Choices

We need now to return to one of the puzzling elements in the opposition between the reductionist account of personal identity and the nonreductionist one, namely, the question of whether the identity of a person is always determinate. This issue is centered on a discussion of future selves. Whatever difficulties spelling out such a notion involves, struggling with these difficulties is not required if the nonreductionist is right. For in that case talk of future selves is nothing more than talk of future states of the person. And these states, like those in the present, are always explainable in terms primarily not of interrelatedness but of that further fact called identity.

Consider, then, the question of future selves. And take the nature of these future persons as indeterminate entities. In the case of future states of what we assume to be our perduring persons, we need to distinguish our descendants from our future selves. We can do so simply by recalling that the psychological interrelatedness between the prior and subsequent events of the same person's life are described in terms of psychological connectedness and psychological continuity. In the case of one's future descendants, we are talking preeminently

---

[12]Strawson 1984:44.

about psychological connectedness, whereas in the case of future selves we are talking mainly about psychological continuity. On the reductionist view both relations matter and neither is understood as more important than the other (301). But when we are talking about future selves as opposed to descendants, what matters most is not so much the genetic propensities that foster in one's descendants the development of certain dispositions connected with one's own. What matters, rather, is the actual psychological continuities, memories, intentions, desires, and so on between our present and future selves. So some of our future states are not so much to be understood as our descendants, to whom we are both physically and psychologically connected, but as our future selves, with whom, additionally and preeminently, we share certain psychological continuities.

We have already seen that in some cases the answer to certain kinds of questions about our future states is not determinate. We need now to carry this result over to our discussion of future selves. The point of that earlier discussion is that, although our relations with our own future selves involve especially psychological continuities, these continuities are subject to variations. Such continuities that may subsist, then, between me and my future selves are always a matter of degree. In some cases the relatedness may be so attenuated that a certain question about the identity of a particular future self may be nothing more than an empty question. But how are we to describe those cases where such a question is not empty?

In the case of future selves we need to introduce the notion of degrees of both connectedness and continuity. We then can say that the degree of psychological continuity is more or less great as a function of just how much memory, intention, and so on is psychologically continuous between me and any one of my future selves. But how are we to determine such matters of degree when one of the key terms in the relation—namely, my future self—does not yet exist? One solution lies in seeing that any one of my future selves is not to be found inalienably fixed to some future time down the course of my as yet unlived life. For my future selves are already anticipated in the present through my imaginings just as my past selves still linger in the present through my rememberings. The difference between these two kinds of selves is that past selves are still present and are so in determinate ways, whereas future selves are already present but only indeterminately. My suggestion is that we stress psychological continuities instead of connectedness, and that instead of the degree of psychological continuity we stress a particular element in such continuity, what I call a basic intention. On this account, then, my first claim is that Rilke's talk of self-transformation may reasonably be construed as signifying the need to care at least as much for oneself as a future self, however indeterminate, as for oneself as an actual person.

LEADING A LIFE AND VIRTUAL PERSONS: A SECOND ACCOUNT

Leading the Life of a Person

I turn now to a second recent account of the nature of the person and personal identity. And just as in the first case, I proceed by sketching the background and aims of this second account, articulating the gist of the account in terms of its basic elements, and then underlining several salient difficulties.

"There are persons," Richard Wollheim begins in his *Thread of Life*, "they exist; persons lead lives, they live; and as a result, in consequence . . . there are lives, of which those who lead them may, for instance, be proud, or feel ashamed. So there is a thing, and there is a process, and there is a product."[13] One striking feature in such a beginning is not so much the tone, which shares a certain directness with the first account. For starting a discussion of the person with an emphasis on things, products, and processes is more concrete than the usual decision to start with an analysis of the concept of a person. The stress here is much less abstract. In fact, the context could almost be characterized as existential were one to overlook the very substantial amount of conceptual analysis which goes into the elaboration of the account. The focus here is not on the definition of a concept but on the meaning of a life. And this focus is sharpened in part by the force of the citations, not from Nietzsche but from Kierkegaard's *Journal* of 1843, which stand at the head of this account. "It is perfectly true, as philosophers say," the citation from Kierkegaard reads, "that life must be understood backwards. But they forget the other proposition, that it must be lived forwards . . . life can never really be understood in time simply because at no particular moment can I find the necessary resting-place from which to understand it—backwards" (1).

The impression that this is an unusual kind of account of personal identity crystallizes once we go on to note a second point, the very important role two elements play in this dramatization. Psychoanalysis— especially certain views on the nature of fantasy, desire, guilt, and death— is the first of these components. And the second is aesthetics, especially a philosophical reflection on the varied resources of literature and painting for comprehending the richness of mental life and the complexities of

---

[13]Wollheim 1985:2. Subsequent references are given in the text.

human motivation. (The color reproduction on the book jacket is the author's choice, a woman releasing into the flowing river water the basket of a child—Poussin's *Exposition of Moses*.) Thus, the context of this second account is far more practically oriented toward understanding the puzzles of everyday deliberation, choices, and actions than the context of the first.

Filling out this account, however, requires adding a third and final element, dialogue with the history of philosophy. For in the background of this account of the person can be found an inhabitual attempt to use the kinds of arguments against reductive views of personal identity that Kant used in his criticisms of Hume's empirical understanding of the self. Conversely, we find a Humean naturalistic orientation against religious views of the person very much like those that are often opposed to Kantian views on morality. For the present account rejects the notion of the person as a temporal entity to be analyzed solely with the help of the observational data available through introspection. When Hume practiced this method he concluded that the self is nothing more than an agglomeration, a bundle of what he called "perceptions." Personal identity thus came to be understood very much as it still is understood (for example, in the previous account), as a set of relations which holds among discrete Humean "perceptions." And the reasons for the rejection of such a view are basically the Kantian ones. For the problem with such an account, the claim goes, is that it assumes that all Humean "perceptions" or impressions are passive. Yet some of our "perceptions" or impressions are active. The person hence cannot be understood in passive terms only, for part of what it means to be a person involves not simply receiving impressions but modifying our world in the very ways in which we deploy our perceptions as agents. "A life which could be described as the life of a person," one commentator summarizes accordingly, "must be unified by a complementary set of states and attitudes whose basic feature is that they relate past experiences and actions."[14]

If the context of this second account, then, is largely antiempirical, although naturalistic, drawing heavily on psychoanalysis and reflection on the arts although relying centrally both on a distinguished capacity for conceptual analysis and on the Kantian view if not of morality then at least of the active component in perception, what then is the aim of such an account?

Two things are going on here—one is the attempt to establish the primacy of the person over the elements, events, and relations that in part make up a person's mental life, and the other is the detailed description of the temporal structure that governs living the life of a person.[15]

[14]See Morton 1985:688.
[15]See Elster 1983.

Although much more of the present account is given over to the elaboration of the second of these matters, the first clearly is meant to be taken as central. Thus, this account aims at providing us with a fresh view of what a person is while using as its main resource not the extensive discussion of puzzles about personal identity but a description of what leading the life of a person really comes to. Hence, the account is proposed as a naturalistic one that has been carefully revised in the light of a critique of empiricist epistemology. More specifically, the aim here is to provide a naturalistic and yet nonreductive account of the nature of the person.

What, then, is the gist of this account?

The view is first developed as a critique of strictly empirical and reductionist views such as those we first considered. The initial claim, thus, is negative. Such reductionist views, the story goes, always try to account for the unity of the person by trying to explain the relations among the various events that make up the physical and psychological continuities and connectedness of a person's life. But this attempt, it is asserted, cannot succeed, because no two events can be construed as part of the unity of a person's life without presupposing the logically prior existence of some underlying entity. This entity is the person, and the existence of persons have priority over the existence of their own mental states. "Once it is recognized," this account goes, "that persons necessarily enter into events that make up the lives of persons, a purely relational theory of a life will not do. For in addition to the relation that holds between different events in the same life, some supplementary requirement must be laid on who enters into these events. . . . What should be required is that one and the same person enters into each and every event that belongs to the same life" (19).

This objection to the first account is then elaborated positively into a rich description of what it means to live the life of a person. The description involves a number of elements. I mention only six.

First, on the present account, the unity of a life is what constitutes the identity of a person. And this unity must be understood, once one has seen the reasons why the Humean account of the self is inadequate, as the unity of a whole not as the unity of a collection. Both a whole and a collection consist of parts. But the parts of a whole exhibit a different kind of unity than that which holds among the parts of a collection. Moreover, unlike the identity of a physical object, the identity of a person cannot be construed satisfactorily in terms of not incompatible but different descriptions. For living a life has consequences that affect what shapes the whole of a life will assume.

Second, unlike the previous account, the present alternative reserves an important place in the understanding of personal identity for the phenomenon of death. Just as some projects have subsequent effects of such an order that the whole of a life is changed, so the thought of death as the limit of life exercises an antecedent effect on the shape the whole of a life may assume. Neither the denial that death is a misfortune nor the affirmation that life is eternal do justice to how the phenomenon of death shapes the unity of a life. For, the claim goes, just because death is both final and a genuine loss, the desire to live a life remains such a persistent concern.

But leading a life involves not only the sense of a whole and continual readjustments to an understanding of death as a loss without reprieve; it involves, third, a continual awareness of being at a crossroads. For being a person involves being in different kinds of relationships with one's own past, present, and future. "A person leads his life at a cross-roads," this account goes, "at the point where a past that has affected him and a future that lies open meet in the present" (31). These relationships are complex. And part of the interest in this account lies in its sensitivity to how the nature of the person is inevitably linked to the subsistence of the different temporal relations within a life. The person stands always at a crossroads in the sense that the person is always moving from a present moment toward the realization of certain future concerns that themselves arise out of past influences.

Fourth, being a person involves living through the fullness of our intentional states—such spasmodic phenomena as "perceptual experiences, attacks of dizziness, dreams, and moments of terror, amusement, lust, or despair" (33). Such states are always about something and hence can be understood as having a mental content. Moreover, the person always experiences such states in a certain peculiar way. Thus, mental states can seem to consist of both an intentional and a subjective component. A life that does not consist of the conjunction of these two claims about the nature of mind— its intentionality and its subjectivity—cannot be the life of a person.

Fifth, being a person not only involves living through these mental states; it especially involves being drawn, through a basic desire to live, to unify the different temporal phases of one's life. The basic attachment of the person to this life is based, then, not on the Hobbesian desire for biological continuation of the species or the Benthamite desire for the pursuit of the varieties of pleasure, but on the personal desire to lead one's life by continually rearticulating the deliberative processes of human agents. Thus, the stress falls clearly on the pursuit of the projects, plans, and proposals of the person as agent.

Finally, being a person involves living through progressive and qualitatively different changes in one's own evolution as a moral agent by attaining a progressively fuller insight into one's own nature as a person. This progression takes place to the degree that the person manages to transform three cardinal relations in the leading of a life—the relation between the person's past and the present, the relation between the person's mental dispositions and mental states, and the relation between the person's conscious and the unconscious or preconscious system of the mind. These qualitative discriminations and transformations are greatly fostered when the actual processes that control the evolution of the person as an agent are comprehended through the theory and practice of psychoanalysis.

These six elements combine and interact in different ways. But the gist of the present account can be put as follows: "we are forced to conceive of our lives as shaped around a substantial self, and . . . part of what it is to live a human life is to be continually revising one's way towards an adequate conception of what that self is."[16]

However sketchy, this summary has the merit of bringing together the two key elements in this account, the reflection on the nature of the person and the reflection on what it means for a person to lead a life. But if we are to understand this account sympathetically yet critically, we need to underline the central role in the description of the person which this account reserves for a process as opposed to either a thing or a product. "In order to understand the thing that is the person, or in order to understand the product that is the person's life, we need to understand the process that is the person's leading his life." (For criticisms of this second view, see section two of Appendix 6A, "The Nonreductive Account.")

Self-concern and Virtual Persons

In a previous section we were able to explore one element in the reductionist account of the nature of the person in relation to our concern with putative moral considerations respecting one's future selves. On the reductionist account we said that in some cases the answer to the question "Am I myself or someone else?" may not be determinate. We then argued that such indeterminate entities are interestingly described as future selves. And we saw that it is rational to be morally concerned with future selves.

Let us now explore several conceptual resources in the rival nonreductionist view of the nature of the person. In particular, we will consider the controversial claim that the identity of persons through time requires something more than psychological and physical connectedness and continuity—namely, a perduring personal unity, which can be understood as a claim about the indeterminateness thesis. On the nonreductionist account in some cases the answer to the question "Is this future

[16]Morton 1985.

person me or someone else?" may be the vaguely determinate reply "This person is virtually me." These vaguely determinate entities might best be understood as virtual persons or fictive selves. Finally, just as it is rational to be morally concerned about future selves, it is rational to be morally concerned about virtual persons or fictive selves. But the kind of moral concern in this case (unlike the former case) is better understood in terms of ethical responsiveness rather than in those of moral obligation.

On the second account of the nature of a person, the nonreductionist account, the central task consists in explaining a process, what it is to live the life of a person. One of the cardinal elements in that process is the relation in which one believes oneself to stand to one's own future states. This relation is called "self-concern" (236–56). And the basic point about self-concern on this account is that it "neither is nor includes an attitude towards myself" (241). How, then, does self-concern differ from basic attitudes toward oneself?

Consider first the attitude one may assume with regard to one's own desires, their fulfillment or frustration—namely, egoism. Egoism consists in one's belief that one's own desires and their fulfillment, regardless of what may be the specific object of such desires, are more important than those of others. By contrast, self-concern involves no preference claim for the superiority of one's own future states over those of others. Thus, self-concern does not do away with egoism, but it does not presuppose it either.

Consider next the attitude one may assume in seeing the course of one's future life in terms of a harmonious equilibrium between pleasure and pain. This attitude is called "finding life worth living." And it consists in two things—a concern with whether some future state will contribute to harmony, and the presupposition that one's present states are already harmonious. But as the case of rational suicide shows, self-concern does not involve finding life worth living in either of these two respects.

Consider finally the attitude that consists in finding in one's life sufficient conditions for fulfilling the desires, plans, and projects one finds important. This attitude is called "finding life worthwhile." And once again such an attitude involves two elements—concern with whether my future states will contribute to the realization of my projects and the presupposition that my present state already does. This attitude is not the same as the previous one, for it is perfectly possible for someone to find life worth living but not worthwhile, as presumably Napoleon did on St. Helena, and life worthwhile but not worth living, as presumably Saint Peter did in Rome (246). But self-concern involves neither, for it is centered on something other than either the realization of harmony or the fulfillment of projects.

If self-concern, then, is neither egoism nor finding life worth living nor even finding life worthwhile, it nonetheless depends on the priority of desire, for without desire there would be no self-concern. But self-concern characteristically is a matter not of the formation or presence of desire but of its motivational force. Thus, self-concern is not an attitude toward oneself or an indifference to one's own future states but a nonpreferential and noninstrumental relation to the importance and value of one's own future states and those of others. Unlike self-love, self-concern depends on no one factor. Nor does self-concern depend on any particular feature of a person's psychology as a whole, and it both derives from and is partly constitutive of the process of living as a person. As such, self-concern is carefully correlated with the capacity to enter into one's past, present, and future states of mind as one's own.

On the present account, then, the nature of self-concern lies in the central contention of the nonreductionist view—namely, that something more is required to account for the nature of the person than interrelatedness. What is required is the presence of ourselves as persisting entities irreducible to mere interrelatedness. This persisting presence is to be understood as our ongoing capacity to enter into the fullness of our own present states and thereby gain that acquaintance with one's present states which enables one both to retrieve states and their influence and to anticipate future states and past concern with them as one's own.

This view of self-concern is inseparable from the nonreductionist view of the person because it depends on the claim that a persisting entity is required for the explanation of the identity of persons over time. That claim, however, includes the view that the question of whether some future person is me or someone else must always have a determinate answer. But since we need not choose between the reductionist and the nonreductionist accounts (see section three of Appendix 6A, "Choosing between the Two Accounts"), we may assert that in some cases such a question may have no determinate answer. In the light of the nonreductionist description of self-concern, I suggest that the set of future states to which I stand in the relation of self-concern described here is usefully described as a "virtual person." I may stand, then, in a relation of self-concern to my future self not just as an entirely indeterminate entity but as a vaguely determinate entity I call a virtual person.

Recall, finally, the discussion of weak and strong kinds of psychological continuity, for this will give us the distinction we need to parse the unfamiliar notion I propose here of virtual person. In cases of those future selves with whom I now enjoy by anticipation strong bonds of psychological continuity, I speak not of future selves but of virtual persons, whereas in cases of those with whom the degrees of continuity are much less strong we may continue to speak of future selves. Virtual persons thus are intimately linked not so much with memory, desire, character, and/or disposition as they are with basic intentions. In thinking of myself in the future, I may entertain a number of scenarios in each of which one of my future selves plays a more or less central role— in short, I may fantasize (see Morton 1985). But when I think of myself in the future, I may just as well articulate a number of scenes in each of which the same virtual person struggles to fulfill a basic intention to realize a life ideal that is already at the basis of my own multiple strivings here and now in the present—that is, I may imagine. In the first case, the entity in question is clearly the object of some of my present psychological states. But no matter how richly detailed such a future self may be or how many such selves may be fantasized, no one of them on the present terms can bear the burden of that peculiar kind of psychological continuity I am calling here my perduring basic intention to realize a life ideal. On these terms, however continuous such similar entities as future selves may be with respect to my present dispositions and desires, only a virtual person can be continuous with my present basic intentions. In other words,[17] all my future selves are clearly my descendants, but they are not all equally my relatives; some, my virtual persons, are more centrally related to me than others. On this account, then, I revise my initial claim to read that Rilke's talk of self-transformation may reasonably be construed as coming into a standing relation of self-concern with at least one of those imagined future selves I call my virtual person.

It could further be added that we need to think of the nature of such moral concern as we have for ourselves as virtual persons not in terms of moral obligations to such beings but in those of ethical responsiveness to the importance and value of embodied mental states (see Appendix 3B, "Moral Obligation and Ethical Responsiveness"). It is then both rationally justifiable and ethically responsive to enter into a relation of moral concern with oneself as a virtual person.

FUTURE SELVES, FICTIONAL CHARACTERS, AND ETHICAL PERSONS

Let us focus now on the relationship between a certain kind of fictive self and the ethical self, and the justification of present concerns for what the poet calls "transformation." It will prove useful to look back at the problem of self-identity, then at the nature of the fictive self, and finally at the key issue of justification by appeal to defining characteristics of a particular virtual person or fictive self.

The character of the kind of construct I call the fictive self or the virtual

---

[17]Parfit 1984:315–16.

person cannot be understood clearly except by contrast with its purported opposite, the "real self" or the "real person." This latter notion we now see conceals a number of issues which should be underlined separately, and this regardless of whether we wish to argue for some other expression as the legitimate opposite of the fictive self than the pretender now in place under the name of the "real self." For the "real self" may refer to those elements that distinguish the class of persons from other similar classes such as that of robots, or mountain gorillas, or corporations.[18] Or the expression may be taken as referring to those individuating features that distinguish one member of the same class of persons from another such member. A third possible referent for the "real person" is the set of criteria which are both necessary and sufficient for reidentifying at different times and under different descriptions the same individual in successive stages of his or her life. Or the expression may refer to the set of essential characteristics which make an individual person just that person and no one else regardless of his or her being differentiated and reidentified in the same way.

Each one of these four problems about the identity of the self is arguably different from any of the others. All four, however, are closely enough related that a position one argues for in any one case usually determines very strongly the position one adopts with respect to the rest. My concern is not so much with the problems of class identity or individuation as it is with those of reidentification and essential self-identity. In the case of reidentification, however, I am less interested in pursuing the issue of just which sets of conditions for a continuing personal identity can arguably be taken as both necessary and sufficient than in seeing how the essential identity of a person is often threatened by the temporal stages or psychological passages a person moves through in living his or her life. Moreover, the essential identity I focus on here must include not only those conditions that define that person as a distinct individual (say, his or her genetic codes) and those that serve to reidentify that person as the same person of a moment ago (say, his or her memories), but also whatever traits the person as well as the person's family and friends and society consider essential to his or her identity. And finally, in talking of essential personal identity rather than looking for conditions that assure survival or those that assure a loose typical identity, I focus the discussion on conditions for a strict notion of identity. This constraint of course, unlike the others, opens up the possibility that a "biological individual may not remain the same person throughout a lifetime."[19]

[18]A. Rorty 1976.
[19]Ibid., 2.

We will find it useful, however, to recall several basic distinctions. Consider first the talk here about the essential identity of the moral self. Notice that two things need to be distinguished, the identity of the moral self with itself (call this self-identity) and the identity of the present self with a future self (call this personal identity). The second kind of identity concerns us, for the question here is what kind of a relation may properly be said to link the present with the future self.

Traditionally, it helps to recall the distinction between numerical identity and qualitative identity. When we talk here of an identity between one's present self and a future self we are not referring to qualitative sameness in the sense of exact likeness (for there are many differences between the two) but numerical sameness in the sense of one and the same (for there is presumably continuity of one and the same person.)[20]

We need also to recall that this relation of numerical identity is not the unity relation. For that relation is one that holds between two or more stages that are already understood as stages of one and the same thing. The problem still remains after one has specified the unity relation as to the nature of what makes these stages of one and the same thing.[21]

If the identity, then, between my present self and my future self is not qualitative but numerical and the relation is not one of unity, what kind of relation can it be? This question turns, however, on still a further distinction between two views of personal identity—the simple and the complex. According to the simple view, two theses are to be conjoined: the indefinability thesis (the view, namely, that personal identity cannot be given a nontrivial and a noncircular account) and the determinacy thesis (namely, the view that statements about personal identity always have a determinate truth-value with the consequence that there are no borderline cases of personal identity). According to the complex view, the indefinability thesis is not settled and the determinacy thesis is not true.

In this first question about the essential identity of the moral self, I qualify the sense of the talk here about identity in terms of a nonunitary relation of numerical identity between my present self and some one of my future selves to be articulated in some complex and not simple account. More specifically, without arguing the case here, I leave the indefinability thesis open for discussion while urging that, *pace* those who hold the simple view, some instances of a putative personal-identity relation between my present self and a future self may well be borderline cases and therefore lack determinate truth-values.

---

[20]Shoemaker 1984:72.
[21]Perry 1975a.

But how are we to mark the difference between the future selves I call fictive selves and fictional characters? Here we can be brief.[22]

In the case of fictional characters, I can come to know in all their exquisite detail the sum total of what exactly in their regard is the case. For fictional characters are surprisingly exhaustible as objects of knowledge since, unlike material objects, they lack the infinity of ever receding perceptual horizons and, unlike self-conscious entities, they lack the inexorable privacy of ever changing varieties of mental states. Fictional characters, in short, are intentional objects of a peculiarly delimited sort; like the stories in which they only appear to have lives of their own, they have a beginning, a middle, and an end.[23]

By contrast, fictive selves are inexhaustible. For such entities, when instantiated, share many of the properties of material objects and hence escape our closest scrutiny while exhausting our most patient descriptions. And such entities, again like the persons with whom they share a numerical identity, must be understood with reference to their mental states and hence exhibit when realized the ineluctable privacy of their causes.

Consequently, when I speak of empathetic identification with one's fictive selves I preserve some distinction between fictional and nonfictional entities.[24] Characters belong among the former, whereas fictive selves belong with the latter.

With these three clarifications in hand let us now look more closely at the details of a recent disagreement.

These distinctions concerning the various issues masked in the expression "the real self" presume that we have a basic interest in being the same person and not just being the same physical object or the same human being. What motivates this basic interest? One thing is the need to know "whom to reward and whom to punish for certain actions." Another is our need to know what we can expect of persons around us, something that is impossible if none of their traits is constant. And still another, a central one for our concerns here, is our need to know what we can reasonably expect of ourselves in the future and what we can reasonably feel pride or shame, gratitude or remorse, about with respect to our past actions. In short, the general philosophical interest of essential personal identity has to do with responsibility, with punishment, blame, and reward.

How, then, are we to understand those conditions that are essential to someone's being a person? Any persistent search for the set of necessary

[22]See Wiseman 1978.
[23]Cf. A. Rorty 1976a.
[24]See Loux 1979.

and sufficient conditions here is likely to be misguided from the start by a basic ambiguity in the concept of person. On the one hand we have the notion of a person as a moral entity, the forensic subject Locke talks about in the *Essay*,[25] the person who is a legally accountable agent and a subject of rights and responsibilities. But we also have the notion of a person as a metaphysical entity, the intelligent, conscious, feeling self that Hume describes in the *Treatise*.[26] If these two notions are as distinct as they seem to be, we will find that instead of one concept of person we have at least two. Consequently, any search for necessary and sufficient conditions of the concept of persons which does not seriously explore this ambiguity cannot be expected to succeed.[27]

If we center our discussion on moral personhood and assume for our purposes that metaphysical personhood is merely one of the necessary conditions for moral personhood, what other conditions on the evidence of the arguments and distinctions in the journals would also seem to be necessary conditions? Recently, six such conditions have been spelled out.

Moral persons, first, are rational beings, as traditional philosophers as different as Aristotle, Aquinas, and Kant have argued. Second, moral persons are beings to which both intentional predicates and states of consciousness are ascribed. Third, whether a being is a moral person depends in part on how other persons treat that being,[28] a point I return to later. Moreover, whether a being is a moral person also depends in part on that being's capacity for reciprocating the personal stance someone assumes in its regard. Fifth, a moral person must be a user of language in the sense that such a being must be capable of communicating through words. And finally, a moral person is a being who is "conscious in a way in which no other species is conscious. Sometimes this is identified as *self*-consciousness of one sort or another."[29]

We now need to specify more carefully the problematic notion of the *self* of a moral person, or what I call more simply the moral self. The notion is problematic in the sense that sometimes some of us might wonder, "Am I the same moral self as yesterday? Will I be the same moral self tomorrow?" And these curious questions in fact involve more than one consideration. For there is an epistemological issue here (what evidence is there for saying that I am the same moral self as yesterday or will be tomorrow?), an ontological issue (what could ever make me the same moral self that was here yesterday and that will be here tomorrow?),

[25]Locke 1975:2, chap. 27.
[26]Hume 1978:251, 259, 633–36.
[27]Dennett 1976.
[28]Dennett 1971 and Van de Vate 1971.
[29]Dennett 1976:178.

and a logical concern (how is one to explain the identity of a moral self?).[30] Granted that our question conceals more than one issue, how can we narrow our focus most usefully in view of our concern with those future selves I call fictive?

Here is one recent view of the self which will help us accomplish that necessary task.[31] The idea is "that relations of psychological connectedness (such as memory and persistence of character and motivation) are what really matter with regard to most questions involving personal identity. The suggestion is that morality should take this seriously as well . . . psychological connectedness (unlike the surface logic of personal identity) admits of degrees. Let us call the relevant properties and relations which admit of degrees, *scalar* items. One of the aims of this view is to make moral thought reflect more directly the scalar character of the phenomena which underlie personal identity. In particular, in those cases in which the scalar relations hold in reduced degree, this fact should receive recognition in moral thought."[32]

When we talk about our moral selves we need to acknowledge not just the scalar items (those of its properties and relations which admit to degrees) but also the related fact of temporalization—the way we were in the past, the way we will be in the future. And here we need to allow further for the distinction between our past and future selves and our past and future characters. If we are ready to grant the general distinction between a moral self and a moral character, then it remains to be seen whether we will go on to hold open the possibility of a changing moral character in a perduring moral self rather than insisting on the multiplication of selves. For some want to maintain that "talk of 'past selves,' 'future selves,' and generally 'several selves' is only a convenient fiction; neglect of this may make the transpositions in moral thought required by the Complex View [that is, Parfit's view above, which this author summarizes] seem simpler and more inviting than they are, since they may glide along on what seems a mere multiplication, in the case of these new 'selves,' of similar interpersonal relations. We must concentrate on the scalar facts."[33]

These considerations are sage counsel. But we need to reflect a moment more if we are to be in a position to apply such counsel. Consider, then, the cryptic suggestion that in all this talk of personal identity, moral persons, and moral selves our several selves or characters are "convenient fictions." (See Appendix 6B, "Describing Persons Indeterminately.")

[30]See Mackensie 1983:163–64 and Gupta 1982:521.
[31]Parfit 1973.
[32]Williams 1976:202.
[33]Ibid., 202–3.

However, take these fictions positively rather than pejoratively. My claim is that we may justify the reasonableness of a certain idea of a future self as a fictive self in terms of imaginative identification between some concerns of our present self and similar concerns of our virtual selves in the future.

The identification I have in mind is related to the kind of phenomenon that occurs repeatedly in our own lives whenever we read literary works with the requisite sympathy. As readers we often identify ourselves with characters in these stories, plays, poems.[34] We practice, in short, a species of empathetic identification. As a result of a peculiar exercise in imagination, we, as readers or as writers, come to believe what it is like to be another person. In fact, most basically we cannot come to understand certain literary works, it has been argued persuasively, without imaginatively identifying ourselves with certain characters. And this is the case "because of the connection between interpretations of characters and conceptions of the self."[35] In short, we can make empathetic identifications between ourselves and fictional characters because in fact we do make such identifications.

We would need, of course, to parse the central term here, "imaginative activity," were we to spell out this view in greater detail. But such detail would not be difficult to generate because the phenomenon of empathetic identification is common across cultures, and several excellent accounts of imaginative activity in different philosophical traditions are already available.[36] For the moment, then, we may be satisfied with construing this activity broadly as something other than the mere practice of postulating possibilities. We may say, rather, that "imaginative activity" here refers to "the ability to seize and act upon a certain course of behavior—including the making of certain statements. . . . This involves a plunge out of a range of alternatives."[37] Of course, we are just as familiar with the imaginative process of empathizing with fictional characters. But here is where I introduce a change in our usual understanding of this process. For the relation I am talking about now is one that subsists between these real persons and the fictional character I call my fictive self.

"Character," thus, is being used here in two different senses: first, as that set of properties, dispositions, relations and events, which I am sometimes able to identify with in reading literary works; and second, a similar set of properties in my future to which I sometimes choose to relate other real persons. In the literary case the other is a character and

[34]Wiseman 1978.
[35]Wiseman 1982:342.
[36]See Casey 1976. For other traditions, see Arbib 1986, Boer 1986, and Tugendhat 1986.
[37]Palma 1983:31–32.

the self is real; in the nonliterary case the other is real and the self, the fictive self, is a character. What, then, is the sense of the cardinal term "character"?

Let us say with one philosopher writing recently that a literary character "is a set of descriptions given by a text, at least one of which is the description of a typical human characteristic, and a character is more than the words on the pages of its text in that it is whatever is both consistent with the words and such that the reader can know what it is like to be it by performing an experiment in imagination."[38] And let us say that nonliterary characters "are all and only what people may imagine themselves to be, and people may conceive of their identity in all and only the ways in which they individuate characters."[39]

My point, then, is that talk of one of my future selves as a fictive self and even as a virtual moral person may be rationally justified in an imaginative way in the sense that I may imaginatively identify my present moral concerns with those of my fictive self. This means that I can understand myself as a fictive self, a character of my own construction (at least in this case, although not necessarily in many other ones), who has moral concerns with respect to his relations with others and with things.

But there is also a stronger imaginative exercise at work here. For in attributing a moral concern to one of my possible selves, I am in fact close to holding not only that such fictive selves have the same rights as persons but the same rights as I myself. For one of the ironies in ascribing moral concerns to the imaginary constructs I call fictive selves is that these concerns may well turn out to be the very same ones I have with respect to my present self. For who is to say that I will not become tomorrow one of those virtual persons whom today I strive to transform myself into? But let us return now to the suggestions of Rilke's late poetry.

FICTION AND FICTIONAL SELVES

*Reinterpreting Fictions of Self-transformation in
Rilke's Late Poetry*

In an initial citation from Sonnets I.5 the critic identifies the speaker as Rilke:

> Erect no gravestone to his memory; just
> let the rose blossom each year for his sake.

[38]Wiseman 1982:374.
[39]Ibid., 348–49.

> For it *is* Orpheus. Whereever he has passed
> through this or that.

Rilke is said to have found in these lines a way of interiorizing and
transforming "the sense of abandonment" which had followed on the
discovery, definition, and relinquishment suggested in the first two elegies, written in 1912.

If this sonnet provides us with a glimpse of Rilke's return to the Orpheus
figure, the third is said to exhibit a breakthrough in the formulation "song
is reality." The breakthrough consists in Rilke's relinquishment, not just
of any residual belief in the genuineness of an unstillable hope for perfect
fulfillment, as in the figure of the angel in "The First Elegy," but in his
relinquishment also of any further representation in his poetry of the
attractiveness of such an illusion.

Creature of habit, Rilke compares us in Sonnet I.3 with Orpheus and
is again dismayed:

> A god can do it. But will you tell me how a
> man can penetrate through the lyre's strings?

A passage in "The Third Elegy" is said to exhibit "the change," from
the earlier relinquishment to the later one. The idea seems to be that in
the transition from the imagery of the passionate voice of desire, the
wooing voice, to that of the pure voice of need, the bird's cry, Rilke has
brought about a transformation not in his poetry but arguably in his own
understanding of himself. And this transformation is said to "culminate"
in "The Ninth Elegy," where the poem is taken to be saying that living
in the world is singing in the sense of praising.

> Perhaps we are *here* in order to say:
> house,
> bridge, fountain, gate, pitcher, fruit-tree,
>   window
> *Here* is the time for the *sayable, here* is its homeland.
> Speak and bear witness.

This kind of saying issues in a speaking, a singing (a making of celebratory
works of art, poems of praise) which transforms our way of being in the
world in such a way that our primary relation to everything else becomes
one of affirmation, to be saying: "Being human . . . is to be constantly
making one's place in language, in consciousness, in imagination. The
work is 'to rise again back into pure relation.' "[40]

---

[40]Hass, in Rilke 1982:xli.

What are we to make of this? I suggest we construe this kind of reading as a serious and thoughtful series of recommendations about what I call the ethical shapes our own future selves might well assume as virtual persons.

Much of the argument for such a suggestion would involve a far more sustained examination of the complicated evolution of Rilke's late work than we have leisure for here. But at least three major notions appear in the course of that work. The initial idea is surely one of change at an abstract level. In "The Seventh Elegy," for example, Rilke writes, "Our life / passes in transformation." "Transformation" here must be understood on larger terms than merely psychological ones, terms that would account for the shift in Rilke's poetry from talk of a turn (*eine Wende*), to change (*eine Wandlung*), and finally to transmutation (*eine Verwandlung*).

A second major notion in this development is the gradual deepening of what is meant by "a relation." Here the movement is from talk of a mere relationship with persons and things (*eine Verhältnis*) to a stress on relation as such (*ein Bezug*), to the insightful idea of standing in a relation to whatever is (*in eine Beziehung stehen*). And finally Rilke's work moves even more richly from a sustained reflection on nothing and nothingness (*das Nichts*) to a richly modulated meditation on the more complex notion of the void, of emptiness (*das Leere*). This extraordinary meditation yields many images, among them the image of a breath. Thus, not long before he died, Rilke wrote in one of his uncollected poems:

> It is nothing but a breath, the void.
> And that green fulfillment
> of blossoming trees: a breath.

Rearticulating the Question

In this chapter I have tried to understand more clearly several issues that questions about putative self-transformation in Rilke's late poetry would seem to raise. And the strategy has been to examine two contrasting views on the nature of the person with a critical interest—first, in whether these accounts are exclusive in the sense that holding one entails not holding the other, and if not then, second, in just what conceptual resources each might make available for pursuing our aims further. The argument has been that even such carefully opposed views as the reductionist and nonreductionist ones examined here can be articulated in other ways than as simple logical contradictories. When so formulated each provides us with at least one central notion that furthers our concern.

On such a reading the reductionist account turns out to offer an important conception of such future entities as indeterminate selves, whereas the nonreductionist account includes an equally important idea about the nature of self-concern. The idea of indeterminate entities provides us with a way of construing the rationality of our concerns with our own future selves; the idea of self-concern makes available a way of construing our ethical responsiveness to ourselves as virtual persons. Thus, Rilke's talk about self-transformations, about becoming a certain type of person in the future, is usefully recast as a question about what it means to be a person and about whether some future persons can be properly taken as the legitimate subjects of both rational and ethical concerns in the present.

Such a conclusion is not so much an answer to our initial question as an invitation to investigate more thoughtfully what responding to such a question involves. This invitation cannot be pursued, although I look at one of the central issues in Chapter 7. But it may be helpful to indicate in a programmatic way at least one of the many directions such further inquiry could take.

The rationality of our moral concern for ourselves as fictive selves and the ethical responsiveness we have for our future selves as virtual persons have at least one major consequence for how we think about future states of those curious entities we call ourselves. Thinking of oneself as rationally and ethically responsible for, although not morally obligated to, one's own fictive self as a virtual person entails that we construe our present selves as those peculiar sorts of fictions I call fictive persons. Such entities are not selves. Rather, they are best understood as selfless persons in the sense that whatever self such entities may properly be thought to have is an illusion. Moreover, fictive persons are not just persons *tout court* because whatever it is we refer to in such a context as "a person" is properly understood not so much as an illusion but as a conceptual construct that is necessarily subsequent to the richness of predicative immediate experience. Rather, fictive persons are better understood on the model of fictional characters. This analogy leads us finally to the view that those peculiar entities who come to understand fictive selves as the ongoing realization of a rational and ethical responsiveness to the deep pathos of things are neither selves nor persons but simply quasi-personal and efficacious fictions, or no persons at all. In the light of such a view we might then be able to see that the general question about peculiar kinds of fictions—how are we to understand the "I" in such lyric utterances of self-transformation as Rilke's "whisper to the silent earth: I'm flowing. / To the flashing water say: I am"?—is neither an open nor an empty question but one that seems to require changes in our usual understandings of personal identity.

Appendix 6A   Describing Persons Impersonally

THE REDUCTIVE ACCOUNT

Parfit's account, for all the sophistication of its presentation and defense, suffers from at least five important difficulties.

First, the account is admittedly a powerful skeptical view, much reminiscent in its major outlines of the later Hume's theory of the self as a mere agglomeration of experiences. But the problem with such skeptical views about the person is whether those views can be accepted outside the relative calm of the Humean study. Parfit is aware of this problem.[41] "I can believe this view at the intellectual or reflective level. I am convinced by the arguments in favour of this view. But I think it likely that, at some other level, I shall always have doubts" (279). But he frankly affirms that his resistance to accepting such views is as irrational as someone's fear of heights. Such a rejoinder, however, does not take skepticism about the person seriously enough.[42] In refusing to argue through the skeptical issues here, the rejoinder turns into a mere assertion.

Second, this account is polarized to an important degree by what it denies—namely, the claim that the essence of the person is an independently existing substance or Cartesian ego. But such a characterization of the traditional view is too general. For it may be pointed out that some traditional views claim that the person is something irreducible, indeed elusive, and yet not properly describable, either as a substance or a soul or a Cartesian ego.[43]

Third, this account does not provide a sufficiently detailed description of how we are to understand one of the central terms, "experience." This term is of course a cardinal one in any discussion of a skeptical and empirical view. Yet we find no attention whatever to the difficult matter of whether experiences can be understood without postulating subjects of experience (see, however, the discussion on 233ff). More specifically, we can see that the stress on experience of physical and psychological continuity and connectedness requires some attention to be paid to the fact that these experiences "are causally dependent on the continued existence (identity) of the individual person."[44] To preserve such experiences seems to require preserving the entity they depend on.

Fourth, this account is too centered on the person as an individual. The critical matter of the person's identity as a social and cultural entity

---

[41]Parfit 1984:279ff. Subsequent references are given in text.
[42]See Scheffler 1984:484.
[43]See H. Lewis 1982.
[44]Strawson 1984:44.

is too often passed over in silence. But no account of personal identity in terms of individual identity alone seems adequate. For example, consider the vast differences in the comprehension of what it means to be a person in such different milieus as say the Faculty Dining Hall at the University of Tokyo and High Table at All Soul's College Oxford.[45] This social dimension of personal identity most basically involves understanding the person in relation to others.

Finally, this account is consistently articulated in third-person terms. The result is an extremely curious picture of the person from the outside only, an exterior view that the account's own occasional recourse to literary examples belies. What we require in an account of the person is an interior view as well, what we may call a first-person account. "Philosophically speaking," one critic writes, "this account views everything from the outside. In dealing with personal identity, this conceals . . . one of the main reasons why people think that it must be a determinate question whether some future experience will be theirs or not: that if it will be theirs, they can, as well as expecting that it will happen, also expect it, in the sense of imaginatively anticipating having it; and there seems to be no reason for the idea that it is simply indeterminate whether I can appropriately do that or not."[46]

It is important to note also that the present account is addressed to a particular set of questions. "We are particular people," the author writes. "I have my life, you have yours. What do these facts involve? What makes me the same person throughout my life, and a different person from you? and What is the distinction between different lives, and different persons?" (ix; see also 202). These questions give a particular slant to this account, one we must scrutinize further once we have in hand an alternative view of how such matters are to be understood.[47]

On this first account, then, of the nature of the person when viewed from the angle of what allows us to explain personal identity over time, we find an attractive conceptual economy that nonetheless leaves both its author and its audience unsure of just how much economy is a virtue. Can we preserve a certain economy in trying to account for the nature of the person that will incorporate a more credible description of the individual and social experiences of the person, in first-person terms as well? Moreover, can we retain the thoughtful awareness that a satisfactory account of the person must involve some attention to both conceptual analysis and questions of value, of exactly what elements in such analyses matter? And finally, is there any room in revising such an account as this

---

[45]Ibid.
[46]Williams 1984:14.
[47]See "Symposium on Derek Parfit's Reasons and Persons," *Ethics* (July 1985).

for such elements as would speak to the phenomenon Rilke's readers have in mind?

The Nonreductive Account

One key difficulty of Wollheim's account of the person surely is the degree to which it relies on psychoanalysis. The problem is not so much the idea that psychoanalysis may have something to offer a more adequate theory of the person. Rather, the difficulty lies in whether some of the usual structures in psychoanalytic theory may not affect this nonreductive account of the person as well. More particularly, the psychoanalytic conceptions of desire, fantasy, and imagination may well lend themselves to philosophical reconstruction. But what of the unargued reliance in this account on a conception of value as "the projection of archaic bliss" and on an understanding of moral values independent of any account of the key notion of intrinsic goodness?[48] In short, is the naturalism this account advocates finally vitiated by an unargued reliance on one particular version of psychoanalytic theory and practice?

A more important difficulty concerns the satisfactoriness of the central claim itself. How good is the argument that purports to show that the concept of a person is logically prior to the mental states that can be predicated of the person? At one point the argument is offered: "If it is true that for mental states to arise, they must be appropriately linked to mental dispositions, then they must essentially belong to things that can house dispositions, and this is where the person is required" (57). But as one of this account's critics points out, mental dispositions could more economically be lodged in the brain of a person considered reductively as no more than a series of psychological and physical states than in the prodigal postulate of a separately existing entity.[49] "The occurrence of a mental state," this criticism runs, "would also be the occurrence of a certain physical state which by physical causality would affect the probability of later physical states and the non-concomitant mental states." So, it is not clear, at least on the sparse and elliptical arguments that accompany this account, that the alternative view must be rejected just because it is a reductive view.

A third difficulty concerns not so much the dependence of this account on obscure and highly speculative psychoanalytic views or the adequacy of the justifications provided for its pivotal claim, as on the model of mind this account proposes. The present account involves a very detailed de-

---

[48]Elster 1983.
[49]Ibid.

scription of mind in terms of mental dispositions, mental states and mental activities. And a large part of the major interest of this account derives from the richness of this description of mind, particularly the distinction between mental acts and actions, and the discussion of desire, fantasy, and imagination. Yet however right in detail, this theory of mind seems to turn on a functional view that "a disposition tends to induce mental states and behavior which reinforce it; moreover, these effects occur *because* they reinforce it."[50] This view, however, is not convincing. For it fails to take account of the fact that exercising some dispositions may result not in the reinforcement of a disposition but in its loss. Eating double desserts may lead not to the desire for even more desserts, but to the desire for none whatsoever. Moreover, not all individual dispositions are to be understood just in the evolutionary terms of contributions to survival since not every single disposition (although some would argue every set of dispositions) is functional; some—for example, certain altruistic behavior among mammals—are in isolation dysfunctional.

Can we articulate a theory of the person, then, that would capture some of the genuine insights offered here into the nature of the person as an activity leading a life both intentionally and subjectively without committing ourselves strongly to a psychoanalytic view of the origin of morality, to a merely functional view of mind, or to an insufficiently argued assertion that some further fact is required for the identity of persons, something more than physical and psychological continuity and connectedness? More particularly, just which, if any, of the numerous elements in this account can satisfactorily address the kinds of concerns with self-transformation that Rilke and some of his readers exhibit?

Choosing between the Two Accounts

These two accounts[51] of the person and personal identity over time clearly conflict. The first view, the reductionist view, explicitly affirms (P) that the personal identity of a person over time consists in nothing more than the continued existence of that person's brain and body and various interrelated physical and psychological events. This claim means: (P1) no separately existing entity is required for a complete description of such an identity; (P2) no distinct although not separately existing entity is required either; and (P3) a complete description of personal identity can be entirely impersonal. By contrast, the second view, the nonreductionist

---

[50]Ibid.
[51]Parfit 1984 and Wollheim 1985. Subsequent references in the text are to *P* and *W*.

view, explicitly denies (P), and consequently denies (P1), (P2), and (P3) also. Thus we seem to be confronted with a clear choice between one or the other; in no case, it would seem, can we hold both, since one cannot rationally affirm and deny the same thing.

The necessity for choosing between these two accounts is apparent only. For although affirming both accounts clearly seems contradictory, the basic opposition between them is not properly described in terms of a pervasive logical incompatibility.

Recall first that more than one question is at issue between the reductionist and the nonreductionist. The central issue, however, seems to be the same: namely, whether the nature of the person is properly understood in relational terms only, or whether some entity in addition to the brain, the body, and mental experiences must be introduced. The reductionist settles for the more economical view. But this interpretation of the discussion strikes me as superficial in two ways. It overlooks the different ways in which the phrase "the nature of the person" is understood in each of these accounts. And it also overlooks several responses in each of these account to more than just this question. Let us look at the first of these points.

For the reductionist, "What is the nature of the person?" is to be understood as the narrow question of whether the identity of a person's existence is composed of physical and psychological continuities and connections over time and no further fact (P:215). By contrast, for the nonreductionist, "What is the nature of the person?" is to be understood as the broader question of whether the identity with itself of the process of living a life as a person can be understood without appealing to some enduring entity other than the interrelatedness of appropriate psychological or physical events (W:11). Evidently, these two questions are closely connected. Each is concerned with whether, and if so then just how, a person can properly be said to perdure as the numerically same person over time. Each is also concerned with specifying certain features that would serve as criteria for the claim that, say, Peter on the garden path is the numerically same person as Peter in the seminar discussion. And each is acutely sensitive to providing an account that, in one way or another, leaves the decision between materialism and immaterialism an open matter.

But, though similar, these two questions are just as clearly different. The reductionist question is much narrower than the nonreductionist one. Indeed, this is one of the charges used in support of the claim that the reductionist account is inadequate (W:15). Moreover, the reductionist question is less exposed to the charge that it conflates the identity relation with the unity relation than the nonreductionist thinks, for the reductionist distinguishes between explaining the unity of consciousness at any time and the unity of a whole life (*P*:216–17). Further, the reductionist question allows for an indeterminate answer in some cases (consider brain bisection or brain transplants or teletransportation of brain states), whereas the nonreductionist question insists that any answer must be determinate. Moreover, the reductionist question involves the claim that an impersonal answer can be a complete one, whereas the nonreductionist question rejects such a claim. And finally, the nonreductionist question, but not the reductionist question, allows an answer in other terms than necessary and sufficient conditions. The reductionist account recognizes that other features may be important in any answer that is proposed to the reductionist question, but those features are seen to be supplements merely to the essence of the solution, which is the conjunction of necessary and sufficient conditions in a criterion for personal identity over time. The nonreductionist account recognizes the interest in including in a reply such a criterion; but it relegates this criterion and those conditions to a subordinate role and reserves the principal role for the provision of as full a set of descriptive features as one can obtain.

These facts suggest that judging the nonreductionist charges against its rival as correct is a mistake. Similarly, something seems to be just as wrong in construing the reductionist charges against *its* rival as correct. The mistake in both cases lies in thinking that both accounts are addressed as answers to one and the same question; they are not. On the one hand, the nonreductionist account asserts that its rival is fatally flawed, but then goes on to provide arguments against an answer proposed to a different question than the one that is the object of the reductionist's concern. However good or bad these arguments may be in themselves (and we have already seen several problems), they are not adduced in support of the central assertion. That assertion is left without adequate support—it is a bare assertion. On the other hand, the reductionist account argues that any further theory, such as the rival one here, is fatally flawed, and it does provide arguments for this assertion. The problem, then, is not a lack of argument but that the arguments remain inconclusive. For on what other grounds than parsimony are we to accept such a thorough-going and barely credible skepticism?

A reasonable verdict is that, although these two views conflict in a number of interesting philosophical ways, we are not compelled to choose between them. For these accounts, however contrary, are not finally logically contradictory. Consequently, the choice between at least these reductionist and nonreductionist accounts of the nature of the person and of personal identity we may legitimately leave open for further inquiry. We are then quite justified in trying to see whether several of the most interesting elements from each account can be integrated selectively into our reflections on self-transformation.

Appendix 6B   Describing Persons Indeterminately

One suggestive element in the reductionist account that we do well to scrutinize is indeterminateness and future selves. The indeterminateness thesis is the view that, despite natural inclinations to believe otherwise, the answer to the question as to whether any future person must be either me or someone else need not be determinate (*P*:214). This claim involves the notion that some questions are properly described as empty questions, questions whose answers would be neither true nor false. The question "Will the entity in the garden tomorrow be either me or someone else?" is, in some cases, an empty question in that the choice we are asked to make is not between two different states of affairs but between two different descriptions of the same state of affairs.

But the indeterminateness thesis articulates an issue arising in some cases only, cases like the "combined spectrum" which suggest that, despite my natural inclinations, my beliefs that any future person must be either me or someone else cannot be true. The case, as I shall describe it (after Parfit and Williams), is that of the neurobiological surgical group that is able to manipulate through electrodes and chemical emplacements and both brain-tissue and body-tissue transplants the full spectrum of my psychological and physical continuity and connectedness.

At the near end of the spectrum the team would activate only a few emplacements and substitute exact duplicates of only a small percentage of my cells. Thus, while losing only a few of my real memories, I would acquire only a few apparent memories that fit the life of someone else; and while losing only a few of my actual cells, I would acquire only a few functioning duplicates of my brain tissue and other body tissue as transplants. At the far end of the spectrum the team would revive from much more complex operations an entity who would have virtually no memories that corresponded to my own past and virtually none of the original cells of my present brain and body. Now, the person reviving from the first operation would almost certainly be me because of the very great, although not full, degree to which psychological and physical continuity and connectedness would have been retained. But the person reviving from the second operation would almost certainly not be me because of the very small degree to which such interrelatedness would have been retained. But "if any future person must be either me or someone else, there must be a line in this range of cases up to which the resulting person would be me, and beyond which he would be someone else" (*P*:277). Yet the combined spectrum case shows merely a neurobiological surgical team making one further psychological change and one further cell transplant. Hence, the question of whether the resulting person is either me or someone else is an empty question in the sense that whatever answer we may provide is simply one of two possible descriptions of the same state of affairs. It is conceivable, then, that, despite our deep-seated inclinations to believe that there must always be a deep difference between some future person being either me or someone else, either being Peter in the garden or not Peter in the garden, in some cases questions about personal identity have no determinate answers.[52]

[52]I thank Jakob Amstutz, Jack Glickman, and Stanley Rubin for their critical comments.

7
Real Fictions

There are no fictive worlds.

—Nelson Goodman

The world is the group of references opened up by all the kinds of descriptive or poetic texts which I have read, interpreted, and loved.

—Paul Ricoeur

There was so much that was real that was not real at all.

—Wallace Stevens

Critical readers of the American poet Wallace Stevens continue to focus attention on his rich and thoughtful construals of the world as a fiction. In much of his most distinguished poetry Stevens is at work in testing such traditional oppositions as that between nature and world, life and art, the real and the imaginary. In the terms of idealist and romantic theories of imagination such oppositions remain unusually problematic in poetry. Very roughly, we may say that part of what Stevens repeatedly presents in his work is a series of emblems for the artist's repeated passage from, in the color symbolism that perfuses his poetry, the green of nature to the blue of the world and the yellow of life. The world in this context is a fiction in that the only world available is the one the artist makes. Yet when fully realized as a work of art the world is not just a fiction; rather, as in the title of one of his most puzzling poems, the world is a "supreme fiction," a fiction of a peculiar sort.

Talk of the world as a fiction is of course no longer unfamiliar, whether in literary circles or philosophical ones. For the terminology of many interpretations of literary works today, in one genre or another, includes such expressions as "the world of Shakespeare" or "the world of Yeats." And one of the central issues which continues to vex philosophers comes under the heading of disputes about realism and antirealism, disagreements in fact inside contemporary versions of the Kantian problem about whether anything can be taken properly as ontologically independent of noetic activity. But however familiar variations on the theme of the world as fiction have become, few at least of the poetic versions confront us with so particular, thoughtful, and suggestive a presentation as Stevens's work. I do not propose to explore that work here. Rather, I explore the notion of a fictional world with some of Stevens's work in mind. More precisely, I propose to bring the notion of a fictional world into clearer view by investigating a contemporary philosophical disagreement about such worlds in the light of Stevens's meditative poetry.

A Supreme Fiction

Stevens's investigation of the world as a fiction is preeminently on exhibit in his poems. We do well, then, at least in the interests of simplicity, to keep his remarks in the essays and letters in the margins and to focus instead on this theme as it is presented in at least several of his most representative poems. Part of what is at stake for Stevens in talk about fictions and part of the difficulty he finds in such talk is summarized in a prominent passage from one of his finest poems, "An Ordinary Evening in New Haven," a stanza that occurs unchanged in both the original short version (stanza 8) and the final much enlarged version (stanza 28).[1]

Some of the interest and the complications of Stevens's thinking about the world as in some sense a fiction is evident here, for example, in the juxtaposition of abstract reflections and proliferating concrete images, in a species of self-reference which partially explores what poetry is, in the linking of questions about the nature of the real and its opposites to those about the nature of art and life, and finally in the musical cadences of a thoroughly rhetorical lyricism—for example, in the line "As it is, in the intricate evasions of as."

A second example representative of Stevens's best work may be taken to complement the first by amplifying this talk of reality, poetry, and life with the suggestion of a fictional world as an artifact that assembles a whole. The example is Stevens's poem "Anecdote of the Jar." In some respects this piece involves a more complex reflection than the former, for it is a complete poem and not just an extract. Moreover, nature appears here explicitly first in the guise of a wilderness and then in some transformed shape. And finally, the speaker seems to claim, in an extremely odd and formal idiom ("And tall and of a port in air"), that the artifact, whether jar or poem, is centrally involved in this transformation.

A final example of Stevens's meditation on the world as a fiction is "The

---

[1]Stevens 1971; shorter versions in Stevens 1953.

Idea of Order at Key West," a longer poem that presents a more fully detailed situation and focuses the themes of reality, nature, art, and life with the help of an elaborate reflection on the world. Since I use this work as a touchstone for what follows, and since I am not able to cite the poem in its entirety here, I must ask readers to look at the poem on their own.

Like the speaker in "An Ordinary Evening in New Haven," the speaker in this poem is in part worrying a series of concerns about the relations between nature and mind. And like the speaker in "Anecdote of the Jar," the speaker here is also busy with just how if at all the echoes of such terms can be caught up in the practices of a poetic art that is preeminently and inexorably self-reflexive. Much, of course, has been said of this poem. What concerns us, however, is the idea that, among other things, the poem presents a fictional world that includes as one of its elements the idea of a fictional world. For the speaker the realm of nature is "meaningless" until it is caught up in the shaping work of the artist, whether the singer or the poet—"There is order in neither sea nor sun" ("Sad Strains of a Gay Waltz"). Then and only then what was undifferentiated is "portioned out" in the verbal ordering of a world. As the speaker says in a related passage in "Tea at the Palaz of Hoon": "I was the world in which I walked, and what I saw / Or heard or felt came not but from myself." Whence the notion on exhibit that whatever world there may or may not be can only be a fictional world in the sense of an artifact of mind. What is on these terms "real" is not the realm of nature but only the worlds fashioned in art. "Say that final belief / Must be in a fiction," says the speaker in "Asides on the Oboe," and later in the same poem the "impossible possible philosopher's man, / The man who has had the time to think enough," cries out, " 'Thou art not August until I make thee so.' "

In order to understand what Stevens is proposing in these meditations on the world as a fiction we need to notice a recurring ambiguity between *the* world as a fiction and *a* fictional world. By the latter we may take Stevens to mean roughly any work of art, but mainly works of verbal art and in particular poetry. Stevens need not be taken to exclude other cultural objects such as scientific theories, religious systems, philosophical accounts, and so on. But clearly the accent falls on poetry. Moreover, we do well to specify successful poems, in the sense of those poems that are acknowledged as good works of art, in order to keep our focus on the central cases.

If *a* fictional world is a successful poem, what then does Stevens mean by *the* world? Here the matter is complicated. Again very roughly we may observe in his work an often varied opposition between what we may call nature and world. The second is the result of imaginative activity, whereas the first is in some obscure sense both dependent on such activity and yet not entirely so. This "not entirely" is what complicates things. Nature here comes in the guise of what Stevens calls the earth, what he describes in such terms as "the rock of summer, the extreme" ("Credences of Summer"), "mute bare splendors" ("On the Manner of Addressing Clouds"), "an old chaos of the sun" ("Sunday Morning"), and "my green, fluent mundo" ("Notes towards a Supreme Fiction"). By contrast, world is exhibited in other terms as a set of "heavenly labials" rather than "a world of gutturals" ("The Plot against the Giant"), "the world / Of Blue" ("The Man with the Blue Guitar"), what is to be read in "the great blue tabulae" ("Large Red Man Reading"), and an irremovable "fiction covering" ("Notes toward a Supreme Fiction"). In short, the contrast here is in terms of the green mundo and a blue world.

Part of the central motive in this body of work is to determine the status of those two poles with respect to what we call reality. Which of these is *the* real world? Stevens, we may say, meditates on this question throughout his work. And the account he arrives at is what we may take to be his description of *the* world, the green mundo. The poet seems to find many serious considerations that incline him to the view that the mundo is in some sense prior to the world. It is "the obscurity of an order" already there to be discovered, or "that which arranged the rendezvous" between mundo and the imagination ("Final Soliloquy of the Interior Paramour"), a "pure reality" where an object exists at the "exactest point, at which it is itself" ("An Ordinary Evening in New Haven"), in a kind of exterior, and "a thing yet to be made" although already there ("The Man with the Blue Guitar"). On this first view the real world is entirely independent of the poet's and anyone else's descriptions.

Yet an equally convincing set of observations also inclines the poet to the opposite view, that the real world is always a fictional world—at best something caught up through imagination in the forms of art, but which even without art is always most basic. Thus the poet speaks of "the rotten names," art as "the place of things as they are," and he writes, "things are as I think they are / And say they are on the blue guitar" ("The Man with the Blue Guitar"). Stevens goes on to worry the theme of language—"It is not in the premise that reality / Is a solid" ("An Ordinary Evening in New Haven")—and seems to plump for the view that the real world is an artifact of words: "said words of the world and the life of the world" ("An Ordinary Evening in New Haven"). The real world, then, is an appearance only—"Let be be the finale of seem," he writes in "The Emperor of Ice-Cream."

Stevens tries to resolve this impasse. Some readers have argued on the basis of such important pieces as "Asides on the Oboe" ("say that final belief / Must be in a fiction"), passages in "An Ordinary Evening in New Haven" such as "We keep coming back and coming back / to the real," and such extended works as "Notes towards a Supreme Fiction" that Stevens finally opts for an antirealist position both in the "existential" sense of there being no real world independent of our thinking and articulating and in the "creative" sense of whatever real world we have

being the one we make.[2] But without arguing the matter in detail, such
an account does a serious injustice to at least some of what Stevens seems
to think. On my view Stevens is the speaker who writes in "Thirteen
Ways of Looking at a Blackbird": "I was of three minds, / Like a tree / In
which there are three blackbirds." For much evidence suggests that Stevens holds neither a realist nor an antirealist view, and even that such a
dichotomy is centrally inappropriate for discussing Stevens's work sympathetically and critically. Rather, Stevens seems to propound a larger
account, which tries to embrace elements from each of such philosophical
exaggerations. Thus, in "The Man with the Blue Guitar" he writes: "Between the two, / Between issue and return, there is / An absence in reality,
/ Things as they are." Or in "Auroras of Autumn" we find the speaker
talking of "the two in one." And in "The Snow Man" we overhear talk
about "the nothing that is." One particularly striking passage can even
be found in one of the major pieces in the account I am contesting, in
"Notes toward a Supreme Fiction":

> He had to choose. But it was not a choice
> Between excluding things. It was not a choice
>
> Between, but of. He chose to include things
> That in each other are included, the whole,
> The complicate, the amassing harmony.

For Stevens, making this kind of choice, a choice of and not between, is a
kind of dying, a being in a barren state but a barrenness at the end of an ex-
hausted fertility, existing in "profounder, physical thunder, dimension in
which / We believe without belief, beyond belief" ("Flyer's Fall").

We do not resolve such questions of interpretation, of course, by ex-
changing lists of purple pages. And surely here we can leave the problem
of attempting a consensus on such a matter to the poets and literary critics
who largely constitute our communities of competent readers. My point
is simply that an alternative reading of Stevens's position is not without
strong evidence in its favor. Such an alternative needs working out with
the proper nuances, such as those that concern the dynamic quality of
Stevens's views (which he keeps deliberately in a state of flux) and his
obscure hopes—"It must be that in time / The real will from its crude
compoundings come," he writes in "Notes toward a Supreme Fiction."
But I will take it as at least not implausible that some such view as the
one I have just described, or a better version of it, is a fair account of
Stevens's reflections on *the* real world.

The real world for Stevens, I suggest, is not a fictional world in the first

[2]Plantinga 1982:49.

sense of that ambiguous expression—that is, a world that is nothing other than some thing invented through those rich imaginings that result in works of art, in successful poems. Rather, the real world is a fictional world in the sense that it exists in a curious way as—and here we need at least for now to borrow Stevens's terms—an absence between issue and return, a "nothing," a "two in one," as simultaneously the philosopher's "interior made exterior" and the poet's "same exterior made / Interior," an "essential bareness," as "the same," "the complicate," "the whitened sky," or in somewhat fairer, fuller, if controversial symbolic terms, as simply an absence of color, a "bowl of white," a whiteness, the whiteness we find in "The Auroras of Autumn."

Whatever qualifications communities of critics finally settle on in trying to answer the difficult question "What is Stevens's poetry about?" I will introduce such poetic work into an investigation of several central accounts in recent philosophy of the nature of fictional worlds. On one of these accounts there are no fictional worlds, whereas on the other fictional worlds not only exist, they actually enlarge the horizons of the real world. Each of these accounts, I shall show, offers important resources in trying to get clear about just how the idea of a fictional world is to be satisfactorily construed. And yet each, for different reasons, falls short not only because of certain internal issues but because neither is rich enough to account for the kinds of fictional worlds proposed in such poetic works as "The Idea of Order at Key West."

My purpose here, then, just as in the studies of Eliot and Rilke in Chapters 5 and 6, is not to interpret a poem, much less Stevens's work as a whole, nor even to treat a theme in that work. Rather, in trying to account for the nature of such examples of a fictional world as we find in lyric poetry generally and in particular in such works as Stevens's "The Idea of Order at Key West," I investigate to what extent we may find good reasons for rearticulating the usual ways we draw our philosophical distinctions between the real and the fictional. Thus I hope to find elements in some recent philosophical reflections on fictional worlds which may enable us to formulate more perspicuously what Stevens calls a fiction. But more centrally, I suggest, if not demonstrate, how trying to articulate an account of the kind of fiction Stevens presents us with forces us to think twice about our habitual and perhaps too narrow philosophical understanding of the world.

Fictive Worlds: A First Account

In this section I examine Nelson Goodman's claim that "there are no fictive worlds." This view in various forms is to be found in many places in his later work, from *The Languages of Art* on. Several central discussions, however, need particular attention because they are recent summary formulations, are worked into a larger context in his latest book, *Of Mind and Other Matters*, and because Goodman has explicitly linked them. Each was first published separately in 1982.

Worlds, Versions, and Categorizations

The first statement occurs as one of five interlocking theses: "(1) All fiction is literal, literary falsehood. (2) Yet some fiction is true. (3) Truth of fiction has nothing to do with realism. (4) There are no fictive worlds. (5) Not all literal, literary falsehood is fiction."[3] Goodman devotes no more than several paragraphs of explanation to each of these elliptical claims, but these discussions do provide at least some initial clarification. Thus, with respect to (1) we are told that "only literary falsehood is fiction," whereas with respect to (2) some fiction is metaphorically true. Whatever truth fiction may involve, this truth (3) does not depend on the "familiarity of symbols used in the telling" but only on what is told. Further, (4) there are many actual worlds and no such thing as *the* actual world or fictive worlds. And finally, since literature includes some biographies and histories that themselves include some falsity, falsity as such does not qualify a work as fiction (5).

Initially, then, we may take Goodman to be making the claim that only actual worlds exist, and since fictive worlds are not actual, fictive worlds do not exist. But why are fictive worlds not actual? And if they are not actual then exactly what are fictive worlds? Possible worlds? Goodman answers no to the last question. His answers to the preceding ones, however, are more difficult to make out.

These theses fall roughly into two groups, one with four claims concerning questions about truth and falsity and another concerning the question of whether fictive worlds exist. Both groups are of course related. For part of the argument against the existence of fictive worlds involves a discussion of several questions about reference, denotation, metaphor, and fictionality. Still, we may be content here with citing the context of his claim about fictive worlds without analyzing this context as such. I shall take it, then, that questions about the truth of a fictive work are, although related, still separate from questions about the existence of fictive worlds.

What, then, are Goodman's reasons for claiming that there are no fictive worlds? The only argument provided here goes as follows:

> Works of fiction, we often hear, are about fictive worlds. But strictly speaking, fiction cannot be about anything nonactual, since there is nothing nonactual, no merely-possible or impossible worlds; for saying that there

[3]Goodman 1982:123–24.

is something fictive but not actual amounts to saying that *there is something such that there is no such thing*. Thus there are no pictures *of* unicorns or stories *about* ghosts but only unicorn-pictures or ghost stories. Fiction, then, no matter how false or far-out, is about what is actual when about anything at all. There are no fictive worlds. . . . Nonfiction and fiction do not differ in that the one but not the other is about actual things. Both are about actual things if anything; and different works of either may be about the same or different actual worlds." (125–26; Goodman's emphasis)

Evaluating such an argument is evidently no easy task because built into the summary comments is a series of elements taken from extensive inquiries in Goodman's other works. We may attempt at least an initial formulation of his views on fictive worlds which, whatever its simplifications, may help us nonetheless to isolate those elements that require further discussion. Thus, there are no such things as fictive worlds, for "fictive worlds" do not exist because they are not actual and only actual worlds exist. Fictions, however, even if not fictional worlds, do exist. Like everything else, fictions are actual. And when they are about something, then such fictions are about actual things. Further, some fictions—namely, verbal ones—although literally false may be metaphorically true. And other fictions—namely, nonverbal ones—although not literally false may be either incorrect of correct versions. Worlds themselves consist of true versions, and a version is true to the degree that it follows upon right categorization. Further, versions are multiple; some true versions conflict and hence are not in specific times; and no true version is compatible with all true versions. Very generally, then, we may say:

1. *Fictive worlds are not actual worlds.* They do not exist. What exists are versions, some of which are fictions not fictive worlds, which if they are about anything are not about *the* actual world but actual worlds. They are at best true versions constructed correctly and chosen among other incompatible true versions as a function of one's interpretive purposes and projects.

On this account we are to construe the supreme fictions of such lyric poets as Wallace Stevens as a version of a world which may be either true or false, and even if false may be either correct or incorrect. When such a version is correct it is true of a construct resulting from the use of right discourse.

But such an initial account remains too general to deal with much of the pertinent detail in the kinds of proposals we find in such worlds as "The Idea of Order at Key West." We need, then, to develop this first formulation in more detail. In particular, we need to look more carefully at the idea that if a fictional world is not an actual world, then perhaps a fictional world can be properly described as a possible world. Exploring this issue involves taking up the themes of reference and denotation.

Reference and Denotation

A second major element in appreciating Goodman's claim that there
are no fictive worlds is his theory and taxonomy of reference together
with his reflections on denotation.

The term "reference" is a primitive and very general term for all kinds
of symbolization.[4] "Reference" has to do with "the various relationships
that may obtain between a term or other sign or symbol and what it refers
to" (*MM*, 55). More generally, reference here has to do with a symbol
system and its objects (on Goodman's theory of reference see Chapter 4
and Appendix 4A).

Goodman's taxonomy of reference shows us several important features
in the background of the central claims we are concerned with—namely,
that there are no fictive worlds. The idea is that fictive worlds cannot in
some strong sense refer. But in order to work out a clearer view of what
is going on here we do well to narrow our focus still further to varieties
of verbal denotation only, the main but of course not the only variety of
reference operative in fictive worlds.

In Russell's classic discussion "On Denoting," the claim is made that
the word "Scott" in the sentence "Scott is the author of *Waverly*" denotes
Scott, and "author" author, and "*Waverly*" the group of books in the
Waverly series. From such a starting point a fuller view has developed,
which is ably summarized as follows: "Denotation is a two place semantic
relation between a symbol and the objects to which it applies. A symbol
denotes whatever complies with it, or satisfies or is an instance of it.
Thus, a name denotes its bearer; a variable, its values; and a portrait, its
subject. A predicate denotes severally the objects in its extension."[5] The
key point in this view is twofold: predicates denote objects and not classes,
and different expressions denote differently—some singly, some generally, and others not at all. In the latter case, expressions that lack compliants, the expressions are said to have "null denotation." Examples of
such expressions are fictive persons ("Elizabeth Bennet" in *Pride and Prejudice*) and fictive entities (unicorns and centaurs). Further, expressions
that have a null denotation include not only tenseless expressions but
may include those in sentences in the future or past tenses where the
denotation is either actual or null.

Goodman's own view comes out when we consider why he thinks
some expressions such as "unicorns" are properly described as having
no referents rather than as having "possible objects" as referents. For
Goodman denotation is "an extensional relation between expressions and

---

[4]Besides Goodman 1982 and 1984 (hereafter *MM*), see also Elgin 1984.
[5]Elgin 1984:29 (hereafter *RR*). Throughout I follow Elgin closely for generalities; further
references appear in the text.

objects" (*RR*, 20) not possible ones. And the reason is that one can individuate clearly between two actual objects but not between two possible
ones. But this rejection of possible objects leads to the further view that
all objects denoted are individuals and hence to a rejection of classes as
well in favor of members or individuals only.

These reflections on reference and verbal denotation allow us to develop
our initial formulation of a fictive world:

> 2. *A "fictive world" is not a possible world.* Whatever kind of deno-
> tation may be going on in a fiction that we mistakenly call a
> fictive world, such a process must be construed as an extensional
> relation between experience and *actual* objects not possible ones,
> because only the former and not the latter can be clearly indi-
> viduated. Further, what a "fictive world" denotes are actual *in-
> dividuals* and not classes of individuals even though almost
> anything whatsoever is to be understood as accommodating its
> description as an individual. Finally, the syntactic and semantic
> interpretation of such actual individuals depends on antecedent
> interests, aims, and projects that determine which general se-
> mantic framework is taken to be the relevant one for the cases
> in question. Such frameworks consist of schemes, realms, and
> systems. In short, a "fictive world" is a construct in the light of
> how particular verbal denotations are sorted, classified, and in-
> tegrated into complex referential chains involving referential re-
> moteness and allusion.

On this account we are to construe what Stevens would call a supreme
fiction as one comprehensive referential framework among others, the
compliants of which are always actual individuals existing in an actual
world and not possible entities subsisting in a possible world.

But this account still falls short of being able to encompass the kinds
of constructs we find in Stevens's work to the degree that while incorporating very general considerations about existence, actuality and possibility, individuals and classes, kinds of reference and the workings of
verbal denotation, it so far merely mentions but does not elaborate on
one of the centrally distinctive features of Stevens's version, its metaphorical character. We require, then, a third and final characterization, a
positive one this time, of "fictive worlds" as metaphorical constructs of
a peculiar sort.

Metaphor and Semantic Systems

The usual bases for applying old words literally to new objects is habit
and stipulation. But when a metaphor is applied to a new object, neither
of these habitual practices suffices. For the metaphorical application both

depends on these antecedent practices and works against them. Metaphorical application of a term depends on the literal application in that we cannot apply the term metaphorically without already knowing its literal application. But the metaphorical application works against this literal application in that the extensions of the literal applications are no longer adequate to encompass the new extensions of the term.

Using a metaphor, however, is not the same thing as introducing ambiguity because, unlike the interpretations of ambiguous terms which are independent of their literal applications, the interpretation of a metaphorical term is not. A tension between the realm of objects which constitutes the literal extension of a term and that which constitutes its metaphorical extension is characteristic of metaphor. When that tension is lost, a metaphoric term degenerates into a merely ambiguous one in which the literal extension now expands to include the metaphorical extension. Thus, as Goodman writes, a metaphor on this account is "an affair between a predicate with a past and an object that yields while resisting."[6]

Such an account, however, needs completion when we return to the metaphorical application of fictive terms. The metaphorical application of nonfictive terms reflects the sorting of objects which its literal application has affected. But in the case of fictive terms, the metaphorical application sorts, rather, the way the term itself is sorted (RR, 60, citing WW, 104). A reclassification is effected. But in the case of fictive terms, instead of denoted objects being reclassified, secondary extensions are reclassified— that is, not the extensions of the terms but the extensions of the parallel compounds of the terms are reclassified.[7] This process occurs in both the cases in which a fictive term is predicated of a nonfictive individual (for example, Sancho Panchez or Charles de Gaulle) and in cases in which a fictive term is predicated of a fictive character (say, Sancho Panchez or Pierre Bezukhov). Further, "the metaphorical application of a term thus brings about a new classification not only of the objects it denotes, but also of the pictures, descriptions, and the like that it mention-selects" (RR, 60).

So far, Goodman's discussion is restricted to metaphoric application where schemes rather than terms are "employed metaphorically to sort objects in a new realm" (RR, 61). The sorting here becomes a novel network of terms as in the expression "the war on poverty," where the objects in the scheme of terms previously clustered around the expression "war" are now made accessible to the scheme of terms previously clustered around the expression "poverty." Sometimes the same term may

<hr>

[6]See Goodman 1976:69 (hereafter LA) and Elgin 1984:6.
[7]See Goodman 1972:231–38; 77–75.

be applied both literally and metaphorically to the same individual, and at other times the literal and metaphorical replicas of the term are even coextensive. Interpretation of which application is the relevant one will require appeals to contexts or even finally to stipulation. The key according to Goodman is to recognize in the contexts just which semantic system is in effect and then to interpret the term accordingly.

Perhaps the most important element in this account is Goodman's accent on a plurality of systems. For whether a token is to be classified as literal or metaphorical depends on which system it is to be situated within. For Goodman, where extensions of terms are construed narrowly as including actual individuals only and neither possibilities nor classes, most applications of a term are to be construed metaphorically, whereas in an alternative system with a broader construal of extensions most terms are to be construed literally. Similarly, where a replica has more than one extension, what determines the issue of whether the replica is to be considered as metaphorical or merely ambiguous is a matter of which system is involved. For it is in terms of the system that a decision is made as to whether the application of a term to objects in one realm is semantically dependent on its application to the objects in another—if so, then the term is metaphorical; if not, then ambiguous.

Besides the talk of metaphorical application of terms and schemes, we have to ask about metaphorical sentences, and particularly about their correctness. For Goodman a correct metaphorical sentence is genuinely true and the metaphorical expressions contained in a correct metaphorical sentence "genuinely denote the objects to which they apply" (*RR*, 65). Thus, a sentence can be true or false without being literally true or false, and the expression of a sentence can denote without literally denoting. The key note here is to be found in the response to the question of whether a particular scheme, when interpreted literally, can be given a truth definition—that is, whether the number of its primitives is finite and certain semantic terms such as "true" are excluded. If yes, then the same scheme when interpreted metaphorically can also be given a truth definition; if no, then not. This means that certain relations of equivalence, inclusion, and exclusion can be the same in the scheme when applied literally and when applied metaphorically. The result is that some systems may include sentences that are metaphorically true even though these sentences are literally false.

Thus, metaphorical applications of sentences, on Goodman's account, need not be interpreted as either false or merely suggestive (Davidson) but as sometimes metaphorically true. Not all true metaphorical sentences need to be understood as cognitively significant, for some are plainly banal. But others, in introducing new ways of sorting and classifying objects under alternative schema than the literal ones that sort them antecedently, and in allowing one to apply metaphorically to a new realm a scheme that has already proved fruitful in another, enable one to extend one's conceptual grasp of a realm of objects.

These comments, however general, enable us to attempt a third—and for now final—formulation of one contemporary philosophical account of those fictions called, on this view, "fictive worlds":

> 3. *A "fictive world" is a metaphorical semantic system*, that is, a kind of semantic framework that sorts and classifies actual individuals and their realms under alternative schema. These schema re-classify antecedent groupings of both primary and secondary extensions of individuals regardless of which kind of referential functions the relevant terms, predicates, or sentences have ful-filled. Further, such reclassifications can come about in more than one way: as an application of an antecedent schema to a new realm altogether or as the reorganization of the same realm through a different use of the antecedent schema. Finally, some such schema when applied metaphorically under certain con-ditions can properly be talked of in terms of truth and falsity.

On this account we are to construe what Stevens calls a "supreme fiction" as a metaphorical semantic system, a single comprehensive ref-erential framework constructed and chosen among others, a version of a world that, when constructed in accordance with right discourse, can be true or false, correct or incorrect.

Recapitulation and Critique

On this first discussion of the nature of fictive worlds, we have the claim that those peculiar fictions we mistakenly call "fictive worlds" are not actual worlds but constructs or versions of a world. Nor are these versions possible worlds but constructs of actual individuals in all their variety. More positively, so-called "fictive worlds" are metaphorical se-mantic systems that, as constructed versions, are functional in such a way as to reclassify at times veridically the terms, realms, and schemata of antecedent systems or their applications.

In such a perspective we may perhaps talk of "fictive world" in the context of Stevens's "The Idea of Order at Key West" at several different levels. We may say that within the poem, the world of the singer, "the world she sang and singing made," is a fictive world in the sense that it is the projection of an artifact that is her song, a semantic projection in which "the meaningless plungings" and all the phenomena of the world of nature take on an interpretation that consists of the interrelationship among the now metaphorical resortings of their antecedent literal exten-sions. The sky is no longer the literal sky but the limit of a version, the horizon of a semantic framework. And at the larger level, the work as a whole, we may perhaps speak as well of "fictive world" in the sense of the metaphorical semantic framework Stevens has constructed under the label "The Idea of Order at Key West." Here the resortings are operative not just at the level of terms and predicates, nor even at the level of sentences as we may imagine them at work in the woman's song, but at the more general level of classifications themselves such that the reading affects actual individuals taken not just as objects but as schemata. Thus, the "ghostlier demarcations" that are said to arise out of the maker's rage "to order words of the sea, . . . and of ourselves, and of our origins" are perhaps to be described not just as constructions but as those kinds of very general versions which claim to be true—that is, true versions constructed with right discourse. A true version is one actual world among many others; it is chosen by virtue of one's interest, aims, and projects over the attractions of its irreconcilable rivals. Hence, as incompatible with other true versions it is a version true in a world, not true in the world—true, we may say, in a fictive world, one that finally is not found but fabricated from others.

This general account of fictive world has already allowed us to grasp certain features of such poetic works as Stevens's "The Idea of Order at Key West." At each stage of our successive elaboration of this account we have looked back to this poem with the aim of articulating more explicitly what it would mean to talk in such a context of a supreme fiction. Yet when we return to the poem with this general account in hand and reread the poem on the interpretive hypothesis that it can be plausibly construed as presenting a fictive world in contributing to metaphorical semantic versions of an actual world of individuals, certain central features of the poetic work go unremarked. Such a perspective does allow us to apprehend some cardinal features of the work—for example, the important contrasts between the world and a world ("She was the single artificer of the world . . . there never was a world for her"), or rich variations among the kinds of correlations of certain referential operations in the work ("beyond the genius of the sea," "the veritable man," "Ramon Fernandez"), or even rhetorical uses of a logical role played by modal considerations in the counterfactual constructions in the third stanza ("If it was only the outer voice of sky . . . it would have been deep air").

But other arguably more central features of this work, features essential to an appreciation of its nature and success, are not captured—for example, the equally important contrast between the world the singer makes in the "medleyed sound" of the sea and her song and the world the speaker makes in the description he proposes to Ramon Fernandez of the lights in the night, or the peculiar species of metaphorical expressions at the level of a story, and not just at that of terms and predicates carefully differentiated in the talk here of "order" ("the idea of order," "Blessed rage for order") and "maker" ("she was the maker," "the single artificer," "the one she sang and, singing, made"), or even the repeated indirect and ambiguous solicitations to a reading in such expressions as "we said," "we knew," "tell me, if you know / Why," "words . . . of ourselves and of our origins." Rereading Stevens's work and noticing what this account of fictive world leaves out and not just what it includes, we see that such an account of fictive world is not without several serious deficiencies.

Among the numerous elements that invite critical comment I focus attention on three. Most generally, a fictive world is taken here as a metaphorical semantic system and is to be understood partly by contrast with a "world" *tout court*, that is, something that "is the creature of and informed by, a version constructed in a symbol system" (*MM*, 28). But such a proposal, whatever further questions may arise about the account of metaphor and the talk of reclassifying extensions, faces the prior compound difficulty of making out clearly the differences between system and theory, world and version. The first part of the difficulty can be glimpsed when we recall in this context the familiar claim in the philosophy of science that languages are theory-laden, although, as Goodman himself reminds us, a language is not the same thing as a theory stated in the language (*MM*, 94). Yet "system" in this account of fictive world as a metaphorical semantic system, a kind of symbol system, blurs such a basic distinction in that the way languages function metaphorically comes to a theory of language and its limits.[8]

The second part of the difficulty arises from the recurring ambiguity in saying both "every right version is a world" and "every right version has a world" (*MM*, 41).[9] Granted that right versions are true in a world, still the question remains as to just how world and version differ, since neither is taken to be independent of the limits of language. Thus, a first difficulty with this account centers on the description here of a fictive world as a symbol system, and on problems with maintaining necessary distinctions between both the language of a system and that of a theory on the one hand and the language of a world and that of a version on the other.

It might be thought that such a problem dissipates once we increase the resolution in our examination and move from this general level to an intermediate one—for example, to that of reference and denotation. But this is not so. For at a less general level we find this account of "fictive world" detailed in terms of certain views about the peculiar objects of terms and predicates in certain kinds of expressions. On this view what refers and what denotes are not speakers of a language but expressions. Moreover, as we have seen, reference itself includes many different kinds,

[8]See Rudner 1978.
[9]I. Scheffler 1980.

both elementary and complex, but one of its kinds, denotation, assumes an inordinate importance.[10] In short, "fictive worlds," whatever their relations to systems and versions, are taken both to refer and to have denotations. More precisely, the expressions that "fictive worlds" include when it is a referring expression have compliants (*MM*, 96–97). These correlates, however, whatever their hierarchies, are always to be understood as individuals.

Yet such a construal raises a serious question about the tenability of Goodman's nominalism. For as Goodman himself concedes, not all expressions can be nominalized. And even though Goodman and Quine have succeeded in reducing the remainder among such expressions (*MM*, n. 51), rather than modify a nominalistic position as Quine does Goodman continues to resort to what he calls "platonic constructions as temporary expedients awaiting eventual nominalization" (*MM*, 51). But this, some might say, is faith and not philosophy. And Goodman's own purposes, others might argue, would be better served were he to abandon such expedients as his talk of "scattered individuals" and frankly enlarge his referents or claimants to include something more than a tendentious understanding of "individuals" as "anything at all." Thus, the basic ambiguity between world and versions, far from being dissipated at the intermediate level of reference and denotation, is in fact complemented by a serious new difficulty with the interpretation of referents as "individuals" only.

Once again, however, it might still be thought that the problems with referents as individuals and worlds as versions are resolvable at the even more particular level of Goodman's views about modality. Unfortunately, this still more finely grained analysis does not deliver the proposal from such problems.

It is true that this view of "fictive worlds" turns on a commitment to all individuals as actual entities rather than possible ones. And a strong argument stands in support of such a radical view, namely, the argument about the conditions for the reidentification of individuals. Nonetheless, a series of difficulties remains. The claim, we recall, is that there are multiple worlds because there are multiple irreconcilable true versions that cannot, therefore, all be true in some world. However, these many true versions of worlds (the ambiguity remains) are said not to exist in space-time (*MM*, 31). But then the key problem arises: how can each of these many worlds or versions, no one of which exists in space-time, be actual? Or, more specifically, how can the referents of the expressions these worlds or versions include be actual, whether such referents are taken always to be individuals or not? The only answer lies in construing

---

[10]Martin 1981.

"actual" in just as controversial a way as both "individual" and "world." (See Appendix 7A, "A Pluralism of Worlds.")

Each of these three recurring difficulties about central features in the account of "fictive world" as a metaphorical semantic system— difficulties about language and conceptual frameworks, about all referents as individuals only, and about all worlds as actual ones only—allows of elaboration. Indeed, these difficulties and many others continue to be raised about Goodman's views as a whole. And although often recognizing their force, Goodman continues to attempt more satisfactory replies. We need not follow all the contours of that discussion, however, to warrant the provisional conclusion that at least these three central difficulties raise reasonable doubts about the satisfactoriness of such an account of fictive worlds. Still, this account includes a number of distinguished suggestions we overlook to our loss. I underline the most important ones after we have looked at some difficulties with a rival version, the account not of fictive but of fictional worlds.

FICTIONAL WORLDS: A SECOND ACCOUNT

In his recent three-volume work *Time and Narrative*, Paul Ricoeur writes: "A more precise reflection on the notion of the world of the text and a more exact characterization of its status of immanent transcendence have convinced me that the passage from configuration to refiguration requires the confrontation between two worlds, the fictive world of the text and the real world of the reader."[11] Whatever problems this claim poses for interpretation, it seems evident that Ricoeur cannot agree with Goodman's claim that there are no fictive worlds. For Ricoeur there are fictive worlds, the fictive worlds of texts. It is useful here to consider several of the general elements of this view so as to attempt a fuller formulation of the key notion, and then to take the critical measure of this new account.

Semantic Innovation, Temporality, and Fiction

In the preface to *Time and Narrative* Ricoeur spells out the general orientations of a series of published studies that stretch over a ten-year period from the appearance of *The Rule of Metaphor* in 1975 to the publication in 1985 of the third and last volume of *Time and Narrative*. One major theme of the several that tie this body of work together is what Ricoeur calls semantic innovation, a phenomenon situated not at the level of individual terms but at the larger level of sentences. This level, which Ricoeur thinks

[11]Ricoeur 1983–85, 3:25. References in the text are to volume and page number. Translations are my own.

of as the domain of speech acts, he calls the level of discourse. Thus, both metaphors and stories are each understood as instances of semantic innovation in the discourse of speech acts.

The central issue for Ricoeur in both the case of metaphor and in that of story is the question of reference and truth. With respect to metaphor, the metaphorical language of poetry is said to retain a referential function even though the usual referential functions of descriptive discourses are suspended. Indeed for Ricoeur it is only when these usual referential functions of description are suspended that certain nondescriptive "aspects, qualities, and values of reality can be articulated" (1.13). With respect to story, Ricoeur takes story as referring especially to the realm of human activity. A plot, thus, is the "imitation" of an action in at least three senses of imitation: "it refers one back to a familiar preunderstanding of the order of action; it is an entry into the realm of fiction; and it is finally a new configuration by means of fiction of the preunderstood order of action" (1.13). This last sense of imitation is said to include a peculiar referential function.

The two kinds of semantic innovation are very closely related since metaphorical redescription is often at the service of dramatic activity, whether in literature or life, and conversely narrative configuration is often caught up in the processes of suffering as well as in those of acting. Thus, for Ricoeur the larger domain is a poetic one that includes within it both narrative discourse and metaphorical utterance. The subject, thus, of the most recent work is specifically the question of how the confused temporal experience is "reconfigured" by the privileged means of inventing plots. And Ricoeur goes on to argue that the referential function of the plot "lies in the capacity of fiction to refigure this temporal experience" (1.13).

Besides this major theme of temporality and the guiding ideas of semantic innovation through metaphor and storytelling, Ricoeur is at some pains in ranging across a variety of materials to articulate his own usage of the cardinal terms in his discussion. Our concern is with the key term "fiction," which Ricoeur opposes to "true story" (1.315). "Fiction" is not to be understood as "imaginary configuration," since both a work of history and one of fiction can exhibit such a feature. Rather, narrative configurations have two forms: true stories and fictional stories.

This terminological clarification puts us in a position to appreciate Ricoeur's attempt to examine more thoroughly the notion of emplotment in connection with reflections on the nature of the world of the work of fiction. Ricoeur draws attention to "a movement of transcendence whereby any work of fiction, be it verbal or plastic or narrative or lyric, projects beyond itself a world which can be called *the world of the work*" (2.14; Ricoeur's emphasis). This world is a "way of inhabiting the world which waits to be taken up in a reading" and in such a reading to be

brought into confrontation with the world of the reader. So far, then, we
have what Ricoeur calls "the world," the "world of the work," and the
"world of the reader." Some of these ways of inhabiting the world are
temporal and Ricoeur devotes his attention to these. On the one hand,
"the temporal ways of inhabiting the world remain imaginary ones to the
degree that they exist only in and through the text; on the other, they
constitute a sort of transcendence in immanence which is precisely what
allows the confrontation with the world of the reader" (2.15). The notion
of "fictive experience," Ricoeur tells us later (2.233), means "a virtual way
or manner of inhabiting the world which the literary work projects by
virtue of its power of autotranscendence." In the light of this initial orientation we may attempt a first formulation of Ricoeur's understanding
of fictional world. In order to mark the difference from the position of
Goodman, however, and to take account of Ricoeur's particular distinction
between "work of fiction" and "fiction," it is useful to articulate our
formulation in terms of the "fictional world," the world to be associated
with the fictional work. We may say informally:

4. *A fictional world is not the world of the text of a fictional work*; rather,
   it is
   a. one kind of configuration only of a preexisting order of action
      and suffering which is projected not only within the limits of
      the text but beyond these limits
   b. through various processes of semantic innovation both at the
      level of predicates and narratives.
   c. Such a projection constitutes a world beyond the textual
      worlds, a world of the fictional work, which is open to indirect
      descriptive and nondescriptive reference only, and which al-
      lows of virtual ways of inhabiting such a domain through
      fictive experiences of time and other phenomena.

Thus, to return to our example in Stevens's poetry, the supreme fiction
with which Stevens is concerned is to be understood on this account as
a configuration of certain possibilities for the reader's own life, possibilities
that the fiction that is the poem projects beyond itself into a domain
inviting the reader's interaction and offering the possibility of a transformation of the reader's experience.

But this initial formulation requires further elaboration.

Fictional Worlds, Refiguration, and Imperfect Mediations

The notion of a fictional world is, as we have seen, not at the center
of Ricoeur's project in *Time and Narrative*. Yet in order to spell out the
passage from the configuration to the refiguration of human time Ricoeur
returns repeatedly to the relation between the worlds of the text, its

readers, and the so-called real world. Early in *Time and Narrative* Ricoeur provides a summary of the previous reflections on world already worked out in *The Rule of Metaphor* (1975) and *Interpretation Theory* (1976). "The world," he writes, "is the group of references opened up by all the kinds of descriptive or poetic texts which I have read, interpreted and loved" (1.121). This is a strong and interesting claim, ambiguous enough to leave open the question of whether anything at all is independent of discourse yet definite enough to suggest that the world may well consist of what our references aim at and not just of the references themselves. Moreover, the claim here mixes a formal mode of speech with talk of "groups," "references," "interpretations" and a suggestion of the importance of factoring into any satisfactory account of the world an affective and a practical as well as a rational component.

Some of the indefiniteness in this initial account of "world" begins to dissipate in the same passage when Ricoeur goes on to talk of understanding texts as a process of transforming an environment into a world. "We owe," says Ricoeur, "a large measure of the expansion of our horizon on reality to works of fiction" (1.121). And he adds that such works succeed "in depicting reality by augmenting reality with all the significations which literary works owe to their virtues of abbreviation, saturation, and culmination" (1.121).

If we narrow our focus in the light of earlier comments to fiction as opposed to literary works in general, we might say that Ricoeur presents us here with an initial contrast between the world as "reality" and as "a simple environment" on the one hand and a world that opens out before us in the practices of interpretive discourse on the other. The former is not described very fully; it is "there" in some ambiguous and as yet uninterpreted sense, although now, unlike the initial comment about a group of referents, it seems clearly not reducible to our discourses themselves. By contrast, the latter notion, a world, is not presented just as a set of references but as an extrapolation from the world.

A further element in this account requires attention: the stress on "refiguration." At the beginning of the fourth and last part of his work, Ricoeur uses this term as one of a pair to capture his general thesis: "the task of thinking a work in all its narrative configuration is completed in a refiguration of temporal experience" (3.9; emphasis omitted). Temporal refiguration has to do with "bringing to light experience where time as such is thematized," with the consciousness of time. Something may not only be configured in a story but refigured in the story, and this difference between configuration and refiguration finally has to be construed not in terms of an analytic notion of reference (historical works referring to a "real" past and fictional works "referring" to unreal events) but in other, more hermeneutic terms (3.13).

We need to add still another element, the notion of intersecting configurations and imperfect mediations. Earlier in his study Ricoeur explored the hypothesis that the peculiarity of lived time or human temporality was a function of the intersecting reference of both historical and fictional narrative. But both history and fiction work such effects on human praxis that time is refigured and becomes a time that is reconnected through the fictionalization of historical stories and the historicalization of fictional ones. The unity of this human time, hence, requires superseding the old distinction between historiography and fiction with a new contrast between historical condition and historical consciousness. Thus, narrative in its largest sense involves refiguration not just of history and fiction but of historical consciousness and the historical condition (3.151), a refiguration Ricoeur goes on to nuance as a process of totalization. This final notion of refiguration, with the help of a critical reflection on Hegel, substitutes the idea of an imperfect mediation between past, present, and future for the impossible ideal of a complete mediation. Thus, the totalization here is always practical, an ongoing refiguration of time through the interlacing narratives of history and consciousness; a dynamic, never completed synthesis of "the future under the sign of a horizon of expectation, the past under that of tradition, and the present under the signs of tumultuous upheaval" (3.151).

So far, then, we have a series of five major themes among the various concerns of this second account—semantic innovation, temporality, fiction, refiguration, and imperfect mediation. Without claiming that these themes can stand for a summary of this major work, we can at least use them to delineate the boundaries of a second view of the notion of fictional world.

In the light, then, of this description we may attempt a second formulation:

> 5. *A fictional world is not the world of the reader.* Rather, such a world is a peculiar species of "imitation" or mimesis involving various semantic innovations at different levels in a fictional work's projection of an immanent configuration beyond the formal closure of the text. These transcendent projections interact with the horizons of a reader's world in such a way as to result in a mediation, a complementarity not of the respective references of history and fiction but of their respective refigurations. Such refigurations concern most centrally not a redescription of certain categorial experiences such as time but the resignification of the reader's consciousness of such experiences, in which some historical matters are fictionalized through imaginative variations and some fictional matters are historicized through their inscription onto lived experience.

On such an account a fictional world such as the one we find in Stevens's "The Idea of Order at Key West" is both the redescription of a world through poetry and the resignification of a world through story. The horizon of such a redescribed and resignified world intersects with the structures of the reader's world, which becomes a mediated totalization of the intersection of history and consciousness. Several issues here, however—matters concerning reference, metaphor, and the passage from configuration to refiguration—require further attention.

Metaphorical Reference, Nonlinguistic Worlds, and Horizons

In commenting that a theory of reading in itself is not sufficient to account for what a fictional work communicates, Ricoeur claims that the world a fictional work projects constitutes its horizon. The key idea here is that the notions of horizon and world are to be taken as correlative (1.118), in the sense that language necessarily refers beyond itself to something extralinguistic. Appropriately, Ricoeur calls this first presupposition an ontological one, a presupposition that now serves to resolve the earlier ambiguity about whether for Ricoeur there is a world independent of discourse. Hence when Ricoeur states that the world of the work intersects with the world of the reader, he insists that this process is at the same time an intersection of horizons rather than what Gadamer has called "a fusion of horizons."

The effects of reference in the fictional work are not simply illusions of reference but veridical modalities "that are profiled against the background of a worldly horizon which constitutes the world of the text" (1.120). For Ricoeur such a horizon cannot finally be constrained within the limits of the work without making it impossible to account for how the world of the work intersects with that of the reader. The movement beyond the immanence of the text takes place largely because of the operations in fictional works of nondescriptive uses of language, especially "metaphorical reference." Independent of any intention on the part of an author, a fictional work is characterized by an internal dynamism that opens out through the nondescriptive reference of metaphorical terms and predication onto a world with a horizon. But the world of the text does not just open out onto the world; to the degree that it intersects with the world of the reader, its configuration helps bring about a refiguration of the reader's world. In this process of refiguration is to be found the signification of the fictional work.

The world of the reader can be taken as either the world the reader constructs in an interpretation of the world the fictional work projects, or it can be taken as the world the reader brings with him or her to the interpretive task, a world at one moment entirely innocent of whatever world the work in hand is yet to project. This second world (that which is antecedent to a reading of the work) Ricoeur opposes to the world of the work in terms of "the reader's real world" being opposed to "the

fictive world" of the work. "The passage from configuration to refiguration," Ricoeur writes, "requires the confrontation between two worlds,
the fictive world of the text and the real world of the reader" (3.231). But
a further idea is presented here as well—namely, the distinction between
the world of the text, which is an inscribed world, and the world of the
work, which is a projected one.

We have, then, something vaguely described as the world or reality;
we have the worlds inscribed and configured in texts, the worlds that
works project; we have the worlds readers arrive at in their interpretations
of the world of a work; and finally we have the world in which readers
go on to live, the refigured world and its successive transformations
through still further interpretive acts. Which of these are we to understand
as the fictive world? Because we owe to works of fiction the expansion
of our horizons on reality, the fictional world for Ricoeur is not the configured world of the text but the refigured world that appears as a consequence of the interaction between the projections of the world of the
work and the ongoing interpretations of the world of the reader. Consequently, when Ricoeur (*pace* Goodman) is taken to hold that there are
fictional worlds, the claim is both that works of fiction present in part
configurations of a world and that some readers of fictional works live
and act in a constantly refigured realm that is no longer properly describable as the real world. For finally, what is refigured, especially in the
imperfect mediation of our ongoing totalizations of historical consciousness and the historical situation, is not just human temporality but the
world itself. The world, the figured world, is in this larger sense a fictional
world.

With these further elements in hand we may make one further attempt
to formulate Ricoeur's notion of a fictional world:

> 6. *A fictional world is a dynamic proposal (a "proposition") for refiguring
>   experience as a reality to be inhabited.* The proposal arises from the
>   interaction between the horizon projected by the world of the
>   work and that projected by the world of the reader. This inter-
>   action is established by a certain operations of the sentences of
>   the fictional text and not their terms, their metaphorical (not
>   literal) reference to an extralinguistic and nondescriptive domain
>   beyond the linguistically closed inscribed world of the text. Ini-
>   tially, a configuration projected beyond the text, the proposal in
>   the interaction process brings about a continual refiguration of
>   both the world of the work which the reader interprets and the
>   world in which the reader inexorably lives, acts, and suffers. This
>   ongoing refiguration expands the reader's horizon of reality and
>   thereby is said to augment reality itself. Further, such a process
>   results in an imperfect ongoing mediation, a partial totalization

of consciousness and history wherein reality is apprehended both from the perspective of human praxis (narrative, whether fictional or historical) and cosmic pathos (lyric poetry).

Returning to our example with such an account before us, a fictional world such as the one Stevens fashions in his poem is a dynamic proposal for the refiguration of the experience of its reader, the enhancement of the possibilities of readers to inhabit a world, and the enlargement of the horizons of a reader's lived world.

Recapitulation and Critique

Just as in the first view, this second account of what we have called a fictional world has allowed us to apprehend a number of salient features in such poetic works as Stevens's poems. For at each stage of its progressive elaboration, we have tried to articulate at least part of what Stevens might be interpreted as pointing toward in such expressions as "a supreme fiction." Thus, we have continued to note the pertinence of such an account to the understanding and interpretation of such works.

But when we return to Stevens's poem with the fuller account in hand, we find once again that still other arguably central features of that poem escape us. It is true that the present account brings into view some elements that were obscured on the first view—for example, the central contrast between world of the text, world of the work, and world of the reader. And some larger lived world now can be surmised in the poem's representation of the world of nature, the singer's world, the world of the speaker, and so on. Further, talk of projective discourse on this account brings out several cardinal features its rival neglected—the notion, for example, of the sky being "acutest at its vanishing," or the measuring "to the hour" of its solitude, or even the final mention of "ghostlier demarcations, keener sounds." And this account also does some justice to the kind of large-scale metaphorical processes going on in the difficult talk of order, maker, singer, and artificer which the first account can deal with only at the level of terms and predicates.

But are there not other perhaps even more central elements to be accounted for? Consider, for example, the complex kinds of denotation and reference at work in such expressions as "what she sang was what she heard," or "Oh! Blessed rage of order, pale Ramon," or even "Ramon Fernandez, tell me, if you know, Why . . ." We require, it seems, an account of reference which is neither too polarized by the exaggerated importance of denotation nor too committed to relational theories, and yet more detailed in its articulation than the striking but overly general talk of suspension of reference, productive reference, or semantic innovation. Consider also the curious kinds of constructs which play such a central role in this work— for example, in the repeated meditations on the song of the singer and the result of her artifice, which is called mysteriously the world, or the peculiar resonances in the changes the poem works on the expression "words" ("words of the sea, Words of the fragrant portals . . . And of ourselves and of our origins"). Here we require not just talk of versions and worlds but sustainable distinctions between such notions, just as we require some attention to whether, and if so at what cost, a distinction can be made between a comparatively external linguistic reality and the limits of our conceptual frameworks. And finally, how are we to construe not just the extensions of the expressions in which this poetic language abounds or just the intentions readers and interpretive communities bring with them to the appreciation of such works but the implicit quasi-intentions that characterize the varied utterances of the poetic work's different speaking voices?

Among the several problematic elements, then, in this second account of fictional world let us focus critical attention selectively once again on three matters only. Most generally, this view is committed to a basic distinction between fictional world and reality. For behind so much of the description here we find continually talk of a preconfigured or "preunderstood" order of human praxis which is ontologically prior to whatever construction such praxis might elaborate. Further, the discourse of any verbal fictional world such as a poetic work is said not only to transcend its own formal closures in being always directed toward or aiming at an unsayable realm that is portrayed in this view as both nondescriptive and extralinguistic. This is the domain that is said to be encompassed by a "worldly horizon," the domain of our "being in the world," the realm we are said to render habitable through the progressive refigurations of human experience. But such a view turns on a central distinction between linguistic worlds and a comprehensive extralinguistic reality which this account presents as both prior to human activity and prior also to the aims of such activity. Extralinguistic domains exist, of course—we need only think of the pictorial or the exemplary, to use examples from the first account. But to characterize such domains as ultimate in the way this second account does requires an extensive range of fundamental arguments about conceptual frameworks that are nowhere to be found. The first problem here, then, is the unsustained claim that there is a reality independent of our versions of it. Thus, if the first account faces the problem of keeping worlds from collapsing into versions, the second faces the related problem of getting world and reality into a unified conceptual framework.

The second difficulty concerns the nature of the "projection" of a world of the work. Ricoeur is at some pains throughout his studies to oppose theories of the work as a set of immanent textual structures, a semiotic system of sorts. His strategy is to oppose the understanding of language which stands behind such diverse and well-elaborated theories, and to substitute for the Saussurian view of language and meaning the larger and less formal view of Bienveniste, of language as discourse and signification. But if the strategy is reasonably clear in outline, the details are sketchy. For what has to be shown is what sense it makes to speak of functions of discourse in the construction and elaboration of the worlds of a work as "aiming" or "moving toward" or "moving beyond." In short, where is the required detailed discussion of what it could mean to say that the discourse of a fictional work "transcends" the linguistic frameworks of its own formal configuration? The move of course is to talk of background beliefs, nonextensional contexts, intentions, and so on. But exactly how these elements, whether individually or as a whole, warrant talk of projection toward an extralinguistic and comprehensive realm is not detailed. A second problem with this view is a difficulty with the nature, function, and justification of projective discourse.

These two difficulties concerning extralinguistic reality and projective discourse lead to a third. For at the more particular level of a theory of meaning we find a very strong claim about the semantic innovation that fictional works are said to bring about. Here the talk is of the suspension of the usual process of reference, of what is called "ordering reference," of the work of the Kantian productive imagination, and the generation of reference not at the level of terms or sentences but at that of the metaphorical significations of story. Much at this level of the account has to do with indirect kinds of reference, what, presumably, Goodman calls complex reference. And indeed Ricoeur's view incorporates in a number of places the fruits of his repeated reflections in *The Rule of Metaphor* on Goodman's views about metaphor in *Languages of Art*. But it is clear, on the arguments Wolterstorff and others have developed, that however bold in conception, the doctrines of semantic innovation cannot stand without substantial revision.[12] Serious difficulties affect the description of so-called "ordering reference." Gaps are present in the discussion of the so-called "suspension" of such reference, and the positive version of what semantic innovation properly consists of adds to the consequences of the previous difficulties further problems of its own. Thus, the major difficulty at this level has to do with categorization, the coherence, and finally the intelligibility of the doctrine of semantic innovation especially at the level of stories.

Each of these three problems—the intelligibility of talk about the worldly horizon of reality *tout court*, at a general level; the construal at the intermediate level of the language of the fictional work as projective discourse; and the coherence, at the more particular level, of the doctrine of semantic innovation with respect to stories—deserves, as in the case

[12]Wolterstorff 1984:141–44.

of the first account, further elaboration. But again, without trying to detail further the extensive discussion of this view provided above, it does not seem unreasonable to conclude that the second view of "fictional world" cannot be endorsed as such. Nonetheless, this second view makes several substantial suggestions toward articulating a less unsatisfactory understanding of the kinds of concerns Stevens and others would seem to indicate in their repeated meditations on supreme fictions.

ELEMENTS FOR AN ALTERNATIVE ACCOUNT

We have seen how both of these accounts of world, as fictive world and as fictional world, whatever their difficulties, make a substantial contribution to our efforts at conceptualizing what is going on in talk about some works of art as supreme fictions. Thus, the first account (despite what I take to be serious problems with distinguishing between true versions and worlds, with interpreting the objects of reference as "individuals" only, and with construing all true worlds as "actual" worlds) has the merit of underlining at least three major features in a satisfactory account of supreme fictions. To move this time from the particular to the general, we may note first the central reflection on modality. The insight here is the realization that something is radically wrong with construing supreme fictions as possible worlds only. The viable alternative does not seem to be to take them as actual either. But an account that does not attend to modal issues falls prey to overgeneralization of supreme fictions in terms of possibility only. A second substantive feature of the analytic account is the sophisticated attempt to systematize the varieties of reference in such a way as to include both elementary and complex referrings but also verbal and nonverbal together with literal and metaphorical ones. We need not follow this account in allowing denotation such a central role that it polarizes the theory of reference nor in taking reference in relational, extensional terms only with the somewhat paradoxical consequences for expressions that have null denotation and blank labels yet play extraordinarily rich referential roles. The key suggestion here is the idea that however we go on to distinguish between our everyday referential practices, say, in nonfiction, we can account for the unusual practices in fictional works only with the help of an account of reference more than merely verbal and richer than merely denotative. Finally, a third substantive feature in this account is the theory of metaphor as an affective reclassification and ordering of at least primary and secondary extensions, as allowing for movement within referential chains and hierarchies, and as operative in more than verbal contexts only, in gesture and the like. Again, we need not follow the account all the way in accepting here what we reject elsewhere—namely, all referents as individuals and all worlds as actual. We need to be critical, however, about the confinement of metaphorical reference to terms and predicates. Still, an account of fiction which skirts metaphor cannot, given the roles of metaphor in fiction, be satisfactory. An emphasis on modality, an account of reference as systematic and larger than merely verbal, and a view of metaphor as the radical recategorization of literal extensions in both verbal and nonverbal realms—each of these invites sympathetic articulation in any account of fictions.

Similarly, the second account (despite serious problems with the notion of an extralinguistic, entirely comprehensive totality in the guise of "reality" before and after our thinking, with the mysterious idea of the discourse of a fictional work as allowing a so-called autotranscendence beyond the work to such "reality," and the arguable errors, gaps, and confusions in a bold theory of semantic innovation) involves at least three distinguished proposals. First, there is indeed something right about the idea that the language of fictional works has to be construed on other terms than merely formal ones because it arises out of and returns to intentional contexts. The key here lies in the claim that tying reference exclusively to expressions, as the first account does, is too narrow; expressions refer, but so do speakers. We need not proceed to adopt a speech-act theory or fictional intentions to accommodate this insight; it is sufficient to pay much closer attention to talk of conventions, backgrounds, and contexts.

Second, this account allows a more extensive interpretation of metaphor than is possible in that of its rival. Thus, metaphorical reference of whatever kind can be operative on a larger scale than just on that of terms and predicates. Indeed, in talking of story the present account allows the possibility—one that a less inadequate theory of supreme fiction requires—of treating versions and conceptual frameworks themselves as metaphors. Moreover, describing metaphysical reference at such levels in terms not just of reclassification and reorderings but as practical refigurations of antecedent and merely formal configurations does more justice to some of the cardinal ways metaphors seem to function in some poetic works. Again, adopting this larger view need not involve accepting the insufficiently detailed theory of reference which this account involves at the level of terms and predicates. Here too we can be selective.

Finally, this hermeneutic account is particularly suggestive in airing the idea that supreme fictions, however we choose to take them, include as some of their central features matters that touch on the dynamic interactions between consciousness and history. Some of the interactions we have seen have to do with fictionalizing the past and historicizing present imaginings in future projects. Such a view calls serious attention to the lived qualities of the world, in particular to the ongoing refigurations of our experience in terms of such incessant convergences between the factual and the fictional. Here too we need not adopt a Hegelian terminology, however qualified in terms of partial totalizations or incomplete mediations, to capture this insight. We need only include in our focus on supreme fictions the cultural world and the historical world as necessary correlates. Thus, three distinguished suggestions to be put with those of the rival view—a stress on language as discourse and not just as system; on metaphorical reference as the figurations of conceptual frameworks and not just reclassifications of extensions; and on culture, history, and consciousnesses as components in any account of supreme fictions.

But talk of accounting for supreme fictions is not completed by merely forcing revisions in each of these accounts and then papering over their different orientations and assumptions by linking loosely their respective insights into a more or less unhappy synthesis. Such an approach cannot succeed because the roots of the suggestions on each account lie in radically different understandings of logic, language, knowledge, and mind. In what follows, then, I map out in a brief and programmatic way only elements of an alternative account that tries to avoid some of the difficulties in the accounts before us while preserving their contributions within at least the contours of an independent synthesis.

Rereadings

When we return to our key example, Stevens's "The Idea of Order at Key West," and reread this poetic fiction in the light of our concern to identify the cardinal elements required for a satisfactory account of whatever it would mean, in the light of such work, to speak of a fictional or fictive world, a number of important features prove suggestive. In order to bring these features out, I take a few steps toward rereading that work and then proceed to isolate and articulate briefly each of these features in turn.

This two-part work begins and ends with a protracted meditation on two different sounds: in the first part the sounds of the movements of the sea and those of a song a woman sings while walking on an ocean beach at night, and in the second the sounds of a conversation between two friends who have been listening to the sounds of the sea and the song and whose own discussion may be taken as ending only sometime after the scene recounted, in the articulation of the poetic work itself. The first sound is the "cry" of the ocean, an inhuman sound that is taken to be both the sea's imitative echo of its own continual movements and a nonhuman kind of creation or making in the natural order of things. The second sound is that of the woman's singing. Her song stands in a curious relation to the sound of the sea. The sound of her singing is not an imitation of the sea's sound but an incorporation of that sound into a different kind of creation, a human making in a human world. Neither of these two sounds is understood as concealing anything the way a mask might conceal an unseen face. Nothing is behind either the grindings and plungings of the sea or the phrasings and the sounds of the woman's singing. Each sound, however, is correlated with the other independent of whatever intentions the singer may have. Yet despite their correlation, the two sounds remain separate— they are not medleyed sound.

Two friends walking on the same darkened beach are represented as having pursued a kind of meditative conversation on the sea sounds and the sounds of the woman's song. A question now arises between them: "Whose spirit is this? we said"—a very general and ambiguous question that seems to be looking for an answer in terms of some kind of a priority. Is it the sound of the sea which evokes the sound of the song, or is it, rather, the sound of the song which generates the sound of the sea? The conversation explores various possibilities. The spirit is not to be identified with the voice of the sea, nor with the closely related but different voice of the sky. The wind in agitating the sea's waves in conjunction with the sea's own tidal movements and currents makes the sea resound. Nor, more complexly, is the spirit to be identified with the voice of the singer, nor finally even with those of the two friends whose discussion continually frames the observations and reflections.

The question is left without an answer when the friends suddenly catch sight of the singer "striding there alone." For this unexpected perception provokes a fresh idea, the idea that questions about the priority of the natural world's productive and generative activity over that of the singer, or her human creative intuitions over that of the world dissolve into the realization that, whatever sense it makes to talk of the world of the singer, the genitive case here is a subjective genitive and not an objective one. "Then we / . . . Knew that there never was a world for here / Except the one she sang and, singing, made." The singer has a world only to the degree that she sings; more strongly, there is no world for the singer except insofar as she sings.

But the singing ends, we are told, as the poem moves into its second part, and the friends turn round to walk back to the town. As they are returning, however, the speaker is struck by how the lights in the fishing boats anchored nearby constitute points of reference in the night sky and on the darkened sea. The speaker then raises a new question, not directly about the spirit but about the reasons that explain why he had just perceived that scene in the way he goes on to describe to his friend, that is, in terms of the lights mastering the night and portioning out the sea, "Fixing emblazoned zones and fiery poles, / Arranging, deepening, enchanting night."

The poem then moves into its concluding stanza, where we overhear the sounds of the continuing discussion and in particular the speaker's implied response to his own question in an unusual rhetorical address to his companion. The suggestion is that the spirit that moves across the water and makes it resound generatively (as in the creation narratives of Western culture) and the spirit that inspires the creative activity of the singer as artist and artificer of the world (in the central myths of the continuing romantic poem) is a quasi-divine rage for order, something "blessed" that influences the speaker's ways of perceiving the world. This same rage for order leads beyond the discursive moments in the reflective discussion, into verbal formulations of the reflection ("Oh! Blessed rage for order"), through a synthesis in the title ("The Idea of Order at Key West"), into the extended symbolic framework that is the poetic work itself, and finally beyond into the world of the work's ongoing interpretations.

Thus, a meditative conversation between two friends walking on a slowly darkening and windy beach at the fall of night and musing on the respective echoing of the sea's sounds and a singer's songs stops short in a perception of the artist's peculiar solitude, as if she did not inhabit a world as she strides alone along the ocean's edge, and expands into a realization that the movements of nature are meaningless until they are fashioned through the activities of a culture into a world. This realization in turn, this idea of a world, reorganizes in the second part of the poetic work the speaker's perception in such a substantive way that he is strongly affected by the puzzling disclosure in which he hears himself describing the boat lights' patterning of the night sky and the dark sea. He then comes to an insight that he can only formulate as a rhetorical expostulation, that the idea of a world itself follows from a rage for order, a rage to order things in words, to make poetic works. And the words that arise from such a rage, the speaker concludes, yield demarcations that are less substantial than either the zones and poles of the night which the lights have arranged. And yet these words yield sounds that are keener even than those of the song of the singer whose voice had "made the sky acutest at its vanishing."

Even within the evident limitations of such a paraphrase of this poetic work, at least six important features stand out sharply in the perspective of our concerns with the notions of a fictive or fictional world.

Six Features

The first salient feature we may pick out under the heading of "contexts." The setting of this fictional work is at once natural, historical, and cultural. The natural realm is everywhere present, from the sea by which the song and the conversation are pursued, to the sky and its curious horizons, to the testimony of the seasons and smells of summer, and to the changing of the time from dusk to deep night. Moreover, the historical past is also evoked in the name "Ramon Fernandez," which is at once a name for any New World cosmopolitan (a Spanish name but most likely that of a South American exile in Key West) and yet also the name of a once prominent literary critic of the thirties and forties. And finally, the context is also a cultural one as well, not just with the presence of the allusions to literature in the name of a critic or the description of the art of song but especially in the suggestive descriptions of the sea in an imagery reminiscent of Genesis, the evocation of a spirit, and in the Arnoldian image of a movement down a darkened beach to the sea. Thus, the fictional work is situated in the selection of its details, the suggestion of its images, and the echoes of its diction in a more than merely formal matrix; the work in short exists in, has been produced inside of, and is taken up for appreciation within a complex context that constitutes an irreplaceable part of its specific contour. *A fictional work is part of a peculiar context*, at least with respect to a poetic work of fiction such as this.

A second feature may be picked out in terms of a peculiar understanding of the language in which the fictional work consists. I call this feature "language as fictional discourse" in order to place the accent squarely on the central importance in this work of a lyrical speaker's monologue represented as arising out of, returning repeatedly to, and finally moving beyond the practice of meditative conversation. The entire work may not implausibly be taken as embodied in a conversation between two friends, one of whom is named and yet is not heard and the other of whom speaks continuously while remaining anonymous. Moreover, the movement of the conversation itself is complex in that different tenses abound, syntactic moods vary, and utterances of more than one type occur. Much needs analysis here. But for our purposes the main point is that whatever claims are represented in the fictional work, and however such claims are presented if not asserted, they are always part of a monologue that itself is nested in a dialogue. Finally, in the figure of the imaginary cosmopolitan who is at the same time a historical personage, a literary critic whose profession is to reorder the words the poet's rage has already ordered, the suggestion arises that the conversation does not end in the poem but only, if ever, outside the poem, once the so far silent interlocutor takes his necessary turn. In short, the fictional work is articulated here with all the resources of a more than merely formal understanding of language. *A fictional work is articulated in a peculiar understanding of language as fictive conversational discourse*.

Besides the contexts of the fictional work and its distinctive uses of conversational discourse and not just systems of language, a third feature this poetic work suggests is a larger interpretation of the referents of such a discourse as merely individuals. We have already noted some of the peculiar kinds of things which occur in this poetic work—a range of items which stretches from the improper proper name "Ramon Fernandez" through the play of pronouns, whether impersonal, personal, possessive

(for one example only consider the uses of "it" in the poem); syncate-
gorematic terms such as the repeated uses of "if"; the proliferation and
juxtaposition of verbs in different and shifting tenses, common nouns
that seem uncommon; expostulations ("Oh!"); and so on. How can we
hope to nominalize our way through the profusions in the discourse of
this work when Quine himself has given up and even Goodman concedes
that temporary expedients are necessary? More than individuals must be
taken as the referents of at least some expressions that not only occur in
but play central roles in fictional discourse. Talk of complex reference,
referential chains and hierarchies, allusion, understatement, irony, and
hyperbole can continue to make good systematic sense without being
centered on overly generous construals of "individuals" as anything at
all except necessary expedients. In short, the discourse of poetic fictions
requires for its proper analysis a nonnominalistic theory of the objects of
reference. Thus, *the referents of the fictive conversational discourses in a fictional
world are more than mere individuals.*

A fourth feature of poetic fictions surely is their pervasive symbolic
character. Here, however, we need to account for at least some of the
complexities that works such as "The Idea of Order at Key West" exhibit
in not just distinguishing between symbols and metaphors but in doing
so somewhat nontraditionally. We need to capture in our terminology
two ideas. For if the constructs we call the poem can, on at least some
interpretations of reflections (like those of a Carnap, a Cassirer, and a
Goodman), be designated as conceptual frameworks or symbolic systems,
we cannot speak of particular symbols in a work in just the same sense
of "symbol." The first use of the term is inevitably linked with constructive
systematic reflection on the nature of language, truth, and the world,
whereas the second use has no other pretentions than to mark the potential of an expression for a general semantic polyphony. By contrast,
"metaphor" in this context is a term that calls attention to a variety of
semantic processes, whether elementary or complex, against the background of an argued account of "literalness," "synonymy," and so on.
When we struggle in reading such works with the semantic fullness of
such terms as "maker" or "order" and the semantic tensions in such
expressions as "And when she sang, the sea / Whatever self it had, became
the self / That was her song, for she was the maker," we require a larger
understanding of symbol than the usual one restricted to the level of
terms. And we require, too, a more perspicuous understanding of metaphorical reference than one that takes reference as necessarily and only
extensional. If blinkered interpretations and blank labels and null denotations are to be avoided, we need to explore the suggestion that some
fictional works both function symbolically, even at the level of conceptual
frameworks, and seem to require a nonrelational account of metaphorical

reference. Thus, *a fictional world may function as a symbolic categorical framework and as a complex instance of nonrelational metaphorical reference.*

Still another central feature of poetic fictions becomes clear on rereading works like Stevens's, what we may call the intersection of projected horizons. Notice initially that part of the way in which some expressions in fictional discourse function is by opening up a domain beyond the formal limits of the fictional work itself. Exactly how such expressions do this I think has to be discussed in a detailed way in relation to individual cases. But the idea that something very much like projection takes place, at least on the evidence of the analysis I began to sketch above (of, say, the peculiar expression "Ramon Fernandez" and other similar cases), is not implausible. The text, we remember, is taken to project a formal configuration. And now we may add that the work projects an informal but nondescriptive schema that includes elements of its background, various contexts, conventions, and its interpretive history in successive communities. It is this second projection that may be taken to intersect with the interpretive schema of the poetic fiction's competent readers. Thus, whatever the formal configurations of Stevens's poem here—and they are both multiple (consider the verbal sound patterns used to represent the ideas of sound patterns) and controversial (how are the self-referential features of the text to be represented perspicuously in a symbolism?)— the text is part of a larger whole called "the work" which, for example, in the talk of a "rage to order words . . . of ourselves and of our origins, in ghostlier demarcations," projects a horizon beyond the work, a horizon that intersects any attempt to offer an interpretation of the work. Accounting, then, for the nature of poetic fictions cannot skirt the task of explaining, not in general but in particular cases, just which uses of fictional discourse can, on a revised understanding of reference and metaphor, refer beyond the formal limits of a text and constitute or generate a horizon of the work which renders interpretation possible. Thus, *a fictional world arises in part from the dynamic intersection of interpretive horizons projected by both the work and the reader.*

A sixth and for now final factor in poetic fictions which comes out in reading such works against the backdrop of the philosophical concerns here may be called the renderings of a work or its refigurations. Recall the unusual sequence in Stevens's poem from the quiet, meditative conversation, to a speculative question, to an end to speculation provoked by a particular observation ("As we beheld her striding there alone"), to an eminently puzzling perceptual experience and its description, to a rhetorical formulation of the idea of a "rage for order," to the fashioning of a poetic work entitled "The Idea of Order at Key West." The suggestion here is that some artifacts like the woman's song project a horizon that intersects with a reader's interpretive schemes in such a way as to allow one to come to know something so novel that the usual perceptual patterns in which one lives one's life are radically transformed into ones no longer understood or operative in the same way. I take it that such occurrences are familiar matters of fact, as many museum goers, concert subscribers, and film viewers continue to testify. What is unfamiliar is the suggestion here that some changes in perception and in action—say, those that concern our categorical schemes and their consequences for our actions—are usefully labeled "refigurations" in that not just our perceptions and our actions but our classifications of experience itself are reshuffled. In short, part of what makes up a poetic fiction is the set of very general and not just specific effects it can work upon the understanding, the classification, the schematization of readers' lived experiences. Thus, *a fictional world may effect central changes in the perceptions, actions and categorical classifications of the experiences of its interpreters.*

Here, then, are six features of poetic fictions which stand out on rereading certain poetic texts with an ear to contemporary philosophical discussions about fictive and fictional worlds. We have the notion of the contexts in which a work is situated dynamically, the language of the controversial discourse of fictional communication in which the poetic work is elaborated, a discourse in which not just expressions but speakers too are taken to refer both to individuals and nonindividuals, one that is largely given over both to symbolic discourse at all levels of language, including that of categorical framework construction and to metaphorical reference of both extensional and nonextensional varieties. We have as well the notion of both a text and a work allowing of semantic projections, which in the latter case transgress the formal closures of the text to constitute a horizon of the work which intersects with the interpretive schemes of its successive readers. And we have the idea that a poetic work of fiction, like other works, has effects, some of which may but need not include the enhancement of perceptual experience and especially the modification of classificatory frameworks.

In this summary perspective, then, I propose a brief description of what may be taken to be neither a fictive nor a fictional world but what I call—in the spirit of what is neither more nor less than an intermittent flickering "realism"—a world that is a real fiction.

Real Fictions

When we ask the question "What does it means to talk of the world of Wallace Stevens as a fictional world?" and when we focus this question sharply on "the world of Wallace Stevens in, for example, the poetic work 'The Idea of Order at Key West,' " we are asking versions of the difficult question "What is a work about?" Part of what makes such a question difficult is that the level at which a satisfactory answer is to be found is not evident. This is especially the case in the philosophy of literature where, unlike the case in criticism, an answer in terms of theme or subject matter cannot suffice, and where such questions require a more generous interpretation in terms of at least some contemporary discussion of realism, antirealism, and even Goodman's "irrealism." My response, unfortunately, must be somewhat mean-spirited, for I want neither to leave such a question at the level of a so-called theme in a work nor take a thoroughly perspicuous position on the still outstanding issue in the realism-antirealism debate. In the first case, that of literary criticism, we do well to leave such matters to the task of building consensus among poets and critics, whereas in the second any position is necessarily controversial and hence requires far more systematic, sustained, and very general argument than is pertinent to our present purposes. What follows, then, is a provisional formulation of the world of Stevens's poem, generated from rereadings of Stevens's work as a whole, presented in particular enough terms to be not wholly inappropriate as an account of part of what Stevens's poem is "about," and yet in general enough terms that at least some of the formulations may be relevant not just to Stevens's poetic work alone but perhaps to many if not all poetic works of fiction as such.

In such works as Stevens's poem, readers find, among other things, the presentations of a symbolic version of the actual world. This version sometimes functions is such a way as to project a horizon beyond the configurations allowed by its own formal structures such that a reader's own most general categorical frameworks for apprehending reality are called into question in the process of attempting to articulate a satisfactory account of what such a fictional poetic work is "about." Again, in some cases the effects of such strains on the categorical framework interpreters bring to a work are such that what the interpreter goes on subsequently to take as "the real" is substantially if only intermittently modified. Such a reader may be said, to borrow one of Stevens's expressions, "to be of three minds." For the world in such a scenario remains "factual" in that it is in some sense prior to the reader's interpretive linguistic strategies and will outlast them. And yet the world is "fictional" also in that whatever world there is can be a world only to the degree that it is referentially apprehended, whether verbally or nonverbally, literally or metaphorically, for reference is varied.

"The world," however, is not be articulated in terms of an opposition between the "fictional" and the "factual" because each of these terms is too heavily compromised either in ordinary usage (where the "fictional" is often wrongly construed as the "not real," because the notion of "the real" is left uninterpreted and uncriticized) or in the philosophical tradition (where "the factual" has historically been wrongly taken as "the neutral," since as our century has shown no facts are independent of observations and values).

Consider, then, the proposal that "the world" of the work becomes "the world" of lived and historical consciousness to the extent that a world is caught up in the refiguration of an interpreter's comprehensive conceptual frameworks in such a way that the world becomes a "real fiction," a fictive world, a fictional world, and a factual fiction at once— a two-in-one, as Stevens would say, neither the world of the green mundo nor the world of the blue guitar not the world of the yellow sun but the white world of the glistening, mineral, ceramic bowl.

Such a real fiction exhibits at least four distinctive features that do not constitute so much a definition of a fictional world or a set of necessary and sufficient conditions but a heuristic description that enables inter-preters to pick up many of the pertinent aspects of a fictional world they encounter in interpreting the world of a fictional work.

First, the world as a "real fiction" involves a quasi-modal feature, for such a world needs specifying neither as an actual world (in some sense it does not exist) nor as a possible world (in other senses it does not exist) but as what I will call a virtual world, a world that on my view exists only intermittently.

Second, the world as a "real fiction" includes the referents of much but not necessarily all of our conversational discourses. Such referents, however, need to be reconstrued not just as the individuals of a nom-inalistic understanding of reference nor as the individuals, situations, events, and sets of a nonnominalistic view, but as the range of individuals, events, and the like of a nonextensional and nonrelational theory of ref-erence along the lines, for example, Joseph Margolis and others have been urging.[13]

Third, the world as a "real fiction" is not just a virtual world full of individuals, events, situations, and sets to which our conversational dis-courses refer in both extensional and nonextensional ways, but a world that works central and at times liberating effects on the persons who are its interpreters. Such effects are centered on cognitive and affective pro-cesses, but most important, on the mechanisms, contours, and ranges of human praxis.

Finally, the world as a "real fiction" is in part an artifact of individual and communal human consciousness as embodiments of varied and changing historical cultures. As such, the world as a real fiction is plural. Moreover, it incorporates both individual and social values. And it com-

---

[13]Margolis 1986.

prises not just productive refigurations of human experience but, most centrally, dynamic rearticulations of concurrent and incompatible versions of truth within different categorical frameworks.

An Exhibit

In concluding I offer no summary of this extended reflection on talk about fictional worlds, with respect to both the worlds of poetic fictions and those of what we like to call "real life." Summaries can be found at each stage in the development of these reflections, from the three formulations of Goodman's notion of a "fictive world" and the three of Ricoeur's notion of a "fictional world," through six related features of a world such as we seem to find in Stevens's poem, to finally the modal, referential, pragmatic, and constructive historical features of a world, whether fictional or factual, a world as a so-called "real fiction," a sometime thing. Rather, I return once again to our starting point in the poetic fictions of Wallace Stevens, the sustained meditation on what he called the world as a "supreme fiction." Perhaps it is enough for now to leave these reflections on fictional and fictive worlds and worlds as real fictions with a reference to still another of Stevens's shorter works, a work exhibiting a more abstract framework for refiguring the virtual world I am calling a real fiction than some of the concrete images we have already alluded to ("the whitened sky," the "bowl of white"), Stevens's "The Snow Man." In the context we have been exploring here, this poem, however unremittingly it invites out repeated interpretations, may be left to speak and to show without a commentary, inviting instead a much more general recapitulation of the nature, kinds, and uses of fictions in the concluding part of this essay.

Appendix 7A   A Pluralism of Worlds

An important feature of Goodman's view of world is his claim that there are many worlds. Behind this claim is a group of arguments to the effect that, since reliable evidence is on hand for conflicting truths about many things (say, the motion of the earth with respect to the sun and the motionlessness of the earth with respect to the individual) and since conflicting truths cannot both hold, there must be more than one world. Moreover, this basic element in Goodman's view about the nonexistence of fictive worlds includes not just this claim about the plurality of worlds but in particular the view that such worlds are not merely possible worlds. The point Goodman wants to make is that accepting his argument that there must be more than one world because conflicting truths cannot exist in the same world is insufficient; we are to grant as well the additional point that this plurality is of actual and not merely possible worlds. This latter point Goodman continually qualifies with his mysterious expression, many actual worlds "if any." Goodman has not found it easy to defend this thesis. But to some extent, as Putnam's own turnabout on some of the complex issues here shows, he has been reasonably successful. But to understand Goodman's view in more detail we need to look more closely at a fuller description of his views about the plurality of actual worlds.

Goodman provides us with some important detail on his view that there are many actual worlds in an article from 1982 whose point is "to review and to clarify some themes from his earlier book *Ways of Worldmaking*."[14] Under the heading of "Monism, Pluralism, Nihilism" we find a summary of the argument for a plurality of worlds together with some reflections on how we are to understand the relations among these many worlds. The argument begins with the familiar assertion that some truths conflict—for example, the truth that the earth is constantly in movement and the truth that the earth is at rest. Talk of a heliocentric system and a geocentric system does not resolve such conflicts, it is claimed, because even though more than one account of how things are is on hand, nothing in either account shows that a particular account is true. Nor does it help to construe statements such as "the earth is at rest" and "the earth moves" as fragments only of fuller statements such as "the earth is at rest relative to Mount Everest" and "the earth moves relative to the sun." For these larger statements themselves are not easy to interpret; even their translation remains controversial. In order to preserve the difference between truth and falsity, an alternative account is presented: each truth in conflict is to be understood as true in a different world. "Versions not applying in the same world no longer conflict; contradiction is avoided by segregation. A true version is true in some worlds, a false version in none. Thus the multiple worlds of conflicting true versions are actual worlds, not merely possible worlds or nonworlds of false versions" (31).

But granted that this alternative account is condensed from a more extensive discussion elsewhere, it is not evident here just why the second attempt to account for conflicting truths fails. Nor is it clear exactly how the proposed alternative differs from the second account because the second is left in such a sketchy state. Further, even if both accounts when described fully were to fail and the alternative were finally to differ essentially from the second, it is not clear either

---

[14]Goodman 1982:30.

how the alternative, on grounds presented here, could be taken as both a reasonable and persuasive account of not just one but of two views, that there are many worlds *and* that these many worlds are not possible but actual ones.

"If there is any actual world, there are many," Goodman summarizes. "For there are conflicting true versions and they cannot be true in the same world" (31). What is said to compel us to accept the plurality of worlds is the "intolerable alternative of a world in which contradictory versions and therefore all versions are true." Such worlds, however, are not to be understood as in space-time, for they are distinct worlds only by virtue of their irreconcilability. Because they conflict irreconcilably, such worlds are themselves totalities and cannot be subsumed under larger totalities. Still, any attempt to interrelate such worlds seems to involve postulating higher orders and finally claiming that, after all, there is only one world. Goodman tries to handle this difficulty by invoking Putnam's doctrine of internal realism according to which we shift from one world version to another and from talk of worlds to talk of versions as suits our purposes, in the way, for example, physicists do when they shift from talk of waves to talk of particles. "One might say," Goodman concludes, "that there is only one world but this holds for each of the many worlds. In both cases the equivocation is stark—yet perhaps negotiable" (33). It is clear enough, then, that a central thesis behind his claim that there are no fictive worlds—namely, the plurality of actual worlds—is both controversial and recognized by Goodman as such.

Another way of handling the problem of conflicting truths turns on a distinction between what is said and how it is said. A further suggestion needs examination, the claim that the difference between conflicting truths is a disagreement about the manner of saying something rather than about objective facts. This new claim to explain away conflicting truths comes to the idea that statements of conflicting truths are really different and indeed artificial ways of describing what after all are neutral facts about the one real world. In reply, Goodman contests the assumption here that there are any neutral facts and brands this assumption just as much a prejudice as any other. "Once we recognize," he writes, "that some supposed features of the world derive from—are made and imposed by—versions, 'the world' rapidly evaporates. For there is no version-independent feature, no true version compatibly with all true versions" (33). Objects, time, space, and the raw material itself of a world are all "version-dependent," that is, features of a construct we call the world. "The world of a true version is a construct. . . . we make versions, and true versions make worlds" (34).

We need to question whether Goodman deals squarely enough with this view. For once again only a skimpy description is put forward for our consideration together with not so much an argument against that account as a series of assertions. Talk of "neutrality" here is said to be a prejudice, and everything in fact is said to be dependent on versions. Note also that this second assertion is in two steps: Goodman moves hastily from the claim that there are no neutral facts to the claim that nothing whatsoever, whether facts or anything else, is neutral. Goodman's discussion elsewhere of motion perception is helpful here,[15] but if it raises questions about "neutrality" of facts about motion, it does not support the kind of generalization Goodman needs in order to dispense with the third account altogether.

Thus, Goodman's recent discussions show that a central thesis behind the claim that no fictive worlds exist—namely, the plurality of actual-worlds thesis—involves several difficulties. For the difficulty is not just holding for some version of internal realism but also elaborating such a doctrine with the help of (at least here) a dubious set of unargued claims that everything is dependent on versions (not all of which are true) and that true versions are precisely what brings distinct worlds into conflict. Goodman recognizes explicitly that talk about true versions making worlds is problematic. He sees that such talk raises questions about how we can be said "to make worlds by making versions" and about what can constitute truth "if there is no independent world to match a version against" (34). Versions are said to make things, however, only if they are true. And yet Goodman denies that such a doctrine comes to saying no more than that "versions can make only what is already there." His reasons are two: the expression "being already there," he says, is not perspicuous, and he suggests and tries to illustrate that "what is already there may turn out to be very much a matter of making." When challenged over the illustration on the grounds that he is simply bringing out a constructive element in the process of cognition and when confronted by a rival illustration that in the case of the stars we cannot say "that we, or versions, make the stars,"[16] Goodman simply ignores the first and answers the second with questions of his own. He concludes by reasserting his thesis. "I suggest that to say that all configurations are constellations is in effect to say that none are: that a constellation becomes such only through being chosen from among all configurations, much as a class becomes a kind only through being distinguished, according to some principle, from other classes" (36). The idea is that drawing boundaries one way rather than another is what enables us to talk of either stars or constellations. And drawing boundaries here and everywhere is a matter of making versions.

Goodman insists here as elsewhere that his relativism is not without

---

[15]See Goodman 1978.
[16]I. Scheffler 1980. For contrasting views see Lorenzen 1986, and Arbib and Hesse 1986.

strict constraints. The difficulty lies in specifying these constraints either within the makeup of versions or in their interrelationships. Since nothing is held to be outside such versions, truth cannot be truth of correspondence, at least in the traditional interpretation of correspondence. Nor will coherence do the job because some versions are false; that is, since some false versions can be coherent, coherence itself cannot make the difference between true and false versions. Goodman takes his cue here as often from his earlier work on the validity of inductive inference, specifically from his theory that formal relations among sentences plus right categorization is what makes induction valid. Even if the conclusion of an induction is true, the induction is valid only when the right categories are used and certain formal relations hold among its sentences. And what makes a category right, Goodman holds, is the entrenchment of some categories rather than others in the successful practices of induction. "Rightness of categorization, in my view, derives from rather than underlies entrenchment" (38). This comes to the view that rightness is a matter of acceptability, and yet unlike acceptability truth must be more than just transient. Accordingly, Goodman moves on to claim that a sufficient condition for truth is "ultimate acceptability," although he quickly adds in a note that his intention is not "to *define* truth as ultimate acceptability" (38) and that ultimate acceptability applies only to versions composed of statements and of what these versions say as statements.

But Goodman immediately broadens the scope, here, to include all kinds of versions, whether verbal or nonverbal. The further claim is added that truth as rightness of what is said is only one kind of rightness, since many nonverbal versions cannot be either true or false but can be either right or wrong. Moreover, truth as rightness of what is said "is a species of but one aspect of rightness, for symbols, verbal or not, may refer not only by denotation but by exemplification or expression or by complex chains make up of homogeneous or heterogenous referential steps, or in two or more of these ways. And a version may be right or wrong in any of these respects" (39). Thus, rightness constrains relativism since some versions are wrong, even though we are left with the view, as Goodman formulated it in reply to Putnam in 1980, of "many world versions—some conflicting with each other, some so disparate that conflict or compatibility among them is indeterminable—are equally right. Nevertheless, right versions are different from wrong versions: relativism is restrained by considerations of rightness. Rightness, however, is neither constituted nor tested by correspondence with a world independent of all versions" (39). What Goodman means by this restriction turns on his qualifications about the nature of right versions. Thus, a version for Goodman is right only if it is well made, that is, constructed from a basis that construes all entities as individuals (53).

Appendix 7B   Semantic Innovation and World

Paul Ricoeur's notion of semantic innovation brings together the issues of metaphor and fiction around the common problem of world. For Ricoeur both metaphors and stories—both historical narratives and fictions—are instances of semantic innovation, and both introduce the problem of the world to which novel forms of discourse refer.

To begin with the simplest case, the metaphor innovates semantically when an unusual application results in a new semantic pertinence in predication. What makes the application unusual is the impossibility of interpreting the new application of the expression by an explication of its literal sense only. The story innovates semantically through "the invention of a plot," which, like the forging of a metaphor, also involves a synthesis of heterogeneous elements, what Ricoeur calls a new congruity in the articulation of incidents. In both cases—new metaphors and new stories—the Kantian productive imagination is said to schematize a certain synthetic operation and, despite the resistance our liberal uses of language and our habitual conceptual patterns raise, to figure it freshly. In both cases a multiplicity is reclassified and assimilated under a novel predication. Thus, Ricoeur wants to talk not just of metaphorical meaning but of metaphorical reference as well in order "to redescribe a reality which is inaccessible to direct description."

Ricoeur follows Benveniste rather than Saussure in taking the basic unit of discourse to be the sentence. His purpose is thereby to resist any limitation of what discourse intends to the immanent system of signs alone. "With the sentence, language is oriented beyond itself"[17] to a world with its own horizon. But the notion of horizon involves two elements, an internal and an external one. All experience is set against a horizon of possibilities. This horizon is internal in the sense that something can always be made more precise inside a set of limitations. And it is external, too, in the sense that what is aimed at in any discourse "stands in a series of possible relations to every other thing under the horizon of a total world which itself never figures as object of discourse" (1.118). Thus, reference itself on this interpretation is correlative with horizon in the sense that language necessarily refers beyond itself to something extra-linguistic. "Metaphorical reference [what he calls the suspension of such reference]—an effacement which in its first approximation refers language to itself—being revealed in a second approximation as the negative condition for liberating a more radical power of reference to some aspects of our being-in-the-world which cannot be said directly. These aspects are aimed at in an indirect but positively assertive way thanks to the new pertinence which the metaphorical utterance establishes at the level of

[17]Ricoeur 1983–85:1.18.

meaning on the ruins of the literal meaning abolished by its own irrelevance" (1.121). Thus, the fictional work refers beyond itself metaphorically. And Ricoeur moves to construe the notion of world and horizon in both nondescriptive as well as descriptive terms. Both metaphorical redescription and narrative refiguration involve nondescriptive reference, the first mainly in the realm of sensory affective aesthetic and normative values, and the second in the realm of action and its temporal values.

Ricoeur proceeds to claim that a fictional work deploys a world in its own right, what he calls a "cultural world" (1.83), the world of the work. More specifically, a fictional work proposes "a world which I could inhabit and in which I could project my most distinctive capacities"(1.122). This "proposal" of a world Ricoeur will go on to qualify as "a movement" of transcendence by which every fictional work "projects beyond itself a world which can be called *the world of the work*" (2.14; Ricoeur's emphasis). Moreover, this "proposal of a world or projection of a world is what Ricoeur takes to be the object of interpretation. Further, the world of the work is taken here to be either a redescription of the world in the case of a poetic work or a resignification of the world in its temporal dimension in the case of a narrative work, the stress on time being only one way of filling out the notion of inhabiting a world. And finally in a very complementary note Ricoeur cites Goodman explicitly and appropriates one of Goodman's chapter titles in *Ways of Worldmaking*, "reality remade," as well as Goodman's maxim of thinking works in terms of worlds and world in terms of works. We are left with an important hierarchy among worlds which includes the world of reality, the representation of a world through the projects of a fictional work, and the making of a lived world on the part of a reader who interprets the world of a fictional work. The major element to be clarified is whether we are to construe the fictional world of Ricoeur as either the world the text projects or the world the reader interprets.

Ricoeur attempts also to reinterpret both the problematic notion of the "real past" in historical works and the equally problematic notion of "unreal entities" in fictional works (3.149). For the first, he resorts to a neologism ("*representance*" or "*lieutenance*") as a way of capturing the peculiar status of a state of affairs which seems to involve genuine construction yet in obedience to definite restraints. The result will be to render problematic the habitual use of the word "reality" with respect to the past. And for the second he appeals to a theory of effects in order to disassociate the varieties of fictive entities from purely negative characterization. The result will be to rearticulate the world of the text as no longer just a transcendence in an immanence but as world brought back through reading into the realm of lived experience, action and suffering (3.149).

The distinctive kinds of reference each of these narrative modes exhibits were originally seen to come together in the notion of a refiguration wherein time was not merely recounted or configured but in some strong sense changed by the practices of history and fiction. This change is effected by the fictionalization of the time of history (a cosmic time) through the practices of imaginative variations and through the historicization of the time of fiction (a lived time) through the procedures reinscribing lived time onto the cosmic times of calendars, chronologies, generations, and so on. The key idea here was the notion of complementarity. But Ricoeur finally abandoned the notion of reference in this context of a complementarity between historical and fictional narrative. The main impetus in the change was the series of reflections on the notion of the "real" just noted. And the result was a final step in the move from an initial dichotomy between historical fictional narrative, to their convergence with the help of the notions of intersecting reference, to the conjoining of their respective effects on the level of human action and suffering in the intersection not of their referential operations but in their respective refigurings (3.150).

Ricoeur claims further that the work of fiction is in some sense both more difficult and yet easier to account for than the work of history. Thus, a specific kind of fictional work—namely, lyric poetry—presents the world as apprehended from the angle of cosmic pathos, whereas narrative works, whether fictional or historical, present the world as apprehended from the angle of human praxis (1.22). In the case of narrative works, Ricoeur holds, "the problem of reference is simpler than in that of lyric poetry" because what is narrated has already been presignified on the level of human action with its symbolic mediations and prenarrative resources. No such resignification or precomprehension exists in the case of lyric functions. Yet with respect to the truth claims of narrative works and their referential claimants the case of narrative works is more complicated than that of lyric fictions because of the referential asymmetries between narrative historical works on the one hand and narrative fictions on the other. These asymmetries cluster around the status of the past in both kinds of narratives, the one "real" the other "unreal," with the result that in the case of history we have reference with respect to traces in the real past, whereas in that of fictional narrative we have reference with respect to signs of an imaginary past.

The world of the fictional work, moreover, has a double character. The world projected by fiction is closed in the sense that the text determines its formal configurations. But this world remains open in the sense that the nondescriptive referential dimensions of the work open out onto a world. "This opening," Ricoeur writes, "consists in the pro-positions of a world susceptible of being dwelt in" (2.150). The world of the work, then, to the degree that it involves both closure and openness, "constitutes what I would call an immanent transcendence with respect to the text" (2.151). But this transcendence of the world of the work must always be understood in dynamic terms as a "relating itself to, a directing itself toward, in short as being subject to" (2.151).[18]

[18]I thank Catherine Elgin for her kindness in letting me see several unpublished pieces by Goodman and her.

Conclusion: Fictions, Relativisms, and Rationality

Here is another unfamiliar text, not a meditative Korean lyric but a short romantic twentieth-century Japanese poem by Shinazaki Toson.

First Love

When I saw you under the apple tree
Your front hair swept back for the first time,
I thought, seeing the flower-comb in front,
That you were a flower too.

Stretching out your gentle, white hand,
You gave me an apple.
I felt a first stirring of love
In the pale crimson of that autumn fruit.

I breathed my love like a sign
Upon your combed-back fringe.
I gave you my heart
Like a cup brimming with the wine of love.

The path lies empty before me now
Under the tree in the apple orchard,
When I ask: "Who walked beside me along
   this narrow path?"
What I am missing is that first love.

When we read this poem, even in its English translation, at least two important aspects stand out. On the one hand, we readily grasp the situation of the poem evident even without the title. A young man recalls the moment when he first fell in love and realizes that he continues to treasure that moment of first love even more than he treasures his friend. On the other hand, certain details of the situation seem obscure. The young woman wears a comb in the front of her hair rather than at the back, and her hair is described implausibly as "swept back for the first time." Not all its details are recognizable; the poem seems at once both familiar and strange.

If we turn to a recent critical discussion of this poem, some of the reasons for its curious effect on Western readers become clear. After noting the suggestion of Adam and Eve in the garden, Donald Keen observes that the lines "Stretching out your gentle, white hand, / You gave me an apple" are particularly effective because they picture, in a manner unknown to earlier Japanese poets, the offering that symbolizes the confession of first love. The girl's beauty is indicated, in Japanese fashion, by mentioning how her hair was arranged for the first time in the style of a girl of sixteen; in the Meiji era the style of a woman's hair, which signified her age and marital status, was a crucial element in any description. The young man responds to her beauty by becoming (in the third stanza) drunk with the wine of love, a Western image.[1]

Just as in the text at the beginning of this book, Han Yong-un's twentieth-century Korean poem "Mountain Hut," so too in the twentieth-century Japanese poem "First Love" by Shinazaki Toson (1872–1943),[2] Western readers recognize certain conventions, whether those of French symbolism or English romanticism, while overlooking the traces of other artistic traditions, whether those of the Buddhist sutras or of Japanese variations on classical Chinese images and forms.

I draw attention to this mixture of familiarity and strangeness in our interactions with literary works of art because it can be taken as emblematic of a more general but more elusive interaction: between poetic representations and philosophical accounts of particular situations and states of affairs in a time of thoroughgoing cultural change.

In the Introduction of this book I made brief reference to increasingly widespread claims that many societies, in North America, Europe, and the Far East, are undergoing fundamental transformation. Thoroughly pervasive change on such a scale, the suggestion was, might be taken as a "cultural revolution" in the sense of a culture substituting one basic paradigm of understanding the totality of its experience for another. In the West such revolutions have already occurred, notably in the early modern period when European cultures substituted the paradigm of the mathematization of nature for the medieval world view of Christian faith. Analyses that have been made in numerous scholarly areas indeed suggest that we are now undergoing a revolution of this kind. The paradigm

[1]Keene 1984:210–11.
[2]In Bownas and Thwaite 1972:1.

in question might be called "the scientific world view," but what the new paradigm will be, as we approach the end of the golden if also uncritical age of science—the twentieth century with its many stunning discoveries and even more numbing and indeed countless horrors—this no one quite knows.

An essential element in this idea of a cultural revolution is the notion that change at such a level cannot leave anything untouched. This explains the main difficulty with describing a cultural revolution while it is in progress. For the very ways in which we observe, perceive, understand, and explain our world are themselves affected profoundly by such a revolution. This is to say a cultural revolution would change also our habitual understanding of what counts as philosophy. If we are indeed undergoing a cultural transformation, then the way we understand philosophy—its nature, its problems, its methods, its importance—must also be in transition.

In this final chapter I reconsider some of the conclusions of our investigation of fictions, philosophies, and the problems of poetics against this background—in the light, especially, of the potential reconception of rationality. In order to sharpen our awareness of the central issues, I once again, as in the Introduction, make use of relatively unfamiliar literary materials. But these materials, like those cited throughout this essay, will be taken from twentieth-century and more specifically modernist work. First, I develop the connection of the idea of a cultural revolution to a currently pervasive reading of rationality. I turn then to a recapitulation, but in a different order and grouping, of the results of the extended analyses of the nature, kinds, and roles of fictions in the seven chapters that make up the body of this book. My intent here is to show with the help of the poetry just how these fictions force us to revise many of our as yet insufficiently critical accounts of reasons and rationality. Finally, I argue for a rehabilitated understanding of fictions which in fact leads us to a novel notion of rationality.

CHANGING CULTURAL PARADIGMS AND RATIONALITY

One problem with our shifting perceptions and understanding of works of art, poetics, and philosophy is getting a sharper focus on what the hypothesis of a cultural revolution actually comprises. For talk of "paradigms," however common in the history of science, remains notoriously ambiguous. But unless we can refine our understanding of exactly what is at stake in trying to rethink at least some of the interactions between poetic and philosophical accounts on the hypothesis that our reflection takes place in an age of cultural revolution, we shall not be able to pull together coherently enough some implicit consequences of our investigations into the nature, kinds, and roles of fictions. My suggestion is that we construe the notion of a cultural revolution as the sustained challenge and the eventual displacement of the dominant and pervasive understanding of rationality in our era. Thus, in place of the necessarily vague and systematically ambiguous talk of the substitution of one paradigm of intelligibility for another, I substitute a more tractable series of reflections on changing understandings of rationality. I take as my guide some recent work that I shall set out in summary form before moving on to a critical reflection that explores a reformulated notion of rationality, a notion of rationality that also draws together the major results of our earlier investigations—not in a merely summary form but in a way that suggests the underlying and potential importance of the issues that have been examined here.

The notion of "rationality," like that of "paradigm," is also systematically ambiguous. We do better to talk of rationality more precisely and in the plural as "concepts of rationality," without overlooking the common thread that runs through these different concepts: that is, the idea of "having or thinking one has reasons for believing."[3]

In the account I cite, this idea of a shared element in different contemporary concepts of rationality arises out of a specific social and intellectual "framework of conviction"; this framework was new in the sense that rationality up to this peculiar moment had been confined to the specific context of doing science, whereas after this moment rationality became a pertinent consideration not only in scientific contexts but in all areas of human life. Each person and not just each scientist was to be responsible for his or her beliefs.

This of course is exactly the framework within which we live and work today. It is the peculiarly modern framework for which the phrase the "Lockean idea of responsible belief" has been proposed. For it is Locke's notion of "the responsible believer" which effectively moves the seventeenth-century concept of rationality into the vaster and plural domains of Enlightenment thought, where the peculiar model for modernity was forged.[4] Moreover, unlike Max Weber's concept of purposive rationality, which is a "deliberative, reflective, calculated rationality, of actions,"[5] Lockean rationality, as we find it in, say, the *Essay*,[6] is a rationality of beliefs. In particular, the claim is made that we find in the *Essay* "the concept of rational belief put to use in a moral framework of conviction which since then has become characteristic of modernity"(41). What needs emphasis is that the concept of rationality according to which beliefs are

---

[3]Wolterstorff 1987:2; cited hereafter in text as "W 1987."
[4]Ibid.
[5]Ibid., 4. Subsequent references are included in the text.
[6]Locke 1975:IV.xviii, 24. For one line of development see Proust 1986.

held for reasons is not itself Locke's contribution; his originality lies, rather, in "the particular framework of conviction within which he used" this concept, namely, the Lockean idea of responsible belief (42).

Nicholas Wolterstorff has articulated the central elements of this framework in eight theses that are decreasingly fundamental. Although these theses derive from a close and extended analysis of Locke's difficult text, they may be summarized, not unfairly I hope, in the following terms. (1) Our beliefs are subject to the governance of our assent. (2) The governance of assent is itself subject to obligations, rules, and norms for directing the mind. (3) Such norms hold without exception for all beliefs susceptible to appropriate governance. (4) All persons ought to strive to achieve the goal of eliminating false beliefs while retaining and acquiring true beliefs. (5) Moreover, none of the various additional properties of our beliefs is to override the eminent importance of their truth or falsity. (6) Further, the central role in "any formulation of the rule to be followed in the governance of belief" must be awarded to having good reasons and to no other consideration. (7) In particular, "one has a good reason for believing P just in case one believes that one's reasons are certain for one, believes that P is either entailed by, or probable with respect to, these reasons, and believes that in the evidence of the *totality* of what one believes to be certain for one, it's not true that not-P is more probable than P" (43). (8) Finally, the attention, consideration, and reflection one pays to a good reason is always a matter of degree. Thus, the specific mandate here is: "Believe only what your Reason, when it is so reflective that you no longer believe it to be less than fully reflective, tells you that you have good reason for believing; and then believe it *for* that reason with a firmness proportioned to what you believe to be the strength of the reason."

In short, the Lockean idea of responsible belief on this account is taken to comprise eight theses about, respectively, governance, obligation, universality, a goal, ultimacy, rationality, good reasons, and a mandate. "There is an ethic of belief, said Locke; it holds for all beliefs; and in that ethic, reasons play a central role . . . we believe only what our Reason, no longer presenting itself to us as less than fully reflective, tells us we have good reasons for believing" (44). Only then can a person claim, in this framework of modernity, to be intellectually justified in his or her belief.

Now, this extraordinary story about modernity is perhaps controversial and may appear especially so in the highly schematic summary I have provided of what is in fact a richly detailed discussion running from Locke back at least to Descartes and forward to Thomas Reid.[7] My purpose here, however, is not to argue this story either in general or in detail but quite simply to make use of it as a way of filling out, for now, the overly vague

[7]See Wolterstorff 1983.

and unqualified talk of cultural revolution and shifting paradigms of intelligibility. My point, then, is not that this story is itself true or false but that it involves a plausible, detailed, and thoroughly argued account of what stands behind the suggestion that the paradigm now in question, on the hypothesis of a current transformation of culture, is "the scientific world view."

The paradigm at issue today, on this hypothesis, is the scientific world view understood as the Lockean framework of conviction controlling the concept of rationality. It is the framework, I hold, which may be yielding to a progressive and renewed revalorization of the notion of the fictional. It would certainly be much to say that in this context the old paradigm, that of modernity, is yielding to a new paradigm, that of fictionality. Such talk is premature. For, on our view, we cannot know the name of a new paradigm except in retrospect, and we are only under way. Still, as I am about to discuss, the various and remarkably rich consequences of renewed reflective attention to the nature, kinds, and roles of fiction both raises serious criticisms about the tenability of the Lockean framework and opens up fresh perspectives on alternative frameworks. With a concrete sketch of modern rationality in hand, we can now consider the various interactions between this conception and the fictions we have been exploring.

RATIONALITY AND FICTIONS

Here, then, is another twentieth-century Japanese poem, this time one that comes not from the earlier part of the century (the Meiji and Taisho periods), but from after World War II in the Showa period.

Remaining Fruit

Its friends have all left the treetop;
They've been carried to the market and sold.

The one remaining survivor
Is what they call the tree-guardian.

Against the deep blue of the sky
Its crimson form is radiant.

On the withered persimmon tree with arms akimbo,
It paints the pupil in a scrawny dragon's eye.

The tree guardian
Is guarding the tree.

Crows and woodpeckers,
Respecting it, leave this fruit uneaten.

Is it waiting for the sleet, for the snow to fall,
For the day, when at last it will die?

Or is it perhaps
Flaunting its present beauty in the cold wind?

Before focusing attention on the several elements of this poem which
are most suggestive in view of recapitulating two of the central themes
we have explored earlier, an historical note will prove useful. "Remaining
Fruit" (1955) is taken from a very late collection, *Momotabi* (After a
Hundred Times, 1962), of the controversial poet Miyoshi Tatsuji (1900–
64).[8] Miyoshi's admiration for the major modern Japanese poet, Hagiwara
Sakutaro (1886–1942), his early service in Korea and later meditations in
his poetry on the Korean Silla monuments and Pulguksa monastery
(known to Han Yong-un), his studies in French literature, his founding
of the Shiki (Four Seasons) group in 1934, his mastery of traditional Japanese poetic traditions, his unbridled nationalistic commitment to the war,
his desolate postwar poetry, his later studies of classical Chinese poetry,
and the final resolution of his poetic art in the dozen years preceding his
death—all make his late work difficult to interpret. My remarks, consequently, are offered as mere observations on one or two points against
the background, as throughout this Conclusion, of Donald Keene's thoroughly informed readings of the movements of modern Japanese poetry
as a whole.

With the substantial qualification in mind, consider briefly two actions
the poem represents—"It paints the pupil in a scrawny dragon's eye"
and "The tree-guardian / Is guarding the tree"—as well as the voice of
the lyrical speaker of the poem: matter of fact, descriptive, allusive, and
questioning. Each of these elements lends itself to pulling together, in a
different order, the main lines of our earlier reflections on actions and
selves.

Consider first this question of the lyrical persona here and its voice.
With the benefit of historical and biographical information (and without
committing biographical and other fallacies), many readers are quickly
aware of the important metaphorical character of this poem. For many
readers sense the possibility of an implicit comparison between the single
fruit left hanging on the withered persimmon tree and the last book of
poems issuing from the work of an aging poet. This hunch may of course
turn out to be unfounded—an informed reader will eventually discover
that Miyoshi did write other poems after "Remaining Fruit." But one
immediate impression surely is that the poem presents the persimmon
tree and its one last fruit in such a way as to suggest something further

[8]In Keene 1984:320.

about the speaker and perhaps the poet and his art. How, then, are we to account for this impression?

In the Introduction we detailed various stages in what I called, very generally, "a linguistic account" of poetic texts. In particular, we saw that one characteristic move in attempting to account for the lyrical voice is to call attention to the way in which linguistic signs function in more than one system simultaneously. More specifically, lyrical voice, the claim went, can be explained by the intersections of a primary and a secondary set of linguistic codes. The result is that the central terms of a system of signs can function univocally as a primary system and they can also function polyvalently as a secondary system. Here the fruit and the tree have more than one semantic tendency, for their respective terms function in such a way as to denote certain particulars while designating much vaguer and more general matters as well. The specific effect is the articulation of a voice that is taken to be that of a fictional self, the speaker in the poem. But the general problem we saw with this account was its failure to address the closely related issues of the relation between the fictional selves of the poem and the actual selves of the poem's readers, which of course include the author-poet.

Exploring this relation with the help of a working hypothesis in the Introduction led us out of poetics in search of relevant conceptual resources in contemporary philosophical accounts of the person to refine the overly vague talk of "fictional selves." In Chapter 6, "Fictional Selves and Virtual Persons," we investigated two related but radically opposed accounts of the person and personal identity: a reductionist account of the person in terms of psychological connectedness and continuity, and a nonreductionist account in terms of leading the life of a person. We were able to demonstrate that, however radically opposed, the accounts were not logically contradictory. But the major consequence was our freedom to select at least one series of reflections from each—the notion of indeterminate selves and the notion of virtual persons. We went on to construct a version of "fictional selves" which seemed large enough to encompass both our concern with certain types of fictive selves and their lyrical voices in poetic works as well as with our own future selves. But this account, however persuasive in its own terms, exhibited a series of further difficulties which became apparent once it was brought into conjunction with the extraordinary richness of the later Rilke's poetry of self-transformation. So, while certainly an improvement on the insufficiently detailed understanding of the self operative in sophisticated contemporary literary theory, the account of fictional selves we arrived at left us puzzled with still further inadequacies.

Now, before suggesting an explanation for these difficulties, we need to return to the Miyoshi poem with an eye on the second of the two themes here, the notion of action and poetic fictions. The critic's gloss on this part of the poem is helpful here. "Mention of the 'pupil in a scrawny dragon's eye,' refers to old Chinese stories of painters who refrain from giving a final stroke of the brush to the eyes of the dragons they painted lest they leap from the wall; here the painting of the final dot suggests a career at its completion, as well as the single brilliant touch of the persimmon against the gaunt, bare branches."[9] The critic picks up on our initial impression of a metaphorical suggestiveness and, with the use of relevant information, begins to spell out some of this suggestiveness. This reading of the poem, however, remains at a level of immediate response—admittedly the response of a knowledgeable reader, but still an intuitive one.

When we move to a more reflective consideration of the poem at the level of, say, poetic theories, we come to a linguistic account of the representation of action in a poetic text. In the Introduction we saw how poetic structures could be described in such a way as to exhibit not just static but also dynamic tensions. The internal dynamisms of the text consist in a series of tensions between elements organized in separate hierarchies as well as between elements organized in the same hierarchy. The "meaning" of the work is said to be the resultant use of the overarching dynamic tension between the general organizing principles of the work's several structured hierarchies and these hierarchies' respective tensions. Thus, in "Remaining Fruit" what is actually a static state of affairs, a poetic text, succeeds in representing actions of different sorts when the text is taken up in a particular reading and its various static representations are made to yield a series of dynamic tensions. The lone red persimmon represented in the bare tree branches becomes, in the reader's performance of the text, the red point of a brush stroke moving to paint the dragon's eye, which in turn moves in the wind to become the wary and restless guardian of the tree. But once again a general problem with this account became evident—its failure to address the closely connected but more complex issues of the relationship between poetic representations of action and how it is that such fictional matters can ever count, as they often seem to, as reasonable grounds for action in the world.

With the help of the working hypothesis presented in the Introduction, we moved to explore this difficulty in Chapter 5, "Action and Poetic Fictions," where we investigated two very different contemporary philosophical accounts of action in the hope of finding further conceptual resources for sharpening our initial understanding of what seemed to be at issue in the relation between actual and fictional actions. Instead of remaining with one philosophical tradition, as we had done in the case of reflection on persons and selves, we widened our search to include

[9]Ibid.

elements from two different traditions of reflection on action: an Anglo-American naturalistic approach and a continental hermeneutic approach. Since both had dealt critically with some of the same central texts, the move here to expand our search seemed both promising and yet prudent. In both naturalistic and hermeneutic accounts of intentional action, however, a close comparison with Eliot's poetry and drama showed up a series of crucial descriptive gaps. In order to span these gaps we went so far in Appendix 5C as to look at what could arguably be taken as the ontology both accounts share. But this brought us to a series of positive and negative aspects of intentional action to which neither view does or can do justice. The result was the suggestion that a fresh philosophical idiom was required both to parse the unresolved difficulties in the analytic and hermeneutic accounts as well as to reconstruct more perspicuously contemporary theoretic attempts in poetics to deal with the relation between fictional representations of actions and their effects—the justification of certain rational actions in the lives of readers.

In the cases of both fictional representations of selves and fictional representations of actions, the varied and sustained moves to retrieve for poetics a series of centrally important conceptual resources from more than one contemporary philosophical tradition have, surprisingly, cut two ways. On the one hand, these resources do indeed provide readers with a much more nuanced grasp of many of the central terms on which much contemporary literary theory continues to rely uncritically. But on the other, the richness of poetic works themselves, at least those from the later work of such representative modernist poets as Rilke and Eliot, continue to elude a comprehensive enough grasp in even these carefully selected philosophical terms. The works seem to call, rather, for readings in neither a purely poetic nor a strictly philosophical idiom but in an idiom that is informed by each and yet subject finally to neither.

The theories and philosophies we have been exploring, however different in their original details and endless ramifications, all show at least one thoroughly pervasive and completely controlling supposition. Each of these accounts incorporates a shared understanding of rationality, what we talked of earlier as the Lockean idea of responsible belief, the Lockean framework of conviction. For each is committed, in different ways certainly but nonetheless centrally, to the cardinal tenet of modernity, the justification of beliefs by the progressive provision of good reasons. We need not claim that each of these theories and philosophies endorses all eight of the claims we spelled out in order to detail the general rationality thesis. It is sufficient to note one key point only—each of the theories we have examined, whatever its interest and whatever its provenience, is if not a theory in the strong sense certainly an explanatory account, designed to articulate the reasons for static states of affairs and dynamic courses of events. But even this minimal notion of theory is a child of modernity in that, since the eighteenth century, propounding an explanation has come to mean, canonically, the provision of reasons as warrants for beliefs.

Before arguing this point in greater detail at the end of the next section, I will extend this summary overview of our explorations in the body of this book. If we began our recapitulation with a summary of salient functions in our understanding of the general themes of fictional selves and fictional actions, we do well, before generalizing further to the theme of fictional worlds, to step back and particularize the results of our other investigations—into the narrower topics of fictional discourses, truths, beliefs, and feelings.

Turn, then to a second postwar Japanese poem and a second set of themes.

The Man with a Green Face

It was a beautiful morning
shoulder to shoulder
we watched the squadron sail out of sight
a huge silence commands
the sea of freedom and necessity
and only illusions are real
we never stopped to question that

of course the squadron never returned
of course reality was an illusion
in all ports, in all fatherlands
shoulder to shoulder
we gazed at the horizon
but freedom and necessity
occurred only within history—
only the man with a green face
tries to leave history
we let go of each other's shoulders
and smashed the morning's beauty
with our dangling arms
we need something to kill our hunger
we need more imagination so we won't dream
we have to leave *we* behind
it won't help to look for the man with a green face
in a crowd or a group
and if you say that only evil exists
then history will whisper back:
all great things are evil

"The Man with a Green Face," taken from Tamura Ryuichi's 1973 collection *Shinnen no tegami* (New Year's Letters),[10] echoes both the title of his 1967 collection *Midori no shiso* (Green Thoughts) and its epigraph from

[10]In Hibbett 1977:335–36.

Andrew Marvell's "The Garden": "Annihilating all that's made / To a green thought in a green shade." Like his much older contemporary Miyoshi, Tamura also exhibits in his poetry a definite shift from the bleakness and despair of his work just after the war to a more varied and complex later lyricism. One of the founders of the Arechi (Wasteland) group in 1947, a contributor to the journal and the yearbook of the same name from 1947 to 1958, and an admirer of both T. S. Eliot and Auden, Tamura (b. 1923) reacted against both the renewed formalism of the pre-war modernist poets and the work of the so-called socialist-realist poets while trying to capture a sense of his times in strikingly polished, un-sentimental, and strongly emotional yet controlled work.

On rereading this poem carefully, at least four related aspects stand out—the presentation of what look like very general assertions, the representations of some beliefs that turn out within the poem to be mistaken, the presentation in the poem of strong feelings and the effect of these presentations on the feelings of a reader, and finally a peculiar mixture of what appears to be both fictional and nonfictional discourse. Each of these four themes can be seen as elements within the larger whole of the lyrical voice of a fictional subject who is represented as exhorting at least an implied reader to action, that is, within the two larger themes of fictional selves and fictional actions we have already looked at. I now summarize our earlier reflection of each of these four more particular themes.

What are some immediate impressions of "The Man with a Green Face" which seem to touch on the first of these themes, namely, the notion of literary or fictional truths? Note initially that a number of general statements are presented, and they are formulated in the present as almost tenseless: "only illusions are real," "we need more imagination," "all great things are evil." Further, other general statements are presented by contrast in the past tense: "reality was an illusion," "freedom and ne-cessity occurred only within history." And at least some general state-ments are embedded in conditional clauses as objects of indirect discourse: "only evil exists," "all great things are evil." Can any such general state-ments be taken as true or false? When we turn to poetics and the linguistic account we find an interesting response in terms of conventions such as pretending which are said to govern either explicitly or implicitly whatever apparent statement may follow. But that response, we recognize, is flawed by reason of its insufficiently nuanced account of sentences, propositions, and assertions. Once again, then, in the hope of identifying a more sharply articulated set of relevant distinctions, we made another move from po-etics to some work in contemporary philosophy.

We recall that in the Introduction we examined the general topic of literature and cognitivity under two related headings: "Art, Knowledge, and Truth" and "Art, Knowledge, Belief." In the first of these investigations we tried in Chapter 2, "Literary Truths," to construct both an analytic and a hermeneutic perspective on the question as to whether literary works can be genuine sources of knowledge. We quickly came to an important contrast between taking the legitimate objects of knowledge to be some concept of truth and taking that object, rather, as some kind of event. Without resolving the tension between such diverse approaches to the putative truths of literary works of art, we turned to a phenomenological account of literary truths as the contents of so-called "quasi-judgments." The move back to Ingarden's work from the more recent analytic and hermeneutic materials was motivated by a desire to retain some of the descriptive rigor in the analytic account while capturing some of the insistence on intuitive approaches in the hermeneutic view. And we reached the tentative conclusion that talk about truth in literary works would seem to call for excluding talk about genuine propositional knowledge while making more room for talk about truth in the sense of verisimilitude, objective consistency, the presentation of certain "metaphysical qualities," and the connection between "ideas" of a work and a positive value as manifested in a particular life situation. But these suggestions remained very open-ended, and whatever hopes we had entertained to remedy some of the inadequacies in the linguistic account seemed finally unfulfilled.

But questions of truth are only one set of concerns about literature and cognitivity and in fact correspond to only one set of initial reactions to Tamura's poem. For many readers immediately notice, however vaguely, not only the general statements in "The Man with a Green Face" and their different tenses and modal contexts; they respond well as to some of these statements being presented as unreliable—not as putative truths but as mere beliefs. "It was a beautiful morning"—and yet it was not: the second stanza falsifies the statement propounded in the first. Other statements turn out to be uncritical: "only illusions are real / we never stopped to question that." And still others assume the form of bare assertions with no reasons offered for their warrant: "we have to leave *we* behind." These statements, unlike the first set, are not presented as putative truths at all but as beliefs only—some false, some unquestioned, and others simply asserted. Are we then to construe some literature as cognitive not in the sense of being a source of truths but as at best a source of beliefs which may or may not be true?

When we look to the linguistic account for some discussion of just how a fictional work could be a source of knowledge we come up quickly with the standard response: that the sentences used to represent fictional states of affairs and courses of events are not to be understood as having propositional content in the same way as sentences used to represent nonfictional ones. Thus, a fictional work like Tamura's poem cannot be a source of knowledge in the sense of representing putative truths or putative beliefs. But we saw that the major difficulty with such an account was its restriction of knowledge to the domain of nonfictional assertions.

We turned to more recent work in contemporary philosophy in hopes of finding a more finely grained account of literature and cognitivity which would enable us to parse the central terms in a more perspicuous fashion than is possible on the linguistic account. A number of important reflections led us then to develop a functional view of the contents of a literary work which drew heavily on an appeal to the notion of abductive implication. It was this notion that led to a revised view of literature as a source of knowledge in the sense that certain beliefs and not truths can be abductively implied from literary works by communities of competent readers rather than by individuals only.

We did not then return to specific texts to test either of these views—the view of literature as a source of truth, in the sense of grasping relations between literary representations and metaphysical qualities, or of literature as a source of beliefs, in abductive implications arrived at by consensus among competent readers within professional communities—but we need only reread "The Man with a Green Face" with such views before us to diagnose an important difficulty that still remains between our patched up theories and our poems. For the abductive account of belief, although very much an improvement on the oversights in the linguistic account, is nonetheless largely restricted to exploring how what some fictional sentences denote and designate can be properly taken; it does not address squarely enough the central distinction between some beliefs properly represented about matters within a literary work and genuine beliefs derived from the literary work about matters outside that work. However, the doctrine of "metaphysical qualities," while again an important improvement over the linguistic account, remains extremely obscure as an account of putative truths a reader is rightly said to come to know as a result of the reading of a literary work. Puzzles of poetics, its seems, resolve themselves once again into puzzles of philosophy.

But Tamura's poem is not only striking because of its many suggestions about what there is and how things really are—its presentations of putative truths and beliefs. The poem also both represents a series of feelings and can, some critics observe, genuinely move its readers. These matters, though related, are separate. In several places the poem suggests some emotion. "We watched the squadron sail out of sight," the poem goes, and many readers are left with the painful ambiguity of the final image whereby the squadron is said to move "out of sight," whether to sail over the horizon or sink under the waters in horrendous battles is not specified. The repetitions—"of course the squadron never returned / of course reality was an illusion"—suggest not just a disillusionment but a touchy exasperation. And the force of the later expressions—"we . . . smashed the morning's beauty / . . . something to kill our hunger"—captures carefully the moving exaggeration of a pervasive mood in the poem. But if the poem represents certain feelings—for example, pathos, exasperation, violence—it also includes a number of additional cues that serve to arouse an emotional reaction in its readers. The suggestion of the depth of disillusion two people are undergoing, the sense of a pervasive cosmic indifference to their plight in the description of "the huge silence" and "the sea of freedom and necessity," the insistence through paradox ("only illusions are real") on a profound inscrutability in the movement of history however persistent one's inquiries, the fatality of a radical individualism ("we have to leave *we* behind"), and the impossible aspiration caught in the title's image ("only the man with a green face tries to leave history")— each of these elements, whether singly or together, is articulated in distinct ways so as not only to inform a competent reader but to move him or her as well.

On the linguistic account we recall that a poetic text is said to be organized as a hierarchy of formal structures unified as a whole and not merely as an aggregate. It is the particularity of the organizations, the ingenuity in the articulation of the details, and the infinitely receding levels of formal hierarchies which are said to account for how it is that a fiction can genuinely move a reader. Like the endless variety within the mental rehearsal of a mathematical proof in, say, non-Euclidean geometry, so too the forever shifting perspectives on the receding and advancing ranks of formal hierarchies in the reading of a poetic text are said to explain the power certain fictions possess to move their readers. And we recall as well the major difficulty with this account in failing to specify whether the referents of the contents of the readers' presumed emotional states are to be found in the fictional worlds themselves or in the minds of actual readers.

The now familiar move from the linguistic account to a more nuanced philosophical view enabled us to undermine in Chapter 4, "Fictions and Feelings," a Fregean account of sense and reference with the help both of an important alternative within analytic philosophy itself, a taxonomy of reference, and a hermeneutic view of reference as productive. In each case, we anticipated a theme that was to preoccupy us in the discussion of fictive and fictional worlds in Chapter 7. Our provisional philosophical conclusion was that fictional works are able to move competent readers generally by soliciting and then guiding the readers' construction of certain mental contents, which themselves become the actual and not merely fictional objects of the readers' emotional states.

Again, we did not test this view against a reading of poetic texts. But when we turn now to Tamura's poem, we are able to bring out more clearly what we found to be disquieting at the end of Chapter 4. For some competent readers on rereading "The Man with a Green Face," while willing to conclude that they find themselves emotionally moved by the poem and that they believe their feelings to be genuine and not self-deceptive ones, claim nonetheless that the objects of their emotional states are not just the actual mental objects they entertain but also the fictional referents of other associated mental objects too. They weep both for themselves and for Hecuba; they are moved both for themselves and for the two who "let go of each other's shoulders" in Tamura's "The Man with a Green Face." So a gap still remains between the amended critical and revised philosophical account on the one hand the the richness of the experience of the poetic text on the other.

We have been talking of certain reactions to a text by way of recapitulating three of the four particular themes of truth, knowledge, and emotion within the larger themes of self and action. The final theme here is fictional discourse, and to capture both the major lines of our treatment of this theme as well as their final limitations it will prove useful to approach Tamura's text in another format. With apologies to the poet, I rewrite his text in the same form in which I had earlier, in the chapter on fictional discourses, rewritten T. S. Eliot's lines from *Four Quartets*.

> It was a beautiful morning; shoulder to shoulder we watched the squadron sail out of sight. A huge silence commands the sea of freedom and necessity and only illusions are real. We never stopped to question that. Of course the squadron never returned. Of course reality was an illusion—in all ports, in all fatherlands. Shoulder to shoulder we gazed at the horizon. But freedom and necessity occurred only within history—only the man with a green face tries to leave history. We let go of each other's shoulders and smashed the morning's beauty with our dangling arms. We need something to kill our hunger, we need more imagination so we won't dream. We have to leave *we* behind. It won't help to look for the man with a green face in a crowd or a group; and if you say that only evil exists, then history will whisper back: all great things are evil.

Our immediate impression on reading a text in this form does not result in a definitive appreciation of the text as a poem. In fact, what is probably most striking are the ways in which the fictional status and the nonfictional status of the poem remain in question. Without the helpful use of title, stanzaic form, spacing, and nonstandard punctuation, the tensions in this text between description and assertion are all the more evident. One plausible reading of such a text surely is to construe it as a brief historical narrative, perhaps from a letter or a diary, but in any case taken from a more personal rather than a public context. On this reading, the text would probably be taken as nonfictional and the puzzling talk of "the man with the green face" as merely some private but still nonfictional way of talking about something actual. Another reading, of course, would be to construe the text as indeed a narrative but a fictional one, in fact an impressionistic story. On this reading the frequent generalities—for example, about freedom and necessity—would be seen as representations of putative truths or beliefs but certainly not their actual assertions. But the point here becomes clear—the more plausible view is arguably the first, the nonfictional, and not the second, the fictional, even though we happen to know that the case is the other way around.

We recall here the move to the linguistic account in hopes of finding an agreed upon procedure for distinguishing fictional from nonfictional discourse. The response there was the series of claims to the effect that the former but not the latter exhibits as its single primary function the focusing of the reader's attention through many varied devices on the peculiarities of its own construction as a coded sign system rather than on its encoder, decoder, context, or message. In short, texts that orient the reader's attention preeminently to their composition as texts are fictional; all others are nonfictional. But this won't do. For the major difficulty we saw here was the particular understanding of language on which this communication model of discourse entirely depends.

In an attempt to relativize this particular model we moved in Chapter 1, "Fictional Discourses," to a contemporary discussion of the resources and liabilities of speech-act theory. But despite our attempts to articulate a more critical version of the speech-act approach to distinguish between fictional and nonfictional discourse, our foray into several different philosophical fields left us with an insistence on the "seriousness" of a particular text as the central criterion we sought. And of course "seriousness" was to be construed, finally, in terms of a renewed examination of a fictional text's capacity to be a source of genuine knowledge. Nonetheless we came to an argued conviction, however provisional, that the relevant properties for justifying the specification of a text as serious and hence nonfictional or its opposite are nonobservable. Accordingly, linguistic appeals to overt features of the text in support of a characterization of the text are to be disallowed.

The difficulty here, however, once we look again at the two forms of our example, is in particularizing this claim. For it is not enough to appeal to nonobservable properties such as conventions, traditions, contexts, relevant background beliefs of a competent reader, the reception of work in successive communities of interpretation, and so on. We require a much more specific account of how we are to analyze some of the most interesting cases—those, namely, that are commonly associated with the term "philosophical." Those cases are difficult enough in the contemporary period, in which some work of Eliot or Stevens or Rilke reads, when recast in prose form, as philosophical observations (conversely, try putting some passages from Wittgenstein's *Philosophical Investigations* in stanza form to appreciate a similar effect). But the situation becomes much more complex when we consider ancient literature and philosophy—think of

Parmenides and Heraclitus, some of the myths in Plato, speeches in Thucydides, atomic analysis in Lucretius, moralizings in Cicero's orations, or meditative prayers in Augustine's *Confessions*. In short, even a relatively critical appropriation of a modified speech-act theory, though it fills some of the gaps in the linguistic account, does not allow of a nonobjectionable account of the distinction between fictional and nonfictional discourse.

I suggested earlier that one recurring problem with the satisfactoriness of both the linguistic account and the more critical philosophical argument is their mutual reliance on the Lockean framework of responsible belief, the commitment to an understanding of both explanatory and interpretive accounts as preeminently the providing of good reasons as warrants for our beliefs. Just as in the case of the still open-ended results of an investigation into representations of fictional selves and fictional actions, so now in the similar results of investigations into the more specific themes of fictional truths, beliefs, knowledge, and feelings we come up against a thoroughgoing and pervasive presupposition. The common assumption, once again, is that the rationality of an account consists preeminently in its provision of good reasons. More specifically, whether the instance at issue is the linguistic or the philosophical account, the maxim these accounts in the humanistic tradition now share with those in the scientific one is the comprehensive Lockean mandate of modernity: "Believe only what you Reason, when it is so reflective that you no longer believe it to be less than fully reflective, tells you that you have good reason for believing; and then believe it *for* that reason with a firmness proportional to what you believe to be the strength of the reason" (W 1987:44).

Yet the burden of these more finely grained reflections on the cognitivity of literature and the closely interlocking issues of belief, truth, knowledge, and discourse is the novel suggestion that the complexity of the fictional may be such that the very understanding of the key element in the Lockean framework—namely, "Reason" with its striking capitalization—is in the process of undergoing radical transformation. With the progressive revalorization of the fictional as something far richer than the putative opposite of the real, the factual, the empirical, the experimental, the true, the warranted, the justified, and so on, the interpretation of the Lockean framework of conviction must itself be undertaken freshly. Before, however, pursuing this one further step in the last section, I will complete our recapitulation of this essay's major themes by turning back to the complex reflections on the nature of "fictional worlds." For in the open-ended results of those considerations we find still further indications of how to pursue our reflection on the relation between fictionality and rationality.

We come, then, to our last theme and still another postwar Japanese poem, this time in two translations.

Still Life

Within the hard surface of night's bowl
Intensifying their bright colors
The autumn fruits
Apples, pears, grapes, and so forth
Each as they pile
Upon another
Goes closer to sleep
To one theme
To spacious music
Each core, reaching its own heart
Reposes
Around it circles
The time of rich putrefaction
Now before the teeth of the dead
The fruits and their kind
Which unlike stones do not strike
Add to their weight
And in the deep bowl
Behind this semblance of night
On occasion
Hugely tilt

Still Life

Autumn fruits
That grow in brightness
Within the solid frame of the vessel of night
Apples and pears and grapes
Each of them
Posed one upon the other
Sinks into slumber
Into a single melody
Moving along towards great music
When each has attained its utmost death
The kernel gently settles down
Surrounding them
Is a luxuriant age of decomposition
Now before the teeth of the deceased
They are quiet as stones
These fruits
Gather weight all the more
Within the deep vessel
In this night's semblance
Once in a while
They tilt sharply

This poem, taken from Yoshioka Minoru's 1955 collection *Seibutsu* (Still Life),[11] which includes four poems with the same title, exhibits some of the celebrated effects associated with both Yoshioka (b. 1919) and his intellectualist colleagues in the Wani (Crocodile) group, which published a journal of the same name between 1959 and 1962.

If one reads this poem carefully in both versions a few initial impressions stand out sharply. The poem seems to present the fruit in the bowl as a kind of self-enclosed cosmos bordered carefully in a deep frame with an overarching black mist of night. Moreover, the fruit are not static; they are represented, rather, as moving through a protracted series of changes which affect their surface colors, intensifying with the advance of a season, as well as their inner composition, where the core and kernel gradually slip downwards. The individual fruits even change location as they move through the progressive stages of ripeness into a thorough decomposition, until suddenly they "hugely tilt." Finally, a theme is said to measure this movement, "a single melody," "a spacious music." In short, the "still life" of the poem is a kind of world; the poem, we say on a first reading, presents a fictional world.

When we turn to the linguistic account in search of an explanation of how it it is that a text might properly be taken as presenting a world, as we did in the Introduction, we are told that the text offers us constructions of a world presented in modeling systems. Just as earlier, in the case of the intersection of two sign systems to explain the lyrical voice of fictional world, an appeal is made to the intersection of two modeling systems. The primary system is basically a particular natural language such as modern Japanese, whereas the secondary system is a much smaller set of signs making a particular poetic discourse, Yoshioka's poem "Still Life." In the interaction between the two systems, the signs of the primary system are affected by those of the secondary system in such a way that their connections with the empirical world are severed. The result is a new relation between those signs of the primary system and their antecedent referents, a modeling relation. A poem presents the construction of a world, then, in presenting not so much a configuration of the actual world as in constructing one out of its many possible models, no one of which is properly speaking a copy of the actual world. And we saw that at least one pervasive difficulty with this ingenious account was articulating the exact nature of this modeling relation in such a way that one could explain the frequent interaction not just between the modeling systems but between the fictional worlds of literary work and the actual world of its readers.

In Chapter 7, "Real Fictions," we went once again in search of conceptual resources in two contemporary philosophical reflections on world,

[11]In Hibbett 1977:339, and in Kirkup and Davis 1978:163.

one in the analytic work of Goodman and the other in the hermeneutic reflections of Ricoeur, in order to resolve the obscurities in the linguistic account. We made use of the putative fictional world presented by Wallace Stevens's poem "The Idea of Order at Key West" as a benchmark for taking the critical measure of both Goodman's talk of "fictive worlds" and Ricoeur's of "fictional worlds." Further, each account was contrasted with the other in the hope of generating a discussion of fictional and fictive worlds which would sidestep objections brought against either one of them while retaining their positive elements. Thus, Goodman's recent and revised views of nondenotational species of reference, together with Ricoeur's recent views on how formal constructions can project a horizon beyond the text, came together in such a way as to suggest, despite some critical difficulties, just how a fictional work can exercise certain revisionary effects on the categorical frameworks of its various readers. The major consequence of such occasional effects is a transformation in the reader's understanding of the actual world from a so-called "real world" into an understanding of the world as a "real fiction."

And yet, despite our efforts to fill out the suggestion in more detail, here too, just as in the cases of our previous moves into various philosophical domains, a new set of difficulties arose about the perplexing matter of nonextensional, nonrelational theories of reference, about the quasi-modal status of world as real fiction, and about the presumed plurality of such worlds. Thus, in the case of Yoshioka's "Still Life," the poem in projecting a world invites its readers not just to consider its projection as a model of something called *the* real world. Rather, some readers in coming to appreciate the projected world of the poem come also to consider important categorial changes in their antecedent understandings of the ontological status of "the real world"—as to whether it is one or many, actual or possible, requires a bipolar or many-valued model of truth, includes extensional or nonextensional referents, and so on. In this perspective, the configuration of "the hard surface of night's bowl," "the solid frame of the vessel of night," the so-called real world lends itself to a radical reconfiguration as *a* real fiction, or, in the images of the poem, "a single melody," "one theme," but "moving along towards great music," a "spacious music," "in this night's semblance."

The provisional character of the conclusions of our investigation of fictional worlds is very much of the same order as those open-ended conclusions to both the themes at the initial level of our inquiry (fictional discourse, truth, knowledge, and feeling) and those at the intermediate level (fictional selves and fictional actions). How is it that in no one of these cases do we seem able to provide an account of fictionality that would not only supplement the uncritical areas of the linguistic account but also resolve in a much less tentative way the problems that keep arising in the interactions between even carefully constructed philosophical accounts and the richness of literary representations of certain central matters in lyric poetry?

My suggestion throughout these recapitulations has been that the very nature of what is to count as a satisfactory story about the interactions between philosophical reflection and literary works of art is freshly in question. This is the case, on the working hypothesis of our essay, because thoughtful persons in many modern societies are pursuing their reflections on works of art as well as on everything else in the context of an ongoing radical cultural revolution. The gist of that story, we have seen, is that one basic paradigm for understanding everything that exists, the scientific world view, is gradually giving way to another paradigm whose nature, elements, and contours remain as yet indistinct. The first paradigm we have parsed as the distinctively modern interpretation of rationality. The second we have as yet left unaddressed.

In order to get on with the task of diagnosing the consequences of such a hypothesis for the interactions of poetics and philosophy, not to mention the more central exchanges between literary works of art and living our lives, we need to push description of the understanding of reasons within the framework of modernity just a bit further.

When we reread our provisional conclusions in conjunction with at least some of the rich representations in poetic texts of the modern era, whether in the West or the East, we find incongruities, whether those between art and life, or between work of contemplation and fruits of actions, or between formal hierarchies of great perfection and historical contexts and conventions of relative obscurity. But one of the important observations we come to in trying to measure the gap between our explanatory accounts of these works of art is the sense of some radical inappropriateness in the very use of a particular idiom for if not measuring that gap, certainly trying to narrow it. Clearly, a particular interpretation of what an explanatory account has to be in the modern era is itself newly in question. For the understanding of the central term that interpretation incorporates—"reason"—no longer seems adequate. The suspicion arises that whatever fate may overtake other attempts to narrow the gap between our thinking and our responding to works of art, at least those attempts that continue to rely on an uncritical interpretation of reason in terms of the mandate of modernity will continue to go awry. More specifically, the mandate that derives from the Lockean framework of conviction, the suspicion goes, is itself overcommitted to the idiom of the "good reasons thesis."

That thesis, we remember says that "one has a good reason for believing P just in case one believes that one's reasons are certain for one, believes that P is either entailed by, or probable with respect to, these reasons, and believes that in the evidence of the *totality* of what one believes to be certain for one it's not true that not-P is more probable than P" (W

1987a:43). But the burden of the investigations here into fictionality, particularly into how we are to interpret the cognitivity of literature in its detailed interconnections with discourse, affectivity, the self, action, and world, is that any such good reasons talk in terms of entailments, certainties, truths, probabilities, evidences, and totalities, and require persistent criticism. That criticism forces revisions not only in our understanding of some of those cardinal topics but especially in our sense of just why such matters, however irreplaceable in scientific explanations, can no longer be construed as equally important in humanistic interpretive ones. On these readings of fictionality, the Lockean framework, which has succeeded in extending the mandate of modernity and the idiom of good reasons beyond the progressive mathematicization of nature in the seventeenth-century rise of the sciences beyond that realm into all realms of reflection whether scientific or not, must now contract. And in its place we find the need for a fresh idiom that incorporates the revalorization of the fictional in such a way that talk of fictionality can move beyond the particular and now newly circumscribed talk of the good-reasons thesis.

But recall that, on the understanding of just what a cultural revolution is, if indeed most of us live and think in societies that are undergoing such a revolution, then the very nature of a revolution that can leave nothing untouched means that we must remain unable to diagnose the nature of such a revolution until after the fact. Hence our considerations here remain necessarily tentative, programmatic only, and lacking in the sustained elaboration of detail which alone can render talk of the necessity for a new idiom finally persuasive. Instead of pursuing this general theme of fictionality and rationality any further in this direct way, I turn instead in the final section to a complementary way of elucidating this suggestion. For the question now arises that, even if it makes sense to talk of a need for a new idiom of rationality, one that would reserve a special place for a ramified understanding of fictionality as opposed to construing good reasons too narrowly in terms of only one kind of thinking, then how is such an idiom to be protected from the arbitrariness that follows on the relativistic consequences of such a proposal? Can a reinterpretation of rationality which awards a central role to fictionality be anything more than a transformation of rationality into relativism?

Reasons and Fictions

It will prove useful in this final section to begin once again with yet another unfamiliar poem, this one, however, from the prewar period that saw the appearance both of the poem with which we began this chapter and the Korean poem of Han Yong-un with which we began the book. This poem is from the work of "the chief figure of modern Japanese poetry,"[12] Hagiwara Sakutaro (1886–1942), to whom I alluded earlier in discussing his great admirer Miyoshi Tatsuji. Here again are two versions of the same poem.

Sickly Face at the Bottom of the Ground

At the bottom of the ground a face emerging,
a lonely invalid's face emerging.

In the dark at the bottom of the ground,
soft vernal grass stalks beginning to flare,
rats' nest beginning to flare,
and entangled with the nest,
innumerable hairs beginning to tremble,
time the winter solstice,
from the lonely sickly ground,
roots of thin blue bamboo beginning to grow,
beginning to grow
and that, looking truly pathetic,
looking blurred,
looking truly, truly, pathetic.
In the dark at the bottom of the ground,
a lonely invalid's face emerging.

Face at the Bottom of the World

Face at the bottom of the world:
A sick, a lonely face,
One invalided out
Of every inner place;
Yet, slowly there uncurled,
Green in the gloom the grasses sprout.

And, as a rat's nest stirs,
Its million tangled hairs
One queasy quivering,
Thinnest of winterers,
The bamboo shoot prepares
Its green grope to the spring.

Sad in the ailing earth,
Tongue-tender with despair,
Green moves through grief's grimace;
And, sick and lonely, there
In the gloom of the under world,
At the bottom of the world, a face.

[12]Keene 1984:260.

Even after many readings this poem,[13] like so many of the central pieces
in Hagiwara's work, remains obscure. Hagiwara's early fascination for
Western culture, particularly French symbolist poetry, modern music, and
traditional Christianity; his highly unusual preoccupation with late romantic themes of nostalgia, morbidity, and the images of Baudelaire's
work; his studies of the sound symbolism in Edgar Allen Poe's poetics;
his early forging of an entirely novel colloquial free verse and his later
return to the classical rhythms of Japanese poetry; his work with the
Kanzo (Feelings) group from 1916 to 1919, which saw in 1917 the appearance of his first major collection, which had the startling title *Tsuki
ni Hoeru* (Howling at the Moon); his later work on Dostoevsky, Schopen-
hauer, and Nietzsche—all of these complex elements render Hagiwara's
poetry not easily accessible. But once again, like Han Yong-un's poetry,
Hagiwara's pervasive debt to a peculiar form of late nineteenth-century
Western sensibility and his participation in a form of twentieth-century
modernism allows non-Japanese readers some purchase on his work.

Hagiwara's poem "Face at the Bottom of the World" presents a number
of perplexing aspects even to Japanese poets and critics such as his fol-
lower Miyoshi. Had we the competence necessary for interpreting such
pieces, we would surely need to explore the very subtle sound contrasts,
rhythms, and cadences of the Japanese text, together with the complex
affinities on exhibit between particular poetic movements in the Japanese
adaptations of European poetry and criticism. Since this competence is
lacking, I call attention to only one aspect of this poem, with a view
towards trying to crystallize our major transitional concern at the end of
this book.

The poem, in the two versions cited, begins and ends with the same
complex image already emphasized in the title:

> At the bottom of the ground a face emerging,
> A lonely invalid's face emerging.
>
> . . . . .
>
> In the dark at the bottom of the the ground
> A lonely invalid's face emerging.
>
> Face at the bottom of the world:
> A sick, a lonely face,
>
> . . . . .
>
> In the gloom of the under world,
> At the bottom of the world, a face.

[13]In Sato and Watson 1981:476 and in Hagiwara 1969:67.

There is surely something inadequate about isolating such lines from their close and various ties with the rest of the poem. And any satisfactory account of the poem would have to include an interpretation of the poem's title, not just with a sensitivity to sound patterns but with an extremely patient and thorough articulation of its connections with the rhythms, images, allusions, and conventions in the poem as a whole. Nonetheless, such an ideal interpretation would still have to make some central room for the particular lines I have isolated here because of their cardinal importance, already evident in their positioning, their repetitiveness, and their respective variations on the image selected for entitling the piece.

The central image of the face, with its many echoes particularly in the medieval texts of several central schools of Japanese Buddhism and in different traditions of Japanese Buddhist portrait sculpture, already appears in a revealing passage in the preface to *Howling at the Moon*. The passage, as Donald Keene points out, is an articulation of a lesson Hagiwara claimed to have found in Dostoevski and which moved his subsequent work away from the influence of Mallarmé and the symbolists. The passage reads:

> People, individually, are always, eternally, perpetually in terrible solitude. . . . Our faces, our skins are all different, one from the other, but as a matter of fact each human being shares traits with all the others. When this commonality is discovered among fellow human beings, "morality" and "love" among human kind are born. When this commodity is discovered among human beings and plants, "morality" and "love" in nature are born. And then we are never lonely again.[14]

This Dostoevskian theme of the possibility of a personal salvation through love permeates the crucial opening and concluding lines of Hagiwara's poem "Face at the Bottom of the World." And in the context of our investigations here of the many suggestions this lyric vision raises, at least one needs closer scrutiny.

If it is arguably the case, as I have tried to show throughout this book, that a composite linguistic account, even with the conceptual resources that arise from a series of nuanced philosophical reconstructions of its central conceptual concerns, cannot adequately capture the crucial links between the works of literary art we prize and the lives we continue to live, then must a poetics understood as a thoroughgoing theory of literary description, interpretation, evaluation, and appreciation always fall short of being entirely rational? In short, how can a poetics maintain its claims on our allegiance when its central concepts seem to allow of no final accounting even in philosophical terms?

More generally, the recurring difficulty that emerges from our inves-

[14]Cited in Keene 1984:269–70.

tigations is just how the richly variegated, revitalized notions of the fictional can still be construed inside the Lockean framework of conviction which determines the understanding of rationality in the modern era. A poetics that would incorporate such notions of the fictional as we have been exploring must consent to its own accounts being labeled "irrational," or the very understanding of rationality which conditions those verdicts must itself be rendered freshly responsive to the larger role of fictions in our interpretations. In other words, a poetics of fiction seems to be nothing more or less than one more version of a rationally scandalous relativism.

We have detailed a standard account of rationality, its sources in the eighteenth century, and its pervasive influence on our understanding of both poetics and philosophy. And we have also seen how the nature, kinds, and roles of fiction both in literary works of art and in our accounts of such works raise serious questions about the satisfactoriness of the standard account of rationality. In the recurring problem of trying to render our accounts of literary works less subjective, we have come up against a basic tension between rationality and the fictional. The rationality ideal imposes on our accounts an exaggerated emphasis on satisfying the general demands of any explanatory theory; this emphasis may promise eventual consensus but it leaves unresolved a central gap between art and life. By contrast, the fictionality story imposes on our accounts an exaggerated stress on the particular requisites of any interpretive attempt that may yield responsive readings of individual texts that turn on the interactions of life and art; but such a stress leaves unaddressed the legitimate demands of interpretive communities for ongoing critical consensus. The oppositions thus seem manifold: art and life, explanation and understanding, general versus particular, individual versus community, theory versus story, reason versus assertion, argument versus intuition, the real versus the imaginary, the rational versus the fictional, and so on. The central opposition arises out of a too facile identification of relativism with the fictionality story. When we examine talk of relativism more closely, we find that the conflation of the fictionality story with relativism is a mistake and that the claims of at least one kind of relativism find strong support from the cardinal elements in the fictionality story. This suggests that the fresh idiom our more perspicuous interactions with literary works of art seem to require, on the evidence at least of these investigations, is plausibly to be construed as the idiom of a revisionary— that is to say, a fictionalizing—relativism.

In one of the most sustained recent inquires into the puzzles of relativism, Joseph Margolis has called attention to the usual charges against relativism, the claim that it either formally contradicts itself or that it entails a thoroughgoing skepticism about cognitive competence.[15] But neither

―――――――――

[15]See Margolis 1986. Subsequent references are included in the text.

of these frequent claims can be sustained. For each overlooks the varieties of conceptual nuance a contemporary relativism is able to incorporate.

Classical relativism is no one doctrine, for it may answer to either an ancient claim that "whatever is affirmed is at once both true or false" or a contemporary one that, for any given investigation such as our inquiries into poetics, "there is no common conceptual ground in terms of which to adjudicate pertinently opposed claims." Moreover, we need to distinguish further each of these relativisms as external ones when contrasted with a third, which is internal. Whereas both what may be called the protagorean and incommensurabilist versions of relativism rely on a shared opposition to a standard two-valued model of truth, another kind of relativism not only opposes that model but argues variously for its replacement with a many-valued model. Now, the many external strains of relativism, it seems, are each susceptible to suitable philosophical therapies, but the internal variety remains resistant to the usual treatments. Accordingly, and not without some irony, such an internal relativism may be called a "robust relativism."

When we survey the usual mistakes in the characterization of relativism from this perspective, we can isolate the conceptual requirements that a robust relativism is designed to incorporate. Accordingly, a viable relativism must not be confused with doctrines that render the rational assessment of "pertinent claims within a domain" impossible, probabilize truth claims, multiply independent conventions for resolving conflicting claims, warrant judgments subjectively and noncognitively in terms of individual feelings and varying psychological attitudes only, conflate empirical relations with empirical cultural relativities, and so on. Rather, in view of much contemporary work on the attempts to reconcile versions of scientific realisms with their various epistemological and ontological challenges, a robust relativism requires "the formation of a thesis that is (i) internally coherent; (ii) intended to account for assigning truth values or otherwise justifying in cognitive terms well entrenched practices and forms of behavior; (iii) at least moderately congruent with the traditions of such practices and behavior; (iv) responsive to well-known and otherwise reasonable conceptual challenges; (v) set within the framework of an articulated philosophical strategy; and (vi) dialectically pitted against its own opponents" (10). The first two of these requirements are particularly important for without internal coherence such a relativism cannot claim to be rational even on some reinterpretation of the standard account of rationality. And without articulating a case for construing a more than bipolar model of truth where truthlike values can function nonsymmetrically, no realtivism can plausibly support claims that on the bipolar model of truth are simply contradictory.

This strategy leads, first, to a strong formulation of necessary and sufficient formal conditions for a robust internal relativism. Such a system must "provide for incongruent judgments"—that is, for judgments that are (1) epistemologically or epistemically eligible within the same context of inquiry; (2) would, on a model of truth and falsity, be contraditions or incompatibles, but do not now so function; (3) are only assigned truth-values weaker than "true" or "false"; and (4) are not detachable in the "evidentiary sense," that is, are not articulated logically in such a way that these judgments can be detached "in the context of argument and entailment from the very evidence in accord with which they are assigned their truth-like values" (17). With these formal conditions on view, the complementary move is to put into place substantive constraints that specify why this putative alternative to a two-valued account of truth cannot be satisfied by merely expanding the standard bipolar model to include both true and false judgments and probabilized judgments, instead of recasting it entirely as a many-valued model of truth that excludes both true and false values for judgments as well as probabilized judgments in favor of incongruent judgments only when construed as taking "plausible," "implausible," "apt," "compatible," and so on as truthlike values. These material constraints in part are (5) that relativism be irreducible either to "any form of skepticism, cynicism, nihilism, irrationalism, anarchism, or the like," or to a pluralism; (6) that relativism preclude "any form of foundationalism, essentialism, logocentrism, or similar doctrines"; (7) that relativism be compatible with forms of historicism without entailing them; (8) that a comprehensive relativism depend not on cognitive limitations of an inquirer but on "properties imputed to a domain of inquiry"; (9) that relativism "should not be construed in terms of judgments merely relativized (or relationalized) to alternative conceptual schemes"; (10) that relativism "should not be construed as precluding comparative judgments . . . (and within restricted domains) cognitive claims . . . that take bi-polar values"; (11) that relativism be construed as neither affirming nor denying but as neutral regarding "the cognitive adequacy of any single or unified conceptual scheme"; (12) that relativism should not be construed as affirming or entailing or denying . . . the facts of cultural diversity"; and (13) that relativism "not be required to be situated in a global or inclusive rather than a restricted form, or a form more inclusive in scope than any non-relativistic theory it contends against" (67–68).

With these formal and material considerations in mind we arrive at, if not a definition, at least a description of a robust relativism. Such a relativism cannot be called a skepticism in any one of the three basic forms of that influential view. Thus it is neither a direct skepticism ("it is not the case that *S* can know *P*"), nor an indirect skepticism ("it is not the case that *S* can know that *S* can know that *P*"), not finally a Pyrrhonic direct skepticism ("there are not better reasons for believing that S can know that P than there are for not believing that it is not the case that S can know that P").[16] Rather, robust relativism is an internal variety of relativism, an empirically motivated (111) and "methodologically positive" theory (58) of how, within a particular domain of inquiry, the alethic properties (24) of incongruent judgments (67) which standardly generate incompatibles are to be reinterpreted inside a many-valued rather than inside a two-valued model of truth. Thus, unlike the external relativist for whom on a particular issue no truth-values could be assigned at all, the internal relativist can coherently maintain that either one or both or neither of any two incongruent claims within a particular domain must be assigned a truthlike value such as "aptness," "plausibility," "compatibility," but other than "probability" (cf. 58). This description shows that a robust relativism can be formulated independent of a particular domain without formal inconsistency. Moreover, when dealing with incongruent judgments within a particular humanist domain such as poetics, this form of relativism is strongly favored, and not just because of the untenability of various forms of foundationalism, essentialism, and so on. Rather, what is at issue in the domain of poetics and the interactions between philosophy and literature are "intensional complexities regarding which the fixity of reference, the boundaries of objects, diachronic shifts in background theory, the contrast between actual and imputed properties and between description and interpretation, become clearly problematic—in such a way, in fact, that systematic relativization cannot but be pertinently eligible" (28).

Now, whatever the quarrels we may have here with some features or other in this description of a robust relativism, it seems clear nonetheless that such a view calls into serious question the standard account of rationality arising from the Lockean framework of conviction. For the kernel of the standard account is not finally the mandate of modernity—"believe only what your Reason . . . tells you that you have good reasons for believing." Rather, as we saw earlier, it is the interpretation of what it means to have good reasons which is crucial. Robust relativism challenges the standard account of rationality precisely in confronting that account with the conceptual scandal of incongruent judgments within a particular domain remaining irreconcilable theoretically while reconciling them in the practical and pragmatic spheres. In short, on the standard account of rationality, the fact of unreconciled incongruent judgments is irrational, whereas from the perspective of a robust relativism, the fact of such judgments is seen as still rational because the judgments are reconcilable. More particularly, behind the standard good-reasons interpretation of rationality we find here an inalienable commitment to a bipolar model of truth sufficiently complex as to accommodate probabilized views but finally incapable of resolving central conflicts between incongruent judg-

---

[16]Klein 1981:11, cited in Margolis 1986:112.

ments. And the reason for this incapacity clearly lies in the strict connection between the bipolar model, and not just the values "true and false" and "probable and improbable" but the interpretation of those values as symmetrical only and not as accommodating truthlike values and nonsymmetries.

If the conflict between Lockean rationality and robust relativism is evident, and if the case for robust relativism, however schematic its summary presentation here, is, to use its own expression, at least not implausible, then we find in robust relativism strong prima facie support for the many elements in an account of fiction which seem to conflict with the rationality story. The fact, then, that in a particular humanistic domain like poetics we find, even on extensively revised philosophical accounts of the cardinal concepts of various poetics, recurring undecidable issues, incommensurable accounts of the relations between art and life, and specific incongruent judgments about the interpretation of particular issues regarding an individual literary work of art—this fact can no longer be construed as a knock-down argument against the rationality of such inquiries. Rather, the strong suggestion now is that the various reconstructions our reflections on poetry have forced in our philosophical poetics require a reconstruction also of the Lockean framework of conviction which generated the modern interpretation of rationality.

This suggestion, however, does not require of us an uncritical allegiance to the version of robust relativism we have been following with interest in Margolis's trilogy. Although this is not the occasion to win some critical distance on that version, it seems clear that on its own terms some serious second thoughts are in order. For example, robust relativism is largely the result of a series of ongoing conceptual discussions in the philosophy of science rather than in the humanities. And even when we grant that this doctrine is not unassailable, suspicions arise nonetheless that robust relativism is overdetermined by discussions whose central concerns differ in important ways from the domain of poetics. Further, although Margolis has argued his case for a particular kind of many-valued model of truth in a remarkable series of recent books, it is not yet clear enough just how the positive content of his own theory includes enough substance that is independent of the self-imposed constraints arising from the need to avoid the deficiencies of a two-valued model. Here, two current disputes in philosophy of science play perhaps too preponderant a role in the construction of a particular version of a many-valued model in robust relativism. And finally this particular many-valued model itself relies on a nonextensional theory of reference which, however attractive over against the exaggerations of both Goodman's view and Ricoeur's, nevertheless requires further explication. For the kinds of justification offered to date in terms of the grammar of natural languages may turn out to be both ad hoc and incapable of sufficient generalization.

We need not try to examine these possible difficulties with robust relativism to justify the more important claim that such a relativism, on the evidence of our investigations of poetics, fictions, and the problems of philosophy, does not seem to go far enough. For what needs relativizing is not just theories of reference, models of truth, and our categorizations of judgments, but the peculiarly modern model of rationality itself. This is the model that has determined the language of the sciences today, continues to adjudicate the quarrels within the diverse philosophies of science, and of course remains just as deeply fixed in the project of poetics. For whether one requires of poetics strong explanatory accounts such as we find in formalist, structuralist, linguistic accounts or the endlessly ramifying weakly interpretive stories we find in the psychoanalytic, deconstructive, poststructuralist accounts, the Lockean ideal of good reasons remains in force, whether positively or negatively. But the burden of these investigations has been that the ideal itself remains insufficiently questioned as long as we continue to allow so little place in our thinking for reflection on the nature, kinds, and roles of our various fictions in both art and life.

In the preface to these inquiries I alluded to Gilles Granger's extremely muted suggestion—carefully qualified over an extraordinary range of work stretching back more than thirty years—that an "epistemological fact," unlike a scientific one, has to do centrally with a "renewal of a domain, a metamorphosis of the types of objects of the discipline in question."[17] With the accumulating evidence increasingly in view that societies like our own are presently undergoing a cultural revolution so pervasive that nothing and surely not the manifold discourses of philosophy is left unaffected, part of the suggestion I take Granger to be making for a domain where the discourse of philosophy and poetics remains entangled is the need for a transformation in our understanding of just what the objects of our inquiry are. At the end of this extended essay, and in a most provisional way, we come upon the idea that the objects of our inquiry in the interactions among fictions, philosophies, and the problems of poetics are gathered up inside a framework of conviction which itself is in the process of dissolution. How to recover, then, a resistance to the arbitrary so strong that it would allow of both a robust relativism and a fictionalized rationality?

At the beginning of this book, on the dedicatory page, I cited a poem by Sappho which reads as follows:

Ἔσπερε πάντα φέρων ὄσα φαίνολις ἐσκέδασ' αὔως,
φέρεις ὄιν, φέρεις αἶγα φέρεις ἄπυ μάτερι παῖδα.

---

[17] Granger 1987:10.

Hesperus, you bring all things homeward
    which the shining dawn dispersed,
You bring the sheep, you bring the goats,
    you bring the child home to its mother.

Whatever the vagaries of that text, arising out of a first contact between the ancient Greeks and another Orient than I have drawn from here, the poem is suffused with a pastoral imagery redolent of its double origins among tamers of horses and nomadic shepherds, and it undergoes myriad transformations across its Hellenistic, Jewish, Christian, Islamic, and even Budhhist readers in successive eras of interpretation up to our own. Sappho's evening star, which is as well Frege's morning star, beckons us to a recovery of the conceptual resources still obscured for us in the blinding light that our scientific canons of rationality project strongly into the past, resources that may enable us to reconstruct that ideal of rationality itself in a post-Fregean and not just a postmodern conceptual landscape.[18]

[18]For help with understanding the Japanese poems I thank Tomonobu Imamichi, Megumi Sakabe, Ryosuke Inagaki, and Noriko Hashimoto.

References

List of Abbreviations

APQ	American Philosophical Quarterly
BJA	British Journal of Aesthetics
CJP	Canadian Journal of Philosophy
JAAC	Journal of Aesthetics and Arts Criticism
JHI	Journal of the History of Ideas
JP	Journal of Philosophy
M	Mind
NLH	New Literary History
PAS	Proceedings of the Aristotelian Society
PMLA	Publications of Modern Language Association
PPR	Philosophy and Phenomenological Research
PR	Philosophical Review
PRAAPA	Proceedings and Addresses of the American Philosophical Association
PWN	Państwowe Wydawnictwo Naukowe
TLS	Times Literary Supplement

Abelson, R. 1981. "Psychological Status of the Script Concept." *American Psychologist* 26:715–29.

Anderson, J. R. 1976. *Language, Memory, and Thought*. Hillsdale, N.J.: Erlbaum Associates.

———.1983. *The Architecture of Cognition*. Cambridge, Mass.: Harvard University Press.

Amstutz, J. 1945. "Einige Beobachtungen über die Frömmigkeit R.M. Rilke." *Schweizerische Theologische Umschau* 4:73–92.

Anscombe, G. E. M. 1963. *Intention*. 2d ed. Ithaca: Cornell University Press.

Arbib, M. A. 1986. *In Search of the Person*. Amherst: University of Massachusetts Press.

Arbib, M. A., and M. Hesse. 1986. *The Construction of Reality*. Cambridge: Cambridge University Press.

Aschenbrenner, K. 1968. "Implications of Frege's Philosophy of Language for Literature." *BJA* 8:319–34.

Audi, R. 1973. "Intending." *JP* 70:387–402

Aune, B. 1975. "Sellars on Practical Reason." In *Action, Knowledge, and Reality*, edited by H. N. Castañeda, 1–25. Indianapolis: Bobbs-Merrill.

——. 1979. *Reason and Action*. Dordrecht: Reidel.

Austen, Jane. 1966. *Emma*. Harmondsworth: Penguin.

Austin, J. 1873. *Lectures on Jurisprudence*. 4th ed. London: John Murray.

Austin, J. L. 1962. *Sense and Sensibilia*. Oxford: Oxford University Press.

——. 1971. *Philosophical Papers*. Oxford: Oxford University Press.

Baier, A. 1985. *Postures of the Mind*. Minneapolis: University of Minnesota Press.

Barwise, J., and J. Perry. 1983. *Situations and Attitudes*. Cambridge, Mass.: MIT Press.

——. 1985. "Shifting Situations and Shaken Attitudes." *Linguistics and Philosophy* 8:105–61.

Beardsley, M. 1958. *Aesthetics*. New York: Harcourt Brace.

——. 1966. *Aesthetics: From Classical Greece to the Present*. New York: Macmillan.

——. 1978a. "Intending." In *Values and Morals*, edited by A. Goldman and J. Kim, 163–84. Dordrecht: Reidel.

——. 1978b. "Aesthetic Intentions and Fictive Illocutions," In *What Is Literature*, 161–77. *See* Hernadi 1978.

——. 1981. "Fiction as Representation." *Synthese* 46:291–314.

Benveniste, E. 1966a. *Problèmes de linguistique générale*. Paris: Gallimard.

——. 1966b. "Le langage et l'expérience humaine." In *Problèmes du langage*. Paris: Gallimard.

Berkeley, G. 1713. *Three Dialogues between Hylas and Philonous*. Indianapolis: Hackett.

Block, N. 1980. "What Is Functionalism?" In *Readings in Philosophy of Psychology*, edited by N. Block, 171–84. Cambridge, Mass.: Harvard University Press.

Boer, S. E., and W. G. Lycan. 1986. *Knowing Who*. Cambridge, Mass.: MIT Press.

Bownas, G., and A. Thwaite, eds. 1972. *The Penguin Book of Japanese Verse*. Hammondsworth: Penguin.

Brand, R. 1984. *Intending and Acting*. Cambridge, Mass.: MIT Press.

Brown, R. L., and M. Steinmann. 1978. "Native Readers of Fiction." In *What Is Literature*, 141–60. *See* Hernadi 1978.

Broyard, A. 1981. "Tolstoy's Metaphor." *New York Times Book Review*, 23 March.

Burke, K. 1941. *Philosophy of Literary Form*. Baton Rouge: Louisiana State University Press.

Carr, D. 1984. "Review of Ricoeur *Time and Narrative* I." *History and Theory* 23:357–70.

——. 1986. *Time, Narrative, and History*. Bloomington: Indiana University Press.

Casey, E. 1976. *Imagination*. Bloomington: Indiana University Press.

Castañeda, H. N. 1975. *Thinking and Doing*. Dordrecht: Reidel.

——. 1976. "The Twofold Structure and the Unity of Practical Thinking." In *Action Theory*, edited by M. Brand and D. Walton, 105–30. Dordrecht: Reidel.

——. 1980. "The Doing of Thinking: Intending and Willing." In *Action and Responsibility*, edited by M. Bradie and M. Brand, 80–92. Bowling Green, Ohio: Bowling Green State University Press.

Champigny, R. 1970. "Implications in Narrative Fiction." *PMLA* 85:988–91.

Charlton, W. 1984. "Feelings for the Fictions." *BJA* 24:206–16.

Chisholm, R. 1976a. "The Agent as Cause." In *Action Theory*, edited by M. Brand and D. Walton, 199–211. Dordrecht: Reidel.

——. 1976b. *Person and Object*. La Salle, Ill.: Open Court.

——. 1979. "Castañeda's *Thinking and Doing*." *Nous* 13:385–96.

——. 1981. *The First Person*. Minneapolis: University of Minnesota Press.
Chisholm, R., and E. Sosa. 1966. "On the Logic of 'Intrinsically Better.' " *APQ* 3:244–49.
Crane, R. S. 1953. *The Language of Criticism*. Chicago: University of Chicago Press.
——. 1972b. *Consciousness and Nature*. Cambridge, Mass.: Harvard University Press.
Culler, J. 1982. *On Deconstruction*. Ithaca: Cornell University Press.
Currie, G. 1985. "What Is Fiction?" *JAAC* 43:385–92.
Danto, A. C. 1983a. "Writing and Its Spokesman." *TLS*, 30 September:1035–36.
——. 1983b. "Margins of Philosophy." *TLS*, 9 December:1374.
Davidson, D. 1963. "Actions, Reasons, and Causes." *JP* 60:685–700.
——. 1967. "The Logical Form of Action Sentences." In *The Logic of Division and Action*, edited by N. Rescher, 81–95. Pittsburgh: University of Pittsburgh Press.
——. 1984. *Essays on Actions and Events*. Oxford: Oxford University Press.
Davis, L. 1975. "Action." *Canadian Journal of Philosophy*, suppl. vol. 1, pt. 2 ("New Essays in the Philosophy of Mind"):129–44.
——. 1979. *Theory of Action*. Englewood Cliffs, N.J.: Prentice-Hall.
Dennett, D. 1971. "Intentional Systems." In *Brainstorms. See* Dennett 1978.
——. 1976. "Conditions of Personhood." In *The Identity of Persons*, 175–96. *See* A. Rorty 1976b.
——. 1978. *Brainstorms*. Montgomery, Vt.: Bradford Books.
——. 1987. *The Intentional Stance*. Cambridge, Mass.: MIT Press.
Derrida, J. 1977a. "Signature Event Context." *Glyph* 1:172–97.
——. 1977b. "Limited Inc. a b c . . ." *Glyph* 2:162–254.
——. 1982. *Margins of Philosophy*. Chicago: University of Chicago Press.
de Sousa, R. 1987. *The Rationality of Emotion*. Cambridge, Mass.: MIT Press.
Dickie, G., and R. Sclafani, eds. 1977. *Aesthetics*. New York: St. Martin's.
Eaton, M. 1982. "A Strange Kind of Sadness." *JAAC* 41:51–63.
Elgin, C. 1984. *With Reference to Reference*. Indianapolis: Hackett.
Elgin, C., and I. Scheffler. 1987. "Mainsprings of Metaphor." *JP* 84:331–36.
Eliot, T. S. 1959. *Four Quartets*. London: Faber & Faber.
——. 1968. *Murder in the Cathedral*. London: Faber & Faber.
——. 1970. *Selected Poems*. London: Faber & Faber.
Elster, J. 1983. "Review of Collins, *Selfless Persons*." *London Review of Books* (2–15 June): 9–11.
——, ed. 1986. *The Multiple Self*. Cambridge: Cambridge University Press.
Evans, G. 1982. *The Varieties of Reference*. Oxford: University of Oxford Press.
Feinberg, J. 1968. "Action and Responsibility." In A. White, ed., *The Philosophy of Action* (Oxford: Oxford University Press), pp. 95–119.
Fine, K. 1985. *Reasoning with Arbitrary Objects*. Oxford: Oxford University Press.
Firth, R. 1981. "Epistemic Merit, Intrinsic and Instrumental." *PRAAPA* 55:5–23.
Fish, S. 1980. *Is There a Text in This Class?* Cambridge, Mass.: Harvard University Press.
Fløistad, G. 1982. "Introduction." In *Contemporary Philosophy*, 1–14. The Hague: Nijhoff.
Fodor, J. 1981. *Representations*. Cambridge, Mass.: MIT Press.
——. 1983. *The Modularity of Mind*. Cambridge, Mass.: MIT Press.
Forbes, G. 1987. *Languages of Possibility*. New York: Blackwells.
Gabriel, G. 1975. *Fiktion und Wahrheit*. Stuttgart: Frommann Holzborg.
Gadamer, H. G. 1975. *Truth and Method*. Translated by G. Barden and J. Cumming. New York: Continuum.
Garvin, P. L., ed. 1964. *A Prague School Reader*. Washington, D.C.: Georgetown University Press.
Geach, P. T. 1960. "Ascriptivism." *PR* 69:221–25.
Geertz, C. 1973. *The Interpretation of Culture*. New York: Basic Books.

Goldman, A. 1970. *A Theory of Human Action*. Englewood Cliffs, N.J.: Prentice-Hall.
Gordon, R. M. "The Volitional Theory Revisited." In *Action Theory*, edited by M. Brand and D. Walton, 67–84. Dordrecht: Reidel.
——. 1976. 1987. *The Structure of Emotions*. Cambridge: Cambridge University Press.
Goodman, N. 1976. *Languages of Art*. 2d ed. Indianapolis: Hackett.
——. 1978. *Ways of Worldmaking*. Indianapolis: Hackett.
——. 1982. "Notes on the Well-Made World." In W. Leinfeller et al., eds. *Language and Ontology* (Vienna: Holder-Pichler-Tempsky), 31–38.
——. 1984. *Of Mind and Other Matters*. Cambridge, Mass.: Harvard University Press.
Granger, G. G. 1987. *Leçon inaugurale*. Paris: Collège de France.
Greenwald, A. 1970. "Sensory Feedback Mechanisms in Performance Control: With Special Reference to the Ideo-Motor Mechanism." *Psychological Review* 77:73–99.
Grice, H. P. 1957. "Meaning." *PR* 66:377–88.
——. 1968. "Utterer's Meaning, Sentence-Meaning and Word-Meaning." *Foundations of Language* 4:1–18.
Griffiths, A. P. 1967. "Ultimate Moral Principles." *The Encyclopedia of Philosophy* (New York: Macmillan), 8:176–78.
Gupta, A. 1982. "Review of Brody, *Identity and Essence*." *JP* 79:518–22.
Gustafson, D. F. 1986. *Intention and Agency*. Dordrecht: Reidel.
Hagiwara, S. 1969. *Face at the Bottom of the World and Other Poems*. Tokyo: Tuttle.
Hamburger, K. 1957. *Die Logik der Dichtung*. Stuttgart: Klett.
Han Yong-un, 1926. *Your Silence*. Translated by Kang Yong-ill. Seoul: n.p.
Harari, J., ed. 1979. *Textual Strategies*. Ithaca: Cornell University Press.
Hart, H. L. A. 1948–49. "The Ascription of Responsibility and Rights." *Proceedings of the Artistotelian Society* 49:171–94.
——. 1968. *Punishment and Responsibility*. Oxford: Oxford University Press.
Hart, H., J. van der Hoeven, and N. Wolterstorff, eds. 1983. *Rationality in the Calvinist Tradition*. Lanham, Md.: University Press of America.
Hass, R. 1982. "Looking for Rilke." In *Selected Poetry*, xi–xliv. *See* Rilke 1982.
Hayes, P. J. 1980. "The Logic of Frames." In *Frame Conceptions and Text Understanding*, edited by D. Metzing, 46–61. New York: Walter de Gruyter.
Hegel, G. F. 1979. *Introduction to the Berlin Aesthetic Lectures of the 1820s*. Oxford: Oxford University Press.
Heidegger, M. 1959. *Unterwegs zur Sprache*. Pfullingen: Neske.
——. 1961. *Was Heisst Denken?* Tübingen: Niemeyer.
——. 1970. *Phänomenologie und Theologie*. Frankfurt: Klostermann.
Hernadi, P., ed. 1978. *What Is Literature?* Bloomington: Indiana University Press.
Hibbett, H., ed. 1977. *Contemporary Japanese Literature*. New York: Knopf.
Hirsch, E. D. 1983. "Derrida's Axioms" [Review of Culler 1982]. *London Review of Books* (21 July–3 August):17–18.
Hornsby, J. 1980. *Action*. London: Routledge & Kegan Paul.
Hospers, J. 1946. *Meaning and Truth in the Arts*. Chapel Hill: University of North Carolina Press.
——. 1960. "Implied Truths in Literature." *JAAC* 19:37–46.
Hull, C. L. 1931. "Goal Attraction and Directing Ideas Conceived as Habit Phenomena." *Psychological Review* 38:487–506.
——. 1943. *Principles of Behaviour*. New York: Appleton-Century-Crofts.
——. 1951. *Essentials of Behaviour*. New Haven, Conn.: Yale University Press.
Hume, D. 1739. *A Treatise of Human Nature*. Bk. I, pt. IV, secs. 1, 5, 6.
——. *A Treatise of Human Nature*, ed. L. A. Selby-Bigge, 2d ed. (Oxford: Clarendon).
Ingarden, R. 1924. "O pytaniach esencjalnych" ["On essential questions"]. *Sprawozdania Towarzystwa Naukowego we Lwowie* 4, no. 3:119–25.
——. 1925. "Essentiale Fragen," *Jahrbuch für Philosophie und phänomenologische Forschung* 7:125–304.

———. 1930a. "O nazwach i wyrażeniach funkcyjnych" ["On functioning terms and expressions"]. *Ruch Filozoficzny* 12, nos. 1–10:204–5.

———. 1930b. "Verbum finitum a zdanie" ["The finite verb and the sentence"]. *Ruch Filozoficzny* 12, nos. 1–10:205–6.

———. 1946. "O różnych rozumieniach 'prawdziwości' w dziele sztuki." ["On various understandings of 'truthfulness' in the work of art"]. *Zagadnienia literackie*, 10, no. 1:12–19, and no. 2:36–43.

———. 1947. "Schematyczność dzieła literackiego." *Szkice z Filozofii literatury*. Łódź.

———. 1966. *Studia z estetyki*. Warsaw: PWN.

———. 1973a. *The Literary Work of Art*. Translated by G. Grabowicz. Evanston, Ill.: Northwestern University Press.

———. 1973b. *The Cognition of the Literary Work of Art*. Translated by R. A. Crowley and K. R. Olson. Evanston, Ill.: Northwestern University Press.

———. 1973c. "On So-Called Truth in Literatures." Translated by A. Czerniawski. In *Aesthetics in Twentieth-Century Poland*, edited by S. G. Harrell, 154–204. Lewisburg, Pa.: Bucknell University Press.

———. 1986. *Selected Papers in Aesthetics*. Edited by P. McCormick. Munich: Philosophia Verlag.

———. 1987. *Ontology of the Work of Art*. Athens, Ohio: Ohio University Press.

Iseminger, G. 1983. "How Strange a Sadness?" *JAAC* 42:81–82.

Iser, W. 1978. *The Art of Reading*. Baltimore: John Hopkins University Press.

Jakobson, R. 1971. "Linguistics and Poetics," In *Style in Language*, 350–77. *See* Sebeok 1971.

———. 1976. "Poetyka w świetle językoznawstwa." In Współczesna teoria . . . , H. Markiewicz (Kraków), 2:23–34.

James, W. 1890. *The Principles of Psychology*, Vol. 2. 1950. Reprint. New York: Dover.

Kambartel, F., and F. Schneider. 1982. "Radical Pragmatics." In *Contemporary Philosophy*, 155–79. *See* Fløistad.

Kant, I. 1977. "Excerpts from *Critique of Judgment*." In *Aesthetics*, 643–88. *See* Dickie and Sclafani 1977.

Kaplan, D. 1978. "Dthat." In *Contemporary Perspectives in the Philosophy of Language*, edited by P. French, T. Vehling, Jr., H. Wettstein, 383–400. Minneapolis: University of Minnesota Press.

Keene, D. 1984. *Dawn to the West*. Vol. 2. New York: Henry Holt and Co.

Kim, J. 1970. "Events and Their Descriptions." In *Essays in Honor of Carl G. Hempel*, edited by N. Rescher et al., 198–215. Dordrecht: Reidel.

———. 1973. "Causation, Nomic Subsumption, and the Concept of Event." *JP* 70:217–36.

———. 1976. "Events as Property Exemplifications." In *Action Theory*, edited by M. Brand and D. Walton, 159–77. Dordrecht: Reidel.

Kirkup, J. and J. Davis, eds. 1978. *Modern Japanese Poetry*. St. Lucia, Queensland, Australia: University of Queensland Press.

Klein, P. D. 1981. *Certainty*. Minneapolis: University of Minnesota Press.

Köhler, H. 1976. *Dichtung and Erkenntnis: Das lyrische Werk in Lichte der Tagebücher*. Bonn: Bouvier.

Krajka, W., and A. Zgorzelski. 1974. *On the Analysis of the Literary Work*. 2d ed. Translated by A. Blaim. Warsaw: PWN.

Kripke, S. 1972. "Naming and Necessity." In *Semantics of Natural Language*, edited by D. Davidson and G. Harmon, 253–355, 763–69. Dordrecht: Reidel.

———. 1982. *Wittgenstein on Rules and Private Language*. Cambridge, Mass.: Harvard University Press.

Krukowski, L. 1981. "Commentary on Beardsley's 'Fiction as Representation.' " *Synthese* 46:325–30.

Kueng, G. 1984. "The Intentional and the Real Object." *Dialectica* 39:143–56.

Kundera, M. 1984. *The Unbearable Lightness of Being*. New York: Harper & Row.

Lamarque, P. 1981. "How Can we Fear and Pity Fictions?" *BJA* 21:291–304.

Langer, S. K., ed. 1958. *Reflections on Art*. Baltimore: John Hopkins University Press.

Lee, P. H. 1965. *Korean Literature: Topics and Themes*. Tucson: Arizona University Press.

Letwin, R. 1984. "The Person Vanishes." *Spectator* (19 May):24.

Lewin, K. 1935. *A Dynamic Theory of Personality*. New York: McGraw-Hill.

——. 1938. *The Conceptual Representation and the Measurement of Psychological Forces*. Durham, N.C.: Duke University Press.

Lewis, D. 1978. "Truth in Fiction." *APQ* 15:37–46.

——. 1979. "Attitudes *De Dicto* and *De Se*." *PR* 87:513–43.

Lewis, H. 1982. *The Elusive Self*. London: Macmillan.

Loar, B. 1982. "Review of Searle's *Expression and Meaning*." *PR* 91:488–93.

Locke, J. 1975. *Essay Concerning Human Understanding*. Oxford: Oxford University Press.

Lombard, L. B. 1979. "Events." *CJP* 9:425–60.

Lord, C. 1984. "A Representational Approach to Fearing Fictions." Unpublished ms.

Lorenzen, P. 1986. *Constructive Philosophy*. Amherst: University of Massachusetts Press.

Lotman, J. 1976. *Analysis of the Poetic Text*. Ann Arbor, Mich.: Ardis.

——. 1977. *The Structure of the Artistic Text*. Ann Arbor: University of Michigan Press.

Loux, M., ed. 1979. *The Possible and the Actual*. Ithaca: Cornell University Press.

McCormick, P. 1971. "De la communication préconventionelle." *Actes du XVe Congrés de d'Association des Sociétés de philosophie française* (Montréal, 1971), 83–101.

——. 1975. "Phenomenologie et critique littéraire: l'esthétique de Dilthey." *Philosophiques* 2:229–52.

——. 1976. *Heidegger and the Language of the World*. Ottawa: University of Ottawa Press.

——, ed. 1986a. *Roman Ingarden: Selected Papers in Aesthetics*. Munich: Philosophia Verlag.

——, ed. 1986b. *The Reasons of Art*. Ottawa: University of Ottawa Press.

McDowell, J. 1986. "Critical Notice of William's *Ethics*." *Mind* 95:377–87.

MacCormac, E. R. 1986. *A Cognitive Theory of Metaphor*. Cambridge, Mass: MIT Press.

Mackensie, P. T. 1983. "Personal Identity and the Imagination." *Philosophy* 58:161–74.

Mackey, L. 1983. "Letters: Margins of Philosophy." *TLS*, 18 November:1279–80.

——. 1984. "An Exchange on Deconstruction." *New York Review of Books*, 2 February:47–48.

Mandelbaum, M. 1965. "Family Resemblance and Generalizations Concerning the Arts." In *Aesthetics*, edited by G. Dickie and R. Sclafani, 500–515. New York: 1977.

Margolis, J., ed. 1962. *Philosophy Looks at the Arts*. Philadelphia: University of Pennsylvania Press.

——. 1977. "The Axiom of Existence." *Southern Journal of Philosophy* 15:91–99.

——. 1983. "Fiction and Existence." *Grazer Philosophische Studien* 19:179–203.

——. 1986. *Pragmatics without Foundations*. New York: Blackwells.

——. 1987. *Science without Unity*. New York: Blackwells.

Martin, R. 1981. "On Some Aesthetic Relations." *JAAC* 39:275–7.

Masterson, F. A., and M. Crawford. 1982. "The Defense Motivation System: A Theory of Avoidance Behaviour" (with commentary). *Behavioral and Brain Sciences* 5:661–96.

Melden, A. I. 1956. "Action." *PR* 65:529–41.

——. 1961. *Free Action*. London: Routledge & Kegan Paul.

Mellor, H. 1968. "Literarische Wahrheit." *Ratio* 10:124–40.

Mew, P. 1973. "Fact in Fiction." *JAAC* 31:329–37.

Mill, J. 1872. *A System of Logic*, 8th ed. 1961. Reprint. London: Longmans, Green.

Miller, G. A., E. Galanter, and K. H. Pribram. 1960. *Plans and the Structure of Behaviour*. New York: Holt, Rinehart, and Winston.

Minsky, M. 1975. "A Framework for Representing Knowledge." In *The Psychology of Computer Vision*, edited by P. H. Winston, 211–77. New York: McGraw-Hill.

Montefiore, A., ed. 1973. *Philosophy and Personal Relations*. London: Routledge & Kegan Paul.

Moody, A. J. 1977. *Thomas Stearns Eliot: Poet*. Cambridge: Cambridge University Press.

Morton, A. 1985. "Making Sense of Oneself." *TLS* 21 June: 688

Mounce, H. O. 1980. "Art and Real Life." *Philosophy* 55:183–92.

Mukařovský, J. 1964. "Standard Language and Poetic Language." In *A Prague School Reader*, 17–31. *See* Garvin 1964.

Muller, G. 1970. "Morphological Poetics." In *Reflections on Art*, 206–7. *See* Langer 1970.

Neville, R. 1971. "The Social Importance of Philosophy." *Abraxis* 1:31–45.

Nietzsche, F. 1963. *The Portable Nietzsche*, ed W. Kaufman. New York: Viking.

——. 1967. "Excerpts from *The Birth of Tragedy*." In *Aesthetics*, 239–68. *See* Dickie and Sclafani 1977.

Nishiyama, Y. 1975. *The Structure of Propositions*. Tokyo: Maruzen.

Novitz, D. 1980. "Fiction, Imagination, and Emotion." *JAAC* 38:279–88.

Ohmann, R. 1971. "Speech Acts and the Definition of Literature." *Philosophy and Rhetoric* 4:1–19.

Palma, A. 1983. "Imaginaiton, Truth and Rationality." *Philosophy* 58:29–38.

Parfit, D. 1973. "Later Selves and Moral Principles." In *Philosophy and Personal Relations*, 137–69. *See* Montefiore 1973.

——. 1984. *Reasons and Persons*. Oxford: Oxford University Press.

Paskins, B. 1977. "On Being Moved by Anna Karenina and *Anna Karenina*." *Philosophy* 52:344–47.

Pavel, T., and J. Wood, eds. 1979. "Literary Semantics." *Poetica*, special issue.

Peacocke, C. 1986. *Thoughts: An Essay on Contents*. New York: Blackwells.

Pears, D. 1987. *The False Prison*. Oxford: Clarendon Press.

Peirce, C. S. 1955. *Collected Papers*, vol 5. Cambaridge, Mass.: Harvard University Press.

Perry, J. 1975a. "The Problem of Personal Identity." In *Personal Identity*, 3–30. *See* Perry 1975b.

——, ed. 1975b. *Personal Identity*. Berkeley: University of California Press.

Plantinga, A. 1974. *The Nature of Necessity*. Oxford: Oxford University Press.

——. 1982. "How to Be an Anti-Realist." *PRAAPA* 56:47–70.

Pollard, D. R. B. 1977. "M. J. Sirridge, Fiction, and Truth." *PPR* 38:251–56.

Prichard, H. A. 1949. *Moral Obligation*. Oxford: Clarendon Press.

Proust, J. 1986. *Questions de forme*. Paris: Fayard.

Quinton, A. 1967. "Knowledge and Belief." In *The Encyclopedia of Philosophy*. New York: Macmillan.

Radford, C. 1977. "Tears and Fiction." *Philosophy* 52:208–13.

Redden, J. 1984. "Defining Self-Deception." *Dialogue* 23:103–20.

Redford, C., and M. Weston. 1975. "How Can We Be Moved by the Fate of Anna Karenina?" *PAS* 49:67–93.

Ricoeur, P. 1950. *Le volontaire et l'involontaire*. Paris: Presses universitaires de France.

——. 1976. "L'imagination dans le discours et dans l'action." *Savoir, faire, espérer*. Bruxelles: Publication des facultés universitaires Saint Louis.

——. 1977. "La structure symbolique de l'action." *Symbolisme: Actes sixième conférence internationale de sociologie de religion*. Lille: Centre internationale des systèmes religieux.

——. 1979. "The Function of Fiction in Shaping Reality." *Man and World* 12:123–41.

——. 1980. "Critical Discussions: *Ways of Worldmaking*." *Philosophy and Literature* 4:107–120.

――. 1981. "Le discours de l'action." *La sémantique de l'action*. Paris: Centre nationale de recherche scientifique.

――. 1983–85. *Temps et récit*. 3 vols. Paris: Seuil.

Riffaterre, M. 1978. *Semiotics of Poetry*. Bloomington: Indiana University Press.

Rilke, R. M. 1982. *Selected Poetry*. Translated by S. Mitchell. New York: Vintage.

Rorty, A. 1976a. "Introduction." In *The Identity of Persons*, 1–15. See Rorty 1976b.

――, ed. 1976b. *The Identity of Persons*. Berkeley: University of California Press.

Rorty, R. 1977. "Derrida on Language." *JP* 74:673–81.

――. 1978. "Philosophy as a Kind of Writing." *NLH* 10:141–60.

――. 1980. *Philosophy and the Mirror of Nature*. Princeton, N.J.: Princeton University Press.

Rosebury, B. J. 1979. "Fiction, Emotion, and 'Beliefs.' " *BJA* 18:31–44.

Rudner, R. 1970. "Show or Tell: Incoherence among Symbol Systems." *Erkenntnis* 12:176–79.

Rummnellhart, D., and D. A. Norman. 1982. "Simulating a Skilled Typist." *Cognitive Science* 6:1–32.

Russell, B. 1911. *The Problems of Philosophy*. London: George Allen.

Ryle, G. 1949. *The Concept of Mind*. London: Hutchinson.

Sato, H., and B. Watson, eds. 1981. *From the Country of Eight Islands*. New York: Doubleday.

Schank, R. 1982. *Dynamic Memory*. Cambridge: Cambridge University Press.

Schank, R., and R. Abelson. 1977. *Scripts, Plans, Goals, and Understanding*. Hillsdale, N.J.: Erlbaum Associates.

Schaper, E. 1978. "Fiction and the Suspension of Disbelief." *BJA* 18:31–44.

Scheffler, I. 1980. "The Wonderful Worlds of Goodman." *Synthese* 45:201–9.

Scheffler, S. 1984. "Ergo: Less Ego." *TLS*, 4 May:484.

Schick, T. 1982. "Can Fictional Literature Communicate Knowledge?" Unpublished ms.

Schiffer, S. 1972. *Meaning*. Oxford: Oxford University Press.

Scriven, M. 1954. "The Language of Fiction." *PAS*, supp. 28:185–96.

Searle, J. R. 1969. *Speech Acts*. Cambridge: Cambridge University Press.

――. 1974. "The Logical Status of Fictional Discourse." *NLH* 6:319–38.

――. 1975a. "Indirect Speech Acts." In *Syntax and Semantics*, edited by P. Cole and J. H. Morgan, 59–82. New York: Academic Press.

――. 1975b. "A Taxonomy of Illocutionary Speech Acts." In *Language, Mind, and Knowledge*, edited by K. Gunderson, 344–69. Minneapolis: University of Minnesota Press.

――. 1976. "The Rules of the Language Game." *TLS*, September:1119.

――. 1977. "Reiterating the Differences: Reply to Derrida." *Glyph* 1:198–208.

――. 1983. "The World Turned Upside Down" [Review of Culler, *On Deconstruction*]. *New York Review of Books*, 27 October:74–79.

――. 1984. "An Exchange on Deconstruction." *New York Review of Books*, 2 February:47–48.

Sebeok, T. A., ed. 1971. *Style in Language*. Cambridge, Mass.: MIT Press.

Sellars, W. 1966. "Thought and Action." In *Freedom and Determinism*, edited by S. Hook, 105–39. New York: Random House.

――. 1973. "Action and Events." *Nous* 7:179–202.

Sen, A. 1985. *Resources, Values and Development*. Oxford: Oxford University Press.

Seuren, P. 1985. *Discourse Semantics*. New York: Blackwells.

Shepard, R. N., and L. A. Cooper. 1986. *Mental Images and Their Transformations*. Cambridge, Mass.: MIT Press.

Shoemaker, S. 1984. "Personal Identity: A Materialist's Account." In *Personal Identity*, 67–132. See Shoemaker and Swinburne 1984.

Shoemaker, S., and R. Swinburne, eds. 1984. *Personal Identity*. London: Blackwells.

Shusterman, R. 1988. *T. S. Eliot and the Philosophy of Criticism*. New York: Columbia University Press.

Sidney, P. 1969. *The Apology for Poetry*. Edited by M. R. Mahl. Northridge, Calif.: San Fernando State College.

Sirridge, M. J. 1975. "Truth from Fiction?" *PPR* 35:453–71.

———. 1977. "The Moral of the Story: A Rejoinder to Pollard." *PPR*, 38:257–59.

Skulsky, H. 1980. "On Being Moved by Fiction." *JAAC* 39:5–14.

Smith, B. H. 1970. "Literature as Performance, Fiction, and Act." *JP* 67:553–63.

Smith, G. 1974. *T. S. Eliot's Poems and Plays*. 2d ed. Chicago: University of Chicago Press.

Spence, K. W. 1956. *Behaviour Theory and Conditioning*. New Haven, Conn: Yale University Press.

Spurgeon, C. 1935. *Shakespeare's Imagery and What It Tells Us*. Cambridge: Cambridge University Press.

Steiner, G. 1975. *After Babel*. New York: Oxford University Press.

Steinmann, M. 1971. "Poetry as Fiction." *NLH* 2:259–81.

Stevens, W. 1953. *Selected Poems*. London: Faber & Faber.

———. 1971. *The Palm at the End of the Mind*. New York: Vintage.

Stocker, M. 1987. "Emotional Thoughts." *APQ* 24:59–71.

Stoutland, F. 1982. "Philosophy of Action." In *Contemporary Philosophy*, 45–72. See Fløistad 1982.

Strawson, P.F. 1964. "Intention and Convention in Speech Acts." *PR* 73:439–60.

———. 1970. *Meaning and Truth*. Oxford: Oxford University Press.

———. 1984. "The Parfit Connection." *New York Review of Books* (14 June):42.

Taylor, B. 1985. *Modes of Occurrence*. Oxford: Blackwells.

Taylor, C. 1964. *The Explanation of Behaviour*. New York: Humanities Press.

Taylor, R. 1966. *Action and Purpose*. Englewood Cliffs, N.J.: Prentice-Hall.

———. 1974. *Metaphysics*. 2d ed. Englewood Cliffs, N.J.: Prentice-Hall.

Thalberg, I. 1977. *Perception, Emotion and Action: A Component Approach*. Oxford: Blackwells.

Thomson, J. J. 1977. *Acts and Other Events*. Ithaca: Cornell University Press.

Tillyard, E. W. 1930. *Milton*. London: Longmans and Green.

Tolman, E. C. 1932. *Purposive Behaviour in Animals and Men*. New York: Appleton-Century-Crofts.

———. 1952. "A Psychological Model." In *Toward a General Theory of Action*, edited by T. Parsons and E. Shils, 279–361. Cambridge, Mass.: Harvard University Press.

Tolstoy, L. 1965. *Anna Karenina*. Translated by C. Garnett. New York: Random House.

Tugendhat, E. 1986. *Self-Consciousness and Self-Determination*. Cambridge, Mass.: MIT Press.

Tuomela, R. 1982. "Explanation and Action." In *Contemporary Philosophy*, 15–43. See Floistad 1982.

———. 1984. "Social Action." In *Social Action*, ed. G. Seebass and R. Tuomela, 103–29. Dordrecht: Reidel.

Van de Vate, D. 1971. "The Problem of Robot Consciousness." *PPR* 32:149–65.

von Wright, G. H. 1971. *Explanation and Understanding*. Ithaca: Cornell University Press.

Walton, K. 1978a. "Fearing Fictions." *JP* 75:5–27.

———. 1978b. "How Remote Are Fictional Worlds?" *JAAC* 37:11–23.

Weitz, M. 1935. "Truth in Literature." *Revue internationale de philosophie* 9:116–29.

Wellek, R., and A. Warren. 1949. *Theory of Literature*. New York: Harcourt Brace.

Williams, B. 1976. "Persons, Character and Morality." In *The Identity of Persons*, 197–216. See A. Rorty 1976b.

———. 1984. "Personal Identity." *London Review of Books* (7–20 June):14.

———. 1985. *Ethics and the Limits of Philosophy*. Cambridge, Mass.: Harvard University Press.

Wimsatt, W. 1954. *The Verbal Icon*. Lexington: University of Kentucky Press.

Wiseman, M. 1978. "Empathic Identification."*APQ* 15:192–15.

Wittgenstein, L. 1961. *Tractatus Logico-Philosophicus*. London: Routledge.

——. 1983. *Philosophical Investigations*. New York: Macmillan.

Wolff, E. 1971. "Der intendierte Leser." *Poetics* 4:141–166.

Wollheim, R. 1985. *The Thread of Life*. Cambridge, Mass.: Harvard University Press.

Wolterstorff, N. 1981. "Response to Beardsley." *Synthese* 46:315–24.

——. 1983. "Thomas Reid on Rationality." In *Rationality in the Calvinist Tradition*, 43–69. *See* Hart et al. 1983.

——. 1984. "Are Texts Autonomous?" *Aesthetics: Proceedings of VIII International Wittgenstein Congress*. Vienna: Holder-Pichler-Tempsky.

——. 1987. "The Emergence of Reality." Unpublished ms.

Ziff, L. 1967. "On Grice's Account of Meaning." *Analysis* 28:1–8.

Index

Library of Congress Cataloging-in-Publication Data

McCormick, Peter (Peter J.)
  Fictions, philosophies, and the problems of poetics.

  Bibliography: p.
  Includes index.
  1. Fiction—Philosophy. 2. Poetics. I. Title.
PN3326.M39 1988   801'.953   88-47783
ISBN 0-8014-2204-3 (alk. paper)
ISBN 0-8014-9519-9 (pbk. : alk. paper)